D1270995

AN INDEX TO ARISTOTLE

AN INDEX TO
ARISTOTLE
IN ENGLISH TRANSLATION

BY TROY WILSON ORGAN

NEW YORK
GORDIAN PRESS, INC.
1966

Originally Published 1949
Reprinted 1966

PREFACE

IT is well-known that the *Corpus Aristotelicum* contains many passages which throw light on one another, but there has been no method by which the student of Aristotle can easily discover this interrelationship. Bonitz' word index is of great help to advanced students of Aristotle in locating terms, but it is of little value to those who are interested in attaining a well-rounded view of Aristotle's analysis of a particular subject. Students of Plato find Abbott's index to Jowett's translations of the dialogues invaluable; but students of Aristotle, who are in much greater need of a synoptic apparatus, have no such work to which they may refer. Consequently, Aristotle is often studied as a biologist, or an orator, or a metaphysician, or an art critic, or a political and moral philosopher without due attention being given to the light thrown upon a particular view by his other works. When approached in this manner Aristotle is open to unnecessary misinterpretations; for example, he has been unduly Christianized by those who have attempted to comment upon the *Politics* or the *Poetics* without appreciating the relevance of his *Ethics* and *Metaphysics*. The intricacies of his terminology and the variety of extant translations add to the difficulty. This English topical index should aid not only the philosopher, but also the student of letters, politics, ethics, or psychology who seeks to evaluate Aristotle's contribution in a specific field.

In the preparation of this index the eleven volume English translation edited by W. D. Ross and J. A. Smith and published by the Oxford University Press (1908-1931) was used. The page numbering is that of the Berlin Academy edition of the Greek text (1831-1870) edited by Immanuel Bekker. This pagination is listed in the margins of the Oxford translations and is likewise indicated in most translations of Aristotle's works. In this pagination, 1284 b 32, for example, refers to line 32 of the second column on page 1284 of the text.

Since the Oxford translations were made by a number of scholars over a considerable period of time, some disagreement is found among the works as to the translation of certain words. For example, σοφία is translated as "wisdom," "reason," or "philosophic wisdom"; φρόνησις as "practical wisdom" or "prudence"; and ἀρχή as "basic truth," "starting-point," "beginning," or "principle." In such cases each translation is

v

listed and the Greek word indicated. The Fragments and the *Constitution of Athens* are not included in this index.

I am indebted to Professor Herbert Martin of the State University of Iowa and to Professor Wilfrid S. Sellars of the University of Minnesota for counsel on the analysis of Aristotle; to Professor Arthur M. Young of the University of Pittsburgh for checking the Greek words; and to my wife, Lorena May, for her painstaking clerical work.

T.W.O.

AN INDEX TO ARISTOTLE

Abdera, 742 b 20

Abdomen, 493 a 19, 655 a 1, 688 b 35, 810 b 17-23

Abomasum, enystrum, 507 b 9

Abortions, 758 b 5, 773 b 18, 1335 b 24; more likely in spring 860 a 19-22

Abscess, 863 a 8, 9, 885 b 31

Absolute attributes, absolute and relative good 49 b 10-14, 115 b 15-35, 116 b 8, 142 b 12, 1129 b 4, 1152 b 26-28, 1155 b 21, 1156 b 14, 1182 b 2, 1228 b 18, 1235 b 30-35, 1237 a 13, 27, 1363 b 5-1365 b 21; definition of 'to belong absolutely' 115 b 29-35; the eternal beautiful 700 b 34

Abstraction (ἀφαίρεσις), 1036 b 6, 1061 a 29, 1142 a 18

Abydos, 1349 a 3-7; insane man of 832 b 18-22; magistrates elected by the people at 1305 b 32; revolution at 1306 a 32; method of raising money at 1349 a 3-7

Acalephae. *See* Sea-anemone

Acanthis, linnet, 616 b 30; diet of 592 b 17; habits of 610 a 6

Accent (προσῳδία), Fallacy of, one of six fallacious refutations dependent on language 165 b 26; examples of 166 a 39-b 9; a form of *ignoratio elenchi* 168 a 30; solution of 177 b 35-178 a 3

Accident, coincident (συμβεβηκός), 83 a 25-32, 101 b 18, 103 b 6, 486 b 5, 649 a 1-12, 1013 b 34-1014 a 19, 1015 b 16-34, 1017 a 7-22, 1026 a 34-1027 b 16, 1030 b 18, 1064 b 15-1065 b 4, 1093 b 17; defined 73 b 4, 102 b 4, 103 b 18, 120 b 35, 1026 b 30; can be no science of the accidental 75 a 19-21, 1064 b 30; never a subject 83 b 18-31; relation between accident and property 102 b 21; commonplace rules governing predications 108 b 37-120 b 7; immortality, an accident of life 126 b 36; tests of accidents apply to all other predicables 155 a 11-13; accidental predicate is the hardest to overthrow 155 a 32; and

substance 1007 a 30-b 18; meanings of 1025 a 14-34, 1031 b 22-27; the same by accident 1037 b 6; nothing is by accident perishable 1059 a 1; error of treating the accident as essential 1401 b 14-18. Cf. Attribute

Accident, Fallacy of, one of the seven fallacious refutations independent of language 166 b 22; examples of 166 b 28-38; fallacy with which amateurs entrap scientists 168 b 6-10; fallacy of consequent is a branch of 168 b 27; solution of 179 a 26-180 a 22

Accountants, 1322 b 11

Accusation, 1368 b 1-1369 b 32, 1426 b 22-1427 a 22; one of the genera of oratory 1421 b 9, 1428 a 6; methods of 1441 b 30-1445 a 29

Acetabulum, 493 a 24

Achaea, Achaeans, 343 b 2, 366 a 27, 368 b 7, 840 b 12, 1269 b 7, 1303 a 29, 1338 b 21; stags of 830 b 22

Achainae deer, gall-bladder of 506 a 25; horns of 611 b 18

Acharnas, 602 a 11; diet of 591 b 1

Achelous River, 350 b 16, 352 a 36, 420 b 12, 535 b 18, 579 b 7, 606 b 15

Achetes. *See* Chirper

Achilles, 97 b 18, 117 b 14, 24, 166 a 38, 239 b 14, 24, 618 b 27, 1071 a 22, 1230 a 20, 1359 a 2, 1363 a 18, 1378 b 32, 1380 b 28, 1396 a 25, b 12, 15, 1397 b 22, 1401 b 17, 1406 b 21, 1416 b 27, 1418 a 35, 1454 b 14, 1460 a 16; 'the sponge of Achilles' 548 b 1, 21; temple of 840 a 12

Acorns, 603 b 31, 615 b 22, 820 b 10, 925 b 32, 930 b 16, 931 a 7; become bitter with age 925 b 38

Acquired characteristics, 806 a 26; can be inherited 585 b 29-34

Acquisition, natural kinds 1256 b 23, 26-1257 a 41, b 19, 1258 b 10-20; kinds contrary to nature 1257 a 6-19, 1258 b 1, 21-26; intermediate kinds 1258 b 27. Cf. Wealth

An Index to Aristotle

Acris. *See* Grasshopper

Acropolis, 399 b 34, 846 a 20, 1347 a 16, 1400 b 32

Action, conduct, doing (πρᾶξις), 431 b 10, 433 a 17, 1113 b 18; example of 2 a 4; admits of contraries and variation of degree 11 b 1; attributed to stars 292 a 14; most varied in man 292 b 2; why thought is sometimes followed by action, sometimes not 701 a 7-b 33; concerned with individuals 981 a 17; defined 1048 b 22; actions are always particular 1110 b 6, 1141 b 6; controlling factors of action and truth 1139 a 18; action and making 1140 a 1-23; good action is the end of practical wisdom 1140 b 7; starting-points of 1144 a 35; final cause is first principle in actions 1151 a 17 (Cf. 1139 a 32); the circumstances of action trivial and unworthy of gods 1178 b 17; the life of action 1265 a 25, 1324 a 5-1325 b 32; superior and inferior actions 1333 a 24-b 3; leisure is the first principle of all action 1337 b 32; seven causes of 1369 a 5; just and unjust actions 1373 b 1-1374 a 17

Action-passion, 315 b 5, 322 b 6-29, 702 a 21, 704 a 1, 705 a 25; must be same in genus and different in species 323 b 1-324 b 25; erroneous theories of its mechanism 324 b 26-326 b 28; explained as a body's actual and potential possession of a quality 326 b 29-327 a 29

Active reason, 430 a 10-25; identical with objects which it thinks 431 b 17. Cf. Reason

Activity (ποιεῖν, ἐνέργεια), 1 b 25, 103 b 22, 1068 a 13-15, 1094 a 4, 1098 a 7, b 31, 1103 a 27, b 21, 1104 a 28, 1175 b 24, 1185 a 27, 1218 b 36, 1219 a 32, 1220 a 8, 1228 a 13, 1237 a 23, 38, 1241 a 40; genus of 'to build' 124 a 21; genus of using 124 a 33; danger of placing a state and an activity in genus-species relationship 125 b 15-19; genus of motion 125 b 17 (Cf. 417 a 16); genus of memory 125 b 19; capacity for activity and potentiality not a property of Being 139 a 4-8; not a means of defining Being 146 a 22,

31, 148 a 18; always superior to passive factor 430 a 18; happiness is an activity 1098 a 17, b 30-1099 a 5, 26, 1102 a 5, 1169 b 28, 1176 b 2, 1177 a 10, 1184 b 32-1185 a 13, 1204 a 28, 1208 a 37, 1219 a 35-b 25, 1325 a 32, 1450 a 17; character determined by activities 1100 b 33, 1122 b 1; of God 1178 b 22; better than state 1190 a 34-b 6

Actors, 901 b 2, 904 b 3, 916 b 35-39, 1405 a 23, 1413 b 12, 1449 b 4, 1450 b 18, 1451 b 37, 1456 a 26, 1459 b 26, 1461 b 33; are imitators 918 b 27; generally of bad character 956 b 11-15; in drama actors count for more than poets 1403 b 33; naturalness of voice of 1404 b 22; increased to two by Aeschylus 1449 a 16. Cf. Theatre

Actuality (ἐνέργεια), 186 a 3, 191 b 28, 262 a 22, 417 a 9, 426 a 1-26, 445 b 30, 734 a 30, b 21, 735 a 10, 740 b 20, 741 b 15, 743 a 23, 1009 a 35, 1047 a 15-b 2, 1048 a 25-1051 a 33, 1065 b 5-1066 a 34, 1071 a 5, b 20, 1076 a 10, 1103 a 27; all causes may be either potential or actual 195 b 4; as used in a definition of movement 201 b 10; and generation 302 a 9; potentiality as explanation of action-passion relationship 326 b 29-327 a 29; form as actuality 412 a 10, 414 a 16; two senses of: (1) possession and (2) actual exercise 412 a 23, 417 a 22; and unity 412 b 9; soul as actuality 413 a 1; and potentiality in sensation 414 a 25, 431 a 5, b 25; and essence 415 b 14; and knowing 417 a 29, 429 b 31, 431 a 3, b 25; do first principles exist potentially or actually? 1002 b 32-1003 a 4; substance as actuality of sensible things 1042 b 9-1044 a 14; defined 1048 a 31; prior to potentiality 1049 b 4-1051 a 3, 1072 a 3-8; the end of potency 1050 a 10; better than potentiality 1051 a 4-21; geometrical truths found by actualization of potentialities 1051 a 22-33; and change 1069 b 16; God's actuality is pleasure 1072 b 16; in rhetorical style 1410 b 36, 1411 b 24-1412 a 8, b 32. Cf. Potentiality, Reality

4

Agathon, 1139 b 9, 1140 a 19, 1230 a 1, 1232 b 8, 1392 b 8, 1402 a 10, 1451 b 22, 1454 b 14, 1456 a 19, 23, 30

Agathyrsi, 920 a 1

Agent, patient and agent must be same in genus and different in species 323 b 1-324 b 25; active and passive 729 b 11

Agesilaus, king of Sparta, 1306 b 36

Aglaia, 1414 a 3

Agora, 1306 b 3; wardens of the agora 1299 b 17, 1322 a 14, 1331 b 9; freemen's agora 1331 a 32; trader's agora 1331 b 1

Agriculture, greater part of mankind engaged in 1256 a 39; a natural means of acquiring wealth 1256 b 1, 1258 b 18; works on 1258 b 40; Spartans not allowed to engage in 1264 a 10; laws to encourage 1319 a 6-19; prior among the arts 1343 a 26; a natural art 1343 a 30; conducive to bravery 1343 b 2

Ague, 947 a 21

Air (ἀήρ), 213 a 25, 216 b 18, 289 a 20, 698 b 18, 787 b 5, 824 b 22, 851 a 17; wind is not air 127 a 6; not its property to be breathable 135 a 33-b 1, 138 b 30-37; thought to be incorporeal 212 a 12; moves upward 269 a 18 (Cf. 939 a 39-b 4); thought to support the earth 294 b 14; both light and heavy 301 b 23; thought by some to be the one element 303 b 11; 'more real' than earth 318 b 29; hot and moist 330 b 4, 348 b 27; an intermediate element 330 b 34, 823 b 5; contrary to earth 331 a 2, 335 a 6; nearest to fire 339 a 18; not the element that fills space between earth and heaven 339 b 30-340 a 18; condensed by cold 341 b 36, 342 a 29, 373 a 28; outermost part potentially fire 345 b 32; a condition of appearance of haloes 346 a 5; thought to be wind, cloud, or water according to its state 349 a 16, 360 a 27; sphere of 354 b 24, 823 b 2, 824 b 23; in the clouds 373 b 20; in oil 384 a 16; in wood 384 b 17; medium of sound 419 a 32, b 33, 420 a 10, 800 a 1-15; medium of smell 424 b 18; air and water form sense organs 425 a 4; propagates movement farthest of all media 435

a 4; digests itself 481 a 15; warm when exhaled 481 b 12; cannot exist in water 482 a 23; akin to soul 483 a 26; agency by which the parts of animals are differentiated 741 b 37; vital heat found in all air 762 a 20; the environing air 777 b 7; colour of 791 a 2, 792 a 18, 794 a 7-15; a transparent medium 794 a 1; problems connected with 937 b 30-940 a 15; not moistened when in contact with water 938 a 17-22, 939 a 16-28; can pass through solids 939 a 10-15; cannot saturate anything 939 a 28-32; smaller amount is warmer than large amount 939 b 23-26; does not become corrupt 939 b 27-32; movement of air in rooms 940 a 3-15; Anaximenes' view of 975 b 24; Democritus' view of 975 b 28; Xenophanes' view of 976 a 33; pure air contributes to health 1330 b 13

Air-ducts (arteries), air passes to bones through air-ducts 482 b 8; not found in plants 482 b 11; in skin 483 b 15, 484 a 34; connect intestines and belly 483 b 25, 30; and veins 484 a 1-5

Ajax, 97 b 18, 117 b 13, 24, 953 a 21

AJAX of Theodectes, 1399 b 27, 1400 a 28

AJAXES, 1455 b 34

Albion Isles, 393 b 13, 16

Alcaeus, 1285 a 37, 1367 a 9

Alcibiades, 97 b 18, 578 b 28, 1390 b 29, 1451 b 11

Alcidamas, 1373 b 17, 1398 b 9, 1406 a 2, 9, 18, b 11

Alcimenes the Sybarite, 838 a 15

Alcinous, 1417 a 13

ALCINOUS, TALE OF, 1455 a 2

Alcmaeon, 581 a 15, 752 b 26, 916 a 33, 986 a 28, 1110 a 27, 1397 b 4, 1453 a 20, b 24, 33; immortality of soul 405 a 29-34; his view that goats inspire through ears 492 a 14

Alcman, 557 a 3

Aleïan plain, 953 a 24

Aletafur tree, 829 a 20

Aleudae, at Larissa 1306 a 31

Alexander the Great, 391 a 1, 1352 a 29, b 26, 1420 a 5

Alexandria, 1352 a 17

417 b 2; 'to perceive by sight' 425 b 20; 'sound' 426 a 8; 'hearing' 426 a 8; 'sense' 426 a 23; 'the sensible object' 426 a 23; 'that which originates the movement' 433 b 14; 'hot' 648 a 20-649 b 8; 'cold' 649 b 7; 'solid' 649 b 9-22; 'fluid' 649 b 9-22; 'impossible' 699 b 18-30; 'from' 724 a 20-35, 994 a 19-b 6; 'prior' 742 a 20; 'eternal' 742 b 27; 'keen' 780 b 14; 'quicker' 848 b 6-8; 'what a thing is' 1030 a 18-26; 'part' 1034 b 33; 'circle' 1035 b 1; 'weight' 1052 b 28; 'speed' 1052 b 29; 'like' 1054 b 3-12; 'other' 1054 b 13-22; 'that which is not' 1067 b 26; 'knowledge' 1087 a 15; 'being' 1089 a 7, 16; 'do' 1136 b 30; 'know' 1146 b 31; 'fortunate' 1207 a 28; 'within the range of action' 1217 a 35; 'work' 1219 a 13-27; 'formidable' 1228 b 17; 'pleasant' 1228 b 18; 'profligate' 1230 a 38-b 13, 1231 a 19; 'all' 1261 b 20; 'both' 1261 b 29; 'odd' 1261 b 29; 'even' 1261 b 29; 'state' 1276 a 24; 'practical' 1363 a 22; 'easily' 1363 a 23; 'difficulty' 1363 a 24; as a line of argument 1398 a 28

Ambitiousness, 146 b 23, 1107 b 28, 1125 b 1-25, 1159 a 13, 1239 a 25; a cause of revolutions 1266 b 38, 1267 a 39, 1309 a 2, 1310 b 19; a cause of crime 1267 a 1-17, 1271 a 16

Ambracia, 1311 a 40; revolution at 1303 a 22-24, 1304 a 32

Ambrosia, food of the gods, 1001 a 12

Amia. *See* Bonito

Amisus, 554 b 16, 1350 b 27; iron of 833 b 23-32

Ammon, 352 b 33

Amneus. *See* Euronotus

Amphiaraus, 1389 a 16, 1455 a 27

Amphiboly, as test of accident 110 b 16-111 a 7; three varieties of 166 b 15-22. Cf. Ambiguity

Amphiboly, Fallacy of, one of six fallacious refutations dependent on language 165 b 26; examples of 166 a 7-14; solution of 177 a 9-33

Amphipolis, 841 b 15; revolution at 1303 b 3, 1306 a 2

Amphitryon, 834 b 26

Amplification and depreciation, 1376 a 34, 1419 b 12; means of 1368 a 10-32; not elements of enthymeme 1403 a 17-24

Amusement, 1108 a 13, 23, 1370 a 16; gives relaxation 1127 b 34, 1176 b 34, 1337 b 38, 1339 b 15; most people delight more than they should in amusement 1128 a 14; necesary element in life 1128 b 3; the lover of amusement 1150 b 16-18; happiness does not lie in amusement 1176 a 30-1177 a 10. Cf. Leisure, Relaxation

Amyntas the Little, 1311 b 3, 14

Anacharsis, 78 b 29, 1176 b 34

Analogy (ἀναλογία), 76 a 37, 99 a 16, 108 a 7-17, 138 b 22-27, 1048 b 7, 1457 b 9, 17; a method of selection 98 a 20; the same by analogy 1016 b 32-1017 a 2, 1018 a 13, 1070 a 32, b 18, 1071 a 4, 26, 1093 b 18. Cf. Like, Metaphor, Proportion

Analysis (ἀνάλυσις), of syllogisms of one figure into another 47 a 4, 50 a 8-51 b 4; of premisses into terms 49 a 19; analytic and dialectic proof 84 a 7, b 3; order of 1112 b 23

Anapaest, 1452 b 23

Anaxagoras, 723 a 7, 11, 756 b 17, 988 a 16, 991 a 17, 1012 a 25, 1063 b 25, 1072 a 5, 1079 b 21, 1091 b 12, 1141 b 4, 1215 b 6, 1216 a 11; Being is one and many 187 a 22-188 a 17; elements are infinite in number 187 a 27, 189 a 17, 203 a 20, 314 a 16, 984 a 11-16; all things mixed together at one time 203 a 22-33, 1007 b 26, 1009 a 27, 1056 b 28, 1071 b 27; why the infinite is at rest 205 b 1-6; refutes existence of the void 213 a 23, 976 b 19-22; mind introduced motion 250 b 24, 252 a 10, 256 b 25, 265 b 22; made ether equivalent to fire 270 b 25, 339 b 23; earth is flat 294 b 14-30; his cosmogony begins with unmoved things 301 a 12; elements are the homoeomerous bodies 302 a 33, b 14, 314 a 20; has not analyzed the notions of light and heavy 309 a 19; distinguishes between coming to be and alteration 314 a 12; on the nature of comets 342 b 27; on nature of milky way 345 a 25-b 9; on

rain 348 b 13; on earthquakes 365 a
19-35; theory of thunder and lightning 369 b 14-24; view of soul 404 a
25-b 7, 405 a 14-18, b 20; mind must
be pure from all admixture 429 a 20;
mind is simple and impassible 429 b
24; all animals breathe 470 b 31;
thinks gall-bladder is cause of acute
diseases 677 a 6; thinks that possession
of hands is cause of man being most
intelligent of all animals 687 a 7; on
sex differentiation 763 b 31-34, 765 a
3-34; says plants are animals 815 a 15;
says plants have intelligence 815 b 17;
thinks plants had respiration 816 b 26;
says seeds of plants came from the air
817 a 27; on sounds 903 a 8-11; on the
water-clock 914 b 9-15; on coming to
be 975 b 16-27; his view of the unlimited 976 a 14; his view of Being
976 a 18; reason as source of world
order 984 b 18; treats reason mechan-
ically 985 a 18; infinite number of
similar atoms 988 a 27; criticism of
989 a 30-b 28; the 'One' 1069 b 21;
'reason' 1075 b 8-10; his description of
the happy man 1179 a 13-16; given
public funeral by the people of Lamp-
sacus 1398 b 15; referred to 1028 b 5,
1069 b 32

Anaxandrides, 1152 a 22, 1411 a 19,
1412 b 17; the *Old Men's Madness* of
1413 b 25

Anaxilaus, tyrant at Rhegium, 1316 a 38

Anaximander, contraries are contained
in the one and emerge from it 187 a
20; identifies infinite and the Divine
203 b 14; earth keeps its place because
of its indifference 295 b 10; the All is
water 975 b 23; the 'mixture' 1069 b
23; referred to 988 a 30, 1052 b 10,
1053 b 15, 1066 b 35

Anaximenes, earth is flat 294 b 14-30; on
earthquakes 365 b 7-20; air as first
principle 975 b 24, 984 a 5; referred to
984 a 28, 988 a 30, 996 a 9, 1001 a 16,
1053 b 15

Anchovy, encrasicholus, 569 b 27

Andria, ancient Spartan name for the
common meals 1272 a 2

Andrians, 1270 b 12

Androcles, 1400 a 9

Androdamas of Rhegium, gave laws to
Chalcidians of Thrace 1274 b 23-25

Andromache, 1239 a 38

Androtion, 1406 b 28

Angel-fish, rhina, 506 b 8, 746 b 6;
breeding of 540 b 11, 543 a 14, b 10;
generation of 565 b 24, 566 a 22; habits of 620 b 30, 622 a 13; skin of 697
a 6

Anger, rage (θυμός, ὀργή), 113 a 36, 403
a 26, 1103 b 8, 1105 b 22, 1106 a 2,
1108 a 4, 1109 b 16, 1125 b 26, 30,
1130 a 31, 1135 b 29, 1138 a 9, 1147 a
15, 1186 a 24, 1191 b 25-38, 1220 b 12,
1221 b 13-15, 1222 a 42, 1225 a 20,
1229 a 5, 1231 b 7, 15, 1250 a 6, 18, 42,
1251 a 6, 1328 a 11, 1354 a 16, 1369 a
4, 1378 a 22, 31-1380 a 4, 1382 a 2-18,
1383 b 6, 1419 b 26, 1456 b 1; not defined as 'pain with a consciousness of
being slighted' 151 a 15 (Cf. 125 b 29,
126 a 6-12); defined 156 a 33, 1378 a
31; how to produce anger in a contentious argument 174 a 20-23; not easily
stopped 453 a 27; often stammer
when angry 804 b 38; voice becomes
high when angry 807 a 14; chest red
when angry 812 a 26-29; makes men
hot 869 a 5, 889 a 15-25, 947 b 23-948
a 12; causes lip to hang down 948 b
4; makes eyes red 957 b 9-17, 961 a 8-
15; harder to fight with pleasure than
with anger 1105 a 8 (Cf. 1315 a 30);
is giving away to anger voluntary?
1111 a 25-b 2, 19, 1135 b 20, 1223 b
18-24; thought to be courage 1116 b
23-1117 a 9; virtues concerned with
1125 b 26-1126 b 10; incontinence in
respect of 1145 b 20, 1148 b 14, 1149
a 4, 24-1150 a 7, 1147 a 15, b 34, 1148
a 11, 1188 a 26, 1201 a 37, 1202 b 10-
28; a species of passion 1220 b 12,
1229 a 21; a species of desire 1223 a
27, 1225 b 25, opposed to reason 1312
b 25-27; accompanied by pain 1312 b
32; in children 1334 b 23; a cause of
action 1369 a 6, b 12-14

Angles, 856 b 24, 857 b 25, 858 a 2, 970
a 12; in triangles 851 a 14; of circles
851 b 24, 38, 855 a 37; in rhombus
855 a 6-24; right angles 857 b 25, 913
b 10, 28, 33, 36; of rebounding ob-

jects 913 b 6-36, 915 b 18-35; notes compared to angles 918 a 21

Animals, not every animal breathes 78 a 23, 444 b 6, 470 b 10-27, 659 b 13, 816 b 27; do not deliberate 199 a 21, 1254 b 23, 1332 b 3; motion of 252 b 22, 253 a 12, 254 b 15, 265 b 34, 290 a 30, 398 b 30-35, 698 a 1-714 b 24; growth of 270 a 31, 916 a 12-17; spatial oppositions in 284 b 14; all animals have sensation 413 b 2, 436 b 11, 467 b 24, 816 a 12; many are voiceless 420 b 9; all animals have five senses 425 a 10; nature of soul of animals 432 a 15; defined as a body with soul in it 434 b 12; cannot exist without touch 434 b 17, 23; body of animal cannot consist of one element 435 a 11, 20; certain lower animals dream 463 b 11; small animals are usually short-lived 466 a 15, 474 b 31; positions of parts in 486 b 23; dwellings of 488 a 21-25; domestication of 488 a 27-31; sleep of 536 b 24-537 b 21, 599 a 29, 894 a 22-29; psychical qualities and habits of 588 a 16-633 b 9; two major acts of: (1) procreation and (2) feeding 589 a 4; drinking habits of 595 a 6-13; study of animals not ignoble 644 b 22-645 b 13; all animals must have some heat 652 b 17; compared with plants 681 a 12, 26 (Cf. 686 b 34), 731 b 4 (Cf. 732 a 13), 741 a 10, 778 b 33, 817 b 32, 818 a 17-21, 819 a 19; all animals except man are dwarf-like in form 686 b 3-35, 689 b 26, 695 a 9; all animals except man have but one mode of defense 687 a 26; tail of 689 b 1, 29-690 a 3; compared with automata 701 b 1-14; why animals have an even number of legs 708 a 22-b 19; swimming of 713 a 4-16; generation of 715 a 1-789 b 21, 897 b 33, 898 b 3-11, 1262 a 21; all animals produce semen 720 a 10; sexes are separated in all animals that can move about 730 b 34; function of animals is to generate and to acquire knowledge 731 a 30; classification of 732 a 25-733 b 22, 737 b 15-738 a 8; formed out of semen 733 b 24; parts of animals differentiated by air 741 b

37; relation of egg and animal 751 b 2-12; ought to be an animal corresponding to fire 761 b 16-23; animals in the moon 761 b 21; cause of long life in 777 b 7; colour of 785 b 17-786 b 5, 797 a 34-799 b 20; some animals do not have female sex 816 a 18; origin of 892 a 26; imitation of parents 894 a 30-37; tame and wild 895 b 22-896 a 11, 1254 b 10; copulation of 896 a 20-29, 1343 b 13-15; marine animals larger than land animals 897 b 14-18; parts which have no functional importance are round 915 a 25-33; extremities are round 915 a 34-36; increase in length more than in any other direction 916 a 12-17; live by appetite, passion, and desire 956 b 35; animals that have memory are more intelligent 980 b 21; why animals are speechless 1253 a 8-17; ruled by man 1254 b 11; modes of life of 1256 a 19-30; exist for sake of man 1256 b 15-22; common life in animals is entirely for procreation 1343 b 15

Animate things, problems connected with 915 b 36-916 a 39

Anise, promotes flow of urine 949 a 2

Ankle, 494 a 10, 516 b 1, 712 a 17; as a physiognomic sign 810 a 25-28

Ant, 199 a 23, 428 a 10, 444 b 12, 488 a 21, 523 b 20, 534 b 22, 594 b 9, 614 b 12; gregarious 488 a 10; generation of 555 a 19-22, 721 a 5; the 'horseman-ant' 606 a 5; habits of 622 b 21, 542 b 30, 623 b 13; intelligence of 650 b 27; tongue of 661 a 17, 678 b 17; teeth of 683 a 6

Antandria, 519 a 16

Antariates, 844 b 10

Antelope, blood of 515 b 33

ANTHEUS of Agathon, 1451 b 22

Anthias. See Aulopias

Anthrena. See Hornet

Anthus, 592 b 25; habits of 609 b 14, 610 a 6, 615 a 27

Anticipation of arguments (προκατά-ληψις), 1428 a 8, 1432 b 11-1433 b 16, 1437 a 2, b 22, 38, 1439 b 3-13, 1440 a 24, 1442 b 5, 1443 a 7, 30, 40, b 13; defined 1432 b 12, 1439 b 4, 1444 a 16-b 7

ANTIDOSIS of Isocrates, 1418 b 28

Antigone, 1373 b 9, 1375 a 34, 1417 a 28, 1418 b 33

ANTIGONE of Sophocles, 1417 a 28, 1454 a 2; quoted 1415 b 19

Antileon, tyrant at Chalcis, 1316 a 32

Antilochus, 513 b 26

Antimachus, 1408 a 2

Antimenes, his schemes for raising money 1352 b 26-1353 a 4, 24-28

Antimenides, brother of Alcaeus, 1285 a 36

Antipheron, oreus, 451 a 9

Antiphon, 172 a 8, 193 a 12, 847 a 20, 1232 b 7, 1239 a 38, 1385 a 9; geometers need not refute his proof of the squaring of the circle 185 a 17; the *Meleager* of 1379 b 15, 1399 b 25

Antiphony, 918 b 30-39; antiphonal notes 919 a 9-13; more pleasing than homophony 921 a 7-30

Antissa, 1347 a 25; revolution at 1303 a 34

Antisthenes, 1024 b 32, 1407 a 9; contradiction is impossible 104 b 21; on definition 1043 b 24-33; fable of 1284 a 16

Antistrophe, 918 b 13-29

Antithesis. *See* Opposition

Anus, 675 b 11

Aorta, 458 a 15, 485 b 7, 510 a 15, 513 a 21, 515 a 30, 586 b 20, 652 b 30, 666 b 26, 670 a 17, 671 b 13, 672 b 6, 678 a 1, 738 a 15; nature and functions of 667 b 15-668 b 32

Aparctias. *See* Boreas

Ape, 502 a 16-b 24, 689 b 32, 810 b 3, 811 a 26, b 10

Apelietes (E. wind), 363 b 13, 394 b 23, 844 a 26, 943 b 35, 946 b 24, 34, 947 a 2, 973 a 13-b 1, 6; does not form clouds 940 a 32-34; blows in early morning 944 a 20; origin of its name 944 a 24; called Potameus at Tripolis 973 a 12; called Syriandus at Rosus 973 a 18; called Marseus at Gulf of Tripolis 973 a 19; sometimes called Hellespontias 973 a 22; called Berecyntias at Sinope 973 a 25; called Cataporthmias in Sicily 973 a 26; sometimes called Thebanas 973 b 1; the most healthful wind 1330 a 40

Aperient, 1199 a 32

Aphrodite, 406 b 18, 838 a 25, 953 b 31, 1269 b 29, 1400 b 22, 1413 a 34; called 'guile-weaving daughter of Cyprus' 1149 b 17

Aphytaeans, democracy of the 1319 a 16

Apis, 1216 a 1

Aplysia, 549 a 3

Apollo, 834 b 24, 838 a 25, 1380 b 28, 1398 b 33; temple of 840 a 20

Apollodorus the Lemnian, 1258 b 41

Apollonia on the Euxine, 511 b 30, 833 a 8, 973 a 23, 1306 a 7; bitumen and burning ground of 842 b 15-27; revolution at 1303 a 38

Apollonia on the Ionian Gulf, 1290 b 11

APOLOGY of Plato, 1419 a 8-12

Apoplexy, 874 b 29, 875 b 7, 37, 903 b 9, 905 a 17, b 35, 954 a 23; effect of seasons on 860 a 34; not infectious 887 a 22-39

Aporeme, defined as an inference that reasons dialectically to a conclusion 162 a 18

Apotome, 968 b 19

Appearance (φαντασία), 1009 a 6-1011 b 23, 1070 a 10; animals other than men live by appearances 980 b 25; not same as sensation 1010 b 3-1011 b 23. Cf. Image

Appetite (ἐπιθυμία, ὄρεξις), 1103 b 18, 1105 b 22, 1117 a 1, 1148 a 21, 1151 b 8, 1224 a 37, b 2, 1225 b 25-30, 240 b 34, 1247 b 20, 38, 1248 a 1, 1250 a 11, b 14, 1369 a 4; genus of desire, passion, wish, etc. 414 b 2, 433 a 25; and avoidance 431 a 12; as source of movement 433 a 5-434 a 22, 701 a 32; contains no deliberative element 434 a 12; is everything in accord with appetite voluntary? 1111 a 25-b 2, 1223 a 29-b 17; contrary to choice 1111 b 10-18; natural appetites 1118 b 15; children are slaves to appetite 1119 b 5; strong appetites 1146 a 2, 10, 1178 b 16, 1246 b 14; incontinence in respect of 1149 a 24-1150 a 7, 1201 a 12-33, 1202 a 14, b 27, 1203 a 5, b 14; some appetites are necessary, others are not 1150 a 18; are acts due to appetite voluntary? 1187 b 38-1188 a 23; a cause of action 1225 a 31, 1369 a 6, b 15; always involves pain 1125 b 31; and temperance 1230 b 21-24; all animals display appetite 1421 a 10

Appetitive element in the soul, 414 a 30, 415 a 14-416 b 31, 432 b 4, 1102 b 30, 1119 b 14, 1185 a 21, 1221 b 31, 1234 b 26, 1249 b 28, 1250 a 10, 1254 b 6, 1277 a 7

Apple, apple-tree, 796 b 13, 819 b 23, 820 b 38, 923 b 25, 1118 a 11

Apprehension, 1250 a 7, 44, 1251 a 12

Appropriateness of rhetorical style, 1404 b 4-25, 1408 a 10-b 21

Apus, cypselus, swift, 487 b 29; habits of 618 a 31

Arabia, 349 a 5, 606 b 6, 906 b 18, 908 a 14; the Arabian camel 494 b 8, 499 a 14, 546 b 2, 830 b 6; hyena in 845 a 24-27

Arabian Gulf, 393 b 17, 27

Arachotae, 499 a 4

Araxes River, 350 a 24

Arcadia, Arcadians, 351 a 3, 388 b 6, 617 a 14, 831 b 14, 842 b 8, 1261 a 26, 1269 b 4, 1270 a 2; winds of 947 a 15-24

Archelaus, king of Macedonia, 954 b 32, 1311 b 8, 30, 1398 a 25

Archias of Thebes, 1306 b 2

Archibius, 1376 a 10

Archicles, 1189 b 20, 21

Archidamus, 1406 b 31

Archilochus, 1328 a 4, 1398 b 11, 1418 b 28

Architect, 1198 a 35

Architecture, 1140 a 7

Archon, 1322 b 29, 1449 b 2; a single archon at Epidamnus 1287 a 7, 1301 b 25

Archytas, 915 a 29, 1043 a 22, 1412 a 12; invented the children's rattle 1340 b 26

Arcturus, 569 b 3, 578 b 12, 598 a 19, 599 b 12, 617 a 30, 859 a 22

Arctus, bear-crab, 549 b 22

Ardiaei, 844 b 9

Areopagus, Council of, 1188 b 33, 1274 a 8, 1275 b 39, 1304 a 21, 1315 b 22, 1354 a 22, 1398 b 27

Ares, 392 a 25, 1269 b 29, 1407 a 16, 1413 a 1, 5, 1457 b 22, 33

Arethusa, fountain of 847 a 4

Argas, 1448 a 17

Argestes. *See* Iapyx

Arginussa, 578 b 27

Argo, 1284 a 25

Argolid, 602 a 9

Argonaut. *See* Nautilus

Argonauts, 1284 a 24; journey of the 839 b 14-840 a 6

Argos, 117 a 27, 352 a 9, 836 b 13, 846 a 22, 1269 b 4, 1270 a 2, 1304 a 25, 1310 b 27, 1365 a 27, 1375 a 5, 1452 a 7; scorpion-fighter of 844 b 24-31; ostracism at 1302 b 18; revolution at 1303 a 7

Argument, four classes of arguments in dialogue form: (1) didactic, (2) dialectical, (3) examination-arguments, and (4) contentious arguments 165 a 39-b 11; incisive (δριμύς) argument 182 b 32; the four general lines of argument: (1) possible and impossible, (2) fact past, (3) fact future, (4) degree 1392 a 8-1392 a 21; twenty-eight lines of argument upon which genuine enthymemes may be based: (1) opposites 1397 a 7-18, (2) modification of the key-word 1397 a 19-22, (3) correlative ideas 1397 a 23-b 11, (4) *a fortiori* 1397 b 12-26, (5) considerations of time 1397 b 27-1398 a 2, (6) turning words of opponent against himself 1398 a 3-14, (7) definition of terms 1398 a 15-27, (8) ambiguous terms 1398 a 28, (9) logical division 1398 a 29-31, (10) induction 1398 a 32-b 18, (11) previous decision or general consent 1398 b 19-1399 a 6, (12) taking separately the parts of a subject 1399 a 7, 8, (13) consequences 1399 a 9-17, (14) contrasting opposites 1399 a 18-27, (15) inconsistency 1399 a 28-32, (16) rational correspondence 1399 a 33-b 3, (17) from results to antecedents 1399 b 4-12, (18) inconsistency 1399 b 13-18, (19) from possible motive to real motive 1399 b 19-30, (20) inducements and deterrents 1399 b 31-1400 a 4, (21) things which are supposed to happen and yet seem incredible 1400 a 5-13, (22) inconsistency 1400 a 14-21, (23) reasons for prejudice

1400 a 22-28, (24) cause to effect 1400 a 29-35, (25) neglect of a better course 1400 a 36-b 3, (26) inconsistency 1400 b 4-8, (27) previous mistakes 1400 b 9-16, (28) meanings from proper names 1400 b 17-24; nine lines of argument of apparent enthymemes: (1) words 1401 a 1-23, (2) confusion of parts and whole 1401 a 24-b 3, (3) indignant language 1401 b 4-8, (4) using of single instance as proof 1401 b 9-13, (5) the accidental as essential 1401 b 14-18, (6) argument from consequence 1401 b 19-29, (7) treating as causes things that happened along with or before the event in question 1401 b 30-33, (8) omission of time and consequence 1401 b 34-1402 a 2, (9) confusion of the absolute with the particular 1402 a 3-27; in oratory 1414 a 30-b 18, 1416 b 18, 1417 b 22-1418 b 38

Ariobarzanes, assassinated by Mithridates 1312 a 16

Ariphrades, 1458 b 32, 1459 a 2

Aristaeus, 838 b 24

Aristeides, 1398 a 10, 1414 b 36, 1494 b 36

Aristippus, 1398 b 30; ridiculed mathematics 996 a 32; referred to 1078 a 33, 1172 a 27 (?)

Aristocracy (ἀριστοκρατία), 1131 a 29, 1160 a 31, b 12, 33, 1161 a 23, 1241 b 30, 1279 a 35, b 5, 1308 b 39; distinguished from oligarchy and constitutional government 1273 a 2-37, 1293 a 35-1204 a 19, 1298 a 34-b 21, 1307 a 5-33; characterized by election for merit 1273 a 26, 1294 a 9, 1310 b 32; the government of the best 1283 b 20, 1293 b 2-21, 1310 b 2; rule of many good men 1286 b 5; people fitted for 1288 a 10; magistrates in 1299 b 21, 1323 a 8; revolutions in 1306 b 22-1307 b 25; a sort of oligarchy 1306 b 25; how preserved 1308 a 4-24; has an educational qualification for citizenship 1365 b 33-38; its end is the maintenance of education and national institutions 1266 a 5

Aristogeiton, 1368 a 18, 1398 a 19, 1401

b 11; conspiracy of Harmodius and Aristogeiton against the Peisistratidae 1311 a 38

Aristogenes, growth of breath due to respiration 481 a 28

Aristomenes, 47 b 22

Aristophanes, 1262 b 12, 1448 a 27; in the *Babylonians* 1405 b 30

Aristophon, 1398 a 5

Aristotle the Rhodian, his schemes for raising money 1348 a 35-b 16

Arithmetic (ἀριθμοί), 153 a 10, 163 b 24, 1005 a 31; differs in genus from geometry 75 a 39; assumptions of 76 b 7, 93 b 25; more exact than harmonies or geometry 87 a 32-36, 982 b 27; arithmetical number 1083 b 16; theorems of 1090 a 15. Cf. Mathematics, Science

Armenia, leopard's bane of 831 a 3-11

Arms, 491 a 29, 493 b 26, 702 a 32; nature and uses of 687 b 25-688 a 3; flexion of 711 b 10, as a physiognomic sign 808 a 33

Arrangement of a speech, 155 b 3-158 a 30, 174 a 17-b 40, 1414 a 30-1420 b 4; three methods of 1438 b 13-27

Arrhabaeus, king of the Lyncestians, 1311 b 13

Art (τέχνη), 89 b 8, 100 a 8, 193 a 15, 740 b 26-28, 847 a 21, 980 b 27, 1013 a 4, 1034 a 20-24, 1097 a 17, 1098 a 24, 1103 a 32, 1112 b 7, 1133 a 14, 1139 b 16, 1140 b 1, 22, 1175 a 24, 1183 a 8, 1221 b 6, 1247 a 6, 16, 1258 b 35, 1279 a 1, 1284 b 7, 1288 b 10; requires knowledge of both form and matter 194 a 22-27; involves purpose 199 b 29, 1094 a 1, 1182 a 33-b 2, 22-32, 1183 a 36; imitates nature 381 b 6, 396 b 11; efficient cause of 640 a 27-33; the starting-point and form of the product 735 a 2; good and bad 895 b 32-39; man-made 955 b 27; origin of 981 a 1-12; considered more truly knowledge than experience is 981 a 13-b 9; knowledge of universals 981 a 17; some directed to necessities, some to recreation 981 b 13-19; difference between science and art 981 b 26; generation by reason, art, or some faculty 1025 b 23; generation by nature, art, or spontaneity 1032 a 12-1034 a 7, 1070 a 6, 17; all arts are potencies 1046 b 2; must be learned 1046 b 36, 1047 b 32; and virtue 1099 b 23, 1106 b 14; always concerned with the harder 1105 a 9; knowledge of how to make things 1140 a 1-22; defined 1140 a 20; no art of pleasure 1152 b 18, 1153 a 24-26; concerned with making 1197 a 12; requires proper instruments 1253 b 23-1254 a 17; some arts aid others 1256 a 10-15, 1258 a 19-37; difference between work of art and a reality 1281 b 12-14; its end is a good 1282 b 15; art and education fill up the deficiencies of nature 1337 a 2; subdivision of the arts 1343 a 5-9; the art of agriculture 1343 a 26; the mercenary arts 1343 a 29; the war-like arts 1343 a 30; the illiberal arts 1343 b 4

Artabazus, 1351 b 20

Artapanes, the assassin of Xerxes 1311 b 37

Artemis, 894 b 34; temple of 839 b 19, 840 b 20-24; golden bull of Orthosian Artemis 847 b 1, 2

Article, 1435 a 36, b 12-16, 1456 b 22, 1457 a 6-10; its use 49 b 10-14

Artisans, 1267 b 16, 1291 b 19; virtue not expected of 1260 a 38, 1278 a 20, 1319 a 26, 1328 b 40, 1329 a 20; admitted to office in a democracy 1277 b 1; can they be citizens? 1278 a 16-34; necessary to state 1291 a 2; must not be too numerous 1326 a 24

Artists, thought wiser than men of experience 981 a 25, b 31; who should judge the artist? 1282 a 1-23

Arum, 600 b 12

Asbamaeon, 845 b 35

Ascalaphus, caeca of 509 a 22

Ascanian Lake, 834 a 32

Ascarid, 551 a 10, b 27

Ascidians, tethya, 528 a 20, 531 a 7-30, 547 b 22, 588 b 20, 680 a 5, 681 a 31-36, 763 b 14; sense of smell in 535 a 24; differ but slightly from plants 681 a 10, 27

Ashes, 389 a 28, 390 a 23, 441 b 4, 442 a 27, 834 b 31; effect on water 213 b 21, 938 b 25-939 a 9; all bodies combustible that dissolve in ashes 387 b 14; porous 470 a 13; colour of 791 a 6

Asia, 350 a 19, 606 b 18, 1271 b 37, 1289 b 40, 1415 a 17; its bounds 393 b 26; natives of Asia are intelligent and inventive, but lack spirit 1285 a 21, 1327 b 27

Asia Minor, 569 a 19, 578 b 27, 606 b 16

Asp, 607 a 21, 612 a 17. Cf. Serpent, Snake, Viper

Aspen, 595 a 2

Ass, 491 a 1; Indian ass 499 b 19; teeth of 501 b 3, 748 b 10; has no gall-bladder 506 a 23, 676 b 27; blood of 521 a 4; milk of 521 b 33, 522 a 28; in Epirus 522 b 20, 606 b 4; breeding of 545 b 21, 575 b 29, 577 a 18-b 18, 747 b 16; diet of 595 b 23-30; diseases of 605 a 16-22; habits of 609 a 31, b 1, 20, 610 a 4, 831 a 23-25; horns and hoofs of Indian ass 663 a 20, heart of 667 a 21; spleen of 674 a 4; stomach of 674 a 27; mammae of 688 b 22; of cold nature 748 a 24; copulation of 808 b 37; insensible to pain 808 b 39; hair of 893 a 27; excrement of 897 b 34-898 a 3; monstrous births in 898 a 11

Assembly, payment of 1293 a 5, 1317 b 32; powers of 1298 a 4-7; in a democracy 1298 a 11-34, 1305 a 30, 1317 b 17-38, 1320 a 23; in an oligarchy 1298 a 34-b 11

Assiduity, physiognomic signs of 811 b 6

Association and dissociation, relation to coming to be and passing away 317 a 13-32; attributed by Empedocles to 'Love' and 'Strife' 333 b 12, 20-334 a 9

Assyritis, 519 a 15

Astacus. See Crustacea, Lobster

Asteius, 343 b 20

Asterias, bittern, a kind of hawk 620 a 18

Astronomy, 46 a 19, 78 b 40, 291 a 30, 297 a 4, 997 b 16, 34, 998 a 5, 1053 a 10, 1077 a 1, 1216 b 12; its procedure similar to arithmetic 76 b 11; compared with physics 193 b 25; a more physical branch of mathematics 194 a

7; a branch of mathematics that studies moving things 989 b 32; the mathematical science most akin to philosophy 1073 b 4

Astyages, attacked by Cyrus 1312 a 12

Astydamas, 1453 b 33

Atarneus, hot waters at 937 b 7-10; siege of 1267 a 33

Athena, 399 b 34, 838 a 25, 846 a 20, 1363 a 18, 1413 a 34; temple of 840 a 28; Heilenia Athene 840 a 32; Achaean Athene 840 b 2; invented the flute 1341 b 4; Athena-on-the-Acropolis 1347 a 15

Athens, Athenians, 5 b 23, 69 a 1, 94 a 37, 176 b 1, 202 b 13, 224 b 22, 559 a 13, 569 b 12, 27, 577 b 30, 618 b 15, 843 b 18, 1010 b 11, 1124 b 17, 1236 a 37, 1242 b 25, 1267 b 19, 1268 a 10, 1274 a 16, 1275 b 36, 1284 a 39, 1291 b 24, 1300 b 29, 1304 a 6, 20, 24, 1310 b 30, 1319 b 21, 1341 a 33, 1353 a 15, 1367 b 8, 1375 b 29, 1384 b 33, 1396 a 8, 1398 b 1, 17, 1406 b 34, 1407 a 5, 1410 a 13, 14, 1411 a 5, 9, 11, 25, 29, 1412 b 4, 1415 b 31, 1418 a 30, 1422 a 40, 1423 a 7, 1429 b 2, 9, 1431 a 17, 1448 a 36; olive tree at 846 a 8; ostracism at 1302 b 18; revolution at 1303 a 8, 1305 a 23; citizens of Athens less democratic than those of Piraeus 1303 b 10; war between Athens and Mytilene 1304 a 5; government of the Four Hundred 1304 b 12, 1305 b 26, 1419 a 28; government of the Thirty 1305 b 26, 1400 a 18, 33, 1401 a 34; the Eleven at Athens 1322 a 20

Atherine, spawning of 570 b 14, 571 a 7; habits of 610 b 5

Athletes, 1111 b 24, 1116 b 12, 1338 b 9-1339 a 10, 1361 b 3-26; jump with weights 705 a 17; swing arms when they run 705 a 18; eating of 768 b 29; development of 768 b 32; diseases usually fatal in 862 b 21-24; do not bear cold 887 b 22-25, 888 a 22-30; pale 967 a 11-19; constitution of 1335 b 5

Athos, Mount, 549 b 17, 607 a 10, 1410 a 11; has no wind 944 b 13

Athribis, Province of, 1353 a 6

Atitania, fire in 833 a 7-9

Atlantic, 392 b 22, 393 a 17, 946 a 29

Atlas, 284 a 20, 1023 a 20; the fable of 699 a 27-b 2

Atomic connexions, defined 79 a 35

Atomists, 1028 b 5, 1084 b 27; on nature of the void 325 b 12-23. Cf. Democritus, Leucippus

Atoms (of Democritus and Leucippus), differ in shape 275 b 30, 303 a 10; in constant movement 300 b 9; infinite in number 303 a 5; Aristotle thinks them in conflict with fact 304 a 25

Atrabilious. See Melancholic

Atreus, 1413 a 33

Atridae, 840 a 7

Atropos, the Fate dealing with the past 401 b 19

'At some time,' defined 222 a 24

Attalus, 1311 b 3

Attelabus. See Locust

Attention, how to secure 1436 b 5-15, 1438 b 21, 1446 a 2

'Attic neighbour,' 1395 a 17

Attica, 942 a 19, 946 b 34, 947 a 2, 1398 a 1, 1411 a 25; thyme of 925 a 8-18; Attic system of economy 1344 b 32, 1345 a 19

Attribute, predicable of a subject 1 a 20, 2 a 20; present in a subject 1 a 23, 2 a 27; the more attributes one has at hand the more quickly is a conclusion reached 43 b 10; types of: (1) true in every instance, (2) essential, (3) commensurate and universal, (4) accidental 73 a 21-74 a 3; non-essential attribute has no demonstrative knowledge 75 a 19; basic truths of inhering attributes are indemonstrable 76 a 17; cannot be an infinite number of attributes in a thing 82 b 39, 84 a 19-27; never a subject 83 b 22; two reasons for attributes being essential in things 84 a 13; makes the cause clear 88 a 5; attributes that belong to species belong also to genus 111 a 21-33; defined as that which may or may not belong to a subject 186 b 19; incidental attribute as a remote cause 195 a 37; are unity and being substances or attributes? 996 a 5-8, 1001 a 4-b 25, 1060 a 36-b 19. Cf. Accident

Audacity. *See* Rashness

Auditors, 1322 b 11, 36

Augeus, 834 b 28

Aulopias, anthias, 620 b 33; spawning of 570 b 20, 610 b 5

Aulus the Peucestian, 836 a 4

Aurochs. *See* Bison

Ausones in Italy, 1329 b 20

Autocles, 1398 b 24

Autocracy, 1199 b 2

Automata, compared with organisms 701 b 1-14

Autophradates, satrap of Lydia, 1267 a 33

Autumn, hailstorms occur usually in spring and autumn 348 a 1, b 27; autumn rain is brackish 358 b 5; hurricanes usually occur in autumn 365 a 2; earthquakes usually occur in spring and autumn 366 b 2; the 'season of mists' 452 a 16; unhealthful season 862 b 11-15

Auxids, 571 a 18

Avarice, greed, 1270 a 14, 1271 b 16, 1273 a 39; a species of injustice 1251 a 30; a cause of crime 1267 b 1, 1271 a 16; a cause of revolutions 1302 b 5

Avernus, Lake, 839 a 12-26

Avoidance, 1189 b 32, 1190 a 7, 1197 a 2, 1199 a 6; and appetite 431 a 12; objects of: the base, the injurious, the painful 1104 b 32; and choice 1190 a 7, 1197 a 2, 1199 a 6, 1215 b 21, 35, 1216 a 14, 1222 a 33, 1233 a 4, 1249 b 2, 16

Axe, 412 b 13, 840 b 4, 853 b 14-24

Axiom (ἀξίωμα), 996 b 26-997 a 14, 1090 a 36; defined 72 a 17; function of axioms in demonstration 75 b 3, 76 b 10, 77 a 5-35; common axioms cannot serve as universal premisses 88 a 37-b 3; philosophy must study primary axioms 1005 a 18-b 34, 1061 b 18-33. Cf. Demonstration

B

Babbling (ἀδολεσχεῖν), to reduce to babbling one of the aims of contentious arguers 165 b 15; defined 165 b

16; how to produce babbling in an opponent 173 a 31-b 16; solution of arguments leading to 181 b 25-182 a 6

Baboon, 502 a 19

Babylon, 1265 a 15, 1352 b 26; fish in 835 b 7-14; size of 1276 a 28

Babylonia, Babylonians, 1284 b 2; astronomical observations 292 a 8

Bacchiadae at Corinth, 1274 a 33

Bacchic frenzy, 1342 b 4

Back, 493 b 12, 498 b 19; as a physiognomic sign 810 b 10-12, 25-34

Backbone, chine, 493 b 12, 496 b 13; only bone in fish that has marrow 652 a 13, 18; center of bones 654 b 12, 702 b 20; related to heart 702 b 20

Back-stay. *See* Epitonos

Bactrian camel, 498 b 8, 499 a 14

Bactrians, 833 b 15

Bactrus River, 350 a 23

Bakers, 863 b 1, 929 b 26, 967 b 19, 1416 b 31

Balagrus, 538 a 15

Balance (συμμετρία), ambiguous term 139 b 21; larger balance more accurate than small 848 b 1-850 a 1; difference in balance depending on whether cord is attached to upper or lower surface of beam 850 a 2-29; moves more easily without a weight upon it 852 a 23-29

Baldness, 518 a 27; a eunuch never becomes bald 632 a 3, 784 a 8, 897 b 23-29; cause of 783 b 9-784 a 22, 893 b 39; a sign of lustfulness 878 b 21-32; those blind from birth do not become bald 957 b 23-32; not a mutilation 1024 a 28. Cf. Hair

Baleros, 602 b 26; spawning of 568 b 27

Ball of foot, 494 a 13

Balsam, 820 b 28

Bapyrus, 973 a 15

Barbarians, 673 a 25, 836 a 12, 840 a 26, 846 a 32, 1420 b 15, 30; counting of 910 b 24-911 a 3; brutish 1145 a 31, 1149 a 10; thought to be natural slaves 1255 a 28; more servile in character than Greeks 1285 a 20 (Cf. 1252 b 7)

Barbarism, 1458 a 25, 26, 31

Bark of plant, 818 b 12, 819 a 32, 820 a 17, b 27, 821 a 12, 827 b 26, 829 a 1, 837 a 20; as a dye 794 a 19; like skin of animal 818 a 19

Barley, 923 b 10-14, 1208 a 23; of Thrace 841 b 3-8; better food for sick person than wheat 863 a 34-b 10; problems concerning 927 a 11-930 a 4; barley-gruel becomes whiter if oil is added 927 a 11-16; less nourishing than wheat 927 a 17-22; grinding of 927 a 23-26, b 15-20; causes catarrh 929 b 26-29, 967 b 19-22

Barley-cake, kneading makes it more indigestible 927 b 23-31; diminishes when kneaded 927 b 31-37, 929 b 8-17; effect of heat on 927 b 38-928 a 4, 929 b 18-25; becomes blacker when kneaded 929 a 6-10

Barley-meal, 929 a 24-39; adheres better when mixed with water 929 a 11-16; cooling makes it more closely packed 929 b 35-930 a 4

Barnacle, 547 b 22, 715 b 17; sense of smell in 535 a 25

Barter. See Exchange

Base, an object of avoidance 1104 b 32

Bashfulness, shyness, 1108 a 33, 1193 a 1, 4, 1220 b 17, 1221 a 1, 1233 b 28; physiognomic signs of 812 a 32

Basic truth. See Principle

Basil, 821 a 30

Basilidae, an oligarchy in Erythrae 1305 b 20

Basse, labrax, 567 a 19; fins of 489 b 26; hearing of 534 a 9, capture of 537 a 28; spawning of 543 a 3, b 4, 12, 567 a 19, 570 b 21; diet of 591 a 10, b 17; has stone in its head 601 b 31; when edible 607 b 25; habits of 610 b 12

Bastard-animals, 606 b 21-607 a 8

Bat, feet of 485 a 18, 487 b 23; habits of 488 a 26; wings of 490 a 8; have cotyledons in womb 511 a 31; part land animal and part bird 697 b 2, 6-13; a misshapen quadruped 714 b 13. Cf. Flying fox

Baths, cure fatigue 863 b 19, 884 b 36; theft from the 952 a 17-b 35. Cf. Vapour baths

Batis, diet of 592 b 17

Batos. See Ray

Batrachus. See Fishing-frog

Bay-tree, 820 b 40; blossoms are same colour as fruit 796 b 10

Beak of birds, 486 b 10, 504 a 20, 743 a 15, 797 b 19; variations of 662 a 35-b 17; formation of 745 a 1

'Beaming Star,' 392 a 24

Beans, 527 b 17, 595 b 7, 890 a 25; a leguminous plant 522 b 33

Bear, paws of 498 a 34, 499 a 29; hair of 498 b 27; mammae of 500 a 22; stomach of 507 b 17, 20; breeding of 539 b 34; temperament of 571 b 27-30, 608 a 33; reproduction of 579 a 18-30, 580 a 7; diet of 594 b 5-16; habits of 595 a 10, 611 b 33; hibernation of 600 a 28-b 12, 835 a 30; blood of 651 a 2; tail of 658 b 1; development of young at birth 774 b 15; white bears 785 b 35, 798 a 26; fat of 835 a 30-32; in Mysia 845 a 17-23

Bear (the constellation), 362 b 9, 1093 a 19

Bear-crab. See Arctus

Beard, 797 b 30, 808 a 23; of the hippelaphus 498 b 34; in women 518 a 34

Beauty (κάλλος), 951 a 4, 1218 a 22, 1362 b 14, 1447 b 3; not as desirable as health 118 b 20; genuine and artificial kinds 164 b 20; the absolutely beautiful 700 b 34; and sexual intercourse 896 b 10-28; and good 1013 a 22, 1078 a 32-b 5, 1091 a 31; present in the beginning 1072 b 31; chief forms of 1078 b 1; implies a certain size 1123 b 7, 1450 b 37; in a city 1326 a 33, 1330 b 32, 1331 a 12; a constituent of happiness 1360 b 22; varies with time of life 1361 b 7-14; matter of size and order 1450 b 34-1451 a 5

Beaver, latax, 594 b 31; feet of 487 a 22

Becca-fico, 592 b 22, 632 b 31

Becoming (γίγνεσθαι), a species of motion 111 b 7; in the full sense 186 a 14, 225 a 13; always assumes a substance that becomes 190 a 14; ways of: (1) change of shape, (2) addition, (3) taking away, (4) putting together, (5) alteration 190 b 5-8; why previous philosophers were bothered

647 b 14; a purifying excretion 677 a
30, b 7; effect of seasons on diseases
due to bile 859 b 5-14; black bile 860
b 24, 861 b 20; hot 862 b 28; those hot
by nature not having sexual intercourse are often oppressed by bile
880 a 22-29; effect of fear on 948 b 10;
effects of black bile 953 a 10-955 a 40.
Cf. Gall-bladder, Liver

Biliousness, causes feet to swell 859 b 1-
4; effect of seasons on 860 b 15-25

Birdlime, 385 b 6, 386 b 14

Birds, 107 a 25, genus and definition of
490 a 12-b 8, 505 b 30; legs of 498 a
28, 693 b 3-17, 694 b 13, 20, 23, 695 a
15, 712 b 22, 895 a 22; characteristics
of 503 b 29-504 b12; spleen of 506 a
15; all have gall-bladder 506 b 5, 20;
caeca of 508 b 15, 509 a 17; crop of
508 b 26-509 a 16, 674 b 23; excrement of 509 a 12; testicles of 509 b 6,
695 a 26, 716 b 22, 717 b 7; womb of
510 b 21, 719 a 3-12; colour changes
with age 519 a 1; have neither mammae nor milk 521 b 26, 692 a 11;
sounds of 536 a 20-33, 800 a 25, b 23,
804 a 23; breeding of 544 a 25-b 12;
generation of 558 b 8-564 b 14, 756 b
14-757 a 13; diet of 592 a 28-594 a 3;
migration of 596 b 20-597 b 30; hibernation of 600 a 10-27, 783 b 12,
835 a 15-22; effect of weather on 601
a 27; bathing of 632 a 29-b 9; metamorphosis of 632 b 14-633 a 28; bones
of 655 b 18; organ of hearing of 657
a 19; eyelids of 657 a 28-b 30, 691 a
22; nostrils of 659 b 5-13; beak of
659 b 9, 21-27, 662 a 35-b 17, 692 b
15-20, 693 a 10-23; tongue of 660 a
29-b 3; lung of 669 a 31; have no
bladder 671 a 14, 891 b 18; liver of
673 b 22; stomach of 674 b 17-34;
have no teeth 674 b 20; hunchbacked
686 b 22, 710 b 17; breast of 688 a 13-
18, 693 b 17; sight of 691 a 26; jaws
of 691 a 30; feathers of 692 b 10-14,
783 b 12-18, 896 b 32; neck of 692 b
21-693 a 9, 694 b 26; wings of 693 a
27, b 14, 27, 712 b 24-29, 713 a 10;
umbilicus of 693 b 22-26; talons and
spurs of 694 a 12-22; flight of 694 a 1-
12, b 19-29, 709 b 20-710 b 4; feet of

694 b 2-12, 15, 714 a 20-b 7; all birds
have an ischium 695 a 1-16; toes of
695 a 17-25; why they can stand on
two legs 710 b 18-32; hip of 710 b 20-
31; do not stand erect 712 b 30;
swimming of 714 a 9-19; have no
penis 717 b 15; eggs of 718 b 17-24,
749 a 10-754 a 21, 755 b 31; discharge
no catamenia 750 b 5; monstrosities
of 770 a 9-23, 898 a 17; development
of young at birth 774 b 27; of Diomedes 836 a 7-19; thick feathered
birds are lustful 880 a 35-b 7, 893 b
10-16; do not eruct 895 b 12-21; most
resemble man of all animals 897 b 11;
have hard frame 898 a 4-8

Birth, difficulty of child-birth 775 b 1-
24; time of 777 a 22-27; why animals
are born head-foremost 777 a 28-31;
birthrights 950 b 5-8; those born il-
legitimately given citizenship in some
democracies 1278 a 29, 1319 b 9; the
gods that preside over birth 1335 b 17

Bisaltae, 842 a 16

Bison, aurochs, 500 a 1, 630 a 18-b 17,
830 a 4-24; mane and horns of 498 b
31, 499 b 34; kidneys of 506 b 31

Bistonis, Lake, 598 a 23

Bithynia, fire-stone in 832 b 29

Bittern. See Asterias

Bitumen, of Apollonia 842 b 15-19

Bitys, statue of 846 a 23

Black, 123 b 26; the privation of white
105 b 36, 1053 b 30; colour of elements in transmutation 791 a 10, b
18-29; due to privation of colour 791
a 13-b 6; harmful to vision 959 a 27

Blackbird, owsel, 632 b 16; breeding of
544 a 26; hibernation of 600 a 19;
habits of 609 b 9, 610 a 13, 831 b 14-
18; nest of 616 a 3; varieties of 617 a
12-17

Black bream, habitat of 598 a 10

Black-cap, blackheaded tit, 592 b 22,
632 b 31; eggs of 616 b 4-9

Black-goby. See Phycis

Black Mountains, 846 a 25-28

Black Sea, 782 b 33, 1148 b 22, 1338 b
22, 1346 b 31, 1347 b 25; its water
whiter than that of the Aegean 932 a
21-38

Bladder, 489 a 8, 497 a 17, 506 b 24-31, 514 b 34, 515 a 3, 519 b 13-22, 748 b 26, 924 a 14, 936 a 31, 949 a 1; stones in 519 b 19; some animals have no bladder 670 b 2, 34, 895 b 1; nature and function of 670 b 34-671 a 26; found in all animals whose lung contains blood 671 a 8; birds have no bladder 671 a 14, 891 b 18; effect of drugs on 863 b 29-864 b 27; in man 895 b 4. Cf. Kidneys

Blame. *See* Vituperation

Blind, defined 143 b 34; those blind from birth do not become bald 957 b 23-32; have better memories 1248 b 2

Blood, 489 a 22, 511 b 2, 11, 512 b 9, 520 b 10-521 b 3,   647 b 30-648 a 22, 723 a 4, 824 b 19; composed of water, air, and earth 384 a 16, 389 a 20, 668 b 10; solidified by cold 384 a 25, 31; naturally hot 389 b 8, 474 a 14, 649 b 22-36, 669 b 5; purest in head, thickest in lower parts 458 a 14, 648 a 1, 656 b 5, 686 a 10; heart is source of 458 a 15, 461 b 12, 480 a 7; ultimate and universal nutriment 481 a 12, 651 a 14, 652 a 7; transformed into flesh 484 a 16; no animal that has more than four feet has blood 489 a 33; of fishes 505 b 1-4; blood-letting 514 b 3; coagulation of 515 a 32-516 a 5; most indispensable part in sanguineous animals 520 b 11; finest and purest in man 521 a 3; developed out of ichor by coction 521 a 18; homogeneous 647 b 13; varieties of 647 b 33; purpose of 650 a 1-b 13; its composition and effect on temperament 650 b 13-651 a 19; no part without blood has sensation 656 b 19, 26; potentially body and flesh 668 a 27; forms viscera 678 a 32; forms all parts of the body 726 b 6; flow of 813 b 7-35; remedies for stanching blood 863 a 13-18; man only animal in which blood flows from nostrils 891 a 13-18; darkens as it dries 967 b 15

Blood vessels, 489 a 23, 495 a 5, 496 a 7, 497 a 5, 511 b 2-515 a 25; heart is center of blood vessels 654 b 11, 666 a 6, 667 b 20; nature and functions of 667 b 15-668 b 32; of women show more

than those of men 727 a 16. Cf. Aorta, Veins

Blow-hole, 697 a 16; in whales and dolphins 489 b 4, 537 b 1, 659 b 16

Blue-bird, wallcreeper, habits of 617 a 24-28

Blueness of eye, a sort of weakness 779 b 13, 780 b 6

Blue-thrush, laius, 617 a 15

Blushing, 701 b 31, 812 a 31; in shame 9 b 30-32, 903 a 3, 905 a 7, 957 b 10, 960 a 36-b 7, 961 a 8-13; in anger 889 a 20, 961 a 14, 15

Boar-fish, caprus, gills of 505 a 13; voice of 535 b 18

Boar, wild, 488 a 31, 499 a 6; temper of 488 b 14, 1229 a 26; penis of 500 b 6; tusks of 502 a 16; habits of 571 b 13-20; breeding of 578 a 25-b 6, 896 a 22; blood of 651 a 3; courage of 806 b 9

Boastfulness, 1108 a 22, 1115 b 30, 1127 a 13-22, b 9-22, 32, 1186 a 25, 1193 a 30, 1221 a 6, 24, 1234 a 2, 1384 a 5

Body, 1101 b 34, 1117 b 30, 1161 a 35; of less value than the soul 118 a 32, 731 b 29; defined as that which has extension in all directions 204 b 20 (Cf. 142 b 24); all sensible bodies are in place 205 b 32; no body is infinite 271 b 1-276 a 17, 699 b 28; either simple or composite 271 b 18; no body beyond the heaven 275 b 5-12; compounded of contraries 407 b 32; a substance 412 a 12, 18; soul is actuality of certain kind of body 414 a 18; soul is source of living body 415 b 8-28; composed of earth as well as air and water 423 a 13, 435 a 11; soul is final cause of body 645 b 15; nobler parts of 665 a 22-25; double 669 b 19; diaphragm separates the nobler and less noble parts 672 b 21; right side stronger than left 684 a 28; how soul moves body 700 b 4; compared to commonwealth 703 a 31-b 2; right side is heavier 705 b 34; movement begins on right side 705 b 20, 30, 706 a 1, 5; all parts of body formed by blood 726 b 6; parts of body participate in soul 735 a 6, 741 a 12; right side is hotter 765 b 2; growth takes place in upper part 779 a 6; influenced by soul 805 a 3, 808 b 11-39, 1254 a 34-b 16; effect of sun on 865 b 28-38; lightened by perspiration 868 a 35-b 10, 965 b 20-35; senses on right side not superior to those on left 958 b 16-27, 959 a 20-23, 960 a 29-33; colder to touch in summer than in winter 964 b 39-965 a 8; problems connected with the whole body 965 b 20-966 b 18; consists of elements 968 a 14; the limits of: (1) surface, (2) line, (3) point, (4) unit 1028 b 17; vices of the body 1114 a 23-31; defined as the soul's congenital tool 1241 b 23; beauty of body easier to see than beauty of soul 1254 b 37; interests of body and soul are same 1255 b 9; soul is more truly a part of animal than is the body 1291 a 25; prior to soul in generation 1334 b 20; body should be trained before the mind 1338 b 6, 1339 a 7; its excellence is health 1361 b 3

Boedromion, 578 b 13, 597 a 24

Boeotia, 559 a 4, 605 b 31, 838 b 4, 842 b 5, 843 b 19, 1407 a 2, 1429 b 14

Bogue, habits of 610 b 4

Boiling, a species of concoction 379 b 12; nature of 380 b 13-381 a 22

Bolbe, Lake, 507 a 17

Bonasus, horns of 663 a 15

Bone, 151 a 23, 379 a 7, 385 a 7, 511 b 6-516 b 30, 517 a 10, 654 a 32-655 b 27, 743 a 18, b 6, 745 a 19-26; combustible 387 a 18, b 1; homogeneous 388 a 17, 389 b 24, 390 b 5, 647 b 17; predominately earth 389 a 12; is breath distributed in bones? 482 b 7; connected by sinews and veins 483 b 32, 654 b 19; nutriment of 484 a 14-b 8; dry by nature 484 a 22; purpose of 484 b 9-485 a 3, 653 b 34; difference of bones in various animals 485 b 20-30; horse's heart has a bone in it 506 a 10, 666 b 19; no bone exists separately 654 a 34; difference between bone and cartilage 655 a 32; formation of 744 b 28-35; growth of 745 a 5-10; as a physiognomic sign 807 a 33

Bonito, amia, gregarious 488 a 6; gallbladder of 506 b 13; 676 b 22; diet of 591 a 11; habitat of 598 a 22, 601 b 20; migration of 598 a 26; habits of 621 a 17

Boorishness, 1104 a 24, 1108 a 26, 1128 a 8, b 1, 1151 b 14, 1193 a 11, 13, 1230 b 28, 1234 a 5-10

Boreas (N. wind), 361 a 22, 363 b 15, 364 a 13, b 4, 21, 29, 365 a 2, 394 b 20, 28, 698 b 25, 941 a 20-26, 973 a 1-3, 12; brings cold 939 b 18, 945 b 3; dispels clouds 939 b 20; blows more frequently than Notus 941 a 27-30; ceases on third day 941 b 34-37; sea becomes dark when Boreas blows 944 b 21-24; strong when it begins to blow 944 b 30-39, 945 a 26-36; follows quickly upon Notus 945 b 5; falls at night 947 a 28-32; called Pegreus at Mallus 973 a 2; favourable to generation 1335 b 1

Borysthenes River, 462 b 25

Bos, ox-ray, breeding of 540 b 17

Bosporus, 353 a 7, 372 a 15, 552 b 18, 600 a 4, 1347 b 4

Bostrychus, 551 b 26

Both, an ambiguous term 1261 b 29

Bowels, effect of sea on 935 b 27-33; loosened by fear 948 b 17, 35-940 a 7

Boxing, 9 a 14, 706 a 7, 1361 b 26

Box-tree, 831 b 24

Brain, 469 a 22, 484 b 16, 491 a 34, 652 a 24-653 b 18, 824 b 20, 963 b 7; coolest part of body 438 b 30, 444 a 10, 457 b 30, 783 b 29-34; originator of motion 484 b 21; place of 494 b 25; in relation to size of body man has largest 494 b 28, 653 a 29; bloodless 495 a 5, 652 b 1; veins of 514 a 15; membranes of 519 b 2; all animals that have blood have a brain 652 a 23, 686 a 6; cold 652 a 33, 743 b 27, 744 a 12; driest of the fluid parts of the body 652 a 35; purpose is to cool the body 652 b 16-653 a 11, 33-b 8, 656 a 22; causes sleep 653 a 12-20; composed of earth and water 653 a 21-28; thought by some to be the organ of sensation 656 a 18-28; most peculiar of the animal organs 656 a 26; why located in front part of the head 656 b 13, 22-27; brain of man larger and more fluid than that of any other animal 658 b

8, 744 a 28; formed with difficulty 744 a 15-23; heaviness of 744 a 32; moist 891 a 11, 896 a 32; source of semen 897 b 25

Braize, habitat of 598 a 14; has stone in its head 601 b 31

Brambles, 819 b 8, 906 b 11

Branchos, in pigs 603 a 31

Brasidas, 1134 b 23

Bravery, 1102 b 28, 1103 b 17, 1104 b 8, 1108 b 19, 24, 1115 a 12-1117 b 21, 1137 a 20, 1144 b 6, 1167 a 20, 1177 a 32, 1178 a 10, 32, b 11, 1185 b 26, 1220 b 19, 39, 1232 a 25, 1249 b 27, 1250 a 6, 44-b 6, 1364 b 35; brave men generally fond of wine 948 a 13-30; law requires all to do acts of a brave man 1129 b 20. Cf. Courage

Bread, lighter if it contains salt 927 a 35-b 5; effect of kneading on 929 a 17-24; toasting of 929 b 30-34. Cf. Loaves

Breaking, 385 a 14, 386 a 12

Breasts. See Mammae

Breath (πνεῦμα), 483 a 18, b 13, 484 a 3, 485 a 7; wind often called breath 394 b 9; uses of 420 b 20; nutrition and growth of 481 a 1-482 a 27; a sort of body 481 a 9; akin to the soul 481 a 17, 483 a 26-35; purest of all substances 481 a 23, 483 b 9; Aristogenes' view that growth of breath is due to respiration 481 a 28; pervades whole body 482 a 33; three functions of 482 b 15-483 a 18; hot breath causes depth of voice 788 a 20; either hot or cold 964 a 10-18

Breathing. See Respiration

Bregma, sinciput, cranial bone, 491 a 31, 495 a 10, 653 a 35; last bone to be formed 744 a 25; has great deal of moisture 785 a 2

Brenthus, habits of 609 a 23, 615 a 15

Briers, 906 b 11

Brigand, 1256 b 2

Brigandry, a natural means of acquiring wealth 1256 b 2

Brimstone, 444 b 33, 792 b 27, 793 b 6, 826 a 3; kills many insects 534 b 21

British Isles, 393 b 13, 16

Broiling, a species of concoction 379 b 12; nature of 381 a 23-b 20

Bronze, coinage of bronze by Timotheus the Athenian 1350 a 24-29

Broom, 627 a 8

Bruises, problems connected with 889 b 10-891 a 5; treatment of 890 a 23-32, b 7-27, 34-37

Brutishness, 1118 a 26, b 4, 1145 a 17, 1148 b 20-23, 1149 a 5-21, b 29, 1154 a 33, 1200 b 6, 9-19, 1203 a 18, 1375 a 7; barbarians are brutish 1145 a 31, 1149 a 10; less evil than vice 1150 a 1-7

Bryson the sophist, 75 b 40, 171 b 17, 172 a 4, 563 a 7, 615 a 10, 1405 b 8

Bryssus, a species of urchins 530 b 5

Bubalus, horns of 663 a 12

Bubbles, bases of bubbles are white and throw no shadow 913 a 19-28; shape of 913 a 29-31; in boiling water 936 b 1-9; air from bubble not wet 939 a 25-27

Budbane, orsodacna, 552 a 30

Buffoonery, 1108 a 24, 1128 a 5, 14, 34, 1193 a 12, 1234 a 6-10, 1419 b 8

Bull, castration of 510 b 2, 717 b 3, 894 b 22, 897 b 27; blood of 520 b 26, 521 a 4, 651 a 2; voice of 538 b 14, 545 a 18, 786 b 16, 787 a 32-b 19; horns of 538 b 23, 663 a 35-b 12; habits of 571 b 21, 609 b 1; urine of 573 a 20; heart of 787 a 19; golden bull of Orthosian Artemis 847 b 1, 2; sacred bulls 938 a 1. Cf. Cattle

Bull-finch, 592 b 23

Bull-head, cottus, hearing of 534 a 1

Bumble-bee, generation of 555 a 12-18

Bura, 395 b 21

Burns, cause and cure of 866 a 6

Bush, 819 b 6

Bustard, oesophagus of 509 a 4; caeca of 509 a 22; breeding of 539 b 31; incubation of 563 a 28

Butterfly, psyche, antennae of 532 a 27; generation of 551 a 13-25

Buttock, 499 b 4; as a physiognomic sign 810 b 1-4

Buzzard, 592 b 3, 620 a 17; habits of 609 a 24

Byzantium, Byzantines, 571 a 17, 598 b 10, 599 a 2, 612 b 8, 1247 a 19, 1291 b 23; hedgehogs in 831 a 15-19; revolution at 1303 a 33; their scheme for raising money 1346 b 13-1347 a 3; aliens at 1347 a 1

C

Cabbage, crambe, raphanus, 551 a 15, b 19, 552 a 32, 819 b 11; stops the ill effects of drinking 873 a 37-b 23

Cabbage-worm, 551 b 19

Caeca, 507 b 34, 508 b 13-25, 509 a 17

Caecias (N.E. wind), 363 b 17, 364 a 15, b 1, 12, 19, 24, 394 b 22, 973 a 9-12, b 1; attracts clouds 940 a 16-34, 943 a 32-b 3; called Thebanas at Lesbos 973 a 9; sometimes called Caunias 973 a 12

Caeneus, 78 a 1

Calamary, 489 b 34, 524 a 24-525 a 13, 590 b 33; breeding of 541 b 1-16; generation of 550 b 12; when edible 607 b 5; habits of 621 b 30, 622 b 19; gladius of 654 a 22; ink of 679 a 8-32; habitat of 679 a 14; feet of 685 a 14-b 12; fin of 685 b 19; uterus of 758 a 6

Calaris, habits of 609 a 27

Calculation, admits of error 100 b 7; only a few beings possess 415 a 9; only in man 433 a 12

Calculative (λογιστικός), part of the soul 432 a 25, b 6; calculative mind 432 b 26; imagination either calculative or sensitive 433 b 30; calculative or deliberative faculty 1139 a 13, b 7, 1196 b 2-33

Calf of leg, 494 a 7, 499 b 5

Callias, 43 a 27, 77 a 18, 83 b 4, 100 b 1, 176 a 1, 179 a 5, 981 a 7, 18, 991 a 7, 1022 a 26, 1030 b 21, 1033 b 24, 1034 a 7, 1035 a 32, 1037 a 32, 1040 b 2, 1058 b 10, 1070 a 12, 1079 b 2, 1356 b 30, 1382 a 5, 1405 a 20

Callicles, 173 a 9, 1432 a 5

Callionymus, gall-bladder of 506 b 11; habitat of 598 a 11

Calliope, 173 b 30

'Calliope's screech,' 1405 a 33

Callippides, 1461 b 34, 1462 a 9

Callippus, 1073 b 32-37, 1373 a 19; the Art of Rhetoric of 1399 a 6, 1400 a 4

Callisthenes, 843 b 9, 1380 b 13

Callistratus, 1364 a 19, 1374 b 27, 1418 b 10; his scheme of raising money 1350 a 16-23

Callyntrum, 553 a 20

Calmness. See Good-tempered

Calumny. See Prejudice

Calydon, 1409 b 10

Calypso, 1109 a 31

Cambyses, 398 a 12

Camel, 499 a 13-30; walk of 498 b 8; mammae of 500 a 30, 688 b 22; genitals of 500 b 15, 16, 23; teeth of 502 a 15, 674 a 32; milk of 521 b 32, 578 a 14; copulation of 540 a 13-19; breeding of 546 b 1-7; temper of 571 b 24-26; reproduction of 578 a 10, 771 a 20; drinking of 595 b 31-596 a 2; age of 596 a 9; diseases of 604 a 10; habits of 630 b 31-34; castration of 632 a 27; stomach of 674 a 33; tongue of 674 b 2; has no distinct gall-bladder 676 b 28, 677 a 34; long-lived 677 a 34; urination of 689 a 34; next largest animal 771 b 10; piety of 830 b 6-10

Camicus, 1271 b 38

Canopus, 351 b 33, 1352 a 31

Cantharides, 721 a 10

Cantharis, 552 b 1; wings of 531 b 24; copulation of 542 a 10

Cantharolethros, beetles of 842 a 5-11

Cantharus. See Dung-beetle

Capacity, faculty (δύναμις), 1105 b 19-1106 a 12, 1170 a 17, 1186 a 15, 16, 1218 b 36, 1219 b 34; indicated by qualitative terms 9 a 15; distinct from disposition 10 b 2; as a disposition 124 a 32; sometimes confusedly used as a genus 126 a 30; always desirable 126 a 37; can never be genus of anything blameworthy 126 b 1; always desirable for sake of something else 126 b 7; male and female distinguished by a certain capacity 765 b 9; is virtue a capacity? 1105 b 19-1106 a 13, 1220 b 7-20; defined 1220 b 15

Caper-plant, does not grow in tilled ground 924 a 1-23

Caphereus, 973 a 22

Capneos, 770 b 20

Capon-fish, epitragiae, 538 a 14

Cappadocia, 831 b 22; mules in 835 b 1

Caprifig, 715 b 25

Caprus. *See* Boar-fish

Capstan, 852 b 11-20

Carabus, stag-beetle, 476 b 31; wings of 531 b 25; generation of 551 b 18, 757 b 32-758 a 25

Carbanians, 973 b 4

Carbas. *See* Eurus

Carbuncle, 387 b 17

Carcinium. *See* Hermit crab

Carcinus, 1150 b 10, 1400 b 9, 1417 b 18, 1454 b 23, 1455 a 27

Caria, 518 a 35, 547 a 6, 548 a 14, 631 a 10, 673 a 18, 844 a 35, 1348 a 5, 1351 b 37; the scorpions of 607 a 15

Carid, prawn, 525 a 33-527 a 34, 547 b 17, 591 b 14; kinds of 525 b 1-3; copulation of 541 b 19-25. Cf. Crustacea

Carp, 538 a 15; gills of 505 a 17, palate of 533 a 29; spawning of 568 a 17, 569 a 4; generation of 568 b 18, 27; sunstroke in 602 b 24

Carpathus, 1413 a 16

Carpentry, 116 a 18, 1098 a 29

Carthage, Carthaginians, 838 a 21, b 27, 841 a 10, 844 a 10, 1307 a 4, 1316 a 34, 1320 b 4, 1324 b 13, 1372 b 27, 1429 b 20, 1459 a 26; criticism of the Carthaginian constitution 1272 b 23-1273 b 26, 1275 b 12, 1293 b 15; has never had a revolution 1272 b 31, 1316 b 6; commercial treaty with the Tyrrhenians 1280 a 37; Carthaginians abstain from wine when on military service 1344 a 33

Carthaginian Islands, 836 b 30-837 a 7

Cartilage, difference between cartilage and bone 655 a 32

Cartilagenous fishes. *See* Selachia

Carts, heavy objects easier moved on rollers than on carts 852 a 30-38

Case, 1456 b 22, 1457 a 19-22; meanings of 6 b 32; cases and nouns 16 b 1-5; terms to be stated in the nominative case 49 a 1

Caspian Sea, 354 a 2

Castanets, 839 a 2

Castor, 594 b 31

Castration, 545 a 20, 589 b 34, 610 b 2, 617 a 26, 618 a 32, 631 b 19-632 a 32, 897 b 27; affects the voice 632 a 5, 787 b 20-788 a 17; causes male to take

on female characteristics 716 b 5, 894 b 19-38

Cat, 580 a 23, 612 b 15, 811 b 10; copulation of 540 a 10

Catamenia. *See* Menstruation

Catana, 1274 a 24

Cataporthmias. *See* Apeliotes

Cataract of eye, 780 a 15

Catarrh, 801 a 15; caused by barley 929 b 26-29, 969 b 19-22

Catarrhactes, oesophagus of 509 a 4; habits of 615 a 14

Category (κατηγορία), 10 b 21, 49 a 7, 83 b 15, 281 a 32, 317 b 6, 319 a 12, 402 a 24, 410 a 15, 1017 a 23, 1024 b 13, 1026 a 36, 1028 a 33, 1029 b 24, 1051 a 35, 1055 a 1, 1058 a 14, 1070 b 2, 1089 a 27, b 24, 1096 a 29, 32, 1385 b 5; enumerated and illustrated 1 b 25-2 a 3, 103 b 20-23, 225 b 6, 1068 a 8; contrary of categories of quality are qualities 10 b 18; substance only category that is independent 185 a 32; all categories come to be only as part of a concrete unity 1034 b 8-19; good is predicated of all the categories 1183 a 9-23, 1205 a 10-16, 1217 b 25-33

Caterpillar, 705 b 27; movement of 709 a 26; scolex of 758 b 9, 19; chrysalis of 758 b 30

Catharsis. *See* Purgation

Catkins, 818 a 16

Catmint, 821 a 30

Cattle, wild cattle 488 a 30, 499 a 5, 643 b 7, 842 b 32-35; temper of 488 b 13; teats of 499 a 18, 500 a 25; horns of 500 a 10, 538 b 23, 659 a 20, 662 a 2; teeth of 501 a 18, b 2, 14-19; heart of 506 a 8, 666 b 18; kidneys of 506 b 29; womb of 510 b 17, 719 b 26; Phrygian cattle 517 a 29; hide of 517 b 30; milk of 521 b 33; rennet of 522 b 10; Epirote cattle 522 b 16, 595 b 18; diet of 522 b 21-523 a 7, 595 b 5-20; dreaming of 536 b 29; breeding of 540 a 6, 545 b 24, 572 a 31, 717 b 3; voice of 545 a 17, 786 b 16, 787 a 32-b 19, 901 b 24-29; reproduction of 573 a 27, 575 a 13-b 20, 732 b 20; drinking of 595 a 9, 605 a 14; diseases of 602 b 13, 604 a 13-21; humped cattle 606 a 15; Egyptian cattle 606 a 22; habits of 611 a 7; rumination of 632 b 2; spleen of 674 a 1; stomach of 674 b 7; mammae of 688 b 25; colour of eye of 779 a 32; hair of 782 b 8, 898 a 32; Umbrian cattle 836 a 20; of the Illyrians 842 b 28-32; do not eruct 895 b 12-21; ox in Egypt 1216 a 1; 'the ox is the poor man's slave' 1252 b 12. Cf. Bull

Cattle-fly, tongue of 661 a 24

Caucasus, 350 a 27, 351 a 9

Caul. *See* Omentum

'Caunian love,' 1402 b 2

Caunias. *See* Caecias, Meses

Caunus, 973 a 3

Cause (αἰτία, αἴτιον), 984 b 6, 1045 b 22, 1098 a 34, 1207 b 5-10; prior to effect 14 b 12; knowledge of cause the essence of scientific knowledge 71 b 11; universal causes are furthest from sense, particular causes are nearest to sense 72 a 4; better knowledge from higher causes 76 a 18; and essential nature 93 a 4, b 22; the four causes as middle terms 94 a 20-95 a 9; causality and time 95 a 10-96 a 19, 98 a 35; plurality of causes 98 b 25-99 b 6; proximate cause preferred to universal cause in demonstration 99 b 6-14; the four causes: (1) material, (2) formal, (3) efficient, (4) final 194 b 16-195 b 30, 415 b 8-11, 455 b 15, 983 a 26-33, 1013 a 24-1014 a 25, 1070 b 26; proper and incidental causes 195 a 28-b 3; potential and actual causes 195 b 4-12; chance and spontaneity are incidental causes 197 a 12, 32; the four causes same as the four meanings of 'why' 198 a 14-22; causes of coming to be and of passing away 335 a 24-337 a 33; first cause 339 a 25, 765 b 13, 981 b 28; if cause is known, then conditions of generation and destruction are known 390 b 17; two modes of: necessity and final cause 639 b 13, 642 a 1, 15; the four causes defined 715 a 3-6; distinction between necessity and final cause 778 a 16-b 19, 789 b 12; not given by sensation 981 b 12; he who knows causes is always wiser 982 a 13; the

four causes were recognized in part by earlier philosophers 983 a 24-993 a 26; definition of 988 b 6; cannot be an infinity of causes 994 a 1-b 30, 1074 a 29; is there one science that studies the four causes? 995 b 6, 996 a 18-b 25; is there a cause apart from matter? 995 b 32-39, 999 a 24-b 23, 1059 a 20-23, 34-38, 1060 a 3-27, b 23-28; all causes are beginnings 1013 a 17; must be eternal 1026 a 17; generable but not generated 1027 a 28-b 16; of natural substances 1044 a 15-b 20; formal and final causes may be the same 1044 a 37; in a sense all things have the same causes 1070 a 31-1071 b 2; causes of human action 1369 a 6. Cf. Final Cause, Middle Term

Cauterization, 863 a 10-12, 1199 a 33, when to be used 863 a 19-24; cures running at the eyes 957 b 25

Caution, 1250 b 11, 1251 a 15

Cavalry, 1274 a 21, 1306 a 36; in oligarchies 1289 b 37, 1297 b 18, 1321 a 9

Cave, of Demonesus 834 b 32-34; in Sicily 836 b 14-27; of the Orchomenians 838 b 4-12

Cedar, 583 a 23, 841 a 16

Cedripolis, 620 a 32

Celery, can endure salt water 923 a 6-8; cultivation of 923 b 10-14

Celeus. *See* Greenpie

Celphanian, 1461 b 7

Celtice, 350 b 2

Celtic tin, 834 a 6-12

Celtoligurians, 837 a 8

Celts, 393 b 8, 748 a 26, 837 a 8, 1229 b 28, 1269 b 26, 1324 b 12; poison of 837 a 13-23; have no fear 1115 b 28; treatment of children 1336 a 16

Censure. *See* Vituperation

CENTAUR of Chaeremon, 1447 b 22

Centaury, 820 a 36

Centipede, scolopendra, 532 a 4, 621 a 9; feet of 489 b 22, 708 b 5; wingless 523 b 18; lives on when cut in two 707 b 1

Ceos, pear of 845 a 15

Cephallenia, Cephallenians, 605 b 27, 1461 b 6; she-goats in 831 a 20-22

32-237 b 22; no change eternal 241 a 27, 252 b 13, 265 a 10; substratum does not change 984 a 22; change is always to opposites or intermediates 1011 b 34, 1057 a 22, 31, 1069 b 3; implies matter as well as form and privation 1042 a 34, 1069 b 3-34; only things subject to generation and change have matter 1044 b 21-28; not a subject 1068 a 19; four kinds: (1) generation and destruction, (2) alteration, (3) growth and diminution, (4) locomotion 1069 b 8-14; change is pleasant 1371 a 26-30

Channa, serranus, 567 a 27, 598 a 13; reproduction in 538 a 20, 760 a 9; diet of 591 a 10; habitat of 598 a 13; no sex differentiation in 755 b 22

Chaonia, 359 a 25

Chaos, 208 b 31, 975 a 12, 1091 b 6

Character, 1127 b 23, 1128 a 11, 1144 b 4, 1165 b 5-12, 1178 a 15, 1250 a 43; determined by activities 1100 b 33, 1122 b 1; purpose is the essential element of character 1163 a 23; affected by pleasures and pains 1172 a 22; bearing of character of speaker, speech, and hearer on rhetorical persuasion 1172 b 16, 1377 b 16-1392 a 7, 1415 a 38, 1417 b 8-12, 1418 b 24-33, 1419 b 17; judged by acts 1219 b 11, 1228 a 13-19; formed by habit 1220 b 1-5; judged from choice 1228 a 3, 13; of citizen 1327 b 18-1328 a 20; of youth, of the prime of life, of old age 1388 b 31-1390 b 11; affected by the gifts of fortune 1390 b 13-1391 b 7

Character, an element in tragedy, 1450 a 2, 14, 36, b 1-4, 1459 b 9, 16, 1460 a 11, b 3, 1461 b 19; defined as that which makes us ascribe certain moral qualities to the agents 1450 a 5; characters are included for the sake of the action 1450 a 21; not necessary in tragedy 1450 a 25; that which reveals the moral purpose of the agents 1450 b 8; rules for characters in tragedy 1454 a 16-b 14

Charadrius, stone-curlew, 593 b 15; habits of 615 a 1

Charcoal, 792 b 27, 833 a 27, 841 a 31

Chares, an Athenian general, 1376 a 10, 1411 a 6, b 3, 1418 a 32; stirred up revolution at Aegina 1306 a 4

Chares the Parian, 1258 b 40

Charicles, leader of party among the Thirty at Athens 1305 b 26

Charidemus, 1399 b 2; his schemes for raising money 1351 b 19-35

Charilaus, tyrant at Lacedaemon, 1316 a 35

Charillus, 1271 b 26

Charisia, on Mount Taÿgetus 846 b 7-9

Charlatanry, 1217 a 4, 1233 b 39, 1234 a 2, 1251 b 2

Charms, 846 a 29-b 25

Charon, 1418 b 30

Charondas, 1252 b 13; a legislator 1274 a 30; first to institute denunciation for perjury 1274 b 5-7; a member of the middle class 1296 a 21; the laws of 1297 a 22

Charopus, 1414 a 3

Charybdis, 356 b 12

'Chasms,' cause of 342 a 35-b 24

Chaste-tree, 819 b 20

Cheek, 492 b 23

Cheese, 384 a 22, 31, 388 b 12, 521 b 28, 522 a 25

Cheese-parers, 1192 a 9

Chelon, 543 b 14, 570 b 1, 591 a 23

Cherry, 820 a 14

Chest, 493 a 12, 497 b 33; as a physiognomic sign 807 a 36, b 34, 808 a 23, 810 b 24, 812 a 26, b 15, 814 b 5

Chia, 499 b 29, 763 b 1, 839 b 5

Chick, 753 b 34; development of 561 a 4-562 a 21

Chick-pea, 846 a 36

Chilblains, treatment of 865 b 29-866 a 7

Children, 1441 a 17; souls of children are restless 248 a 1; diseases of 588 a 3-12; crawling of 709 a 10; dwarf-like 710 b 14-17; hair of 797 b 24-29, 798 a 30; voices of 801 b 5, 803 b 19; moist and hot 861 b 8; not fond of wine 872 a 3-8; communications of young children 895 a 14, 902 a 5-35; hesitate in speech 902 b 16-29; slaves to appetite 1119 b 5; as chattel 1134 b 10-17; life of a child is not desirable for an adult 1174 a 1-4, 1215 b 22;

not happy 1185 a 2; virtue of 1259 b 30-1261 a 32; deliberative faculty immature in 1260 a 13; Plato's community of women and children criticized 1261 a 5, b 16-1262 b 36; citizens in a qualified sense 1275 a 14, 1278 a 4; education of 1295 b 16-25, 1310 a 12-36; Guardians of Children 1299 b 19, 1300 a 4, 1322 b 39; anger in 1334 b 23; exposure of 1335 b 20-23; way in which they should be reared 1336 a 3-1337 a 6; care should be taken in stories that children hear 1336 a 30-33, 1340 a 35; crying and screaming of children contribute to their growth 1336 a 35; slaves are not good company for 1336 a 41; gymnastic exercises for children ought to be light 1338 b 39-1339 a 10; training in music 1340 b 20-1341 a 15; a constituent of happiness 1360 b 21, 38-1361 a 11. Cf. Education

Chill, problems connected with 887 b 10-889 b 7; makes body livid 887 b 10-14; prevents sleep 887 b 15-18, 889 b 3-6; of feet 887 b 28-31; fat persons liable to 887 b 31-34; effect on speech 888 b 6-15; the chilled feel pain if warmed too quickly 888 b 39-889 a 14, 966 a 35-39; caused by fear 889 a 24, 948 b 13-19. Cf. Cold

Chilon, 1389 b 4, 1398 b 13

Chin, 492 b 23, 797 b 31

Chine. See Backbone

Chionides, 1448 a 33

Chios, 343 a 1, 1259 a 13, 1284 a 40, 1291 b 24, 1303 a 34, 1398 b 11, 1409 b 27; revolution at 1306 b 6; method of raising money in 1347 b 35-1348 a 4

Chiron, 1230 a 3

Chirper, achetes, 532 b 16

Chloreus, habits of 609 a 7, 26

Choaspes River, 350 a 24

CHOEPHOROE, 1455 a 5

Choerilus, 157 a 16, 1415 a 3

Choice, purpose (προαίρεσις), 700 b 18, 1111 b 6-1113 a 14, 1139 a 32-b 13, 1144 a 20, 1189 a 1-b 8, 1199 a 6, 1200 a 2, 1225 b 18-1228 a 18, 1233 a 32, 1237 a 31, 1238 b 3-5, 1240 b 33, 1241 a 21, 1243 a 33, b 2, 9, 1244 a 28; belongs both to intellect and desire 700 b 23; moves organism 701 a 5; cannot exist without thought 1065 a 32; objects of: noble, advantageous, pleasant 1104 b 31; virtue involves choice 1106 a 4, b 36; defined as the deliberate desire of things in our own power 1113 a 11, 1225 b 38, 1226 b 18; justice as involving choice 1135 a 15-1138 b 14; the efficient cause of action 1139 a 32; the principle of an act 1187 b 15; distinction between voluntary act and purposive act 1189 b 1; choice and avoidance 1190 a 7, 1197 a 2, 1199 a 6, 1215 b 21, 35, 1216 a 14, 1222 a 33, 1233 a 4, 1249 b 2, 16; and voluntary acts 1223 a 19, b 38, 1224 a 6, 1225 b 2; man only animal that has power of choice 1226 b 22; a man's character ought to be judged by his choices, but since it is hard to see the nature of choices we must judge him by his acts 1227 b 13-1228 a 19; virtue implies deliberative choice 1230 a 27, 1234 a 25. Cf. Final cause

Choking, 883 a 2-10, 964 a 25-32

Chomis, has stone in its head 601 b 31

Chones, 1329 b 22

Choria, 739 b 32

Chorion, 746 a 1, 753 b 30, 754 a 10

Chorus, 1347 a 12, 1351 b 38, 1449 a 17, b 1, 1452 b 17, 1456 a 25-32; practices before eating 901 b 2, 904 b 3; large chorus keeps better time than small one 919 a 36-39, 922 a 30-39

Chough, 617 b 16

Chremetes, 350 b 14

Chremps, hearing of 534 a 8

Chromis, sciaena, hearing of 534 a 9; voice of 535 b 17; breeding of 543 a 2; has stone in its head 601 b 31

Chrysalis, pupa, 551 a 19, 557 b 22, 733 b 14, 759 a 1

Chrysophrys. See Gilt head

Churlishness. See Unfriendliness

Chytians, quarrelled with inhabitants of Clazomenae 1303 b 8

Cicada, tettix, 532 b 11-18, 550 b 34, 605 b 26; sound of 535 b 8; generation of 556 a 14-b 20, 721 a 5; sloughing of 601 a 7; mouth and tongue of 682 a 20; diet of 682 a 25

Cicadelle, tettigonium, 532 b 18, 556 a 19

Cicigna. *See* Chalcis

Cilicia, whirlpool in 832 b 4-6

Cimon, 1233 b 13, 1390 b 31

Cinadon, stirred up revolution at Sparta 1306 b 35

Cinclus, 593 b 4

Cinnabar, 378 a 25

Cinnamon bird, 616 a 6

Circaean Mountain, poison of 835 b 35-836 a 7

Circaeum, 973 b 21

Circias. *See* Thracias

Circle (κύκλος), 845 b 32, 852 a 30-38, 1407 b 27; squaring of 185 a 17; locomotion not always circular 217 a 19; 'human life is a circle' 223 b 24, 916 a 18-39; time thought to be a circle 223 b 29; and movement 240 a 29-b 7, 248 a 19-b 7, 261 b 29, 262 a 15, 264 b 18, 265 a 13; a perfect thing 269 a 20; the divine body 286 a 12; the primary figure 286 b 24; properties of the 847 b 17-848 a 37; made up of contraries 847 b 19; larger circle revolves easier than small 851 a 14-22; can revolve in three different ways 851 b 16-21; paths of large and small circle differ when rolled separately and when placed about the same center 855 a 28-856 a 39; movement of rolling circular object 915 a 37-b 5, why magnitudes of uneven weight travel in circle 915 b 6-17; meanings of 1035 b 1; only continuous movement is circular movement 1071 b 11, 1072 a 21, 1073 a 32. Cf. Round

Circular bodies, why easily moved 851 b 15-852 a 13

Circular motion, rotation (κυκλοφορία, περιφορά), 227 b 18, 847 b 20, 848 a 19, 851 b 35; the primary kind of locomotion 223 b 19, 265 a 13-266 a 9; only circular motion continuous and infinite 261 b 27-265 a 12, 337 a 1, 32, 1071 b 11, 1072 a 21, 1073 a 32; natural movement of a certain body 269 b 1; has no contrary 270 a 19, b 32-271 a 34; cause of coming to be 337 a 1, 338 a 14-b 5; eternal 407 a 23. Cf. Motion

Circular proof, defined 57 b 18; in the three figures 57 b 18-59 a 43

Circus, 620 a 17; nest of 599 a 12; habits of 609 b 2

Citharus, caeca of 508 b 17

Citizen, citizenship, 1130 b 29, 1160 a 5, 1165 a 31, 1252 a 16; legislators make citizens good by forming habits in them 1103 b 4; citizens are equal in most constitutions 1259 b 5; defined and characterized 1274 b 31-1278 b 5; is the virtue of a good man and a good citizen the same? 1276 b 16-1277 b 32, 1278 a 40, 1288 a 38, 1293 b 5, 1333 a 12; defined as one who shares in governing and in being governed 1283 b 44; Guardians of Citizens 1305 b 29; character of citizen 1327 b 18-1328 a 20; should be moulded to fit the government 1337 a 14; at Byzantium one may become citizen even though only one parent is a citizen 1346 b 28; the good citizen 1446 b 32-36

City, state (πόλις), 1115 a 32, 1167 a 26; best life for state and individual is the same 1094 b 8-10, 1323 a 14-1325 b 31, 1334 a 12; friendship holds state together 1155 a 23, 1157 a 26; proper size of 1170 b 31; highest form of community 1252 a 1-6; aims at the highest good 1252 a 5; formed by union of villages 1252 b 28-34; a natural organization 1252 b 31-1253 a 37; prior to family and individual 1253 a 19-31; criticism of the state in *The Republic* 1260 b 27-1264 b 25; not to have too much unity 1261 a 10-23, 1263 b 30-37; friendship is the greatest good of states 1262 b 7; criticism of the state in *The Laws* 1264 b 26-1266 a 30; criticism of the state of Phaleas of Chalcedon 1266 a 38-1267 b 21; criticism of Hippodamus' state 1267 b 22-1269 a 28; defined as a union of people sufficing for the purposes of life 1275 b 21, 1328 b 17; an ambiguous word 1276 a 24; sameness of state consists in sameness of the constitution 1276 b 11; purpose of state is to satisfy man's social instinct and to promote well-being 1278 b 15-

An Index to Aristotle

29; exists to promote the good life 1280 a 32-1281 a 10; Aristotle's ideal state 1325 b 33-1342 b 34; population of state must be limited 1326 a 5-b 25; territory of state must be limited 1326 b 26-1327 a 3; position of the ideal state in relation to sea 1327 a 4-b 17; the ideal state will be composed of citizens like the Greeks 1327 b 18-1328 a 21; classes of people in the ideal state 1328 a 22-1330 a 33; site of ideal state 1330 a 34-b 17; walls of the city 1330 b 32-1331 a 18; defined as an aggregate made up of households, land, and property 1343 a 10

Cius, 834 a 35

Civet, thos, 580 a 27, 610 a 14; stomach of 507 b 18; habits of 610 a 14, 630 a 9-17

Clam, cockle, 528 a 22, 26, 547 b 14, 548 a 5

Classification, by dichotomy is impractical 642 b 5-644 a 11; of animals 705 a 27, 732 a 25-733 b 22, 737 b 15-738 a 8

Clavicles, 809 b 26; as a physiognomic sign 811 a 6-10

Clay, a remedy for bruises 890 a 26

Clazomenae, 984 a 11, b 19, 1215 b 6; revolution at 1303 b 8; scheme for raising money at 1348 b 17-32

Cleander, tyrant at Gela, 1316 a 37

Clearchus, 1203 a 22

Clearness of rhetorical style, 155 b 23, 1404 b 2-6, 1458 a 34; how obtained 157 a 14-17, 1435 a 33-b 24, 1446 a 11, 1458 b 4; three kinds of 162 a 35-b 2; due to words or facts 1438 a 27; the perfection of diction 1458 a 18

Cleidemus, his theory of lightning 370 a 10-22

Cleisthenes, tyrant at Sicyon, 1315 b 17, 1316 a 32

Cleisthenes the Athenian, 1275 b 36, 1319 b 19

Cleomenes the Lacedaemonian, 1303 a 7; his schemes for raising money 1352 a 17-b 25, 1355 b 1-7

Cleon, 43 a 26, 182 a 33, 420 b 4, 425 a 26, 1040 b 2, 1055 b 35, 1378 a 33, 1407 a 27, 1408 b 27, 1457 a 27

Cleontimus, stirred up revolution at Amphipolis 1306 a 2

Cleonymus the Spartan, 836 a 5

Cleopatra, the widow of Perdiccas, 1311 b 15

Cleophon, 174 b 27, 1375 b 32, 1408 a 15, 1448 a 12, 1458 a 21

Cleotimus, leader of revolution at Amphipolis, 1306 a 2

Clepsydra, 213 a 27

Cleverness, 1197 b 18-27, 36; and practical wisdom 1144 a 23-b 14; and incontinence 1152 a 9-12, 1204 a 13-18; may degenerate into madness 1390 b 27

Climate, affects character of a people 806 b 16, 1327 b 20-32; its effect on plants 824 b 36-825 a 39

Clock, water-clock, 866 b 12, 868 b 23, 914 b 9-915 a 24

Clothes-moth, ses, 557 b 2

Clotho, the Fate dealing with the present 401 b 22

Clouds, 146 b 28, not formed in the ether 340 a 19-341 a 13; distinguished from mist 346 b 32, 369 a 15; lightning produced when clouds contract 364 b 32; rainbow purest when clouds are blackest 375 a 9; described 394 a 26; colour of 791 a 25, 793 b 9

Clover, 595 b 27

Clytaemnestra, 1453 b 23

Cnecus, 550 b 28

Cnidos, 569 a 13, 831 b 20; revolution at 1305 b 12-18, 1306 b 6

Cnips, sense of smell in 534 b 18

Coa, 499 b 28

Coal, 134 b 29, 138 b 19, 387 b 18

Coan throw, 292 a 30

Cocalia, 528 a 9

Cock, 559 b 18, 614 a 7, 757 b 29, 811 a 39; copulation of 488 b 4, 539 b 32, 544 a 31, 564 b 12; crest of 504 b 12; crop of 508 b 27; caeca of 509 a 21; cry of 536 a 27, 800 b 24, 807 a 19; habits of 631 b 5-18; tail of 710 a 6; generation of 730 a 4-13; bravery of 806 b 12

Cockchafer, 523 b 19, 682 b 15; wings of 490 a 7, 15, 532 a 23; generation of 552 a 16

Cockle. See Clam, Shell-fish

30

Cocoon, 551 b 14

Codrus, king of Athens, 1310 b 37

Coinage, 1345 b 21, 23, 1347 a 8; of tin by Dionysius of Syracuse 1347 a 33-37; of iron at Clazomenae 1348 b 26; of bronze by Timotheus the Athenian 1350 a 24-29

Coincident. *See* Attribute

Cold, defined as that which brings things together 329 b 30; air condensed by 341 b 36; rain, snow, and hail condensed by 347 b 12, 349 b 23, 371 a 8; why mountains are cold 352 b 7; condenses vapour into water 360 a 1; why it is cold at sunrise 367 a 26, 888 b 27-38, 938 a 32-36, 939 b 5-8; an active quality 378 b 12; adverse to putrification 379 a 26; iron solidified by 384 b 14; bodies consisting of water are commonly cold 389 a 25, 31; an actual existence, not a mere privation 649 a 19; ambiguous 649 b 7; its effect on plants 825 b 24, 828 a 40; its effect on animals 835 a 15-21, 845 a 10-14, 887 b 28-34; its effect on those who are ill, in pain, or angry 887 b 19-21; source of stagnation, contraction, and downward movement 908 a 24; cold climate promotes brutishness 909 a 13-17; cold climate promotes courage 909 b 9-24, 910 a 37-b 8; accustoming children to cold is conducive to health 1336 a 13-21. Cf. Chill

Coleoptera, 552 b 30; have no stings 490 a 19; sloughing of 601 a 3

Collyrion, fieldfare, habits of 617 b 9

Colon, 675 b 8

Colophon, 1290 b 15; revolution at 1303 b 9

Colour, 373 b 24, 388 a 13, 791 a 1-799 b 20; Democritus denied the reality of colour 316 a 2; unmixed colours are red, green, and purple 372 a 7; visible only in lights 418 a 30-b 3; moves the transparent, not the sense organ 419 a 14; all bodies are coloured 437 a 7; nature of 439 a 6-440 b 25; defined as the limit of the translucent in determinately bound body 439 b 12; of animals 785 b 17-786 b 5, 797 a 34-799 b 20; simple colours 791 a 1-b 29; secondary and tertiary colours 792 a 3-b 32; causes of the variety of 792 b 33-794 a 15; always blent 793 b 14-794 a 15; coloration by dyeing 794 a 16-b 11; of plants 794 b 12-797 a 32

Coly-mackerel, migration of 598 a 24, b 27; habits of 610 b 7

Combination (μίξις), 315 b 4, 322 b 8, 324 b 35; some predicates combine to form one predicate 20 b 31; presupposes contact 322 b 25; defined 327 a 30-328 b 24; implied in coming to be 334 b 8-20

Combination (σύνθεσις), Fallacy of, one of six fallacious refutations dependent on language 165 b 26; examples of 166 a 22-32; solution of 177 a 34-b 34, 179 a 12

Combustible, 385 a 18; wood is combustible 384 b 15; why some bodies are combustible 387 a 17-22, b 14, 18

Comedy, 1128 a 22, 1447 a 14, b 26, 1449 a 3, 10, b 20, 1451 b 12, 1453 a 37; comic writers 1230 b 19, 1384 b 10; portrays men worse than in actual life 1448 a 18, b 37, 1449 a 32; etymology of the term 1448 a 35-b 2; origin and development of 1449 a 32-b 8; proper names in 1451 b 11-15

Comets, 392 b 4; cause of 342 b 25-345 a 10; frequent comets foreshadow wind and drought 344 b 20; some think comets are reflection of sun 345 b 12; usually found outside tropic circles 346 a 14; why so few 346 b 8; described 395 b 10

Comfrey, 616 a 1

Coming to be and passing away, qualified and unqualified senses 186 a 14, 193 b 21, 225 a 13, 317 a 32-319 b 4; and alteration 314 a 6, 315 a 26; relation to association and dissociation 317 a 13-31; changes of substance 319 b 5-320 a 7; causes of 335 a 24-337 a 33; sun is efficient cause of 336 a 15-337 a 33; always continuous 336 b 25; if necessary then cyclical 338 a 5-b 7. Cf. Becoming, Combination

Commerce, three kinds of 1258 b 21-26; advantages and disadvantages of 1327 a 11-b 17

COMMOE, 1452 b 20, 24

Common meals, 1331 a 21; at Crete 1263 b 41, 1271 a 28, 1272 a 2, 13-27, 1329 b 5, 22; at Sparta 1263 b 41, 1265 b 41, 1271 a 27-37, 1272 a 2, 15, 1294 b 27; in *The Laws* 1265 a 8; of Carthage 1272 b 34; destroys tyranny 1313 b 1; of magistrates 1317 b 39, 1331 a 25; in Italy 1329 b 7; necessary in a well-ordered city 1330 a 3-8; of priests 1331 b 5; the young not allowed at 1336 b 9

Commonplaces, 1396 b 12

Common sense (κοινὸν αἰσθητήριον), 425 a 14, 453 a 23, b 3, 454 a 30, 456 a 22, 458 b 4, 461 a 32, 467 b 29, 478 b 35, 667 b 24, 702 b 22; why more than one sense? 425 b 14; discriminates between sensations of different genera 426 b 8-427 a 15; general faculty of perception is one 426 b 8-29, 449 a 5-b 30; *sensus communis* 450 a 10-13; sleep an affection of 454 a 22, b 10, 455 a 26, b 10, 456 b 9, 458 a 26; each sense has a peculiar and a common element 455 a 14-b 13; dreams and sleep pertain to the organ of sense-perception 459 a 12-22, 461 a 6; found in the heart 469 a 10-33, 647 a 25-b 9, 656 a 30. Cf. Common sensibles, Heart, Perception, Sensation, Sense

Common sensibles (κοινὰ αἰσθητά), 425 b 9, 442 b 10, 14, 458 b 5; list of 418 a 18; do not have a special sense organ 425 a 14; perceived especially through sight 437 a 8

Commonwealth, timocracy, 1160 a 31, b 16, 1161 a 4, 1241 b 31; body compared to a commonwealth 703 a 31-b 2; justice holds commonwealths together 1194 a 17

Commos, a lamentation sung by chorus and actor in concert 1452 b 20, 24

Community, 1160 a 9-30; of women and children criticized 1261 a 5, b 16-1262 b 36

Compassion, physiognomic signs of 808 a 34-b 2

Complaisance, 1192 b 30, 1233 b 35

Complete (τέλειον), 207 a 8, 265 a 23, 1023 a 35, 1092 a 13, 1185 a 2-9; meanings of 286 b 20, 1021 b 12-1022

a 3, 1055 a 10-18; complete and incomplete goods 1184 a 8-14. Cf. Whole

Complex term, rules for testing the definition of 148 b 23-149 b 38

Complexion, as a physiognomic sign 806 b 4, 807 b 7, 32, 808 a 17, 22, 33, b 5, 812 a 12-b 13, 813 b 12-26. Cf. Skin

Complication, 1455 b 23-1456 a 4; defined 1455 b 25

Composition, three degrees of: (1) physical substances, (2) homogeneous parts, (3) heterogeneous parts 646 a 6-24; relation of the three degrees of 646 a 25-647 b 9

Composition, a written composition should be easy to read and to deliver 1407 b 11-25

Compound, composite (σύνθετος), 1029 b 23, 1043 a 30, 1075 a 8, 1088 b 16; compound bodies are formed from simple bodies 334 a 16-335 a 23; of shape and matter 1023 a 32; compound words 1404 b 28, 1405 b 35, 1406 a 6, 1457 a 12, 34, 1459 a 4, 8

Compressible, 385 a 17, 387 a 15

Compulsion, force, 1220 b 5; actions due to 1109 b 35-1110 b 17, 1111 a 21, 1223 a 30, 1224 a 9-1225 a 37; voluntary acts defined as those not done under compulsion 1187 b 35; defined 1188 b 1-14; pains attend compulsory acts 1206 a 14-16; a cause of action 1369 a 6, b 5, 6

Conception (ὑπόληψις), 449 b 24; genus of knowledge 114 a 18, 119 b 3, 125 a 9-11, 703 b 19; a cause of desire 701 a 36; has same effect as object conceived 701 b 19

Conciseness in rhetorical style, how obtained 1438 a 39-41

Conclusion (συμπέρασμα), 32 a 6-14, 701 a 12; conclusion will be half the number of the premises 42 b 4; universal conclusion most difficult to establish, easiest to overthrow 43 a 1; particular conclusions are easiest to establish 43 a 9; the more attributes one has at hand, the more quickly is a conclusion reached 43 b 10; rules for drawing true conclusions from false premisses 53 b 4-57 b 17; demonstrative conclusion is necessary 73 b 14; as essential and eternal 75 b 21; homogeneous with basic facts of science 76 a 30; reciprocal with premisses in mathematics 78 a 10; less numerous than basic truths 88 b 5; number of conclusions is indefinite 88 b 9. Cf. Attribute, Cause, Demonstration, Middle Term, Premiss

Concoction, 776 b 34; due to heat 379 b 12, 765 b 17; its species are ripening, boiling, and broiling 379 b 12, 380 a 11-381 b 22; defined 379 b 18; of food 650 a 11, 670 a 21; of blood 651 a 16, 668 b 5-16; of brain 744 a 17; a kind of heat 753 a 18; in plants 822 a 27-b 25, 825 a 30; in earth and sea 822 b 33-824 b 2. Cf. Digestion

Concrete (σύνολος), 999 a 33, 1029 a 5, 1035 b 22, 1037 a 26, 31, 1077 b 7; concrete and abstract terms 48 a 1-28; defined 995 b 35

Condalus, his methods of raising money 1348 a 18-34

Condition. See Disposition

Conduct. See Action

Confidence, confident, 1105 b 22, 1107 b 1, 1115 a 8, b 10, 1117 a 29, 1221 a 18, 1228 a 28, 33, 1229 a 5, 10, 22, 27, b 21-24, 1232 a 25-27, 1234 b 12, and fear 1190 b 9-21, 1383 a 14-b 11

Confirmation, of facts 1438 b 29-1439 b 2, 1442 b 34-1443 a 5; of statements 1446 a 21

Conger, fins of 489 b 27, 696 a 3, 708 a 4; gills of 505 a 14; smooth-skinned 505 a 27; gall-bladder of 506 b 18; oesophagus of 507 a 11; egg of 517 b 8; spawning of 571 a 27; diet of 591 a 9; habitat of 598 a 12; hibernation of 599 b 6; habits of 610 b 15; body of 696 a 4; movement of 707 b 29

Conjunction, 1413 b 33, 1456 b 22, 39-1457 a 5; proper use of 1407 a 20-30, b 12, 39, 1434 b 13

Connexion and sense-perception 88 a 12; how to select a connexion for demonstration 98 a 1-23

Conon, 1399 a 5, 1400 b 18

Conopes, 721 a 10

Conops. See Gnat

Consequences (τὰ ἀκόλουθα, τά παρεπόμενα), as tests of accidents 111 b 17-23, 112 a 16-23; as means of distinguishing between values 117 a 5-15; two kinds: prior and later 117 a 12; as tests of definition 145 b 11-20

Consequent, Fallacy of, one of the seven fallacious refutations independent of language 166 b 25; examples of 167 b 1-20; solution of 181 a 22-30

Considerateness, 1143 a 19-24, 1198 b 34-1199 a 2, 1251 b 34

Consonant, 535 a 32, 895 a 9, 10, 1434 b 36

Constitution, 1103 b 6, 1163 b 5-12, 1181 b 6-20, 1360 a 23; the ancient constitutions 1113 a 8; three kinds of: (1) monarchy, (2) aristocracy, (3) timocracy 1160 a 31-b 15, 1241 b 13-40; friendships corresponding to the kinds of constitutions 1161 a 10-b 10; criticism of the Spartan constitution 1269 a 29-1271 b 19, 1293 b 17, 1294 b 19-34, 1333 b 11; criticism of the Cretan constitution 1271 b 20-1272 b 22; criticism of the Carthaginian constitution 1272 b 23-1273 b 26, 1275 b 12, 1293 b 15; characteristics of Plato's constitution 1274 b 9-14; classification of constitutions 1278 b 6-1295 a 24; defined as arrangement of magistrates in a state 1278 b 9; three good and three bad forms 1279 a 23-b 10, 1289 a 26-29 (Cf. 1288 a 35); defined as the organization of offices in a state 1289 a 15, 1290 a 7; the same constitution may be administered democratically or oligarchically 1292 b 12-22; four forms of: (1) democracy, (2) oligarchy, (3) aristocracy, (4) monarchy 1365 b 30; a subject of deliberative oratory 1423 a 24, 1424 a 9-b 27, 1446 b 20. Cf. Government

Constitutional Government. See Polity

Consumption, 518 b 22, 846 a 4, 1150 b 33

Contact (ἄψις), 122 b 26, 1002 a 34, 1051 b 24, 1070 a 11, 1082 a 20; and movement 202 a 7; and organic union 213 a 9, 227 a 16; defined 226 b 23, 231 a 22, 322 b 1-323 a 24; of whole with whole 330 a 3; of point with point 971 a 27, b 4-972 a 6; of point with line 972 a 25-30; numbers do not have contact 1085 a 3

Contemplation, 1095 b 19, 1096 a 4, 1166 a 26, 1169 b 34, 1174 b 21, 1216 a 13; as the good for man 1095 b 19, 1177 a 17; contemplative intellect 1139 a 27; source of greatest happiness 1177 a 11-1179 a 32, 1324 a 28; the activity of God 1178 b 22, 1213 a 1-8

Contempt, 1251 a 22, 1378 b 14-16

Contentious (ἐριστικός) reasoning, 185 a 8, 186 a 6; defined 100 a 24; defined as reasoning to a conclusion from premisses that appear to be generally accepted but are not so 165 b 8; the aims of: (1) refutation, (2) fallacy, (3) paradox, (4) solecism, (5) to reduce opponent to babbling 165 b 13; compared with dialectical reasoning 171 b 3-172 a 8; it is foul fighting in disputation 171 b 23; when a contentious argument is most incisive 183 a 7-14

Contentiousness. See Unfriendliness

Contiguous, 236 a 12, 971 a 26; defined 227 a 6, 1069 a 1-14; nothing without parts can be contiguous 237 a 7

Continence, self-control, 1102 b 15, 1128 b 34, 1145 a 15-1152 a 35, 1168 b 34, 1188 a 18, 1200 a 37-b 8, 20-1204 a 18, 1206 a 37, 1223 b 12, 18, 1224 b 16, 1227 b 16, 1231 b 3, 1246 b 24, 1249 b 28, 1250 b 13-15, 1361 a 7, 1390 a 14, 1441 a 18; and temperance 949 a 23-950 a 19, 1151 b 32-1152 a 3, 1203 b 12-23; approve most of continence in the young and wealthy 949 b 20-25; acts with choice, but not with appetite 1111 b 15; and endurance 1150 a 14, 34, 1202 b 29-33; virtue and continence 1227 b 15-20; a virtue of the appetitive soul 1249 b 28, 1250 a 9-11

Contingency, 32 a 16-b 37, 1223 a 2; contradictory of propositions expressing 21 b 10-22 a 2; syllogisms with two contingent premisses 32 b 38-33 b 34, 36 b 26-37 a 18, 39 a 4-b 6; syllogisms with one contingent and one pure premiss 33 b 25-35 b 22, 37 b 19-38 a 13, 39 b 8-40 a 3; syllogisms with one contingent and one necessary premiss 35 b 23-36 b 25, 38 a 13-39 a 3, 40 a 4-b 16; enthymeme and example deal with what is contingent 1357 a 14-22

Continuous (συνεχής), 185 b 10, 211 a 30, 217 a 3, 242 b 27, 445 b 30, 446 b 15, 968 b 23, 970 a 24, b 27, 971 a 18, 19, b 2, 980 a 4, 1016 b 9, 1023 b 32, 1040 b 14, 1061 a 34, 1220 b 21-26; quantity discrete or continuous 4 b 20; motion belongs to class of things that are continuous 200 b 17, 228 a 20; all magnitude is continuous 219 a 12, 234 a 7; time both made continuous and divided by the 'now' 220 a 4, 222 a 10; defined 200 b 18, 227 a 10-17, 231 a 22, 232 b 24, 239 a 17, 971 b 28, 1069 a 5-14; every continuum composed of continuous and divisible parts 231 a 20-233 b 32; everything essentially in motion is continuous 257 b 1; only continuous motion is that caused by the unmoved mover 267 b 16; by nature and art 1016 a 1-17, 1023 b 34

Contracts, 1164 b 13, 1193 b 24; Ephors decide suits about contracts at Sparta 1275 b 9; often nullified after a revolution 1276 a 7-11; a form of persuasion 1375 a 24, 1376 a 33-b 31; law suits about contracts 1421 b 13, 1446 a 22; a subject of deliberative oratory 1423 a 25, 1424 b 28-1425 a 8

Contradiction (ἀντίφασις), 93 a 34; defined 17 a 34, 72 a 12; contradictories of two contraries may both be true 17 b 24; admits of no intermediates 18 a 28-19 b 4, 77 a 30, 88 a 39, 1011 b 24-1012 a 28, 1055 b 2, 1057 a 34, 1069 a 4; contradictory opposition 59 b 8; relation of contrariety to contradiction and privation 73 b 21, 1055 a 33-b 29; law of 1005 b 5-1011 b 23, 1061 b 34-1063 b 35; in poetry 1461 b 15-18

Contradictory propositions, example of 17 b 17, 20 a 25-31; in a pair of contradictories one must be true, the other false 18 a 30; contradictories of contrary propositions 20 a 16; each

34

proposition has but one proper contradictory proposition 20 b 3; of possible propositions 21 b 10-22; of contingent propositions 21 b 23-22 a 2; of necessary propositions 22 a 3-6; of impossible propositions 22 a 7

Contradictory terms, as tests of ambiguity 106 b 13-20; as tests of accident 113 b 15-26; as tests of genus 124 b 7-14; as tests of property 136 a 5-b 2

Contrary (ἐναντίος), 188 a 19, 286 a 22, 441 b 16, 448 a 2, 453 b 27, 454 b 1, 941 b 6, 1011 b 16, 1013 b 12, 1018 a 25-38, 1054 a 25, b 32-1055 a 2, 1061 a 19, 1078 a 26; substance has no contrary 3 b 24 (Cf. 1018 b 2); quantity has no contrary 3 b 28, 5 b 11-6 a 18; substance admits contrary qualities 4 a 12, 6 a 1; statement and opinion incapable of admitting contrary qualities 4 b 12; space appears to admit of a contrary 6 a 11; some relatives have contraries 6 b 15; one quality may be contrary of another 10 b 12; action and affection have contraries 11 b 1; opposites as 11 b 33-12 a 25; with and without intermediates 12 a 1, 312 b 1; contrary attributes must be present in subjects belonging to same species or genus 14 a 16; of universal propositions 17 b 4; is contrary found in denial or in another affirmation? 23 a 27-24 b 8; contrary opposition 59 b 10; rules for testing the definition of 145 a 32-b 25; contrariety of motion 229 a 8-231 a 4; contrary nourishment to contrary 260 a 31; one thing may have more than one contrary 261 b 16 (Cf. 1055 a 19); essential to generation 270 a 13; as one of the elements of bodies 328 b 26-329 a 5; the four contrarieties 329 a 6-330 a 29; harmony out of contraries 396 b 8, 11, 23-25, 921 a 3; every object involves contrariety 445 b 25; contraries in a circle 847 b 19-848 a 36; contraries sometimes have same effect 874 b 36, 888 a 32; contraries destroy one another 889 a 6, 1092 a 2; a kind of difference 1004 a 21, 1054 b 32, 1055 a 4, 16, 1058 a 12; one of two contraries always privative 1004 b 28,

1011 b 18, 1055 b 14, 26, 1061 a 20, 1063 b 17; being and substance composed of contraries 1004 b 30; contraries do not come from one another 1044 b 25, 1057 b 22; capacity for contraries 1051 a 10; the greatest difference possible between things 1055 a 3-32; its relation to contradiction and privation 1055 a 33-b 29; primary contrariety 1055 a 33; intermediates composed of contraries 1057 a 18-b 34; contraries are other in form 1058 b 27 (Cf. 1032 b 2); sensible contraries 1061 a 32; contrary in place 1068 b 31; others make all things out of contraries 1075 a 25-39; contraries do not affect one another 1075 a 30; 'there is nothing contrary to that which is primary' 1075 b 22-24; contraries involve matter 1075 b 22, 1087 b 1; theory of Forms treat contraries as first principles 1087 a 28-1090 a 1; contraries always predicable of a subject 1087 b 1; contraries are equally possible 1392 a 9-b 11; objection from a contrary statement 1402 b 4-6; in enthymemes 1430 a 23, 1431 a 31. Cf. Opposite

Contrary propositions, 974 b 29; examples of 17 b 5, 21, 20 a 25-31

Contrary terms, 151 a 32-b 3, 187 a 17-26; as tests of ambiguity 106 a 9-b 12; to show that contrary terms belong to the same thing, look at the genus 111 a 15; of predications of accident 112 b 27-113 b 14; six ways in which they can be conjoined 112 b 27-40; as tests of genus 123 a 20-124 a 14; as comparative estimates of properties 135 b 8-16; five ways in which contraries are assumed 163 a 14-28; principles must be contraries 188 a 18-189 a 10; contraries defined as things furthest from each other 1108 b 33

Controllers, 1322 b 11

Conversion (ἀντιστρέφειν), 113 b 15-26, 124 b 7-14, makes no difference in meaning 20 b 1; assertoric 25 a 6-25; necessary 25 a 27-36; possible 25 a 37-b 26, 32 a 30, 36 b 35; all propositions except particular negative are convertible 53 a 8; in the three figures

59 a 1-61 a 17; defined 59 b 1; of terms of syllogism 67 b 27-68 a 25; of subject and predicate 103 b 8; not a necessary process in accidents 109 a 25

Conviction, 125 b 29-126 a 2, 128 a 35, of pure science must be unshakable 72 b 4. Cf. Opinion

Cookery, 1206 a 27, 1255 b 26

Co-ordinates (σύστοιχα), as tests of accidents 114 a 26-b 5; as tests of genus 124 a 10-14; as tests of definitions 147 a 21, 153 b 25-35; as tests of sameness 151 b 28-33

Coot, 593 b 16. Cf. Porphyrio

Copper, 377 b 21, 378 a 28, 385 a 33, b 13, 386 a 17, b 19, 387 b 25, 388 a 14, 389 a 7, 390 a 17, b 11, 552 b 11, 793 a 19, b 6, 794 b 9; in Cyprus 833 b 1-3; Indian copper 834 a 1-6; of Demonesus 834 b 19-31; of the Mossynosci 835 a 9-14; good material for surgical instruments 863 a 25-30; burns caused by copper heal quickly 863 a 31-33; as treatment for bruises 890 b 20-27

Copula, 24 b 17, 25 b 22; 'to possible' of same rank as the copula 32 b 1

Copulation, 539 b 16-546 a 14, 892 a 23-38, 1147 a 15; love more dependent on friendship than on sexual intercourse 68 b 3; animals use their power of singing in connection with 488 b 1; season of pairing 542 a 20-544 b 12; time of life best adapted for 544 b 12-546 b 14; sex determined in 723 a 23-35; pleasure of 723 b 33, 727 b 8, 34, 728 a 9, 32, 739 a 29, 878 b 1-13, 879 a 36-880 a 5, 896 b 10-28, 1118 a 31, 1147 b 26, 1152 b 17, 1154 a 18; exhaustion in 725 b 6-25, 726 b 12; no animal that copulates has many young 755 b 25; makes men cold 783 b 30; sexual excess beneficial to diseases caused by phlegm 865 a 31, 878 b 14-16; drunkards incapable of 872 b 15-25, 875 b 39-876 a 14; position of eyes during 876 a 30-36; if too frequent the eyes and flanks sink 876 a 37-b 23; effect on vision 876 b 24-31, 880 b 8-13; man grows hair on face and body when capable of 876 b 32-

877 a 4; bareness of feet prejudicial to 877 a 5-15; man more languid after sexual intercourse than any other animal 877 a 16-22, 879 a 4-10; turgid state necessary for 877 a 35-b 4; one can have sexual intercourse more readily when fasting 877 b 5-9; the young feel loathing after 877 b 10-14; horseback riding makes one more inclined for 877 b 15-20; those capable of sexual intercourse have an evil odour 877 b 21-39, 879 a 22-25; man is less able to have sexual intercourse in water 878 a 35-39; stomach is cooled and dried by 878 b 17-20; those who wish to pass urine cannot have 878 b 33-35; accompanied by an emission of breath 879 a 1; men are less capable of sexual intercourse in summer, women more so 879 a 26-35, 880 a 11-21; shame felt in admitting desire for 880 a 6-10; those hot by nature not having sexual intercourse are often oppressed by bile 880 a 22-29; why the melancholic are particularly inclined for 880 a 30-34; frequency of 896 a 20-29; sexual desire due to presence of breath 953 b 34; effect on temperament 955 a 22-28; women have passive role in copulation 1148 b 32; unnatural sexual pleasure 1149 a 15; in animals based on instinct 1343 b 13-15; rules for copulation in man 1344 a 13

Coracine, crow-fish, 602 a 13; spawning of 543 a 32, 570 b 22, 571 a 26; hibernation of 599 b 3; when edible 607 b 24; habits of 610 b 5

Corax, 1421 b 2; the *Art of Rhetoric* of 1402 a 17

Coraxi, 351 a 12

Corcyra, 1350 a 31

Corcyraean jars, 839 b 8

Cordylus. *See* Newt

Corinth, Corinthian, 345 a 5, 808 a 31, 1265 b 12, 1274 a 32, 1280 b 13, 1310 b 30, 1315 b 23, 1363 a 15, 1375 b 31, 1429 b 18; revolution at 1306 a 24

Coriscus, 85 a 25, 166 b 33, 173 b 31, 175 b 20, 179 a 1, b 2, 28, 182 a 19, 219 b 20, 227 b 34, 450 b 31, 461 b 23, 462 a 5, 644 a 23, 767 b 25, 768 a 1, 7,

1015 b 17, 1026 b 17, 1037 a 6, b 6, 1220 a 19, 1240 b 25

Cormorant, water-raven, 593 b 18

Corn, 750 a 25; colour of 797 a 19; of Pontus 909 a 18-21; of Scythia 925 a 26; affected by lakes 935 a 18-34; corn measurers 1299 a 23

Corncrake, migration of 597 b 17

Coronea, moles of 842 b 5, 6

Correlation, is reciprocal if statement is accurate 6 b 37-7 a 4; sometimes must coin a word to express 7 a 5

Correlatives, all relatives have correlatives 6 b 26, 7 a 21; correlated terms must be exactly stated 7 b 11; thought to come into existence simultaneously 7 b 15; apprehension of its correlative 8 a 35; opposites as 11 b 23-33

Corsica, 393 a 13

Corycian cave, 391 a 21

Cos, woman of 551 b 15; revolution at 1304 b 26

Cosmi, of Crete similar to Ephors of Sparta 1272 a 6; worse than the Ephors 1272 a 28-b 10

Cosmologists. See Physics

Cottabus, 1373 a 23

Cottus. See Bull-head

Cotyledons, 527 a 25, 745 b 33, 752 a 22; of womb 511 a 30, 586 a 31, 746 a 5, 10

Cotys, king of the Odysians, 1311 b 21; his schemes for raising money 1351 a 18-32

Couch-grass, 552 a 15

Coughing, 700 a 26, 962 a 22; why some animals cough 891 a 8-12; some cough when they scrape their ears 960 b 35-39

Council of Elders, at Sparta 1270 b 35-1271 a 17; at Carthage 1272 b 38

Counter-earth, a Pythagorean invention 293 a 21-b 16, 986 a 12

Counting, 910 b 23-911 a 3; defined 968 b 2, 969 a 31

Coupled term (συνδεδυασμένον), 1043 a 4; does it have essence or definition? 1030 b 14-1031 a 14

Courage, 112 a 34, 150 b 36, 1104 a 25, 35, 1108 b 32, 1109 a 3, 8, 1115 a 7-1117 b 21, 1118 b 29, 1185 b 8, 31, 1186 b 7, 1190 b 9-1191 a 36, 1228 a 23-1230 a 36, 1258 a 10, 1269 b 35, 1277 b 20, 1323 a 28, b 34, 1334 a 23, 1362 b 13, 1366 b 1, 6, 12, 1367 a 21, b 2, 1440 b 20, 1441 b 7, 1447 b 5; more desired in youth than in old age 117 a 31; not defined as control of fears 125 b 22-27; not defined as daring with right reasoning 151 a 4; physiognomic signs of 806 b 6, 27, 807 a 31-b 4, 812 a 15, b 3, 5, 24, 34; problems connected with fear and courage 947 b 12-949 a 20; brave men generally fond of wine 948 a 13-30; honoured by states 948 a 31-34; has no excess nor deficiency 1107 a 22; the mean between fear and confidence 1107 b 1; civic courage 1116 a 15-b 2, 1191 a 5-13, 1229 a 14, 29, 1230 a 21; of citizen soldiers 1116 a 16-b 2; of experience 1116 b 3-22, 1190 b 23-32, 1229 a 15, 1230 a 5, 13; of passion 1116 b 23-1117 a 9, 1190 b 36-1191 a 4, 1229 a 21, b 28; of hope 1117 a 10-22, 1191 a 13-16, 1229 a 19; of inexperience and ignorance 1117 a 23-27, 1190 b 33-35, 1229 a 17, b 26; relation to pain and pleasure 1117 a 29-b 21; of men and women 1260 a 23-31; 1277 b 20-25; promoted by gymnastic exercise 1337 b 27. Cf. Bravery

Cow. See Cattle

Cowardice, timidity, 846 b 35, 957 b 12, 1103 b 18, 1104 a 20-26, b 8, 1107 b 3, 1108 b 19, 24, 1109 a 2, 9, 1115 a 21, b 34-1116 a 9, 1130 a 18, 1138 a 17, 1149 a 5, 1166 b 10, 1186 b 8, 1187 a 11, 1220 b 19, 39, 1221 a 19, 1228 a 28, 31, b 2, 1229 b 2, 21, 1249 b 29, 1250 a 18, 1251 a 11-16, 1366 b 13, 1368 b 18, 1383 b 21, 1384 a 21; physiognomic signs of 806 b 6, 27, 807 b 5-11, 810 a 24, 811 a 16, b 6, 812 a 12, 17, b 1, 3, 10, 29, 32, 813 a 21; why those living in warm regions are cowardly 909 b 9-24, 910 a 37-b 7; has no mean 1107 a 19; less voluntary than self-indulgence 1119 a 22-33; actuated by pain 1119 a 23. Cf. Fear

Crab, 487 b 8, 490 b 11, 525 a 34-527 b 34; varieties of 525 b 3-11; feet of 530 a 26, 590 b 25; copulation of 541 b 26-34; sloughing of 601 a 15; teeth of

679 a 32; stomach of 679 a 36; habitat of 684 a 5; head of 686 a 1; claws of 691 b 17, 714 b 18; movement of 712 b 13-21; legs of 713 a 26-714 a 7; not a swimming creature 713 b 31

Crake, crex, habits of 609 b 9, 616 b 20; toes of 695 a 22

Crane, 644 a 32, 1231 a 16; gregarious 488 a 4, 10; changes colour with age 519 a 2, 785 a 22; copulation of 539 b 32; migration of 597 a 30; habits of 614 b 18-27, 615 b 17, 616 b 20

Crangon. *See* Squilla

Crannon, crows of 842 b 10-14

Crastonia, 842 a 15-24

Crataeas, assassin of Archelaus 1311 b 8, 15

Crates, the Athenian poet, 1449 b 6

Crathis River, 846 b 34

Cratylus, 987 a 32, 1010 a 12, 1417 b 1

Craurus, in pigs 603 b 7; in cattle 604 a 17

Crawfish, spiny-lobster, 487 b 16, 523 b 8, 525 a 31, 527 a 1-9, 530 a 28; bloodless 489 a 32; swimming of 490 a 1; feet of 525 a 15; antennae of 526 a 34; generation of 529 a 20, 549 a 14-b 29; capture of 534 b 26; sleep of 536 b 34-537 b 4; copulation of 541 b 19-25; diet of 590 b 12-30; sloughing of 601 a 10; legs of 713 b 23; tail of 713 b 30

Creon, 1375 a 34, 1454 a 2

CRESPHONTES of Euripides, 1454 a 6

Cretan Sea, 393 a 28

Crete, 393 a 13, 572 a 13, 598 a 17, 612 a 2, 973 a 21, 1102 a 11, 1229 a 24, 1252 b 14, 1269 a 39, 1274 a 27, 1324 b 8, 1418 a 24, 1461 a 13; she-goats of 830 b 20; black poplars in 835 b 2; has no wild beasts 836 b 28; birthplace of Zeus 836 b 29; common meals at 1263 b 41, 1271 a 28, 1272 a 2, 13-27, 1329 b 5, 22; forbids slaves to take gymnastic exercises 1264 a 22; criticism of the Cretan constitution 1271 b 20-1272 b 22; classes in 1329 b 3

Crex. *See* Crake

Crime, ambition and avarice are the motives of 1267 a 1-17, 1271 a 16; defined 1427 a 31-33

Crimea, 821 b 7

Critias, 1375 b 32, 1416 b 28; soul as blood 405 b 5-7

Crocodile, 503 a 9-14, b 4, 505 b 32, 589 a 26, 609 a 1, 1236 b 9; legs of 487 a 22, 498 a 14, 713 a 17, b 19; jaws of 492 b 24, 516 a 24, 660 b 26, 691 b 6, 16, 26, 831 a 11-14; tongue of 502 b 34, 660 b 15, 26-34, 690 b 20-691 a 4; spleen of 506 a 20; stomach of 508 a 5; testicles of 509 b 8; generation of 559 a 18-24; hibernation of 599 a 31; habits of 612 a 20, 1236 b 9; ears of 691 a 13-18; has horny plates 691 a 17; eyelids of 691 a 21; feet of 691 b 7; oviparous 713 a 16; eggs of 926 a 9; regarded as a deity in Egypt 1352 a 24

Croesus, 834 a 23, 1407 a 39

Crop of birds, 508 b 26-509 a 16

Croton, 581 a 15, 752 b 26, 840 a 18, 986 a 28

Crow, 606 a 25, 844 b 7; inclined to chastity 488 b 5; oesophagus of 509 a 2; habits of 563 b 12, 609 a 8, 610 a 8; breeding of 564 a 15; diet of 593 b 14; beak of 662 b 9; young of 774 b 28; of Crannon 842 b 10-14; does not change colour 891 b 16. Cf. Raven

Crow-fish. *See* Coracine

Crown (the constellation), 362 b 10, 392 a 23, 399 a 11

Crowns of olive at Olympia, 834 a 16

Crustacea, malacostraca, 476 b 30, 487 b 16, 523 b 5, 525 a 30-527 b 33, 589 b 21; swimming of 490 a 2; sensation of 534 b 13-535 a 25, 681 b 21-31; make no sound 535 b 13; sleep of 536 b 34-537 b 5; sex in 537 b 26; generation of 541 b 19-34, 549 a 14-b 29, 550 a 32, 757 b 32-758 a 25; diet of 590 b 10-30; hibernation of 599 b 28; when edible 607 b 3, 727 b 3; shell of 654 a 1-8; have no eyelids 657 b 32; have hard eyes 657 b 34; tongue of 661 a 13, 678 b 11, 679 a 33; have no viscera 678 a 29; teeth of 678 b 10, 679 a 32; stomach of 679 a 36; feet of 683 b 25; genera of: (1) Carabi, (2) Astaci, (3) Carides, (4) Carcini 683 b 27; claws of 683 b 31-36, 684 a 25; tail of 684 a 2; uterus of 717 a 4; copulation of

D

Death, 469 b 19, 898 b 20-25, 1115 a 11,
27, 1229 b 4, 36, 1230 a 2, 1382 a 26,
1398 b 27, 1412 b 17; cause and nature of 472 a 11-17, 478 b 21-479 a 27,
33-b 4; hair grows after death 518 b
22, 745 a 18; why likely to occur during the hundred days following each
solstice 862 b 7-10; by drinking 874 a
35-b 7; must we wait until a man dies
before we call him happy? 1100 a 10-
1101 b 9; fear of 1116 b 20-22, 1128 b
13

Debt, 1162 b 28, 1165 a 2; should debts
be paid after a revolution? 1276 a 10

Decamnichus, assassin of Archelaus
1311 b 30

Decay, a subordinate kind of motion
700 a 27-b 3; caused by heat 784 b 7;
grayness is a sort of decay 785 a 26
(Cf. 784 b 12); generation and decay
balance one another 975 b 34

Decrease, 253 b 22; contrary of increase
201 a 14, 226 a 26; loss of magnitude
is the limit of 241 b 1. Cf. Diminution

Deduction, 809 a 20-26

Deer, 488 b 15, 499 a 3, 545 a 1; foot of
499 b 10, 17; horns of 500 a 6, 517 a
23, 538 b 19, 663 a 10, b 13, 835 b 29;
genitals of 500 b 23; has no gall-bladder 506 a 22, 676 b 17, 677 a 32; maggots are found inside the head of 506
a 27; intestines of 506 a 32; blood of
515 b 33, 520 b 24, 650 b 15; rennet of
522 b 12; copulation of 540 a 4, 578 b
7-579 a 18; habits of 611 a 15-b 32;
castration of 632 a 11; rumination in
632 b 4; doe has no horns 662 a 1,
664 a 4; heart of 667 a 20; stomach of
674 b 8; long-lived 677 a 32; mammae of 688 b 25; white deer 798 a 26;
timidity of 806 b 7; voice of 807 a 20;
neck of 811 a 16; nose of 811 b 2;
hide when they shed their horns 830
b 20-831 a 2

Deer Mountain, Elaphoeis, 578 b 27

Defect (ἔνδεια), 859 a 1, 1186 a 30, 38,
b 3-25, 1189 b 29, 1191 b 1, 35, 1192
a 6, b 12, 1193 b 26, 1200 a 34, 1220 b
10, 1222 a 9-b 10, 1227 a 37, 1231 a
35, b 16, 1233 b 17, 1234 b 8, 1249 b
20; contrary of excess 14 a 2, 123 b

28, 187 a 17, 189 b 11, 486 b 17; moral
virtue destroyed by defect and excess
1185 b 14-32; excess and defect are
painful 1204 b 12; in friendship 1210
a 28-35. Cf. Excess, Extreme, Mean

Defence, 1426 b 27, 1427 a 23-b 11; a
subject of political oratory 1360 a 6-
11; one of the genera of oratory 1421
b 9, 1428 a 6; methods of 1441 b 30-
1445 a 29

Defendant, position of in a law court
951 b 15-19; wins case if votes are
equal 951 b 20-952 a 16, b 36-953 a 2

Deficiency, 1108 b 12; has no mean
1107 a 25

Definition, formula (λόγος, ὅρος, ὁρισ-
μός), 43 b 2, 50 a 11, 103 b 6, 703 a 4,
1006 b 1, 1012 a 23, 1016 a 34, 1042 a
28, 1043 a 19, 1050 b 33, 1087 b 12,
1183 a 5; never predicable 2 a 30; defined 72 a 22, 92 b 28, 101 b 21, 38,
153 a 15, 154 a 32; definition of substance is premiss of demonstration 75
b 31; and hypothesis 76 b 35-77 a 4;
possible only if attributes are finite 82
b 39, 84 a 27; compared with demonstration 90 a 35-91 a 12, 407 a 25;
definition of a thing does not give
knowledge of it 90 b 15; not everything demonstrable can be defined 90
b 18; basic premisses of demonstrations are definitions 90 b 24; reveals
essential nature of a thing 91 a 1;
does not touch question of existence
92 a 34-b 39; three elements of 92 b
26-39; definition of attribute revealed
by demonstration 93 a 3-b 20, 94 a 1-
9; types of 93 b 28-94 a 19; how to
obtain a definition of substance 96 a
20-97 b 40; rules of definition by division 97 a 22, 1037 b 28-1038 a 35, universal and commensurate 97 b 26;
sciences built through definition 99 a
22; always consists of a phrase 102 a
5, 148 b 35; consists of genus and differentiae 103 b 16, 139 a 28, 143 b 8,
153 b 14; as a test of ambiguity 107 a
36-b 13; examination of likeness useful to making definitions 108 b 8, 20;
terms are to be defined 110 a 5; commonplace rules governing predications of definition 139 a 24-151 b 24;

obscurity and redundancy to be avoided 139 b 12-141 a 22; a certain type of contemplation 141 a 8; must be made through terms that are prior and more intelligible 141 a 23-142 b 19; rules for testing whether a formula is a definition 141 a 23-151 b 24; purpose of definition is to make known the term stated 141 a 27; rules for establishing a definition 153 a 6-154 a 12; more difficult to establish than to overthrow 154 a 24-155 a 36; definition of the essence is the starting-point of demonstration 402 a 25; 'closed groups of terms' 407 a 30; must state fact and ground 413 a 15; Socrates was first to fix thought on definitions 987 b 1; by genera 998 b 13; prior in 1018 b 31, 1028 a 32, 1038 b 27, 1049 b 12, 1054 a 28, 1077 b 1, 1078 a 9; and essence 1030 a 6-b 13, 1034 b 20-1038 a 35; the formula of the essence 1030 a 6-1031 a 14; only substance is definable 1031 a 1; is of universal and form 1036 a 28; unity of an object of definition 1037 b 7-1038 a 35; substance as formula 1039 b 20, 1058 b 10, 1074 a 34; a scientific process 1039 b 32; Platonic Forms undefinable 1040 a 8-b 4; a sort of number 1043 b 34-1044 a 14; unity of 1044 a 3, 1045 a 6-b 24; cause as definition 1070 a 22; aim of 1182 b 19, 33. Cf. Attribute, Cause, Demonstration, Middle Term

Degree, as a line of argument 1363 b 5-1365 b 21, 1374 b 24-1375 a 21, 1393 a 9-21

Degree, Variation of, none in substance 3 b 32; some qualities admit of 4 a 3, 10 b 26; quantity does not admit of 6 a 19; some relatives have 6 b 20; action and affection have 11 b 1

Deiope, tomb of 843 b 1-5

Delachia, skin of 505 a 26

Deliberation (βούλευσις), 1139 a 13, b 7, 1140 a 27, 31, 1189 a 28, b 37, 1197 b 13; deliberative imagination 434 a 6; appetite contains no 434 a 12; a form of inference 453 a 14; nature of the objects of 1112 a 18-1113 a 14, 1196 b 30, 1226 a 20-1227 a 30; im-possible to deliberate about necessary things 1140 a 36; and practical wisdom 1141 b 8-20; error in 1142 a 20; excellence in 1142 a 32-b 33; faculty of 1196 b 28; slave has no deliberative faculty 1260 a 11; deliberative element in the state 1297 b 35-1299 a 2; seeks to determine means to ends 1362 a 19; the most divine of human activities 1420 b 20

Delirium, 847 b 9

Delivery, its importance in speaking 1403 b 20-1404 a 19; spoken style admits of dramatic delivery 1413 b 9

Delos, 580 a 19, 1099 a 26, 1214 a 2

Delphi, 395 b 29, 1398 b 33; revolution at 1303 b 39-1304 a 4

Delphian knife, 1252 b 2

Delphium mountain, 839 a 34-b 8

Delphys. See Hystera

Demades, 1401 b 33

Demagogue, 1310 a 3; likes extreme democracy 1274 a 5-15, 1292 a 5-38, 1319 b 6-20; causes revolutions in democracies 1304 b 20-1305 a 7; sometimes wins favor by wronging the wealthy 1305 a 3-7, 1320 a 5; most ancient tyrants were originally demagogues 1305 a 8-12, 1310 b 14; the oligarchical demagogue 1305 b 22-36

Demaratus, madness of 847 b 7-10

Demeter, 836 b 27, 1349 a 15; temple of 843 b 2

Demiurge (Plato's), 406 b 32

Democracy (δημοκρατία), 1131 a 27, 1160 b 16-21, 1161 a 7, b 9, 1241 b 31, 1265 b 36, 1266 a 2, 7, 1278 a 27-34, 1316 b 31-1320 b 16, 1360 a 25; may be founded on violence 1276 a 14; people are supreme 1278 b 12, 1296 a 27; perverted form of constitutional government 1279 b 6, 1289 a 29; has in view the interest only of the needy 1279 b 9; rule of the free and the poor 1279 b 18-1280 a 7, 1290 b 1-20; liberty and equality are characteristic features of 1280 a 5, 1291 b 30-37, 1294 a 12, 1301 a 28-30, 1308 a 11, 1317 a 40-b 17, 1318 a 6, 1319 b 30, 1366 a 4; must destroy the outstanding men 1284 a 36; suitable to large countries 1286 b 21, 1293 a 2, 1297 b

22-25; most tolerable of the perverted forms of government 1289 b 4; governments sometimes divided into two forms: democracy and oligarchy 1289 b 27-1290 a 29, 1291 b 12, 1301 b 40; forms of 1290 a 30-1292 a 38, b 23-1293 a 11, 1296 b 26-31, 1298 a 11-33, 1318 b 6-1319 b 32; akin to tyranny 1292 a 18-22, 1312 b 3-5; may become a tyranny 1296 a 3, 1305 a 7-34, 1308 a 21; more permanent than oligarchy 1296 a 14, 1302 a 8; democratic devices to keep power in hands of the people 1297 a 35-37; arises from notion that men equal in one respect are equal in all respects 1301 a 29; leads to revolution 1301 a 38, safest of the imperfect forms of government 1302 a 8-15; revolutions in 1302 b 28, 1303 a 11, b 7, 1304 b 19-1305 a 35; difficulty in the preservation of 1307 b 26-1309 a 32, 1319 b 33-1320 b 16; extreme democracies have false idea of liberty 1310 a 25-36; enjoyed by women and slaves 1313 b 33-38; more likely to change into an oligarchy than into a monarchy 1316 a 25; characteristics of 1317 a 40-1318 a 10; defined as form of government in which citizens distribute offices among themselves by lot 1365 b 32; final appeal is to law 1420 a 21; rules governing elections in 1424 a 13-20; legislation 1424 a 21-39, b 10; worst and best forms of 1446 b 20-23

Democrates, 1407 a 6

Democritus, 213 a 34, 252 a 34, 313 a 23, 325 a 2, b 7, 327 a 20, 640 b 32, 1009 b 16, 1069 b 23, 1078 b 20; first principles of nature are an infinite many, one in kind but differing in shape or form 184 b 21; void and full 188 a 22, 985 b 5-19, 1009 a 27; says little about forms and essence 194 a 21; infinite number of elements 203 a 20, 303 a 3-b 8, 314 a 18; separateness of elements 203 a 34; time is uncreated 251 b 15; whole exists as parts separated by void 275 b 30; earth is flat 294 b 14-30; elements in perpetual movement 300 b 9; on generation of elements 305 a 35; gives shape to the elements 307 a 17; makes careful study of coming to be 315 a 34-b 15; primary reals are indivisible bodies 315 b 30; denies reality of colour 316 a 2; agent and patient as identical 323 b 10-16; his theory of the nature of comets 342 b 27; on nature of milky way 345 a 25-b 9; thinks sea is diminishing 356 b 10; on earthquakes 365 b 1-6; his view of soul 403 b 28-404 a 16, 405 a 8-13, 406 b 17, 409 a 34; spherical atoms 409 a 11; on sight 419 a 16; eye composed of water 437 b 5; all objects as objects of touch 442 b 1; on images and emanations 464 a 5-27; on respiration 470 b 28, 471 b 30-472 b 6, 482 a 29; first to come near notion of substance 642 a 27; his notion why viscera are not found in bloodless animals 665 a 31; on development of animals 740 a 13, 36; on causation 742 b 20; why mules are sterile 747 a 30; on sex differentiation 764 a 6-765 a 2; on cause of monstrosities 769 b 31-37; on teeth 788 b 10, 25, 789 b 3; plants have intelligence 815 b 17; existing things are same but differ in rhythm 975 b 28; says there is no truth 1009 b 12; identifies substances with indivisible magnitudes 1039 a 9; thinks there were three differentiae 1042 b 11-14; referred to 1029 b 21

Democritus of Chios, 1409 b 27

Demodocus, 1151 a 8

Demonesus, copper of 834 b 19-31; cave of 834 b 32-34

Demons, 846 a 37, b 25

Demonstration, scientific proof (ἀπόδειξις), 14 a 38, 40 b 23, 402 a 16, 992 b 32, 1140 b 33, 1141 a 2, 1143 b 10, 1147 a 20, 1196 b 39, 1403 a 16, 1414 a 35; the subject of the *Analytica Priora* 24 a 11; demonstrative and dialectical premiss 24 a 22; difference between demonstration and syllogism 25 b 28; demonstrative syllogism concerned with things that are natural 32 b 20; develops from universals 71 b 1; defined as syllogism productive of scientific knowledge 71 b 18, 100 a 27, 1140 a 32; impossible without knowl-

edge of primary premisses 72 a 25, 99
b 20; futility of circular demonstration 72 b 18, 27-73 a 20; knowledge
of immediate premiss is independent
of demonstration 72 b 19; not all
knowledge is demonstrative 72 b 19-
24, 84 a 32, 1140 a 33; must be based
on premisses prior to the conclusion
72 b 25; defined as inference from
necessary premisses 73 a 23, 74 b 5-75
a 38; often err in demonstration because conclusion is not commensu-
rately universal 74 a 5-b 4; demonstrative knowledge obtained through
necessary middle term 75 a 13, 84 b
23; premisses and conclusion in a
demonstration must fall within one
genus 75 a 38-b 20; elements in: (1)
conclusion, (2) axioms, (3) subject-
genus 75 a 40, 76 b 12; only external
connexions can be demonstrated 75 b
21-36; does not imply forms 77 a 5;
cannot develop an infinite regress of
premisses 81 b 10-84 b 2; proves the
inherence of essential attributes in
things 84 a 11; superiority of universal to particular demonstration 85
a 13-86 a 30; superiority of affirmative to negative demonstration 86 a
31-b 39; superiority of affirmative and
negative demonstration to *reductio ad
impossibile* 87 a 1-30; may have several demonstrations of one connexion
87 a 5-18; chance conjunctions are not
demonstrable 87 b 18-27; not possible
through sense perception 87 b 27-88
a 17; compared with definition 90 a
35-91 a 12, 407 a 25; basic premisses
of demonstrations are definitions 90
b 24; essential nature exhibited
through demonstration 93 a 18;
knowledge of cause is scientific
knowledge 94 a 20; how to select a
connexion for demonstration 98 a 1-
23; relation of dialectical problems
and theses to demonstration 105 a 8;
demonstrations are infinite in number 170 a 23; each demonstration also
a refutation 170 a 24; definition of
the essence is the starting-point of 402
a 25; should science that studies first
principles of substance also study

demonstration? 995 b 8, 996 b 26-997
a 14; demonstrative science 997 a 5-
32; not everything demonstrable 997
a 8, 1006 a 9; educated person knows
of what things to demand demonstration 1006 a 6; negative demonstration
1006 a 16-28; starting-point of demonstration is not demonstration 1011
a 13; a necessary thing 1015 b 7; is of
necessary truths 1039 b 31; substance
cannot be demonstrated 1064 a 9; science deals with that which admits of
1197 a 21, 34; persuasion is a form of
1355 a 4-17. Cf. Definition, Knowledge, Predication

Demosthenes, 1397 b 7, 1401 b 33, 1407
a 5

Denial, 1444 b 16; defined 12 b 7, 17 a
26; possible to contradict any denial
17 a 30; of a single affirmation is
single 17 b 37-18 a 7; when a denial
is single 18 a 13-26; does not affect
circumstances 18 b 38; requires a verb
19 b 12

Denouement, 1454 b 1, 1455 b 23-1456
a 4; defined 1455 b 27

Dentex. *See* Synodon

Dentist, why he can extract teeth more
easily with tooth-extractor than with
the bare hand 854 a 16-31

DEPARTURE OF THE FLEET, 1459 b 7

Derdas, assassin of Amyntas 1311 b 3

Derivatives, when things are named de-
rivatively 1 a 12; and qualities 10 a 27

Desirable (αἱρετόν), rules for comparison of desirable and undesirable objects 68 a 25-b 7, 116 a 1-119 a 10;
three meanings: (1) expedient, (2)
honorable, (3) pleasant 105 a 27, 118
b 28; means 'proper object of pursuit'
133 a 27; distinguish from what is to
be desired 1208 b 38

Desire, desiderative (βούλησις, ἐπι-
θυμητικός, ἐπιθυμία, ὄρεξις), 700 b 18,
22, 710 a 1, 1218 a 31, 1219 b 42, 1247
b 37, 1248 a 6, 1266 b 29; the seat of
friendship 113 b 2; the seat of pleasure and pain 126 a 9, 413 b 23; not
well defined as connotation for the
pleasant 140 b 27, 146 b 12, 147 a 2;
desiderative soul 407 a 5, 432 a 25, b
6, 433 b 4, 1139 b 4; appetite the

genus of 414 b 2, 433 a 25; in imperfect animals? 434 a 1; the efficient cause of movement 701 a 35, 703 a 5; caused by perception, imagination, or conception 701 a 36; has no control over sleep, waking, or respiration 703 b 9; proceeds only from sensation 815 b 20; deliberative desire 1113 a 11, 1139 a 24; the efficient cause of choice 1139 a 32; voluntary is not action in accord with desire 1223 a 25-b 37, 1224 b 22, 1225 b 2; three sorts of 1223 a 27, 1225 b 25; desire and reason do not always agree 1224 a 24, 1225 a 3, 1241 a 19; and choice 1226 b 17, 1227 a 4; unlimited 1258 a 1; in young children 1334 b 23; defined as the craving for pleasure 1370 a 18; found in all animals 1421 a 10

Despondency, physiognomic signs of 813 a 34

Destruction (φθορά, φθείρεσθαι), 994 b 6, 1000 a 6, 27, b 25, 1027 a 29, 1043 b 15-22, 1068 a 25, 1069 b 11, 1070 a 15; as movement 15 a 13-32, 111 b 5-7; contrary of generation 15 b 2; Empedocles on destruction of world 279 b 15; Heraclitus on destruction of world 279 b 15; meanings of destructible and indestructible 280 b 21-34; nothing is by accident perishable 1059 a 1; defined 1067 b 24

Deucalion, 352 a 34

Dew, 378 a 31, 399 a 25, 938 a 34, 939 b 36; cause of 347 a 14-b 12, 394 a 15; described 394 a 24

Dexander, leader of revolution at Mytilene 1304 a 7

Diagoras of Eretria, 1306 a 36

Dialectic (διαλεκτική), 46 a 30, 81 b 18-22, 987 b 32, 995 b 22, 1078 b 26; dialectical questions 20 b 22-30; demonstrative and dialectical premiss 24 a 22; begging the question in dialectical arguments 65 a 37; the two forms of: syllogistic and inductive 71 a 5, 105 a 12; not confined to a single genus 77 a 32; dialectical proof 84 a 7, b 2, 86 a 21, 88 a 18; defined 100 a 30; value of the study of dialectics 101 a 25-b 4; the prior nature of 101 b 1; four sources of arguments: (1)

how to secure propositions, (2) how to distinguish ambiguous meanings, (3) how to note differences, (4) how to note resemblances 105 a 20-108 b 36; how to frame questions in dialectics 155 b 3-159 a 14; principally a matter of framing questions 155 b 8; in dialectics a premiss is valid if it holds in several instances and if no objection is raised 157 b 2; how to answer questions in dialectics 159 a 15-161 a 15; one of chief aims of dialectics is to lead into paradox 159 a 18; four ways to prevent an opponent from arguing to a conclusion 161 a 1-15; ought to use as few steps as possible 162 a 24; three kinds of clearness in arguments 162 a 35-b 3; the dialectician is a skilled propounder and objector 164 b 3; art of examining is a branch of 169 b 25, 171 b 4, 172 a 22; compared with contentious reasoning 171 b 3-172 b 8; dialectician defined 171 b 7, 172 a 35; proceeds by questioning 172 a 17; in a sense everyone is a dialectician 172 a 30; task of 183 a 38; history of dialectics and rhetoric compared 183 b 16; and sophistic 1004 b 18-26, 1061 b 8; relation of rhetoric to 1354 a 1-11, 1356 a 25-35, 1359 b 10-18, 1402 a 5; its business is the study of syllogisms 1355 a 9, b 16; deals with classes of men rather than individual men 1356 b 26-1357 a 7; a practical faculty 1359 b 13. Cf. Proposition, Syllogism

Diameter, 264 b 16, 910 b 11-23

'Diapason,' why so called 920 a 14-18

Diaphragm, midriff, phrenes, 482 a 17, 496 b 12, 15, 514 a 36, 670 b 31, 738 b 15; found in all blooded animals 506 a 5, 672 b 13; nature and function of 672 b 9-673 b 2; separates the nobler from the less noble parts 672 b 21

Diares, 418 a 21

Diarrhoea, rennet is a cure for 522 b 11; in elephants 605 a 27; cabbage as a cure for 873 b 4

Dicaeogenes, 1455 a 2

An Index to Aristotle

Dice, 1247 a 23, b 17, 1371 a 2; loaded dice 913 a 35, 915 b 8

Dichotomy, inadequacies of 642 b 5-644 a 11. Cf. Classification

Dictatorship. *See* Aesymnetia

Diction, 1449 a 20, 1450 a 14, 29, 36, b 13-15, 1455 a 23, 1456 b 9, 1459 a 16, b 12, 17; teachable 1404 a 16; defined as the composition of verses 1449 b 34; perfection of 1458 a 18; needs to be elaborate only where there is no action 1460 b 2

Dictum de omni et nullo, 25 b 32

Didales, his deception of his soldiers 1350 b 16-32

Differentia, difference (διαφορά), 1 b 18, 21, 74 a 37-b 4, 83 b 1, 96 b 12-97 b 6, 998 b 26, 1016 a 25, 1020 a 33, 1057 b 5, 1058 a 29-b 26; cannot be present in a subject 3 a 22, predicated univocally 3 a 33; predicated of both species and individual 3 b 1; definition of differentia applicable to species and individuals 3 b 5; as a test of ambiguity 107 b 27; usually distinguish the essence by means of the differentia 108 b 5; as tests of genus 122 b 12-123 a 19; the differentia of a thing is never its genus 122 b 15, 1058 a 8; rules for distinguishing genus from differentia 128 a 20-30; as a test of definition 143 a 29-145 b 33; never an accidental attribute 144 a 25; has a wider range than species 144 b 6; posterior to genus, but prior to species 144 b 10; not an affection 145 a 3; less familiar than the genus 149 a 29; things called the same if they do not differ in differentia 223 b 7-14; rules for differentia in dichotomous classification 642 b 5-644 a 11; generic differentia must be subdivisible 642 b 25; a kind of otherness 1004 a 21, 1054 b 23, 1055 a 5, 17, 1058 a 12; meanings of 1018 a 13, 14, 1054 b 23-31; definition by 1037 b 7-1038 a 35, 1043 a 19; types of 1042 b 11-24; of numbers 1083 a 1-1085 a 2

Digestion, requires heat 474 a 27; one means of nutrition 481 a 7; caused by breath 481 b 2, 21. Cf. Concoction

Dignity, reserve (σεμνότης), 1192 b 30-39, 1221 a 8, 1233 b 34-38

DILIAD of Nicochares, 1448 a 14

Dimension, three sorts of: (1) length, (2) breadth, (3) depth 209 a 5; six in number: (1) superior, (2) inferior, (3) before, (4) behind, (5) right, (6) left 704 b 20, 705 a 27-706 a 26, b 25

Diminution, as movement 15 a 14, 406 a 12; contrary of increase 15 b 3. Cf. Decrease, Increase

Diminutives, 1405 b 28-33

Diocles, an Olympic victor 1274 a 33-b 4

Diogenes of Apollonia, 322 b 15; view of soul 405 a 22-24; all animals breathe 470 b 31; on the nature of veins 511 b 30-512 b 11; air as first principle 984 a 5; referred to 996 a 8, 1001 a 16

Diogenes the Dog, 1411 a 24

Diomede, 1116 a 22, 1136 b 9, 1396 b 15, 1399 b 27

Diomedeia, birds of 836 a 7-19

Diomedes, 836 a 8, 15, 1416 b 12; arms of 84 b 1-19

Diomedon, 1397 a 25

Dion of Syracuse, 1344 b 35, 1373 a 20, 1429 b 16; the assassin of Dionysius the Younger 1312 a 5, 35-39, b 9-17

Dionysiac contests, 1323 a 2, 1416 a 32

Dionysius (anyone), 1401 b 12

Dionysius the Brazen, 1405 a 32

Dionysius the Elder, tyrant of Syracuse, 838 a 20, 949 a 25, 1203 a 22, 1259 a 28, 1286 b 38, 1305 a 26, 1306 a 2, 1307 a 38, 1310 b 31, 1313 b 27, 1344 b 36, 1357 b 31, 1385 a 10, 1390 b 29; his schemes for raising money 1349 a 14-1350 a 5, 1353 b 20-27

Dionysius, the painter, 1448 a 7

Dionysius the Sophist, 808 a 17; his definition of life 148 a 28

Dionysius the Younger, the assassination of 1312 a 5, 35-39, b 9-17, 1429 b 17

Dionysus, 842 a 27, 953 b 31, 1023 b 11, 1361 b 38, 1405 a 23, 1407 a 16, 1457 b 21; temple of Dionysus in Crastonia 842 a 19; the feast of 1347 a 27

Diopeithes, 1386 a 14

Diophantus, 1267 b 19

Dioscuri, 1245 b 33

Diptera, stings of 490 a 20

Disarrangement, 1251 a 21

Discovery in tragedy, 1450 a 34, 1452 a 17, 30-b 10, 1454 a 4, 1455 b 34, 1459 b 11; defined 1452 a 31; forms of 1454 b 19-1455 a 21

Diseases, 123 b 17, 1115 a 11, 17, 35, 1148 b 25, 1149 b 29, 1150 b 33; disease is a greater evil than debility 157 b 20; of children 588 a 3-12; of fish 602 b 12-30; of pigs 603 a 30-604 a 3; of sheep 604 a 2; of dogs 604 a 4-12, 612 a 6, 31; of elephants 604 a 12, 605 a 23-b 4; of cattle 604 a 13-21; of horses 604 a 22-605 a 2; of asses 605 a 16-22; of bees 605 b 16, 626 b 16-20; defined as acquired old age 784 b 34; can be caused and cured by excesses 859 a 1-8; effect of seasons on 859 a 9-24, b 1-14, 21-860 b 25; contagiousness of 886 b 4-8, 887 a 22-39; all diseases are caused by excretions 959 b 30

Disgrace, 1115 a 11

Dishonour, 1250 a 16, 28, b 35, 1251 b 17, 22

Disorder, 1251 a 21

Disposition, condition (διάθεσις), 1218 b 38, 1220 a 19, 26, 29, 1229 b 20, 1231 b 24, 1235 a 5, 1239 b 39, 1246 a 15, 1248 b 38, 1250 b 32, 40, 1251 a 8, 15, b 28; contrasted with habit 8 b 27-9 a 15; defined 8 b 35; relative nature of 11 a 22; the genus of knowledge 111 a 23, 121 b 38, 125 a 1, 145 a 36; the genus of virtue 121 b 38; physiognomic signs of gentle disposition 808 a 24-27; meaning of 1022 b 1-3; three kinds of 1108 b 11; the worse act is the one prompted by the worse disposition 1374 b 24-1375 a 21; manner of speaking that corresponds to 1408 a 29-32

Dissection, 474 b 9, 478 a 36, 511 b 21-23

Dissuasion, one of the genera of oratory 1421 b 9, 1444 b 25; defined 1421 b 21; topics of 1421 b 24-1423 a 12; methods of 1439 b 14-1440 b 4

Distinctive mark, of substance 4 a 10; of quantity 6 a 26; of quality 11 a 19

Distribution, both subject and predicate cannot be distributed 17 b 13-16

Dithyrambic poetry, 918 b 18, 1402 b 2, 1409 a 25, b 26, 1413 b 14, 1415 a 9, 1447 a 14, b 25, 1448 a 15, 1449 a 11, 1459 a 9; suitable to the Phrygian mode 1342 b 7

Dittany, 830 b 21

Diver. See Aethyia

Divers, ear-drums burst in the sea 960 b 8-14; tie sponges around their ears 960 b 15-17; slit their ears and nostrils 960 b 21-34; pour olive oil in ears 961 a 24-30

Divination, 284 b 5, 449 b 12; by dreams 462 b 12-464 b 18; vagueness of 1407 b 1

Divine, divinity, 1026 a 20, 1064 a 37, 1247 a 28; the divine is not jealous 983 a 2; encloses the whole of nature 1074 b 2; all things have something divine in them 1153 b 32

Divisible, all magnitudes divisible 315 a 26-317 a 13

Division (διαίρεσις), 46 a 31-b 37, 222 a 19, 969 a 29; proper uses of 91 b 29-32; does not involve inference 91 b 33; proper order in division is important 96 b 31; as test for accident 109 b 13-29, 111 a 33-b 11, 120 a 34-b 6; as test of genus 121 a 27-37; as test of property 132 a 27-b 3; infinity in respect of addition 204 a 7, 206 a 15, b 3, 233 a 20, 236 b 14; time has infinite number of divisions 263 a 21; by similar and dissimilar parts 818 a 22-30; definition by division 1037 b 28-1038 a 35. Cf. Definition

Division, Fallacy of, one of six fallacious refutations dependent on language 165 b 26; examples of 166 a 33-38; solution of 177 a 34-b 34

Dizziness, more likely to occur in those standing than in those sitting 885 b 35-886 a 2

Dodder, 827 a 1

Dodona, 352 a 36

Dodonis, 1398 b 3

Dog, 488 a 24, 31, 840 b 5, 1235 a 12, 1401 a 16-19; temper of 488 b 21, 572 a 7, 894 b 12; hair of 498 b 27, 658 a 30, 893 a 4; feet of 499 b 8; mammae of 500 a 26, 688 a 35; teeth of 501 a 17, b 4-13, 575 a 5-12; mouth of 502 a 7; stomach of 507 b 17, 21, 508 a 28, 674 a 26, 675 a 29; womb of 510 b 17, 719 b 26; skull of 516 a 17; dreaming of 536 b 29; copulation of 540 a 9, 24, b 14, 546 a 28-34, 572 b 25, 808 b 37; bark of 545 a 5; reproduction of 545 b 4-9, 574 a 16-b 34, 742 a 9, 771 a 22, 892 b 1, 894 b 13; lice on 557 a 17; Laconian hound 574 a 17, b 10, 575 a 2, 607 a 2, 608 a 27; vomiting in 594 a 28; diseases of 604 a 4, 612 a 6, 31; Indian dog 607 a 4, 746 a 33; Molossian dogs 608 a 28; habits of 612 a 5, 31, 630 a 11, 1380 a 25; spleen of 674 a 3; digits of 688 a 4-12; viviparous externally and internally 718 b 30; development of young at birth 774 b 17; nostrils of Laconian hound 781 b 10; railing of 808 b 38; Melitaean terriers 892 a 21; wild dogs 895 b 25; monstrous births in 898 a 12

Dog-days, 1026 b 32

Dog-fish, 505 a 18, 540 b 28, 565 a 25; gills of 505 a 5; gall-bladder of 506 b 7; liver of 507 a 16; caeca of 508 b 16; womb of 510 b 35; copulation of 540 b 18, 543 a 18; egg-shell of 565 a 22; generation of 565 b 24, 566 a 20

Dog-rose, 555 b 2

Dog-star, 547 a 14, 566 b 22, 569 a 14, 599 a 18, 600 a 3, 602 a 27, b 22, 633 a 13, 821 b 6, 859 a 22, 1401 a 16; the South wind blows at time of 941 a 37-b 23, 944 a 4-9

Dolon, 1461 a 12

Dolphin, 476 b 13-29, 589 a 31-b 20, 598 b 2; viviparous 489 b 2, 732 a 33; has no ears 492 a 27; testicles of 500 b 1, 509 b 9, 510 a 9, 716 b 27, 719 b 9, 720 a 34; mammae of 504 b 23, 521 b 24; has no gall-bladder 506 b 4, 676 b 29, 677 a 34; bones of 516 b 12, 655 a 17; hearing of 533 b 10-28, 534 b 8; voice of 535 b 35; blow-hole of 537 b 1, 566 b 2, 589 b 1, 697 a 16; sleep of 537 b 1; copulation of 540 b 22, 756 b 1; generation of 566 b 3-26; mouth of 591 b 25, 696 b 26; habits of 631 a 7-b 4; long-lived 677 a 34; lung of 697 a 16, 26-31; viviparous externally and internally 718 b 30. Cf. Cetacea

Dolphin (the constellation), 345 b 22

Dolphin's louse, 559 a 31

Dorado, caeca of 508 b 20

Dorian mode, 1276 b 10, 1290 a 21; produce a moderate and settled temper 1340 b 3, 1342 a 29; the gravest and manliest music 1342 b 14

Dorians, claim they discovered tragedy and comedy 1448 a 30

Dorieus, 1357 a 19

Dormouse, hibernation of 600 b 14

Dorylaeum, 973 b 15

Dough, increases when kneaded 927 b 31-37, 929 b 8-17; effect of heat on 927 b 38-928 a 4, 929 b 18-25; becomes white when kneaded 929 a 6-10

Dove. See Ring-dove, Rock-dove, Turtle-dove

Dove-hawk, dove-killer, 592 b 2, 615 b 7, 620 a 19

Down, 365 a 26; not for all things what it is for the Cosmos 416 a 2

Drachma, 1243 a 28

Draco, 1274 b 15-17, 1400 b 21

Dragon, habits of 612 a 29

Drama, 1404 a 33, 1448 a 29, 1456 a 14, 1459 a 18, 1462 a 17; actors count for more than poets in 1403 b 33; etymology of the term 1448 a 35-b 2

Dramatic ability, a natural gift 1404 a 15

Draughts, 1253 a 6, 1371 a 2

Drawing, a customary branch of education 1337 b 24, 1338 a 18. Cf. Painting

Dreams, 458 b 1-464 b 18, 1102 b 12; a sort of sense-impression 456 a 27; not perceived by sense-perception 458 b 8, 459 a 1; not perceived by opinion 458 b 9-25; defined as a sort of presentation which occurs in sleep 462 a 16, 30; not every presentation that occurs in sleep is a dream 462 a 19; the interpretation of 462 b 12-464 b 18; not sent by God 462 b 22, 463 b 12-23; as causes, tokens, and coincidences 462 b 27-463 b 10; certain lower animals dream 463 b 11; found in animals 536 b 30; man most given to dreams of all animals 537 a 14-19; those who sleep deeply see no visions 956 b 38-957 a 35; reveal dispositions 957 a 26-35

Drepanis, 487 b 26

Dropsy, 846 a 4, 1150 b 33; drunkards liable to 871 b 25; why not infectious 887 a 22-39

Drought, 360 b 5, 365 b 9, 366 b 3, 368 b 16; foreshadowed by comets 344 b 20

Druggist, 1346 b 22

Drugs, when to be used 863 a 19-24; effect on stomach and bladder 863 b 29-864 b 27; properties of 865 a 3-18

Drum, 839 a 2

Drummer-bird, habits of 609 a 26

Drunkenness, 953 a 33-954 a 11, 957 a 2, 1113 b 32, 1114 a 27, 1117 a 14, 1151 a 4, 1152 a 15, 1154 b 10, 1195 a 32-34, 1202 a 2-4, 1205 a 24, 1231 a 9; physiognomic signs of 811 b 15, 812 a 33; problems connected with the drinking of wine and drunkenness 871 a 1-876 a 29; drunkards are unable to endure cold 871 a 1-6, b 32-872 a 2; the slightly intoxicated are most troublesome 871 a 7-15, 875 a 29-40; drunkards generally infertile 871 a 23-26; why drunkards tremble 871 a 27-b 31, 874 b 22-875 a 28; men are more sensitive to salty and bad water when drunk than when sober 872 a 9-17, 873 b 38-874 a 4; effect on vision 872 a 18-b 14, 874 a 5-21, 875 b 9-18; drunkards incapable of sexual intercourse 872 b 15-25, 875 b 39-876 a 14; takes place when heat is in region of head 872 b 30, 873 a 2, 874 b 13; effect of physical exercise on 873 a 12-22; cabbage stops the ill effects of drinking 873 a 37-b 23; death by drinking 874 a 35-b 7; drunkards are easily moved to tears 874 b 8-10; drunkards delight in warmth of sun 875 b 5-8, 34-38; effect on speech 875 b 19-33; young drunkards wet their beds 876 a 15-25; oil prevents drunkenness 876 a 26-29; sipping prevents drunkenness 876 a 26-29; effect on voice 900 b 39-901 a 6, 903 b 7-12, 904 b 1-6, 905 a 24-30; makes men braver 948 a 30; despondency in 954 b 37-955 a 22; drunkard acts in ignorance, not by reason of ignorance 1110 b 24-27, 1147 a 13, b 7; impedes action 1206 a 5; effect on tongue 1235 b 38; law of Pittacus regarding 1274 b 18-22

Dry (ξηρόν), derivative forms of 329 b 32-330 a 24; and moist are primary contraries of touch 330 a 24-29; passive quality 378 b 13; nature of drying 382 b 10-28; old age is dry and cold 466 a 21, 875 a 15

Duck, 593 b 16; oesophagus of 509 a 3; caeca of 509 a 21

Duck-killer, 618 b 25

Dullness of sense, physiognomic signs of 806 b 22, 807 b 20-28, 810 b 19, 811 a 9, 30, b 32, 812 a 6

Dung-beetle, cantharus-beetle, scarabaeus, 552 a 17; wings of 490 a 15; sloughing of 601 a 3; body of 682 b 26; flight of 710 a 10

Duration, name for eternal existence of the universe 279 a 23-32

Dwarfs, 467 a 32; have weak memory 453 b 2; all animals except man are dwarf-like in form 686 b 3-35, 689 b 26, 695 a 9; children are dwarf in shape 686 b 11, 710 b 14; dwarfs are deficient in intelligence 686 b 27; cause of 749 a 4, 892 a 6-22

Dyad, two, 192 a 12, 987 b 26, 34, 988 a 13; the first number 999 a 8, 1085 b 10; the indefinite dyad 1081 a 15, 22, b 21, 32, 1082 a 12, b 31, 1083 b 36, 1085 b 7, 1087 b 7, 1088 b 29, 1089 a 36, 1091 a 4; the ideal dyad 1036 b 14, 1081 a 23, 1082 b 9, 20. Cf. Great and small

Dyes, 375 a 22, 794 a 16-30, 795 b 10-20

Dysentery, effect of seasons on 860 a 32, 861 b 1-20

E

earth causes eclipse of moon 88 a 1, 93 a 31, 98 b 18, 297 b 30; Mars eclipsed by moon 292 a 5; wind usually occurs during 942 a 22-28

Economics, compared with politics 1343 a 1-16; makes proper rules for husband and wife 1343 a 24; qualities of the economist 1344 b 23-1345 b 3

Economy, the Attic system 1344 b 31-33; the Persian system 1344 b 31, 34, 1345 a 2; the Laconian system 1344 b 31, 1345 b 2; royal economy 1345 b 12, 14, 20-27; satrapic economy 1345 b 13, 15, 1346 a 5-7; political economy 1345 b 13, 15, 1346 a 5-7; personal economy 1345 b 13, 16, 1346 a 8-12

Ecphantides, 1341 a 36

Education (παιδεία), 1104 b 12, 1172 a 20, 1260 b 15, 1283 a 25; educated man 639 a 5; universal education 639 a 10; educated person knows of what things to demand demonstration 1006 a 6; educated man knows precision to be looked for in a study 1094 b 12-27; 1098 a 27; the means of uniting the state 1263 b 37; confined in *The Republic* to guardians 1264 a 32; ought to have equal education 1266 b 32; contributes most to permanency of constitutions 1310 a 13-35; destroys tyranny 1313 b 1; in the ideal state 1331 b 24-1342 b 34; care of body must precede care of soul 1334 b 25; Directors of Education 1336 a 30, 40; two periods of: (1) from seven to puberty, (2) from puberty to twenty-one 1336 b 39; art and education fill in the deficiencies of nature 1337 a 2; ought to be the same for all 1337 a 23; possible aims of: (1) the useful, (2) the virtuous, (3) higher knowledge 1337 a 41; branches of: (1) reading and writing, (2) gymnastic exercise, (3) music, (4) drawing 1337 b 24; three principles of: (1) the mean, (2) the possible, (3) the becoming 1342 b 34; aristocracy has an educational qualification for citizenship 1365 b 33-38; the preserver of the mind 1421 a 17

Eel, 567 a 21, 569 a 5, 608 a 6; fins of 489 b 28, 504 b 31, 696 a 4, 708 a 6, 709 b 12; gills of 505 a 15, 696 b 23; smooth-skinned 505 a 27; gall-bladder of 506 b 9; oesophagus of 507 a 11; has no egg 517 b 8; capture of 534 a 20; sex and reproduction of 538 a 2-13, 570 a 2-24, 741 b 1, 762 b 24; migration of 569 a 8; diet of 592 a 1-27; body of 696 a 4; movement of 707 b 6-708 a 21, 709 a 25, 710 a 1

Effeminacy, 1145 a 35, 1150 b 2, 1229 b 1, 1251 a 27, 1384 a 1, 2; physiognomic signs of 808 a 10, 813 a 15

Effrontery. See Impudence

Eggs, 478 b 31, 559 a 15-561 a 3, 737 b 24; defined 489 b 6; development of chick in egg 561 a 4-562 a 21; double-yolked 562 a 24-b 2, 770 a 19, 898 a 18; of fish 564 b 24-565 a 2, 718 b 6-16, 33-719 a 2, 749 a 19-27, 754 b 1-33; the hatching of 665 a 36, 752 b 17-754 a 21; of birds 718 b 17-24, 749 a 10-754 a 21; difference between scolex and egg 732 a 29, 758 b 11, 34; egg-shells are soluble in liquids 743 a 17; reasons for colours of 751 a 25-752 a 9; shape of 752 a 10-23; growth of 752 a 24-b 12; laying of 752 b 13-16; uria or rotten eggs 753 a 22; raw eggs cannot be spun around 885 b 37; as cure of weals 889 b 11-19

Egypt, Egyptians, 274 b 16, 298 a 3, 343 b 10, 28, 351 b 27, 394 a 1, 557 a 29, 559 b 1, 562 b 26, 581 a 1, 584 b 7, 30, 597 a 5, 617 b 31, 805 a 27, 812 a 12, 821 a 34, b 8, 926 b 5, 1216 a 1, 1235 b 2, 1352 a 8, 17, 1393 a 33, 1417 a 6; astronomical observations 292 a 8; becoming drier 351 b 28; Egyptians most ancient of men 352 b 21, 1329 b 32; animals of 502 a 9, 606 a 22, 608 b 33, 612 a 16, 845 a 11; animals more fertile in 770 a 36; sandpipers of 831 a 11-14; effect of hot climate upon Egyptians 909 a 27-31; South wind in 945 a 19-25; mathematics founded in 981 b 23; physicians in 1286 a 13; pyramids of 1313 b 21; classes in 1329 a 40-b 24

Egyptian Sea, 393 a 29

Eileus, in horses 604 a 29

An Index to Aristotle

Elaitic Gulf, 973 a 11

Elaphebolion, 571 a 13, 579 a 25

Elaterium, 864 a 5

Elbow, 493 b 26, 702 a 27, b 4, 12, 813 a 10

Elea, 1400 b 6

ELECTRA of Sophocles, 1460 a 31

Electric ray. *See* Torpedo fish

Elegiacs, 1447 b 12

Eleginus, habits of 610 b 5

Elements (στοιχεῖα), 187 a 26, 188 b 28, 270 b 22, 354 b 5, 389 b 1, 393 a 1, 437 a 20, 646 a 14, 791 a 1-792 a 3, 972 a 9, 975 b 12, 992 b 18, 1001 a 18, 1059 b 23, 1086 b 13-1087 a 25, 1091 a 30; importance of knowing 184 a 11; three in number 189 b 16, 276 a 33, 277 b 14, 1070 b 25; each has a proper place 208 b 10, 214 b 14, 330 b 30, 334 b 35, 335 a 20, 337 a 7-15, 355 b 1, 823 b 3, 824 a 8, 1103 a 20-25; have natural movements 276 a 22-277 b 8, 300 a 20-301 b 32; view of Leucippus and Democritus 300 b 9, 303 a 3-b 8, 975 b 28; the primary constituents of bodies 302 a 12, 16; view of Anaxagoras and Empedocles 302 a 29, 984 a 7, 985 a 32, 988 a 27, 998 a 30; finite in number 302 b 10-303 a 2; cannot be reduced to one 303 b 9-304 b 23; not eternal but generated out of each other 304 b 24-305 a 33, 331 a 7-332 a 2 (Cf. 975 b 4); not to be differentiated by shape 306 b 3-307 b 24; explanation of their movements 310 a 14-311 a 14; heaviness and lightness of 311 a 16-312 a 22; because of their mutual generation may regard them as composed of one matter 312 a 23; homoeomerous bodies regarded by Anaxagoras as elements 314 a 20; real elements are prime matter and certain contrarieties 328 b 26-329 a 5; the qualities of the four simple bodies 330 a 30-331 a 6, 441 b 12; the simple bodies are similar to but purer than earth, air, fire, and water 330 b 22-30; how simple bodies form compound bodies 334 a 16-b 30, 703 a 27; motion of 339 a 15, 340 b 33; material causes of meteorological

events 339 a 29; originate from one another 339 b 1; have four qualities 378 b 10; earth and water are material elements of all bodies 382 a 6; homogeneous bodies consist of 389 b 27; agreement of 396 b 33-397 a 8; soul not composed of 409 b 19-411 a 6; no fifth element 425 a 12; body of animal cannot consist of one element 435 a 11, 20; have no odour 443 a 10; when pure show no variation 960 a 31; indivisible 968 a 16-b 3; corporeal elements 969 a 21; of Forms 987 b 17; do they exist only potentially? 1002 b 33-1003 a 4; meanings of 1014 a 26-b 15; defined 1041 b 32; eternal entities not composed of 1088 b 14-34. Cf. Principles

Elephant, 298 a 13; easily tamed 488 a 29; temper of 488 b 22; trunk of 492 b 17, 497 b 25-32, 658 b 28-659 a 36, 661 a 28, 682 b 32-683 a 3, 692 b 16; legs of 497 b 22, 498 a 4-13, 709 a 11, 712 a 10; mammae of 498 a 1, 500 a 18, 688 b 5-20; sleep of 498 a 9; least hairy of quadrupeds 499 a 9, 782 b 9; genitals of 500 b 7, 509 b 11, 719 b 16; teeth of 501 b 30-502 a 2; tongue of 502 a 3; has no gall-bladder 506 b 1; intestines of 507 b 35; liver of 507 b 39; has no nails 517 a 32; sperm of 523 a 27; sound of 536 b 21; copulation of 540 a 20, 546 b 8-14; reproduction of 578 a 16-24, 771 a 19, 777 b 16, 847 b 5, 6; diet of 596 a 3-8; age of 596 a 12, 630 b 23-25, 777 b 15; diseases of 604 a 12, 605 a 23-b 4; habits of 610 a 15-32, 630 b 18-30, 659 a 32; feet of 659 a 27; largest of animals 663 a 6, 771 b 9; semen of 736 a 4; foetus of 773 b 6; has longest period of gestation 777 b 4, 16

Eleus, 592 b 11, 609 b 9

Eleusis, 843 b 2

Eleven, the, at Athens, 1322 a 20

Elis, 586 a 3, 722 a 10, 834 a 21, b 26, 842 a 25-b 2, 1416 a 1; revolution at 1306 a 16-20

Elk, tarandos, hair of 832 b 8-17

Elm, 595 b 11, 628 b 26, 828 b 24

Elops, gills of 505 a 15; gall-bladder of 506 b 16

Elymeia, 1311 b 12

Elysian Plains, 943 b 23

Emathiotae, pigs in 835 a 34

Embryo, nutrition begins in 483 a 13; defined as first mixture of male and female 728 b 34; development of 733 b 23-735 a 28, 739 b 34-741 a 5, b 25-745 b 21; movement of 734 b 16; has as much life as a plant 736 a 35, b 13; possesses soul potentially 737 a 17; abortion of 758 b 5, 773 b 18; causes of sex in 763 b 20-767 a 35; sleep of 778 b 20-779 a 27

Emetics, to be avoided at changes of seasons 859 b 25-27

Emotion. *See* Passion

Empedocles, 126 b 18, 294 a 25, 305 a 3, 325 b 17, 382 a 1, 387 b 3, 399 b 26, 410 a 3, b 27, 420 a 28, 731 a 4, 929 b 17, 972 b 29, 988 a 16, 1000 b 13, 1015 a 1, 1091 b 12, 1147 a 21, b 12, 1155 b 7, 1208 b 12, 1212 a 15, 1235 a 12, 1373 b 14, 1407 a 35, 1447 b 18, 1457 b 24, 1461 a 24; the elements of 105 b 17, 187 a 26, 302 a 29, 314 a 16, 26, 329 a 4, 330 b 20, 984 a 8, 985 b 1, 988 a 27, 998 a 30, b 30; Being is one and many 187 a 22-188 a 17; finite number of principles 189 a 16; says little about forms and essence 194 a 21; uses the term 'chance' 196 a 22; his 'man-faced ox-progeny' 198 b 33, 199 b 6; Love and Strife 250 a 27, 252 a 7, 26, 265 b 20, 295 a 30, 300 b 29, 301 a 16, 314 a 17, 315 a 7, 17, 333 b 12-334 a 9, 985 a 1-9, 22-30, 988 a 33, 994 a 7, 996 a 8, 1004 b 33, 1072 a 6; on destruction of world 279 b 15, 284 a 24; movement of heavens prevents movement of earth 295 a 17; the vortex keeps the earth still 300 b 2; fire, earth, and related bodies are elements 302 a 30, b 23; his view of generation of elements 305 b 1-27; does not analyse the notions of light and heavy 309 a 19; distinguishes between coming to be and alteration 314 a 12; no coming to be 314 b 8, 315 a 25; some bodies have pores 324 b 33, 325 b 6-12; elements immutable 329 b 1; criticism of the four elements of 333 a 16-334 a 15, 989 a 19-29; theory of thunder and lightning 369 b 12; view of soul 404 b 8-15, 408 a 18; on growth of plants 415 b 28; on light 418 b 20-26, 446 a 27; identification of thinking and perceiving 427 a 22; eye composed of fire 437 b 12, 25, 910 a 14; on water 441 a 5; on respiration 473 a 15-474 a 24; thinks warmest animals live in sea 477 a 32-478 a 10; says nothing about purpose of respiration 482 a 29; nail is formed from sinew 484 a 39; on nature of bone 485 b 27; thinks many of characteristics of animals are result of incidental occurrences 640 a 20; ratio as essence of things 642 a 19; men hotter than women 648 a 32; on generation 722 b 8, 723 a 24; 'Reign of Love' 722 b 19; why mules are sterile 747 a 34; on sex differentiation 764 a 2-5, 12-765 a 2; on milk 777 a 9; on colour of eye 779 b 16, 910 a 14; plants have sex 815 a 15, 817 a 2, 10, 36; plants have intelligence 815 b 17; on origin of plants and animals 817 b 36; on formation of rocks and stones 937 a 15; melancholic 953 a 27; some things come to be and others are eternal 975 a 39-b 15; his view of the void 976 b 23-33; nothing exists by virtue of the ratio in it 993 a 17; all except God proceeded from strife 1000 a 24-32; God least wise of all beings 1000 b 4-8; unity is love 1001 a 13, 1053 b 15; relativity of knowledge 1009 b 17-21; the 'mixture' 1069 b 22; made love the good 1075 b 1-7

Empis, midge, sloughing of 601 a 3. Cf. Gnat

Emprosthuretic animals, 509 b 3

Emulation, 1105 b 22, 1388 a 29-b 30, 1419 b 26; defined 1388 a 31

Emys, has neither kidneys nor bladder 671 a 32

Encomium, 1219 b 9, 15, 1367 b 28, 1368 a 18

End. *See* Final Cause, Limit

Endive, 612 a 30

Endurance, 1145 a 36, b 8, 15, 1147 b 22, 1221 a 9, 1250 b 6, 1334 a 23; and continence 1146 b 12, 1150 a 14, 34, 1202 b 29-33

Endymion, 1178 b 20

Enmity, 1382 a 1-16

Enna, cave of 836 b 14-27

Enthymeme, 70 a 3-b 38, 71 a 10, 701 a 25-39, 1354 b 22, 1394 a 9-18, 1419 a 19, 1428 a 20, 1430 a 23-38, 1431 a 30-38, b 26, 1432 b 26, 1433 a 25, 1434 a 35, 1438 b 34, 1439 a 5, 20, 34, 1440 a 23, 1441 a 19, 39, 1442 b 38, 1443 a 2, b 43; defined 70 a 10, 1430 a 23; examples and fables preferred to enthymemes in rhetoric 916 b 25-34; the substance of rhetorical persuasion 1354 a 14; a rhetorical syllogism 1355 a 8-13, 1356 b 1-25, 1359 a 10, 1394 a 26; deals with the contingent 1357 a 14-22; its materials are probabilities and signs 1357 a 33; two kinds of: demonstrative and refutative 1358 a 2-35, 1396 b 25-28, 1400 b 25-33, 1403 a 25-33, 1418 b 2; most suitable to forensic speeches 1368 a 31; compared with maxims 1394 a 26-b 6; use of 1395 b 20-1397 a 6; twenty-eight lines of argument upon which genuine enthymemes may be based: (1) opposites 1397 a 7-18, (2) modification of the key-word 1397 a 19-22, (3) correlative ideas 1397 a 23-b 11, (4) a fortiori 1397 b 12-26, (5) consideration of time 1397 b 27-1398 a 2, (6) turning words of opponent against himself 1398 a 3-14, (7) definition of terms 1398 a 15-27, (8) ambiguous terms 1398 a 28, (9) logical division 1398 a 29-31, (10) induction 1398 a 32-b 18, (11) previous decision or general consent 1398 b 19-1399 a 6, (12) taking separately the parts of a subject 1399 a 7, 8, (13) consequences 1399 a 9-17, (14) contrasting opposites 1399 a 18-27, (15) inconsistency 1399 a 28-32, (16) rational correspondence 1399 a 33-b 3, (17) from results to antecedents 1399 b 4-12, (18) inconsistency 1399 b 13-18, (19) from possible motive to real motive 1399 b 19-30, (20) inducements and deterrents 1399 b 31-1400 a 4, (21) things which are supposed to happen and yet seem incredible 1400 a 5-13, (22) inconsistency 1400 a 14-21, (23) reasons for prejudice 1400 a 22-28, (24) cause to effect 1400 a 29-35, (25) neglect of a better course 1400 a 36-b 3, (26) inconsistency 1400 b 4-8, (27) previous mistakes 1400 b 9-16, (28) meanings from proper names 1400 b 17-24; nine lines of argument of apparent enthymemes: (1) words 1401 a 1-23, (2) confusion of parts and whole 1401 a 24-b 3, (3) indignant language 1401 a b 4-8, (4) using of single instance as proof 1401 b 9-13, (5) the accidental as essential 1401 b 14-18, (6) argument from consequence 1401 b 19-29, (7) treating as causes things that happened along with or before event in question 1401 b 30-33, (8) omission of time and consequence 1401 b 34-1402 a 2, (9) confusion of the absolute with the particular 1402 a 3-27; four methods of refutation: (1) by directly attacking your opponent's statements, (2) by putting forward another statement like it, (3) by putting forward a statement contrary to it, (4) by quoting previous decisions 1402 a 29-1403 a 16; based on probabilities, examples, infallible signs, or ordinary si͘͘ 1402 b 14; amplification and de͘ ation are not elements of 1403 . 24; as an argument 1418 a 2-16, ͘ 4, 34-38

Enunciation, 72 a 11

Envy, jealousy (φθόνος), 807 a 5, 1105 b 22, 1108 a 35, 1115 a 22, 1192 b 18, 1221 a 3, 38, 1229 a 39, 1234 a 30, 1354 a 25, 1386 b 17, 1387 b 21-1388 a 28, 34, 1419 b 26, 1443 b 17; defined 109 b 36, 1233 b 19, 1387 b 22; has no mean 1107 a 11; how aroused 1440 a 35, 1445 a 12-29

Enystrum. See Abomasum

Epeus, tools of 840 a 27-34

Ephemeron, dayfly, 490 b 1, 552 b 18-23; diet of 682 a 26

Ephesus, 371 a 31, 1201 b 8; raised money by asking women to give gold ornaments to the state 1349 a 9-13

Ephialtes, 1274 a 8

Ephors, 1419 a 32; selected by the people 1265 b 39, 1294 b 30; criticism of the Ephoralty 1270 b 7-34; decide suits about contracts 1275 b 9; Pausanias attempted to overthrow Ephoralty 1301 b 20 (Cf. 1333 b 34); established by Theopompus 1313 a 25-33

Epic Cycle, 1417 a 15

Epicharmus, a Sicilian poet, 1010 a 5, 1086 a 18, 1167 b 25, 1410 b 3, 1448 a 33, 1449 b 6; the climax of 724 a 29, 1365 a 17

Epichireme, defined as a dialectical inference 162 a 16

Epic poetry, 1406 b 3, 1415 a 12, 1447 a 14, b 14, 1449 a 6, 1456 a 12, 1458 b 16; compared with tragedy 1449 b 9-19, 1459 b 8-1460 b 5; episodes in 1455 b 16; must have unity of action 1459 a 18-b 7; compared with history 1459 a 22-29; length of epic compared to that of tragedy 1459 b 18-31; metre of 1459 b 32-1460 a 4; the improbable in 1460 a 13, 1461 b 13, 14; possibility and impossibility in 1460 a 26-b 5, 1461 b 9-12; a higher form of imitation than the tragedy 1461 b 26-1462 b 15

Epidamnus, 1267 b 19, 1287 a 9; revolution at 1301 b 21, 1304 a 14-17

Epidaurus, 1411 a 12

Epiglottis, 476 a 34, 492 b 34, 495 a 29, 504 b 4; function of 664 b 22-665 a 25

Epilais, 592 b 23

Epilepsy, 457 a 9, 954 b 30, 1149 a 12, 1150 b 34; cure of 831 b 25, 835 a 29, b 34; man only animal subject to epilepsy in infancy 896 b 6; the sacred disease 953 a 16; man more liable to suffer from epilepsy than any other animal 960 a 10, 17

Epilogue of a speech, 1414 b 1-7, 12, 1419 b 10-1420 b 4

Epimenides, 1252 b 14, 1418 a 24

Epipetrum, a long-living plant 681 a 24

Epirus, 572 b 19, 595 b 18, 606 b 4; large quadrupeds of 522 b 16-20; stags of 835 b 29

Episode, 1451 b 34, 1452 b 18, 21, 1455 b 1-22, 1459 a 37, b 30; plurality of episodes 1449 a 28

Epithets, 1407 b 32; misuse of 1405 b 21-27, 1406 a 12-b 4

Epitonos, back-stay, 515 b 10

Epitragiae. See Capon-fish

'Epitrite,' 920 a 36

Epomis, 493 a 9

Equality, 1001 b 23, 1021 a 12, 1075 a 33, 1082 b 7, 1087 b 5, 1088 b 32, 1089 b 6, 1091 b 35, 1158 b 30, 1310 a 31, 1332 b 27; predicated of quantity 6 a 27; how opposed to great and small 847 b 28, 1055 b 30-1056 b 2; of ratios 1131 a 32; friendship is equality 1157 b 36, 1168 b 8; two kinds of: numerical and proportional 1241 b 33-40, 1301 b 29-1302 a 7; of property 1266 a 39-1267 b 19, 1274 b 9; justice as equality 1280 a 8-31, 1282 b 15-1284 b 34, 1301 b 36, 1310 a 31, 1325 b 8, 1332 b 27; legislation is only for those who are equal 1284 a 3-18; one form of democracy based strictly on equality 1291 b 30-38; democracy has numerical equality 1291 b 30, 1301 a 28, 1308 a 12, 1310 a 30, 1317 b 3-9, 1318 a 6; demanded on grounds of freedom, wealth, or virtue 1294 a 19; inequality is chief cause of revolutions 1301 b 26, 1302 a 23-31. Cf. Proportion

Equinox, 942 b 26, 30, 36, 943 a 2

Equity, 1137 a 32-1138 a 3, 1143 b 20, 31, 1198 b 24-33, 1199 a 2, 1251 b 34, 1372 b 18, 1374 a 25-b 23, 1375 a 31

Equivocal, 1030 a 32, 1046 a 6, 1060 b 33, 1461 a 26; when things are named equivocally 1 a 1; relation of equivocal terms 249 a 23. Cf. Ambiguous terms, Obscurity

Eretria, 94 b 1; cavalry of 1289 b 39; revolution at 1306 a 35

Ergophilus, 1380 b 12

Eridanus River, 836 a 31

Eriphyle, 1453 b 24

Eristic, 1012 a 19, 1402 a 2, 14, 1414 b 28

Erithacus. See Robin

Eros. See Cupid

Error, 66 b 18-67 b 26, 427 b 3, 465 a 23, 1052 a 2; three kinds of 67 b 6; as formal fallacy 77 b 20-33; as inferential in atomic connexion or disconnexion 79 b 23-80 b 16; two kinds occur in problems 109 a 27; in sensation 442 b 8; may occur in two ways 1226 a 35; defined 1427 a 34; plea of 1429 a 15, 1444 a 8-15. Cf. Fallacy

Erythe, 843 b 31

Erytheia, 359 a 27, 843 b 15-844 a 6

Erythrae, 838 a 9; revolution at 1305 b 19-21

Erythraean Sea, 383 b 3

Erythrinus, 567 a 27; reproduction in 538 a 20, 760 a 9; habitat of 598 a 13; no sex distinction in 741 a 36, 755 b 22

Erythus, 843 b 15-844 a 6

Eryxis, 1231 a 17

Essence (τί ἦν εἶναι), 993 a 13, 1007 a 20, 1025 b 29, 1038 b 14, 1045 b 3; essence of things is in the individual 731 b 33, 742 b 34; in the doctrine of Forms 988 a 34-b 16; cannot be reduced to another definition fuller in expression 994 b 17; substance as essence 1029 b 12-1032 a 11; and definition 1030 a 6-27, 1034 b 20-1038 a 35, 1182 b 19; defined 1343 a 13. Cf. Being, Substance

Essential nature. See Definition

Etelis, 567 a 20

Eternal, 263 a 3, 465 b 29, 974 a 2, 975 a 35, 1015 b 15, 1051 a 20, 1091 a 12, 1218 a 12; as an individual 731 b 33, 742 b 32; ambiguous 742 b 27; the elements are eternal 975 b 5; God is eternal 977 a 22; objects of mathematics are eternal 987 b 15; eternal sensible substance 1069 a 31, b 25, 1071 b 3-1072 a 17; can eternal things consist of elements? 1088 b 14; philosophy has to do with the eternal 1197 b 7

Etesian winds, 395 a 2

Etesiae, 361 b 24, 35, 362 a 12, 363 a 15

Ether, aither, 365 a 20, 369 b 14, 20, 699 b 25; name for the primary body 270 b 23; Anaxagoras made it equivalent to fire 270 b 25, 302 b 5; moves in circle 339 a 11; element that fills space between earth and heaven 339 b 19; clouds and water do not form in 340 a 19-341 a 13; substance of heaven and stars 392 a 5; in continual motion 392 a 7

Ethics, 1197 b 28; a branch of politics 1181 a 24-b 29; etymology of 1185 b 38-1186 a 2

Ethiopia, Ethiopians, 167 a 12, 349 a 5, 362 b 22, 517 a 18, 523 a 18, 722 a 10, 736 a 11, 812 b 32, 820 a 5, 1290 b 5; said to be flying serpents in 490 a 11; sheep in 573 b 29; hair of 782 b 34; teeth of 898 b 12-19; effect of climate on 909 a 27-31

Ethiopian mountains, 350 b 11

Etna, 395 b 21, 400 a 34, 840 a 5, 846 a 9; eruptions of 833 a 18

Etruria, 837 b 34; mine in 837 b 28-33

Euboea, 366 a 27, 393 a 13, 496 b 26, 677 a 3, 846 b 37, 973 a 21, b 22, 1411 a 10

Eubulus, tyrant of Atarneus, 1267 a 33, 1376 a 9

Euclees, 343 b 5

Euclid, 1458 b 7

Euctemon, 1374 b 37

Eudoxus, 847 a 7, 991 a 17, b 11, 17, 1073 b 18-31, 1079 b 21, 1101 b 27; thinks pleasure is the good 1172 b 9-25; referred to 1172 a 27

Eulogy, 1425 b 37-1426 b 21; one of the genera of oratory 1421 b 9, 1428 a 3; methods of 1440 b 5-1441 b 29

Eunuchs, 879 b 8; never become bald 632 a 3, 784 a 8, 897 b 23-29; have poor sight 876 b 25; have sore and ulcerated legs 876 b 31, 895 a 31-35; resemble female 894 b 19-38; never suffer from varicocele 894 b 39-895 a 4; voice of 900 b 15-28, 903 a 26-38, 906 a 2-20

Euphrates, snake of 845 b 12-16

Euripides, 443 b 30, 957 b 11, 1110 a 27, 1136 a 12, 1142 a 2, 1155 b 2, 1208 b 17, 1209 b 36, 1210 a 14, 1212 b 27, 1244 a 10, 1252 b 8, 1277 a 18, 1310 a 34, 1311 b 31, 1328 a 16, 1339 a 18, 1384 b 16, 1400 b 22, 1404 b 25, 1405 a 28, 1415 a 19, 1416 a 29, 1433 b 10, 1453 a 24, 28, 1455 b 9, 1456 a 17, 27, 1458 b 19, 24, 1460 b 34; referred to 1111 a 12, 1129 b 28, 1154 b 29, 1167 a 33, 1168 b 7, 1169 b 7, 1177 b 32. Cf. Cresphontes, Medea, Oeneus, Tyro

Euripus, 547 a 6

Euronotus (S.S.E. wind), 394 b 33; sometimes called Eurus 973 b 7; sometimes called Amneus 973 b 7

Europe, 224 b 21, 579 b 7, 606 b 15, 1415 a 17; its bounds 393 b 22; natives of Europe are full of spirit, but lack intelligence and skill 1285 a 21, 1327 b 24

Eurus (S.E. wind), 363 b 20, 364 a 17, b 3, 20, 23, 26, 394 b 20, 23, 947 a 4; a rainy wind 943 a 5-27, 945 a 37-b 4; makes all things appear larger 946 a 34; sometimes called Phoenicias 973 a 5; called Scopeleus at Aegae 973 b 2; called Carbas at Cyrene 973 b 2

Euryphon, the father of Hippodamus, 1267 b 22

Eurypylus, 1459 b 6

Eurystheus, 1245 b 32

Eurytion of Heraclea, 1306 b 1

Eurytus, 1092 b 10

Euthycrates, a Phocian 1304 a 12

Euthydemus, 177 b 13, 1401 a 27

EUTHYDEMUS of Plato, 74 b 25, 1097 a 26, 1098 b 12

Euthynus, 1392 b 12

Euxenus, 1406 b 31

Euxine, 350 b 4, 354 a 17, 543 b 3, 566 b 10, 567 b 16, 568 a 4, 571 a 15, 597 a 15, 598 a 24, 603 a 25, 604 b 22, 606 a 10, 1303 a 38; why fish penetrate into 598 a 30, 601 b 17

Evaeses, his trickery 1352 a 8-16

Evagoras, tyrant of Salamis in Cyprus, 1311 b 4, 1399 a 5

Evaporation, exhalation, two kinds of: moist (vapour) and dry (a kind of smoke) 341 b 8, 346 b 32, 357 b 25, 358 a 21, 359 b 28, 360 a 8, 365 b 21, 369 a 13, 378 a 18, 384 b 33, 394 a 8; ignited by motion 341 b 35, 342 a 17; of brain 744 a 17

Even, even and odd are the differentia of number 120 b 5, 123 a 13, 142 b 10; the Pythagorean conception 986 a 18, 990 a 9; an ambiguous term 1261 b 29

Evenus, 1015 a 29, 1152 a 31, 1223 a 32, 1251 a 35; quoted 1370 a 10

Evidence. See Testimony

Evil, vice (κακία, κακός), 985 a 1, 1115 a 18, 1140 b 19; contrary of virtue 113 b 31; that which is cause of evil is more objectionable than what is evil *per accidens* 116 b 5; any con-

trary of a good thing is evil 119 a 36-b 16; genus of disease 123 b 17; genus of defect and excess 123 b 28; soul as well as body has its vice 153 b 10; does not exist apart from evil things 1051 a 17; a first principle? 1075 a 35, 1091 b 34; belongs to the class of the unlimited 1106 b 28; responsible for bad as well as good actions 1113 b 3-1115 a 6; destroys itself 1126 a 12; multiform 1192 a 12; man only animal that has sense of good and evil 1253 a 16. Cf. Virtue

Evil eye, 926 b 20-31

Example (παράδειγμα), 68 b 38-69 a 19, 1357 b 25-1358 a 1, 1428 a 19, 1431 a 24-29, 1438 b 40, 1439 a 5, 1443 a 1, b 37; a rhetorical induction 71 a 10, 1356 b 1-25, 1357 b 25, 1393 a 25; preferred in rhetoric to enthymemes 916 b 25-34; deals with the contingent 1357 a 14-22; most suitable to deliberative speeches 1368 a 30; varieties of 1393 a 25-1394 a 18; as a basis of an enthymeme 1402 b 14, 17, 1403 a 5-9; as an argument 1418 a 2; nature of 1429 a 21-27; kinds of 1429 a 28-b 24; methods of using 1429 b 25-1430 a 13

Excess (ὑπερβολή), 737 b 6, 992 b 6, 1004 b 12, 1042 b 24, 1186 a 30, 38, b 3-25, 1189 b 29, 1191 b 1, 35, 1192 a 6, b 12, 1193 b 26, 1200 a 34, 1222 a 9-b 10, 1220 b 22, 1221 b 11, 1227 a 35, 1231 a 35, b 16, 1233 b 17, 1234 b 8, 1249 b 20; contrary of defect 14 a 2, 123 b 28, 187 a 17, 189 b 11, 486 b 17; cause and cure of disease 859 a 1-8, 861 a 22; moral virtue destroyed by defect and excess 1185 b 14-32; defect and excess are painful 1204 b 12. Cf. Defect, Extreme, Intemperance, Mean

Exchange, 1132 b 31, 1133 a 2, 19-30, b 11-27, 1194 a 24, 1258 b 21; voluntary exchange 1132 b 11; kinds contrary to nature 1256 b 40-1257 a 19, b 1-24, 1258 b 1-7; kinds according to nature 1257 a 6-30, 1258 a 38-40

Excluded middle, 18 a 28-19 b 4, 77 a 30, 88 a 39, 1011 b 24-1012 a 28, 1055 b 2, 1057 a 34, 1069 a 4

Excrement, 676 a 33, 830 a 18-25, 831 a 6, 897 b 34-898 a 3; the opposite of nutriment 677 a 28; of birds 679 a 19; passages for 719 b 29-720 a 36; not found in plants 817 b 19

Excretions, 305 b 4, 380 a 1, b 5, 487 a 5, 511 b 10

Executioner, 1322 a 23

Executive element in the state, 1298 a 2, 1299 a 3-1300 b 12, 1321 b 4-1323 a 10

Exercise, physical, promotes health 865 a 1-3, 884 a 23-25; distends the body 885 b 24; voice is shrill after violent exercise 901 a 30-34; harms vision 958 b 29-33

Exode, 1452 b 18, 22

Expedient, 1422 a 4-15, b 25-1423 a 7, b 1, 1425 b 40, 1427 a 27, b 40, 1430 a 28, 1436 a 14, 1438 b 20, 32, 1439 a 11, 37, 1440 a 11, 1442 a 18, 1445 b 9; a topic of persuasion 1421 b 24

Expenditure, a department of royal economy 1345 b 21; must not exceed income 1346 a 16

Experience (ἐμπειρία), 703 a 9, 1143 b 13, 1250 a 35; experience gives the principles that belong to a subject 46 a 18-21; developed from memory and produces skill and knowledge 100 a 6; science and art come to men through 981 a 2; art considered more truly knowledge than experience is 981 a 13-b 9; knowledge of individuals 981 a 16; courage of experience 1190 b 24-32, 1229 a 15, 1230 a 5, 13; should not disregard the experience of ages 1264 a 2 (Cf. 1329 b 35)

Exports, 1348 b 33, 1352 a 22; a department of royal economy 1345 b 21

Exposition, 645 b 1; a means of demonstration 28 a 22, 30 a 9, b 32

Extension. See Interval

Extravagance. See Prodigality, Vulgarity

Extreme (ἄκρον), anything that admits of extreme heat also admits of extreme cold 860 a 1; extremes opposed to each other and to the mean 1108 b 11-1109 a 19, 1220 b 30; one extreme is sometimes more opposed to the mean than the other 1109 a 1-19, 1222

a 23-b 4, 1234 b 6-14; sometimes the extremes meet 1234 a 34-b 5

Exyris, 1231 a 17

Eye, 491 b 18-492 a 13, 495 a 11, 520 b 4, 734 a 18; eye is an eye only as long as it fulfills its function 412 b 20; composed of water, not fire 437 a 18-438 b 29; loses its power from too long use 454 a 28; colour of 492 a 3, 779 a 28-780 b 12, 892 a 1-5, 910 a 12-25, 1247 a 11, 37; size of 492 a 7; reason for position of 656 b 30; last part of the body to be formed 743 b 32-744 b 12; only sense-organ having a bodily constitution peculiar to itself 744 a 5; differences in visual ability 779 b 34-781 a 14; as a physiognomic sign 807 b 2, 8, 23, 28, 36, 808 a 4, 9, 12, 31, 34, b 6, 811 b 14-29, 813 a 20-31, 814 b 4; position of eyes during sexual intercourse 876 a 30-36; man has smaller distance between eyes in proportion to size than any other animal 892 b 4-14, 960 a 14; problems connected with the eyes 957 a 38-960 a 33; rubbing eye stops sneezing 957 a 38-b 4, 961 b 27-32, 962 a 25-31; see more accurately with one eye than with two 957 b 5-8, 18-22, 959 a 38-b 4; anger makes eyes red 957 b 9-17, 961 a 8-15; those blind from birth do not become bald 957 b 23-32; affected by smoke 957 b 33, 34, 959 b 5-14; movements of 957 b 35-958 a 34; those who see with one eye are less liable to visual disturbances 958 b 10; double-vision 958 b 12-15, 959 a 9-19; physical exercise detrimental to acuteness of vision 958 b 28-33; only part of body that does not feel cold 959 b 15-19; left eye closed more easily than right 959 b 31-35; eye of the soul 1144 a 29; 'shame dwells in the eyes' 1384 a 33. Cf. Sight

Eyebrows, 518 b 7, 798 a 31; shape indicates disposition 491 b 15; protect the eyes 658 b 14; often grow bushy in old age 658 b 19, 878 b 28; right eyebrow raised more than left 671 b 33; right eyebrow more arched than left

671 b 34; as a physiognomic sign 808 a 9, 812 b 25-27

Eyelashes, 491 b 20, 498 b 23, 518 b 10, 798 a 31, 834 b 29; all animals with hair on body have eyelashes 658 a 11; man is only hairy animal that has eyelashes on both lids 658 a 15; protect the eyes 658 b 14; loss of eyelashes is sign of lustfulness 878 b 21-32

Eyelids, 421 b 29, 493 a 29, 518 a 2, 657 a 25-658 a 10; hard-eyed animals 444 b 26; droop when drowsy 456 b 32, 457 b 4; animals are late in getting control of 744 a 36-b 9; as a physiognomic sign 807 b 29, 811 b 14-18, 813 a 23

F

Fable. *See* Plot

Fables, 1393 a 30, b 9-1394 a 8

Face, 491 b 9, 662 b 20; as a physiognomic sign 807 b 14, 26, 32, 808 a 28, 31, 811 b 5-13, 814 b 5; why face gives off most perspiration 867 a 23-27, b 34-868 a 4, 965 b 4-12; chosen for portraits 965 b 1-3; eruptions appear most frequently on 965 b 13-17

Fact (τὸ ὅτι), 1095 b 6; the reasoned fact 75 a 18, 76 a 12, 85 b 22, 87 a 31; difference between knowledge of fact and knowledge of reasoned fact 78 a 22-b 31; relation to perception and knowledge 88 a 2, 89 b 23, 90 a 25, 93 a 17; can opine both fact and reasoned fact 89 a 15; fact past and fact future as lines of argument 1392 b 14-1393 a 8. Cf. Cause, Demonstration, Knowledge, Middle Term

Faculty. *See* Capacity

Faggot-bearer, 557 b 13-25

Fainting, 880 b 29-33

Falcon. *See* Hawk

Falconry, 841 b 15-27

Fallacy, 108 a 26-36; four senses in which an argument may be fallacious 162 b 4-15; all types of fallacy consist in ignorance of what refutation is 168 a 17-169 a 22; how to show

172 a 9-28; solutions of 175 a 1-183 a 26; use of studying solutions of 175 a 5-17; apparent and genuine solutions of 175 a 32-177 a 8; nine lines of argument of apparent enthymemes: (1) words 1401 a 1-23, (2) confusion of parts and whole 1401 a 24-b 3, (3) indignant language 1401 b 4-8, (4) using of single instance as proof 1401 b 9-13, (5) the accidental as essential 1401 b 14-18, (6) argument from consequence 1401 b 19-29, (7) treating as causes things that happened along with or before the event in question 1401 b 30-33, (8) omission of time and consequence 1401 b 34-1402 a 2, (9) confusion of the absolute with the particular 1402 a 3-27. Cf. Error

Fall of Ilium, 1459 b 7

False cause, 65 a 38-66 a 15

False cause, Fallacy of, one of the seven fallacious refutations independent of language 166 b 27; examples of 167 b 21-36; solution of 181 a 31-35

Falsity (ψεῦδος), 88 a 25-30, 980 a 10, 1089 a 20, 1234 a 33; truth and falsity imply combination and separation 16 a 11; argument made false by first false statement 66 a 16; not same as impossibility 281 b 3-25, 1047 b 13; defined 1011 b 26; meanings of 1024 b 17-1025 a 13; not-being as falsity 1027 b 17-1028 a 5, 1051 a 34-1052 a 12; not in all things 1027 b 25. Cf. Not-being

Fame, a constituent of happiness 1360 b 24, 1361 a 25, 26

Family, 1252 a 26-b 27, 1261 b 12, 1265 b 14; association to supply man's everyday wants 1252 b 12; members of the family called 'companions of the cupboard' and 'companions of the manger' 1252 b 14; village formed out of families 1252 b 15, 1260 b 13, 1269 b 15; ruled by the eldest 1252 b 22; three parts in 1259 a 37-b 16. Cf. Household

Fat, 511 b 9, 520 a 6-b 9, 521 b 10; fumes of 387 b 6; composition and purpose of 388 a 7, 651 a 20-b 19; on kidneys 672 a 1-b 8; fat animals are less fertile 725 b 30-726 a 6, 727 a 33; a healthy secretion 726 a 6; floats on surface of water 823 a 30; of bear 835 a 30-32; consumed in exercise 880 b 37, 38; not natural 882 a 22; difference in place of fat in animals 891 a 19-25

Fate, use of the word means God 401 b 9; the three Fates 401 b 14-24; external principles sometimes work against man's plans 463 b 27

Fatigue, 809 a 10; cure of 863 b 19-28, 861 a 4-39, 884 b 36-885 a 5; induces sleep 874 b 17; the fatigued emit semen during sleep 876 a 10, 884 a 6-15; problems connected with 880 b 15-885 b 11; in walking 880 b 15-28, 881 b 18-27, 37-882 a 2, 29-39, 883 a 21-28, 884 b 9, 10, 885 a 14-b 9; more fatiguing to throw with hand empty than with stone in it 881 a 39-b 7; more fatiguing to lie on flat than concave surface 881 b 28-36; in knees and thighs 882 b 25-36, 883 a 29-b 2; why those of equable temperament throw off fatigue easily 883 a 11-20

Fear (φόβος), 1105 b 22, 1106 a 2, 1107 b 1, 1110 a 4, 1115 a 8-b 7, 1116 a 31, 1117 a 30, 1121 b 28, 1128 b 11, 1179 b 11, 1185 b 24-32, 1191 a 25, 30-36, b 17, 1220 b 12, 1228 b 13, 1229 a 34, 1378 a 22, 1380 a 23, 32, 1382 a 19-1383 b 11, 1386 a 27; animals having cold and watery blood are subject to fear 650 b 28; bloodless animals more timorous than sanguineous 650 b 31, 679 a 25; animals having large heart are subject to fear 667 a 20; a refrigeration which results from deficiency of natural heat 692 a 26; makes men cold 889 a 24, 898 a 6, 903 b 12, 947 b 23-948 a 12, b 14-19; problems connected with courage and fear 947 b 12-949 a 20; causes thirst 947 b 15-22, 35-948 a 8, b 14-19; causes trembling 947 b 12-14, 948 a 35-b 13; affects bile 948 b 10; makes sexual organs contract 948 b 10, 949 a 8-20; loosens bowels 948 b 17, 35-949 a 7; those who are afraid keep silent 948 b 20-34; makes men desire to pass urine 948 b 35-949 a 7; some define

fear as expectation of evil 1115 a 10; a feeling 1186 a 14; and confidence 1190 b 9-21, 1228 a 28; as a cause of revolutions 1302 b 22-25, 1311 a 26, b 37; will unite bitterest enemies 1304 b 23; helps preserve the state 1308 a 26; defined 1382 a 21; in tragedy 1449 b 27, 1452 a 2, b 1, 32, 35, 38, 1453 a 6, b 1, 12, 1456 a 38

Feathers, all birds are feathered 692 b 10, 697 b 12; feather wings of insects 692 b 12, 713 a 11; birds shed their feathers 783 b 12-18; thick-feathered birds are lustful 880 a 35-b 7, 893 b 10-16

Feeling. See Passion

Feet, 494 a 12, 499 b 7, 734 b 29; of quadrupeds 690 a 4-28; of man 690 a 28-b 11; man has largest feet of all animals in proportion to size of body 690 a 28; etymology of 706 a 33; as a physiognomic sign 809 b 10, 810 a 15-24, 814 b 6; swelling of 859 b 1-4; bareness of feet prejudicial to sexual intercourse 877 a 5-15; chill in 887 b 28-31; why animals have even number of feet 893 b 20-26, 894 a 17-21

Female, 1024 a 36; differences of male and female 538 a 22-24, 544 b 33, 608 a 22-b 25, 727 a 26, 729 b 13, 757 b 17, 766 a 22-b 26, 806 b 33, 809 a 26-810 a 13, 814 a 9, 891 b 21-24, 894 b 27, 963 b 20; naturally inferior to male 648 a 12, 951 a 12, 1254 b 14, 1259 a 39, 1260 a 9, 1343 b 30; contains the material cause of generation 716 a 7, 724 a 10, 727 b 31, 729 a 11, 34-730 b 32, 738 b 20-27, 740 b 25 (Cf. 763 b 33); defined as animal that generates in itself 716 a 15; has no semen 726 a 28-729 a 33; a mutilated male 737 a 28; needs the male in generation 741 a 6-b 24, 748 a 19, 817 a 5, 1343 b 13; residual secretion in 762 b 2; nature does not give weapons for fighting to any female 769 b 2; some animals have no female sex 816 a 18; pass urine with effort 892 b 36-893 a 2; shorter lived than male 896 a 35; damp climate makes birth of females more likely 909 a 32-34; not a species 1058 a 29-b 26; a common life is natural to male and female 1162 a 17, 1252 a 28, 1343 b 8-1344 a 7; difference between female and slave 1252 b 1-8. Cf. Male, Sex, Woman

Fennel, 803 a 42, 905 b 7, 923 b 25; blow of 889 b 28-890 a 9, 37-b 6

Ferret, 580 b 26

Fever, 123 b 36, 861 b 33-862 a 2, 874 b 18, 875 a 13, 948 a 26, 1357 b 15, 21, 1370 b 17; effect of seasons on 859 b 21-860 a 10, 861 b 1-20, 862 b 25-863 a 5; effect of south winds on 862 a 17-25, 946 b 4-9; treatment of 866 a 8-b 6; why not infectious 887 a 22-39; occurs more frequently in coldest season 909 a 22-26; tongue as an indicator of 963 b 34

Fibre, 489 a 23, 511 b 4, 515 b 28-516 a 6

Fieldfare. See Collyrion

Fieldmouse, 606 b 7, 842 b 8

Fiery Star, 399 a 9

Fig, 541 b 24, 552 b 2, 595 b 10, 626 b 8, 930 a 10, b 21; fig-juice curdles milk 552 b 2, 729 a 12, 737 a 15, 771 b 23, 772 a 25 (Cf. Rennet); wild fig 554 a 16, 557 b 26-31; fig-tree 715 b 25, 818 b 35, 820 a 35, b 39, 821 a 23, b 15; rue grafted on fig-tree 924 b 35-925 a 5; dried figs 930 b 33-931 a 5; destroy teeth 931 a 28-33

Figure ($\sigma\chi\tilde{\eta}\mu\alpha$), first 25 b 27-26 b 33, 85 a 3, 93 a 9; second 26 b 34-28 a 9, 85 a 7; third 28 a 10-29 a 18, 85 a 10; common properties of the three figures 29 a 19-b 28; all syllogisms may be reduced to universal syllogisms in the first figure 29 b 1, 40 b 17-41 b 5; three figures only 41 a 17; kinds of propositions to be treated in each 42 b 27-43 a 19; location of middle term in the three figures 47 a 1; analysis of syllogisms of one figure into another 50 b 5-51 b 4; first figure the most scientific 79 a 17-32; conclusions in second figure are negative 90 b 6; no conclusions in third figure are universal 90 b 7

Fig-wasp. See Psen

Final, defined 1097 a 34

Final cause, purpose, end ($o\tilde{v}$ $\check{\epsilon}\nu\epsilon\kappa\alpha$), 646 a 28, 742 a 21, 983 a 31, 994 b 9, 1013 b 26, 1044 a 36, 1059 a 37, 1072 b 2, 1074 a 30, 1139 a 32, b 2, 1189 a 1-b 8, 1218 b 10, 1252 b 34; end more desirable than means 116 b 23; defined as 'that for the sake of which' 194 a 27, 200 a 22, 34, 1013 a 33; and nature 198 b 10-199 b 33, 271 a 34, 290 a 31, 415 b 16, 432 b 21, 434 a 30, 455 b 17, 471 b 26, 476 a 13, 485 a 3-27, 641 b 12, 645 a 24, 661 b 24, 677 a 16, 704 b 15, 708 a 10, 711 a 7, 18, 717 a 16, 738 b 1, 741 b 4, 744 a 38, 788 b 22; ambiguous 415 b 2, 20; and cause in living things 639 b 12-641 a 17; constitutes nature of an animal more than matter 642 a 18; soul is final cause of body 645 b 15; distinction between necessity and final cause 663 b 14-23, 778 a 16-b 19, 789 b 12; everything exists for a final cause 778 b 11, 1050 a 8; some ends are activities, others products 1094 a 4, 1184 b 10, 1185 a 9, 1197 a 3-10, 1211 b 27-32, 1219 a 13-17; final end 1097 a 25; wish relates to the end, choice to the means 1111 b 27, 1113 b 3; deliberate about means, not about end 1112 b 12, 34; each thing is defined by its end 1115 b 23; practical wisdom determines the end, virtue the means 1145 a 5; in actions the final cause is the first principle 1151 a 16; virtue aims at both ends and means 1190 a 8-33; foolish not to select an end for living 1214 b 6-11; end is the limit of the means 1256 b 35, 1257 b 27; means and end may agree or disagree 1331 b 29; contains some pleasure 1339 b 32; deliberation seeks to determine means to ends 1362 a 19. Cf. Cause, Necessity

Finch-titmouse, 592 b 18

Fingers, 493 b 28; of man 687 b 7-21, 690 a 33; a finger of a dead man is a finger only in name 1035 b 24

Finite, relation of finite and infinite space and time 233 a 22-b 15, 237 b 23-238 b 22, 239 b 5-240 b 8; relation of finite and infinite force and magnitude 266 b 25-267 b 23. Cf. Infinite

Fins, 709 b 10-19, 713 a 10, 714 b 1

Fire ($\pi\tilde{v}\rho$), 652 b 8, 699 b 25, 826 a 9, 832 a 27, 968 a 15, 1210 a 18-22; body

are oviparous internally, viviparous externally 718 b 32; generation without males? 750 b 28, 757 b 22, 759 a 10; in India 835 b 5; in Babylon 835 b 7-14; in Pontus and Rhegium 835 b 15-23; in Paphlagonia 835 b 24-27; some have no bladders 895 b 1

Fisherman, 1256 b 3, 1291 b 23

Fishing, a natural means of acquiring wealth 1256 b 2

Fishing-frog, batrachus, 489 b 33, 505 a 6, 540 b 18, 564 b 18, 620 b 13; generation of 505 b 3, 565 b 29, 570 b 30, 749 a 24; gall-bladder of 506 b 16; body of 695 b 14-17; fins of 696 a 27-30; egg of 754 a 26-34, 755 a 8. Cf. Frog

Fissile, 385 a 16, 386 b 25-387 a 11

Flame, 134 b 28, 146 a 17, 342 b 19, 437 b 22; the ebullition of a dry exhalation 341 b 22; process of becoming, involving a constant interchange of moist and dry 355 a 10; fire becomes flame when accompanied by wind 366 a 2. Cf. Fire

Flank, 493 a 18, 810 a 5

Flat-fish, psetta, breeding of 538 a 20, 543 a 2; habits of 620 b 30

Flattery, 1108 a 28, 1121 b 7, 1125 a 2, 1127 a 10, 1173 b 32, 1193 a 22, 1199 a 17, 1208 b 21, 1221 a 7, 26, 1239 a 24, 1371 a 23, 1383 b 35; physiognomic signs of 811 b 37, 813 a 17; loved by most men 1159 a 3; flatterer is a friend in an inferior position 1159 a 14; loved by tyrants 1292 a 21, 1314 a 2

Flat-worm, 551 a 10

Flavour, 380 b 32, 422 a 17, 426 a 14, 796 b 21, 1196 b 19; of sea 354 b 1, 357 a 16, 358 a 3; of water 356 a 13, 357 a 9, 358 b 22, 378 b 1; of rivers 359 b 9-22; of wine 387 b 12; of homogeneous bodies 388 a 12; a tangible quality 414 b 11; species of 422 b 10-14

Flax, 821 a 32

Flea, 537 a 6; spontaneous generation of 539 b 12, 556 b 23, 721 a 10, 723 b 4

Fleabane, 534 b 28

Flesh, 385 a 8, 390 a 2, 486 b 1, 519 b 26-520 a 5, 647 b 14, 653 b 19-654 a

31, 734 b 31, 743 b 5; destroyed by burning or putrefaction 379 a 8; squeezable 386 b 8; a homogeneous body 388 a 16, 389 b 24, 390 b 5, 16, 647 b 14; medium of touch 423 b 26, 653 b 24-29; not ultimate sense organ 426 b 15; blood transformed into flesh 484 a 16; different kinds in various animals 485 b 20; not primary organ of touch 656 b 35; softest in man 660 a 13; composed of small blood vessels 668 a 32; as a physiognomic sign 806 b 22-24, 807 b 13, 808 a 25, b 7; must be rare to promote health 865 b 18-38, 884 a 26-b 8; why flesh has unpleasant odour when sexual powers are present 877 b 21-39; produced by friction 965 b 36-966 a 34, b 10-18; dry friction makes flesh solid 966 b 1-9; darkened by sun 966 b 20-24, 967 b 23-27

Flexion, in movement 708 b 22-709 b 33; why flexion of legs is different in man and quadrupeds 711 a 8-713 b 21; four modes of 712 a 1-20

Flood, the, 222 a 23, 910 a 35

Flower-honey, 831 b 19-21

Flowering reed, 627 a 8

Flowers, 818 a 15, b 9, 819 a 38, 825 a 19, 828 b 38, 909 a 1; a source of dye 794 a 18; colour of 794 b 13, 796 b 6-797 a 14; odour is less perceptible at short distance 907 a 22-35, b 35-908 a 4, 24-28; have unpleasant odour when rubbed 907 b 34

Fluid, easy to heat or chill but will not hold the affection long 648 b 33, 658 b 9; ambiguous 649 b 9-22

Flute, 900 a 31; enjoyed both by the happy and the unhappy 917 b 18-20; as accompaniment to song 918 a 22-28, 922 a 1-20; compared to voice 918 a 29-34; requires great skill 1341 a 17; arouses the passions 1341 a 21-b 8, 1342 b 2; invented by Athene 1341 b 4; flute-playing 1447 a 15, 25, 1448 a 9, 1461 b 31

Fly, 488 a 18, 628 b 34; sting of 490 a 20; proboscis of 528 b 29, 678 b 16; tongue of 532 a 14, 661 a 21; wings of 532 a 20; sound of 535 b 11; copulation of 539 b 12, 542 a 7, b 30; generation of 552 a 21-28; diet of 596 b 13; legs of 683 a 30; spontaneous generation of 721 a 10, 723 b 4

Flying-fish, sea-swallow, 535 b 28

Flying-fox, wings of 490 a 8

Foam, 823 b 13; nature of 736 a 14-20; as source of dye 794 a 20

Folly, 1249 b 29, 1250 a 17, b 44-1251 a 10; physiognomic signs of 811 a 26

Food, 416 b 11, 786 b 2; changed in process of digestion 416 a 33; must be composite 445 a 18; of plants 650 a 20; growth impossible without food 650 a 3, 655 a 32; enjoyment of 690 b 30; not to be taken after exercise 883 b 33-36; natural foods 928 a 33-b 22; easily sated by sweet food 930 a 14-39; supplied by nature to all 1256 a 19-b 26, 1258 a 35; of slaves 1344 a 36-b 4

Fop, physiognomic signs of a 813 a 22

Force, 699 a 33-39, 703 a 9, 1188 b 1-12, 27, 1255 a 13; a source of movement from outside a thing 301 b 19, 1188 b 14; no loss of 699 b 9; and necessity 1224 a 14, b 1, 13

Fore-arm, 493 b 27

Forehead, shape indicates temperament 491 b 11; as a physiognomic sign 807 b 3, 23, 808 a 3, 811 b 30-812 a 5, 814 b 4

Foreigner, friendship with a foreigner 1211 a 8, 12

Forewaters, 586 a 30

Form (εἶδος) (Aristotle), 192 a 14-24, 193 a 30, 201 a 4, 245 b 7, 310 b 16, 312 a 12, 336 a 1, 640 a 17, 645 a 32-37, 701 b 20; everything comes to be from both shape and matter 190 b 20; art requires knowledge of both form and matter 194 a 22-27; to each form there corresponds a special matter 194 b 9; subject matter of physics is things whose forms are separable but which do not exist apart from matter 194 b 12; first philosophy examines the truly separable form 194 b 15; as cause 198 b 3, 199 a 31, 379 b 25, 1044 b 1, 1070 b 31; contains the infinite and matter 207 a 36; place is neither matter nor form 209 a 2-210 a 13, 211 b 10-13; form and matter as

proof that there is only one heaven 277 b 26-278 b 9; as embodied in and as separate from matter 324 b 5-22; as actuality 412 a 10, 414 a 16; and thinking 431 b 2, 432 a 1; of greater importance than matter 640 b 29, 1029 a 5; image created by conception and imagination 703 b 19; as shape 999 b 16, 1015 a 5, 1017 b 25, 1033 b 6, 1044 b 22, 1052 a 22, 1060 a 21, b 26; as definition 1016 b 9, 1035 a 21, 1036 a 29, b 5, 1043 a 19, 1044 b 13, 1069 b 33, 1084 b 11; matter and form cannot be primary substance 1029 a 27-33; substance is form 1032 b 1, 1035 a 8, 1041 a 6-b 34, 1050 b 2, 1084 b 11; as essence 1032 b 1, 1033 b 7, 1035 b 32; only combination of form and matter come to be 1033 a 24-1034 a 8; as art 1034 a 24, 1070 a 16; ungenerated 1034 b 8, 1042 a 30, 1043 b 16, 1044 b 22, 1069 b 35, 1070 a 15; relation of parts and form 1036 a 26-1037 b 6; not subject to generation and change 1044 b 23; same as proximate matter 1045 b 18; neither matter nor form comes to be 1069 b 35-1070 a 3

Form (εἶδος) (Plato), 187 a 19, 278 a 17, 404 b 21, 987 b 5-22, 988 a 10-13, b 1-5, 1028 b 19-27, 1031 b 14, 1033 b 25-1034 a 8, 1036 b 14-31, 1045 a 16, 1050 b 35, 1059 a 10-14, 1069 a 35, 1071 b 15, 1075 b 18, 28, 1077 a 12; demonstration does not imply Forms 77 a 5; mathematical sciences concern Forms 79 a 8, 81 b 4; 'mere sound without sense' 83 a 30; motionless 113 a 27, 148 a 20; intelligible 113 a 28; recognize Form in individual through sense of sight 113 a 32; as tests of property 137 b 3-13; as tests of definition 143 b 23-33, 147 a 7-11, 148 a 13-22; one of most effective tests 154 a 19; an attempt to separate the objects of physics 193 b 35-194 a 6; not in space 203 a 8; infinite present in the Forms 203 a 9; thought by some to account for coming to be 335 b 9-24; and essence 988 a 34-b 16; criticism of doctrine of Forms 990 a 33-993 a 10, 1078 b 6-1079 b 11, 1217 b 19-25; as numbers 991 b 9-20, 1073 a 18, 1076 a 20, 1080 b 12, 23, 1081 a 1-1083 a 20, b 2, 1086 a 6, 1088 b 34, 1090 a 16, b 33, 1091 b 27; do Forms exist as well as sensible things and mathematical objects? 997 a 34-998 a 19, 1002 b 11-32; Forms are not substances 1039 a 24-b 19; indefinable 1040 a 8-b 4; doctrine of Forms assigns separate existence to universals 1040 a 9, 1078 b 31, 1086 a 18-1087 a 25; existence of 1040 b 28-1041 a 5; universal 1042 a 15, 1086 a 33; for all natural objects 1070 a 18; thought by some to be substances 1076 a 17-33; do not explain changes in sensible world 1079 b 12-1080 a 11; theory of Forms treat contraries as first principles 1087 a 28-1090 a 1; examination of the Form of good 1095 a 27, 1096 a 11-1097 a 14, 1182 b 9-16, 1183 a 24-b 8, 1217 b 1-1218 b 26

Form of expression, Fallacy of, one of six fallacious refutations dependent on language 165 b 26; examples of 166 b 10-19; solution of 178 a 4-179 a 10

Formula. *See* Definition

Fortuitous, defined 18 b 8; nothing is 18 b 10-17. Cf. Spontaneity

Fortune, 1183 b 33, 1213 a 28, 1215 a 13; its effect on the character of men 1390 b 13-1391 b 7. Cf. Good Fortune

Fossils, metals and fossils are the two kinds of bodies that originate in the earth 378 a 20

Fountain, healing fountain at Scotussae 841 b 9-14; of Arethusa at Syracuse 847 a 4; officers in charge of fountains 1321 b 26

Four Hundred, government of the Four Hundred at Athens 1304 b 12, 1305 b 26, 1419 a 28

Fox, 607 a 3; temper of 488 b 20; genitals of 500 b 24; reproduction of 580 a 6-10, 742 a 9; diet of 580 b 25; habits of 609 b 1, 31, 610 a 12; crossed with dog 746 a 33; development of young at birth 774 b 15; in Aesop's fable 1393 b 24-1394 a 1

Fox-shark, 565 b 1, 566 a 31, 621 a 12

Francolin, 617 b 25; dust bath of 633 b 2

Frankincense, 583 a 23, 818 a 5, 1407 a 10

Freedom. *See* Liberty

Freeman, some think the distinction between slave and freeman exists by law only 1253 b 21, 22; distinction between slave and freeman is natural 1254 a 19-1255 a 2; will not endure a tyranny if he can escape it 1295 a 23; the life of 1325 a 20; government of freemen nobler than despotic government 1333 b 27; may learn certain arts 1337 b 15-22

Frenum, 493 a 30

Friendship (φιλία), 126 a 12, 203 b 13, 1105 b 22, 1126 b 20, 1155 a 3-1172 a 15, 1202 a 30, 1208 b 2-1213 b 30, 1234 a 18-1246 a 25, 1362 b 19, 1371 a 17, 1380 b 34-1382 a 18, 1439 b 15, 20, 1440 a 26, 40, 1447 b 5; love more dependent on friendship than on sexual intercourse 68 b 3; contrary of hatred 113 b 1; more desirable than wealth because it is prized for its own worth 116 b 37; things that can be shared with friends more desirable than those that cannot be shared 118 a 1; excess of friendship more desirable than excess of money 118 b 7; a creditor is not a friend 950 a 32; a good friend 1126 b 21; necessary and noble 1155 a 3-32; and justice 1155 a 22-28, 1159 b 25-1162 a 33, 1211 a 6-15, 1234 b 26-1235 a 3, 1241 b 11-1242 b 1; better between the like or the opposite? 1155 a 33-b 7, 1208 b 7-20, 1210 a 6-23, 1235 a 4-29, 1446 b 7-16; can there be friendship between the bad? 1155 b 9-16, 1208 b 26-35, 1235 a 29-35, 1236 b 10-21; three kinds of: (1) friendships of utility, (2) of pleasure, (3) of goodness 1155 b 17-1158 b 11, 1209 a 4-b 37, 1236 a 32-1237 b 7, 1238 b 15, 1239 a 1, 1242 b 2; and goodwill 1155 b 33-1156 a 5, 1166 b 30-1167 a 20, 1211 b 40-1212 a 13, 1241 a 1-14; essence of friendship is living together 1157 b 19, 1158 a 9, 1171 a 2, b 29-1172 a 15, 1211 a 4, 1280 b 38; a state of character 1157 b 29-37; limit to the number of friends 1158 a 10, 1170 b 20-1171 a 20, 1213 b 3-17, 1237 b 35, 1245 b 20-25; unequal friendships 1158 b 1-1159 a 12, b 10-24, 1238 b 15-1240 a 7; political friendship 1161 a 10-b 11, 1163 b 34, 1167 b 2, 1171 a 17; between relations 1161 b 11-1162 a 33, 1241 b 40-1242 a 11, 27-b 1; between equals 1162 a 34-1163 a 23, 1242 b 23-31; between unequals 1163 a 24-b 27, 1242 b 2-21; in which the motives on the two sides are different 1163 b 33-1164 a 22, 1243 b 15-38; when to be broken 1165 a 37-b 36; definitions of a friend 1166 a 1-9, 1236 a 15; self-love is the basis of 1166 a 1-b 29, 1210 b 32-1211 a 5, 1240 a 8-b 39; sense in which a man may have friendship towards himself 1166 a 33, 1210 b 33, 1211 a 16-b 3; and unanimity 1167 a 22-b 15, 1212 a 14-26, 1241 a 15-35; between father and son 1167 b 17-1168 a 27, 1211 b 18-39, 1213 b 22, 1241 a 36-b 10; why happy man needs friendship 1169 b 3-1170 b 19, 1244 b 1-1245 b 19; desirable both in good and bad fortune 1171 a 21-b 27, 1245 b 26-1246 a 25; a partnership 1171 b 32; perfect friendship 1210 b 23-32; equality in 1211 b 4-17, 1287 b 33; a friend is a second self 1213 a 24, 1245 a 30; a sort of a moral habit 1234 b 28; a stable thing 1237 b 18-1238 a 29; misfortune is best test of 1238 a 15-20; weakened by communism 1262 b 1-23; the greatest good of states 1262 b 7; friends have all things in common 1263 a 30; a constituent of happiness 1361 b 35-38.

Friendlessness, 1115 a 11, 1386 a 10

Friendliness, 1108 a 27, 1126 b 12-1127 a 12, 1193 a 20-27, 1221 a 7, 1233 b 29-34

Frog, 530 b 34, 589 a 28, 626 a 9, 810 b 16; habitat of 487 a 27; spleen of 506 a 20; womb of 510 b 35; tongue of 536 a 9; croak of 536 a 12, 606 a 5, 800 a 25; female larger than male 538

a 27; copulation of 540 a 32; spawn of 568 a 23; in Cyrene 835 a 33; in Seriphos 835 b 4; abundance of frogs is sign of an unhealthy year 862 a 10-16. Cf. Fishing-frog

From (ἐκ τινος), meanings of 724 a 20-35, 991 a 20, 994 a 19-b 6, 1023 a 26-b 11, 1044 a 24, 1092 a 23

Frost, 348 b 4, 361 b 25, 366 b 5, 371 a 6; prevents growth 466 b 28, 470 a 28

Fruit, 380 a 11, 15, 28, 390 b 1, 822 a 2-8; predominantly composed of earth 389 a 16; formation of 728 a 28; production of 765 b 30, 827 a 7-b 6; monstrosities in 770 a 15; as source of dye 794 a 19; colours of 795 a 25-797 a 14; differences in 820 a 29-b 25; flavour of 829 a 36-830 b 4; some are bitter near the root 925 b 30-38; problems connected with 930 a 5-931 a 33; preserving of 930 b 1-4, 939 b 12-14; dried fruits 930 b 12-14; wine to be taken while eating fruit 930 b 20-32; chaff concocts hard fruits 931 a 23-27

Fulcrum, 850 a 35, 38, b 2, 6, 11, 14, 16, 33, 39, 851 b 1, 4, 853 a 10, 13, 15, 18, 22, 29, 854 a 10, 13, 28, b 1, 8, 10, 857 b 13, 18

Fulfilment. See Actuality, Reality

Full, 985 b 5, 1009 a 29

Fumes, 387 a 23-b 13, 385 a 18, 388 a 5, 389 a 17

Function, work, product (ἔργον), 645 b 35, 1094 a 5, 1152 b 19, 1153 a 23, 1168 a 9; organ made to fulfill function 687 a 11; determines dimensions 705 a 27-b 8; of man 1097 b 25-32, 1098 a 7; meanings of 1098 a 7-17, 1219 a 13-27; of men and women 1162 a 22; final cause of a state 1219 a 1-18; of soul 1219 a 24. Cf. Final Cause

Funeral Speech, 1411 a 32; of Socrates 1415 b 30

Fungi, 819 a 31, 825 b 17

Future (τὸ μέλλον), 463 b 29; impossible to remember the future 449 b 10

G

Gades, 844 a 25

Gadfly, oestrus, generation of 487 b 5, 551 b 22; tongue of 490 a 20, 528 b 31, 532 a 10, 661 a 24; diet of 596 b 13

Gain, 1132 b 18, 1163 b 3, 1221 a 4, 23; incontinence in respect of 1145 b 20, 1148 b 14

Gait, as a physiognomic sign 807 b 35, 808 a 6, 11, 15, 21, 813 a 3-9

Gaius, 836 a 4

Galeodes. See Shark

Gall-bladder, 496 b 23, 506 a 21-b 23; nature and functions of 676 b 16-677 b 10. Cf. Bile, Liver

Gallic Gulf, 393 b 10

Gallic Sea, 393 a 27

Gall-stones, man only animal that suffers from 895 a 36-b 11

Gamblers, physiognomic sign of 808 a 32

Ganymede, 1461 a 29

Gargaria, 840 a 27

Garland-makers, 1206 a 27

Garlic, 925 b 10, 926 a 2; promotes the flow of urine 865 a 22, 907 b 7, 908 a 28-b 10, 924 b 22, 949 a 5; effect on voice 903 b 27-29; cultivation of 926 a 11-15; sprout when stored 926 a 16-20; smell of 926 a 26-32

Gastrocnemia, 499 b 5

Gaul, 606 b 5

Gazelle, horns of 499 a 9, 663 a 13, b 26

Gecko, spotted lizard, female larger than male 538 a 27; hibernation of 599 a 31; sloughing of 600 b 23; bite of 607 a 26; habits of 609 a 28, 614 b 4; legs of 713 a 17

Gela, 1316 a 37

Gelo, tyrant of Syracuse, 1302 b 33, 1312 b 9-16, 1315 b 34, 1316 a 34

Gelon, 1373 a 23

Geloni, 832 b 8

Genealogy, use of genealogy in eulogistic oratory 1440 b 29-1441 a 12

Generation (γένεσις), 416 b 15, 479 a 29, 489 b 18, 1068 a 25; as movement 15 a 13-17; man begotten by man 193 b 12, 198 a 26, 202 a 11; man begotten

either by man or by the sun 194 b 14; depends on interaction of contraries 270 a 15; meanings of 'generated' and 'ungenerated' 280 b 1-20; Melissus and Parmenides deny generation 298 b 17; examination of bodies subject to generation 302 a 10-307 b 24; sun causes generation when approaching the earth 336 b 7; a natural act 415 a 27; a means of partaking of the eternal and the divine 415 b 1-7; organs of 509 a 28-511 a 34; from egg 561 a 4-562 a 21; anterior in actual development to logical essence 646 a 26, 36; defined 646 a 31, 1067 b 22; a subordinate kind of motion 700 a 27-b 3; of animals 715 a 1-789 b 21, 897 b 30-33, 898 b 3-11; male contributes formal and efficient cause, female the material cause 716 a 7, 724 a 10, 727 b 31, 729 a 11, 34-730 b 32, 738 b 20-27, 740 b 25; of man 737 b 26-739 b 33; male is necessary 741 a 6-b 24; male imparts the sensitive soul 741 b 5; of fish 754 a 22-756 b 13, 757 a 14-34; of bee 759 a 8-761 a 11; of testacea 761 a 12-763 b 16; nothing comes into being by putrefaction 762 a 15; nothing comes into being out of the whole of anything 762 a 17; why children are like their progenitors 767 a 36-769 b 10; number produced at birth 771 a 18-772 b 12; generative principle derived from sun 817 a 26; effect on temper 894 b 12-18; generation and decay balance one another 975 b 34; two types 994 a 22-b 6; only things subject to generation and change have matter 1044 b 21-28; neither matter nor form comes to be 1069 b 35-1070 a 3; four kinds: (1) art, (2) nature, (3) luck, (4) spontaneity 1032 a 13, 1033 a 24-1034 a 7, 1070 a 6, 1140 a 15. Cf. Becoming, Copulation, Spontaneous generation

Generosity. See Liberality

Genitals, movements of are involuntary 703 b 7; in a sense a separate vital organ 703 b 22 (Cf. 666 b 17); contracted by fear 948 b 10, 949 a 8-20. Cf. Penis, Testicles, Uterus

Glaucus, 1136 b 9, 1236 a 36

Glaucus, grey-back, caeca of 508 b 20; habitat of 598 a 13; hibernation of 599 b 32; when edible 607 b 27

Glistening star, 392 a 26

Glottis, migration of 597 b 16

Glow-worm, 523 b 20, 551 b 24, 642 b 37

Glue, 517 b 30

Gluttony, 1221 b 2, 17, 1231 a 19; physiognomic signs of 808 b 3, 810 b 18

Gnat, conops, sting of 490 a 20, 532 a 14; sense of taste in 535 a 3; generation of 551 b 27-552 a 8, b 4, 721 a 10. Cf. Empis

Gnomon, 203 a 14, 912 a 4, b 8

Goat, 499 b 10, 557 a 16, 812 b 7; wild goat 488 a 31, 612 a 2; ears of 492 a 14; milk of 522 a 27, 30, 891 b 4; diet of 522 b 34, 596 a 13-b 9; dreaming of 536 b 30; reproduction of 545 a 23, 546 a 1, 572 b 32, 573 b 17-574 a 15; temper of 571 b 22; urine of 573 a 18; habits of 610 b 25-611 a 6, 830 b 20-23, 831 a 20-22; rumination in 632 b 2; spleen of 673 b 33; stomach of 674 b 7; usually have gall-bladder 676 b 36; mammae of 688 b 25; monstrosities in 770 b 35-37, 898 a 12; colour of eye 779 a 33; of Pedasa 844 a 35-b 8; change of colour in 891 b 13-20

Goatberry, 819 b 21

'Goats,' cause of 341 b 1-342 a 35

Goat-sucker, habits of 618 b 2

Goby, gudgeon, 601 b 21; caeca of 508 b 16; spawn of 567 b 12, 569 b 23; diet of 591 b 13; habitat of 598 a 11; habits of 610 b 4, 621 b 12. Cf. Phycis

God (θεός), 336 b 32, 407 b 10, 955 b 23, 1001 b 30, 1096 a 24, 1166 a 22, 1182 b 3, 1212 b 34, 1217 a 24, 1222 b 22, 1238 b 27, 1239 a 18, 1243 b 12, 1247 a 24, 1248 a 38, 1252 b 24, 1264 b 12, 1287 a 28, 1336 b 16; cannot be injured or wronged 109 b 33; better than man 116 b 13-15; an immortal living being 122 b 13, 128 b 20, 136 b 7; has capacity to do bad things 126 a 35; living being that partakes of knowledge 132 b 12; use of number three in worship of 268 a 15; all men have some conception of 270 b 6; connected with the heavens 270 b 7, 284 a 12; as creative 271 a 33; God's activity is immortality 286 a 9; preserver of universe 391 b 12; position in universe 396 a 33-397 b 8; attributes of 397 b 9-401 b 29; of Empedocles 410 b 4; not the sender of dreams 462 b 22, 463 b 12-23, 464 a 21; Xenophanes' view of 977 a 13-979 a 9, 986 b 24; a first principle 983 a 8; enjoys a continuous single and simple pleasure 1154 b 26; no friendship between God and man 1159 a 4 (Cf. 1242 a 33), 1208 b 30; activity of God is contemplation 1178 b 22, 1213 a 1-8; superior to virtue 1200 b 13; not the giver of material goods 1207 a 7-17; needs no friends 1244 b 7-15, 1245 b 14-19; self-sufficient 1245 b 19, 1249 b 16, 1253 a 29; cause of all movement 1248 a 26; greater than knowledge and intellect 1248 a 29; divine form of good luck 1248 b 3; happy by reason of his own nature 1323 b 24, 1325 b 28; holds together the universe 1326 a 32. Cf. Divine, Prime Mover

Gods, the, 105 a 6, 115 b 32, 1101 b 19, 1122 b 20, 1123 a 19, b 19, 1134 b 28, 1137 a 28, 1145 a 23, 26, 1159 a 7, 1160 a 24, 1162 a 5, 1164 b 6, 1179 a 25-32, 1207 a 6, 1250 b 20, 1251 a 31, 1336 b 16, 1454 b 5, 1460 b 37, 1461 a 30; in human form 997 b 10, 1074 b 6; stars thought to be gods 1074 b 1-14; happiness is the gift of the gods 1099 b 11-17; surpass men in all good things 1158 b 36; the happiness of 1178 b 8-32; good of 1182 b 3; drink nectar 1205 b 15; some say the gods have a king 1252 b 24, 1259 b 13; statues of the gods 1254 b 35; tyrant to give appearance of honouring the gods 1314 b 40; to be worshipped only by the citizens 1329 a 29; fear of 1185 b 24; that preside over birth 1335 b 17

Gold, 164 b 23, 378 a 28, 380 b 29, 384 b 32, 388 a 14, 389 a 7, 793 a 19, 837 b 3; small particles of gold can float on water 348 a 10; inodorous 443 a 17; why it sinks in water 823 a 25;

mines in Macedonia 833 a 29-31; in
Paeonia 833 b 6-14; of the Oxus 833 b
15; of the Theodorus 833 b 17; of
Pieria 833 b 19-22; gold solder 834 b
21

Goldfinch, 592 b 29

Good (ἀγαθός), 433 a 29, 701 a 24, 1078
a 32, 1091 a 30, 1109 a 29, 1158 a 25,
1173 a 4; absolute and relative 49 b
10-14, 115 b 15-35, 116 b 8, 142 b 12,
700 b 35, 1129 b 4, 1152 b 26-28, 1155
b 21, 1156 b 14, 1182 b 2, 1228 b 18,
1235 b 30-35, 1237 a 13, 27, 1332 a 7-
27, 1363 b 5-1365 b 21; an ambiguous
term 106 a 5, 107 a 6, 1096 a 23, b 13,
1152 b 27, 1182 b 6-9, 1217 b 25, 1218
b 3, 1228 b 18; that which is cause of
good more desirable than what is
good *per accidens* 116 b 1; that which
is good by nature more desirable than
good that is not so by nature 116 b 11;
that which is nearer the good is more
desirable 117 b 10; the more conspic-
uous and more difficult good is more
desirable 117 b 28; has no genus 123
b 8-12 (Cf. 121 a 1); cannot be defined as contrary of evil 147 b 18-25;
final cause of nature is a good 455 b
18, 983 a 31, 996 a 28, 1013 a 22, 1059
a 36; actual and apparent 700 b 29,
1013 b 27, 1113 a 16, 1114 a 32; how
present in universe as order of parts
and ruler 1075 a 12-24; relation between first principles and the good
1091 a 29-1092 a 21; defined as that
at which all things aim 1094 a 2, 1095
a 14, 1182 a 33; Form of the good
1095 a 27, 1096 a 11-1097 a 14, 1182
b 9-16, 1183 a 24-b 8, 1217 b 1-1218 b
26; has as many senses as being 1096
a 23, 1217 b 25; two senses of 1096 b
13, 1152 b 27, 1182 b 6-9, 1238 a 4;
chief good is something final 1097 a
27; final good is self-sufficient 1097 b
8; external and in the soul 1098 b 12-
15, 1184 b 1-6, 1218 b 32-36, 1360 b
27; better when it is harder 1105 a 9;
divided into activity and state 1152 b
34-1153 a 7; as an object of love 1155
b 18; desired by all men 1166 a 20;
good as the end 1182 a 34-b 5; of the

gods 1182 b 3; no one science deals
with good in general 1183 a 8-23;
goodness always difficult 1187 b 37;
all things aim at the good 1205 b 36;
as the pleasant and useful 1209 a 7,
20, 29; predicated of all the categories
1217 b 25-33; has many meanings
1236 a 7; all men's actions directed
toward some good 1252 a 2; man is
only animal that has sense of good
and evil 1253 a 15; definitions of 1362
a 15-1363 b 4, 13-15

Good birth. *See* Noble

Good counsel, 1142 a 32-b 33, 1199 a 4-
13

Good fortune, good luck, prosperity,
1124 a 14, b 19, 1155 a 8, 1206 b 30-
1207 b 18, 1246 b 37-1248 b 7, 1250 a
15, 28, b 35, 1251 b 17, 1361 b 39-
1362 a 11, 1389 a 1, 1441 a 13; and
happiness 1098 b 26, 1099 b 8, 1153 b
22, 1214 a 26, 1323 b 26; the goods of
1129 b 2; need friends in prosperity
1169 b 15, 1171 a 21-b 28; not every
one can bear prosperity 1308 b 14; defined 1361 b 39; effect on character
1391 a 30-b 3. Cf. Chance

Good Genius, 1233 b 3

Good judgement, 1250 a 36, 39

Good moral character, physiognomic
signs of 807 b 34-808 a 2

Goods, divided into: (1) the honourable,
(2) the praiseworthy, (3) potencies
1183 b 20-36; choiceworthy goods
1183 b 38-1184 a 2; as ends or means
1184 b 3-14; some within the range of
human action, some not 1217 a 30-40;
limit of external goods is amount conducive to contemplation of God 1249
a 21-b 23; virtue preferred to external
goods 1271 b 9, 1323 a 35-b 21, 1334
b 5; three classes of (1) external
goods, (2) goods of body, (3) goods
of soul 1323 a 25; external goods not
cause of happiness 1323 b 24, 1332 a
26

Good spirits, cheerfulness, physiognomic signs of 808 a 3-7

Good temper, gentleness, calmness, 125
b 21-27, 1103 a 8, b 19, 1108 a 6, 1109
b 17, 1125 b 26-1126 b 10, 1129 b 22,

1186 a 23, 1191 b 23-38, 1220 b 38, 1222 a 42, 1231 b 5-26, 1249 b 27, 1250 a 4, 40-43, 1339 b 18, 1366 b 1, 1380 a 5-b 33; physiognomic signs of 811 b 29, 813 b 4; productive of friendship 1158 a 3

Goodwill, 1158 a 7, 1378 a 19; and friendship 1155 b 33-1156 a 5, 1166 b 30-1167 a 20, 1211 b 40-1212 a 13, 1241 a 1-14; defined as inactive friendship 1167 a 11; sometimes identified with justice 1255 a 17; how to secure the goodwill of one's hearers 1436 b 17-29, 1441 b 37-1442 a 21, 1443 b 17, 1444 b 35-1445 a 10, 1446 a 29-33

Goose, 560 b 10, 593 b 22, 597 b 31; temper of 488 b 23; foot of 499 a 28; oesophagus of 509 a 3; caeca of 509 a 22; penis of 509 b 32; wind eggs in 559 b 27; brooding of 563 a 28, 564 a 9

Goose-skin, due to change of temperature in heart 701 b 31

Gorgias, 183 b 37, 1406 a 1, b 9, 15, 1408 b 20, 1416 a 1, 1418 a 33; views of 979 a 11-32; criticism of 979 a 33-980 b 21; his definition of virtue 1260 a 27; his definition of a citizen 1275 b 27; first to give oratory a poetical colour 1404 a 25; the *Olympic Speech* of 1414 b 31; his view of jests 1419 b 3

Gorgias of Plato, 173 a 9

Gorgus, father of Psammetichus, 1315 b 26

Gossiping, 1117 b 35, 1125 a 5

Gourds, grow large if buried 923 b 16-29; storing of 924 a 36-b 14

Government, 1252 a 14; true and perverted forms of 1275 a 39, 1279 a 18-b 10, 1288 a 34-b 3, 1289 a 26-b 11; people suited to each form 1287 b 36-1288 a 33; the study of 1288 b 10-1289 a 25; governments sometimes divided into two forms: democracy and oligarchy 1289 b 27-1290 a 29, 1291 b 12, 1301 b 40. Cf. Constitution

Graces, temple of the 1133 a 2

Grafting of trees, 820 b 29-41, 924 b 35-925 a 7

Grain, compared with seed 724 b 18-21

Grammar, 1003 b 20, 1205 a 19-22, 1226 a 37, 1246 b 28; a single science 104 a 18; a kind of knowledge 111 a 38, 124 b 19, 126 a 5; defined 142 b 31-35

Granny-crab, maia, 525 b 5, 527 b 12; legs of 684 a 10

Grape, 820 a 30, 909 a 21; colour of 792 b 3, 795 b 25, 796 b 28; dried grapes sweeter than fresh 925 b 15; stones of 925 b 24

Grape-beetle, 604 b 18

Grass, 594 a 29, 923 a 31; of Chalcis 832 a 2

Grasshopper, acris, 550 b 34; gut of 532 b 10; sound of 535 b 13, 804 a 22; generation of 555 b 18-556 a 7; sloughing of 601 a 6; announces the solstices 835 a 23-26

Great and small, 187 a 18, 189 a 7, 192 a 7, 12, 203 a 15, 206 b 27, 209 b 36, 987 b 21, 26, 988 a 26, 992 a 12, 998 b 10, 1083 b 23, 1085 a 10, 1087 b 14; how opposed to equal 1055 b 30-1056 b 2. Cf. Dyad

Greatness of soul. *See* Magnanimity

Grebe, 593 b 16; wings of 487 a 23

Greece, Greeks, 152 a 14, 182 a 34, 270 b 8, 351 a 7, 352 a 9, 584 b 11, 606 a 22, 819 a 21, 832 a 12, 836 a 11, b 7, 837 a 10, 839 b 25, 840 b 6, 27, 842 a 28, 845 b 16, 956 b 24, 1348 a 33, 1384 b 33, 1397 b 26, 1401 b 17, 1411 a 5, 32, b 30, 1414 b 32, 1420 b 15, 1448 a 32, 1454 b 2, 1460 a 15; counting of the Greeks 910 b 24-911 a 3; Greeks superior to barbarians 1252 b 7, 1255 a 29, 1285 a 20; formerly under royal rule 1252 b 20, 1297 b 17; ancient Hellenes carried arms 1268 b 40; effect of climate on the Greeks 1327 b 20-30; best governed of any nation 1327 b 31, 1333 b 6; politicians of Greece used reason first, then deeds 1420 b 28

Greed. *See* Avarice

Greek language, 919 a 24, 1407 a 20-30, 1413 b 7

Green, beneficial to vision 959 a 23-37

Greenfinch, green linnet, diet of 592 b 16; habits of 615 b 33

Greenpie, green woodpecker, celeus, 593 a 8; claws of 504 a 18; habits of 609 a 19, 610 a 9

Grey-back. *See* Glaucus

Grin, as a physiognomic sign 808 a 17

Gristle, 487 a 6, 511 b 7, 516 b 31-517 a 5

Groin, 493 b 8, 808 a 23

Ground-wasp. *See* Tenthredo

Growth (αὔξεσθαι), 315 b 2, 319 b 32, 325 b 4, 327 a 22-25; a species of motion 111 b 5, 406 a 13; nourishment does not always produce growth 111 b 25; a change of magnitude 314 b 15, 320 a 8-322 a 34; three characteristics of: (1) the growing thing persists, (2) grows by accession of something, (3) every perceptible particle of it becomes larger 321 a 19, b 12; distinguished from nutrition 322 a 20-28; Empedocles makes growth impossible 333 a 35; heat is direct cause of 441 b 30, 442 a 4, 669 b 4; affects memory 450 b 7; impossible without food 655 b 32; a subordinate kind of motion 700 a 27-b 3; of bones 744 b 30-745 a 9; of hair 745 a 11-17; of teeth 745 a 18-b 9; takes place in upper part of body 779 a 5; dimensions of 916 a 13-17. Cf. Increase

Grub-picker. *See* Tree-creeper

Grubs, 489 b 9, 539 b 12, 550 b 27, 831 b 7; of the king bee 760 a 26

Grumbling, 1251 b 25

Guardians, Plato's guardians 1260 b 27-1264 b 25; of the laws 1287 a 21, 1298 b 28, 1322 b 39, 1323 a 8; of children 1299 b 19, 1300 a 4, 1322 b 39; of women 1299 b 19, 1300 a 4, 1322 b 38; of the citizens 1305 b 29; of shrines 1322 b 25

Gudgeon. *See* Goby

Guinea-fowl, eggs of 559 a 25

Gull, larus, 593 b 14; oesophagus of 509 a 3; eggs of 542 b 17; habits of 609 a 23

Gum 388 b 20, 829 a 15-24; gum-arabic 818 a 5

Gums, 493 a 1; salt and purslane stop inflammation of 863 b 11-18, 887 b 1-9

Gurnard, lyra, 'voice' of 535 b 17

Gust, 395 a 6

Gyaros, mice of 832 a 23

Gyges, 1418 b 31

Gymnastic exercise, 1096 a 34, 1106 b 5, 1112 b 6, 1143 b 27, 1180 b 3, 1288 b 17, 1323 a 1, 1331 a 36, 1441 a 35; discouraged among poor in oligarchies 1297 a 30; Directors of Gymnastics 1323 a 1; a customary branch of education 1337 b 24; promotes courage 1337 b 27; promotes health and strength 1338 a 20, 1426 a 9; carried to excess in Sparta 1338 b 9-38; ought to be light for children 1338 b 39-1339 a 10

Gymnesiae Islands, 837 a 30-b 7

H

Habit (ἕξις), 928 b 23-929 a 5, 955 b 1-3, 1148 b 18-34, 1180 a 7, 1204 a 1, 1220 b 18-20, 1222 a 18, 27, b 5-14, 1228 a 37, 1232 a 34, 1234 a 14, b 28, 1370 a 5, 1428 b 9; contrasted with dispositions 8 b 27-9 a 12; a sort of quality 8 b 27; difficult to displace 9 a 5, 1152 a 30; habits are relative 11 a 22; force of 995 a 5; meanings of 1022 b 4-14; moral virtue produced by habit 1103 a 14-b 26, 1105 a 18, 1179 b 21, 1220 a 38-b 6, 1227 b 7; strength of law is in habit 1269 a 20; an element in virtue 1332 a 39-b 11, 1334 b 8; a cause of action 1369 a 6, b 7, 16. Cf. Custom

Haemon, 1417 b 20, 1418 b 32, 1454 a 1

Haemorrhage, 738 a 16; widest passages of body most subject to 668 b 17

Haemorrhoids, aporrhaids, 521 a 18, 30, 530 a 19, 587 b 33

Hail, 369 b 32, 388 b 10; cause of 347 b 34-349 a 10, 394 a 16, b 2

Hair, 387 b 1, 389 a 12, 664 b 23; homogeneous 90 b 5, 388 a 16; tractile 386 b 14; of hedgehogs and porcupines 490 b 28; all viviparous quadrupeds are hair coated 498 b 17; nature of 517 b 2-519 a 29; turns grey or white as animal grows old 518 a 7-17; grows after death 518 b 22, 745 a 18; distribution of hair in animals 658 a 16-b 11; man has more hair on front than back 658 a 17, 896 b 29-39; serves as a protection 658 a 19; why man has more hair on head than any other animal 658 b 2-7, 898 a 20-30; formation of 745 a 1; growth of 745 a 11-18; hairiness is a sign of abundance of residual matter 774 b 1; colours of 778 a 20, 794 a 23, 797 a 34-799 b 20; only hair of men and horses turns grey with age 780 b 5, 782 a 11; differences of hair in animals 781 b 30-785 b 16; final cause of 782 a 20-b 12; cause of length of 782 b 13-18; cause of straightness or curliness 782 b 19-34, 909 a 30, 963 b 10; cause of fineness and coarseness of 783 a 2-b 8, 893 a 36-b 9; cause of baldness in men 783 b 9-784 a 22; greying of 784 a 23-785 b 16, 891 b 1; effects of drinking water on 786 a 5; why reddish in young children 797 b 24; as a physiognomic sign 806 b 6-21, 807 a 31, b 5, 17, 808 a 19, 23, 27, b 6, 8, 812 b 14-813 a 2; why man grows hair on face and body when capable of sexual intercourse 876 b 32-877 a 4; baldness a sign of lustfulness 878 b 21-32; thick hair a sign of lustfulness 880 a 35-b 7, 893 b 10-16; why hair bristles 886 b 25-30, 888 a 38-40, b 16-20, 889 a 26-b 2, 965 a 9; does not grow on human scars 890 b 38, 893 b 28-894 a 6, 13-16, leprosy turns hair grey 891 b 1, 896 b 6-8; grows hard if plucked out 893 a 17-35; longer the hair grows in man the softer it becomes 893 a 36-b 9; man only animal in which hair turns white 898 a 31-37; all who work in sea have reddish hair 966 b 25-28; free men have long hair at Sparta 1367 a 29

Hake, hibernation of 599 b 33; habits of 620 b 30

Halcyon, kingfisher, 542 b 21-25, 593 b 9, 615 b 29; pairing of 542 b 4-16; habits of 616 a 14-33

Halcyon days, 542 b 6

Halcyone, 1274 a 34

Haloes, appear to follow sun and moon 344 b 4, 377 b 34; cause and nature of 346 a 5, 371 b 19-25, 372 a 17-21, 395 b 1, 912 b 34; significance of 372 b 17-33; why they are circular 373 a 1-32; compared to rainbows 373 b 34-374 b 7.

Halys, 1407 a 39

Hand, 493 b 27, 690 a 33, 702 b 4, 712 a 21, 734 b 30, 972 b 30; a tool of tools 432 a 1; hand is not a hand unless attached to a living body 640 b 35, 726 b 22, 1036 b 30; nature and functions of 687 a 5-b 21; Anaxagoras thinks that possession of hands is cause of man being most intelligent of all animals 687 a 7; not one organ but many 687 a 20; as a physiognomic sign 807 b 9, 808 a 14, 813 a 10

Hanno, 833 a 11; conspiracy of 1307 a 4

Happiness (εὐδαιμονία), 1095 a 14-1102 a 4, 1214 a 1-1215 b 14, 1250 a 4, 1362 b 11; usually thought to be the good for man 1095 a 19, 1217 a 22; as pleasure, honour, wealth, or contemplation 1095 b 13-1096 a 10, 1098 b 24-26; chosen only for its own sake 1097 b 1; defined as activity of soul in accordance with virtue 1098 a 17, b 30, 1099 b 26, 1102 a 5, 1177 a 11, 1184 b 23-1185 a 13, 1204 a 28, 1219 a 35-b 25; composed of wisdom, virtue, and pleasure 1098 b 24-29, 1214 a 31-b 5, 1215 a 33; an activity 1098 b 30-1099 a 5, 1169 b 28, 1176 b 2, 1177 a 10, 1208 a 37, 1325 a 32, 1450 a 17; most pleasant thing in the world 1099 a 24, 1214 a 1-9; needs external goods 1099 a 31-b 8; how acquired 1099 b 9-11, 1214 a 10-26; not a matter of chance 1099 b 9-1100 a 9; must we wait until a man dies before we call him happy? 1100 a 10-1101 b 9; is above praise 1101 b 21-26, 1219 b 11-16; constituent parts of 1129 b 18, 1360 b 19-1362 a 14; most people think happiness involves pleasure 1152 b 6, 1153 b 15; a perfect thing 1153 b 17; found in virtuous activity, not in amusement 1176 a 30-1177 a 10, 1325 a 16-34; the end of human

animals is hollow 494 b 34, 656 b 13; of man has no flesh 656 a 14, b 8-13; some think man would live longer if he had more flesh on his head 656 a 16; organs of sight, hearing, and smell located in head 656 a 32-b 7; some think blood vessels originate in head 665 b 28; all animals that have blood have a head 685 b 34; functions of 686 a 1-18; as a physiognomic sign 808 a 14, 812 a 6-8, 814 b 4; head of female smaller than head of male 809 b 5; effect of running on 881 b 8-17; movement of 892 b 19-21; most divine part 962 a 23, 35

Health (ὑγίεια), 444 a 14, 480 b 23, 1362 b 14; desired as an end 111 a 1, 116 a 29; more desirable than beauty 116 b 18, 118 b 21; no intermediary between health and disease 123 a 17; poorly defined as balance of hot and cold elements 139 b 21, 145 b 8; consists in balance of hot and cold elements 246 b 5; achieved in various ways 292 a 22-27, b 11; presupposes life 436 a 17; reduction of diet and increase of exercise promotes 865 a 1, 884 a 22-25; why not contagious 886 b 3-8, 951 a 3; effect of climate on 910 a 1-4; must be considered in choosing site for a city 1330 a 38-b 17; a constituent of happiness 1360 b 22, 1361 b 3-26

Hearing (ἀκοή, ἄκουσις), 106 a 30, 425 b 30, 426 a 29, 445 a 10, 532 b 33, 744 a 2, 801 a 21-40, b 15-22, 803 b 40-804 a 8, 1231 a 22; medium is air 419 a 32; nature and objects of 419 b 3-421 a 5, 422 a 23, 980 a 13, b 24; contributes most to growth of intelligence 437 a 11; in fish 533 b 4-534 a 11; reasons for position of the organs of hearing 656 b 14-20, 28; position of organ of hearing in quadrupeds 657 a 14-18; accuracy and keenness of 781 a 15-b 29; sense most likely to be defective from birth 898 b 27-899 a 3; one hears less when yawning 902 a 9-15, 904 a 16-22, 961 a 36-b 6; hear better when holding breath 903 b 34-904 a 3, b 11-14; painful 1154 b 7; has more connection with morality than

any other sense 1340 a 29-b 19. Cf. Ear

Heart (καρδία), 474 b 1-9, 496 a 4-34, 506 b 32-507 a 9, 520 b 15; hottest bodily part 439 a 3, 743 b 27, 744 a 29; origin of veins 456 b 1; source of blood 458 a 15, 461 b 12, 521 a 9, 666 a 8, 667 b 17; first organ to be developed 468 b 28, 666 a 10, 21, 735 a 24, 740 a 18, b 3, 741 b 16, 742 b 37, 743 b 27; organ of common sense 469 a 10-33, 702 b 22; its activities 479 b 17-480 a 15; breath distributed from the heart 482 b 6; pulse originates from the heart 482 b 33; sinews of 484 a 17, 485 a 8, 666 b 14; found in all blooded animals 506 a 5, 665 b 10; cavities of 513 a 27-38, 666 b 22-667 a 7; the origin of sinews 515 a 28; center of sensation, movement, and nutrition 647 a 25-b 9, 656 a 30, 678 b 3, 703 b 24, 743 b 26; homogeneous and heterogeneous 647 a 33; center of blood vessels 654 b 11, 665 b 14, 666 a 6, 667 b 20; taste and touch are in immediate connection with 656 a 30; nature and function of 665 a 26-667 b 14; occupies most honorable position of body 665 b 19-24; central source of heat 665 b 32, 670 a 24, 701 b 31, 766 b 1, 897 a 3; origin of sensation 666 a 12-37, 672 b 17, 703 b 24, 741 b 18, 743 b 26; position of 666 b 2-13; originates movement 666 b 15; size of 667 a 7-32; unable to suffer serious affection 667 a 33-b 13, 677 b 3; its 'jumping' 669 a 18; necessary to every animal 670 a 23, 678 b 3; small change in heart has great effect 701 b 25; soul resides in heart 703 a 2, b 38; why it is the material cause of movement 703 a 6-b 2; movements of the heart are involuntary (i.e., palpitation) 703 b 7 (Cf. 479 b 19, 480 a 14); in a sense a separate vital organ 703 b 22 (Cf. 666 b 17); first principle of a natural body 738 b 16; origin of blood vessels 740 a 23, 743 a 1, b 27, 787 b 27; life fails in heart last of all 741 b 19; animals with two hearts 773 a 12; passages of all sense organs run to heart 781 a 21; not controlled by the mind 882 a 33-35; effect of fear on 947 b 29. Cf. Common sense

Heat, 802 a 13; essential property of fire 330 b 3, 441 b 11; stars impart heat to earth 340 a 21; why earth is heated by sun 341 a 13-37; affection of sense 341 a 15; all heat moves upward 342 a 16; raises moisture 347 a 8; thrusts clouds upward 348 a 20; cause of spontaneous generation 379 b 7; dry heat or cold solidifies 382 b 33, 384 b 13 (Cf. 385 a 31); foreign heat 389 a 26, b 1, 19; causes growth 441 b 30, 442 a 4, 669 b 4; bodily heat 456 b 21, 470 a 5, 481 b 4, 13, 483 b 19, 485 a 28, 809 a 7, 813 b 6-35, 875 a 14; necessary for life 470 a 20, 474 a 25; from within and from without 649 a 1, 784 b 8; causes both coagulation and melting 649 a 29; animals and plants have natural source of heat 650 a 6; all animals must have 652 b 17; indicated by an abundance of blood 669 b 5; natural heat tends to make the body erect 669 b 6; heart is source of 670 a 24, 766 b 1, 897 a 3; heat promoted by tickling armpits 673 a 3; requires sustenance 682 a 23; causes expansion 701 b 15; generative elements preserved by 748 b 1; vital heat found in all air 762 a 20; causes decay 784 b 7; in illness whole body is deficient in natural heat 784 b 27; perishes either by dying down or by being extinguished 875 a 4; makes water lighter 900 a 8; excessive heat causes brutishness 909 a 13-17. Cf. Hot

Heaven, heavenly sphere, universe (οὐρανός), 196 a 33, 213 b 24, 217 a 13, 392 b 33, 1076 a 2; in constant motion 211 a 13, 391 b 17, 700 b 31; in place indirectly 212 b 12-22; Plato thinks universe and time created together 251 b 19; perceive that it moves in a circle, yet can prove that circular motion is impossible 272 a 5; no body beyond the heaven 275 b 5-12; cannot be more than one heaven 276 a 18-279 b 3; meanings of the term 278 b 10-20; no place or void or time outside the heaven 279 a 12-b 3;

ungenerated and indestructible 279 b 4-283 b 22 (Cf. 699 b 29); plurality of movements and bodies in the heaven 286 a 3-b 9; necessarily spherical 286 b 10-287 b 22; has swiftest movement 287 a 26; outermost circle the swiftest 291 b 1; greatest of all subjects 391 a 25-b 8; its composition 391 b 10, 393 a 1; abode of the gods 391 b 15; spherical 391 b 20; place of God in 396 a 33-397 b 8; harmony of the universe 396 b 23-397 a 5, 399 a 12, 400 a 4; God as creator of 397 b 13-24; origin and final cause? 641 b 17-23; Prime Mover must lie outside the universe 699 a 12-700 a 26; called father 716 a 17; removed from life and death 816 a 33; but one heaven 1074 a 32-39; more divine than man 1141 b 2

Heavenly bodies, 259 b 30, 816 a 24; nine in number 910 b 35; appear always to have same shape 911 a 4-13

Heavy, contrary of light 106 a 18, 201 a 8, 255 b 9, 703 a 27; natural locomotion of heavy things is downward 205 b 27, 212 a 25, 269 b 20; dense 217 b 18, 260 b 11; not applicable to the primary body 269 b 19, 276 a 16; heavy the privative, light the positive, term 286 a 26; may be absolute or relative 307 b 28-308 a 33, 311 a 16-312 a 22; examination of the theories of heaviness and lightness 308 a 34-310 a 13

Hebrus, 350 b 18

Hecate, 847 a 7

Hecatombaeon, 543 b 12, 571 a 13

Hector, 1009 b 28, 1116 a 22, 25, 32, 1145 a 21, 1191 a 8, 1230 a 19, 1380 b 28, 1396 b 16, 1397 b 22, 1460 a 15, b 27

Hecuba, 1400 b 22

Hedgehog, spines of 490 b 30, 517 b 25, 781 b 34; testicles of 509 b 8, 719 b 16; copulation of 540 a 3, 717 b 26-31; habits of 612 b 4, 831 a 15-19, 835 a 27; in Aesop's fable 1393 b 27

Heel, 494 a 12

Hegemon of Thasos, 1448 a 13

Hegesippus, 1398 b 32

Hegiaenon, 1416 a 29

Helen, 1109 b 10, 1363 a 18, 1399 a 2, 1401 b 36, 1414 b 28

HELEN of Isocrates, 1414 b 27

Helen of Theodectes, 1255 a 37

Heliaea, court at Epidamnus 1301 b 24

Helice, 395 b 21; cuckoos of 830 b 11

Hellanocrates of Larissa, a conspirator against Archelaus 1311 b 18

Hellas, Hellenes. *See* Greece, Greeks

HELLE, 1454 a 8

Hellebore 864 a 4, 1137 a 14, 1199 a 32

Hellen, 1024 a 33

Hellespont, 366 a 27, 393 b 1, 398 a 28, 34, 548 b 24, 549 b 16, 568 a 5, 946 b 35, 39, 973 a 24, 1410 a 10

Hellespontias. *See* Apeliotes

Helots, 1264 a 35, 1269 a 38, 1271 b 40, 1272 b 19

Hemlock, 1225 b 5; death by drinking hemlock 874 b 1

Hemys. *See* Tortoise

Hen, 560 b 7, 613 b 15; copulation of 544 a 31, 558 b 12-28, 757 b 5; Adrian hen 558 b 18; eggs of 559 a 17, 751 a 9; wind-eggs in 559 b 27, 730 a 5, 751 a 10, 757 b 1; development of chick in egg 560 a 1, 561 a 4-562 a 21; dust bath of 560 b 8, 633 b 1; crowing of 613 b 8; brooding of 753 a 20; generation of 894 b 17

Heneti, jackdaws of 841 b 29-842 a 4

Heniochi, savage tribes about the Black Sea 1338 b 21

Hepatus, caeca of 508 b 20

Hephaestus, 369 a 32, 1253 b 36

Heptagon, a musical instrument 1341 a 41

Hera (the goddess), 838 a 17, 25, 1418 b 22

Heraclea, 840 a 13, 1327 b 14; fish in 835 b 15-23; revolutions at 1304 b 32, 1305 b 5, 37, 1306 a 37; method of paying their army 1347 b 3-15

Heracleia, 367 a 1

HERACLEID, 1451 a 21

Heracleidae, 1396 a 14

Heracleides of Aenos, 1311 b 20

Heracleitus, on anger 1315 a 30; punctuation is difficult in writings of 1407 b 7

Heracleodorus, leader of revolution at Oreum, 1303 a 18

Heracleotis, crabs of 525 b 5, 527 b 12, 684 a 10 •

Heracles, 359 a 27, 392 a 25, 834 a 17, b 26, 837 b 6, 838 a 30, 33, b 2, 18, 20, 840 a 20, 843 b 27, 953 a 14, 1213 a 13, 1245 a 30, b 30, 1284 a 24, 1451 a 22

Heraclidae, 1058 a 23

Heraclitus, 396 b 20, 401 a 11, 645 a 17, 908 a 30, 1005 b 25, 1010 a 13, 1012 a 24, 1062 a 32, 1063 b 25, 1078 b 14, 1146 b 30, 1155 b 5-7, 1176 a 7, 1201 b 8, 1223 b 22, 1235 a 26; all things are in motion 104 b 22, 987 a 33; good and evil are the same thing 159 b 30; criticism of 185 a 7, b 21; all things become fire 205 a 3, 1067 a 5; on destruction of world 279 b 15; everything generated 298 b 33; view of soul 405 a 25-28; on odours 443 a 22; on the formation of the earth 934 b 34; fire as first principle 984 a 7; 'all things are true and all are false' 1012 a 35; 'it is harder to fight with pleasure than with anger' 1105 a 8; referred to 984 a 28, 989 a 2, 1001 a 16

Heraea, revolution at 1303 a 15

Herb, 821 b 28, 825 a 5, 828 b 15, 923 a 31; defined 819 b 11; lance-herb of the Lycormas River 847 a 1

Hercules, 585 a 14, b 22

Hercules, Pillars of, 298 a 11, 350 b 3, 354 a 23, 362 b 22, 393 a 19, 24, b 10, 22, 32, 462 b 25, 833 a 10, 836 b 30, 844 a 25, 1388 a 10

Hercules, Road of, 837 a 8-12

Hercynian mountains, 350 b 5

Hercynian woods, 839 b 10

Here, the god, 580 a 20

Heredity, 585 b 29-586 a 14, 891 b 32-38, 1390 b 25-30; scars are transmitted 721 b 29-34; children resemble parents 722 a 4-16, 769 a 1-25

Herioni, 491 a 2

Hermeias, 1351 a 33

Hermes, 190 b 7, 1002 a 22, 1017 b 7, 1048 a 32, 1050 a 20, 1401 a 20; temple of 1116 b 18

Hermes, Promontory of 844 a 8

Hermes (the star), 399 a 8

Hermit crab, carcinium, 476 b 31, 529 b 20-530 a 7, 17; spontaneous growth of 548 a 15-21

Hermocaicoxanthus, 1457 a 36

Hermotimus of Clazomenae, reason as source of world order 984 b 19

Hero, the tragic hero 1452 b 30-1453 a 39

Herodicus, 1243 b 23, 1400 b 19; a healthy man 1361 b 5

Herodorus, 563 a 7, 615 a 10, 659 a 20; says the trochus has two pudenda 757 a 5

Herodotus, 736 a 10, 1236 b 8, 1407 a 39, 1409 a 27, 1417 a 6, 1451 b 2; thought Ethiopians ejected black sperm 523 a 19; on conception of fish 756 b 6

Heroic rhythm, 1408 b 33, 1448 b 33, 1459 a 9, 1460 a 3; the gravest and weightiest of metres 1459 b 34

Heron, diet of 593 a 29; habits of 609 a 30, b 6, 21-28, 610 a 8, 616 b 32-617 a 8; species of 609 b 22; tail of 710 a 13; feet of 710 a 15

Hesaenus Mountain, 830 a 5

Hesiod, 601 b 1, 879 a 28, 892 a 29, 975 a 11, 976 b 16, 989 a 10, 1000 a 8, 1095 b 9, 1132 b 27, 1153 b 27, 1164 a 27, 1252 b 11, 1312 b 4, 1343 a 20, 1344 a 15, 1381 b 17, 1388 a 16; chaos came first into being 208 b 28; everything generated 298 b 28; makes love a principle 984 b 23-29; referred to 1023 a 20, 1091 b 6, 1155 b 1

Hesione, 1416 b 2

Hestia, 369 a 32

Hestiaea, revolution at 1303 b 32-38

Heterogeneous parts (ἀνομοιομερῆ), 640 b 21, 655 b 33-697 b 30, 722 a 18; active functions of body carried on by 646 b 13 (Cf. 722 b 32); relation to homogeneous parts 646 b 32, 724 b 25, 740 a 19; serve for active functions 647 a 24

Heteroglaucia, found in horses and men 779 b 4, 780 b 3-12

Hexameter poetry, 1404 a 34, 1449 a 27, b 20

Hibernation, of fish 599 a 4-19, 30-600 a 9, 835 a 15-18; of insects 599 a 20-29; of birds 600 a 10-27; of quadrupeds 600 a 28-601 a 23, 818 b 25; of snakes 845 a 10-14

Hiccups, treatment of 961 b 9-26, 962 a 1-16, b 32-34, 963 a 37-b 9

Hiera, an island in the Aeolian group 367 a 1

Hiero, tyrant of Syracuse, 1312 b 12, 1313 b 14, 1315 b 34, 1391 a 9

Himera, 1393 b 10

Hipparchus, 1401 b 12

Hipparinus of Syracuse, 1306 a 2

Hippasus of Metapontium, fire as first principle 984 a 6; referred to 996 a 8, 1001 a 15

Hippelaphus, hair of 498 b 33; horns of 499 a 1

Hippias, 1356 b 34; the Athenian's schemes for raising money 1347 a 6-17

Hippias of Thasos, 1461 a 21

HIPPIAS MINOR of Plato, 1025 a 6

Hippo, 984 a 4; soul as water 405 b 1-4

Hippocrates, 1247 a 17, 1326 a 15; his method of squaring the circle 171 b 15; theory of the nature of comets 343 a 1-20, 344 b 15

Hippodamus of Miletus, 1330 b 24; criticism of his state 1267 b 22-1269 a 28

Hippolochus, 1368 a 17

Hippomanes, 572 a 21-30, 577 a 8-13, 605 a 2

Hippopotamus, 499 b 10, 502 a 9-15, 589 a 26, 605 a 13

Hippos, Promontory of, 844 a 9

Hippurus, growth of 543 a 22; breeding of 543 a 24; hibernation of 599 b 2

Hips, as a physiognomic sign 807 b 1, 22, 809 b 7

History, compared with poetry 1451 b 1-7, 1459 a 22-29

Hoar-frost, 378 a 31, 388 b 12, 940 b 9; cause of 347 a 14-b 12, 394 a 16; same as snow 347 b 16; described as congealed dew 394 a 26; frozen vapour 784 b 17; falls at dawn 888 b 30, 938 a 34

Holm-oak, 821 b 20, 1407 a 3

Holothuria, 681 a 18; motionless 487 b 15

Holy-fish, 620 b 35

Holy-snake, 607 a 31

Homer, 157 a 16, 166 b 2, 171 a 10, 222 a 1, 351 b 35, 1113 a 9, 1160 b 26, 1161 a 14, 1230 a 19, 1234 a 2, 1252 b 23, 1259 b 12, 1338 a 25, 1363 a 18, 1375 b 30, 1398 b 11, 1447 b 17, 1448 a 12, 22, 25, 1454 b 14, 1459 a 31, b 13, 1460 a 5-12, 19, 1461 b 3; Homeric scholars 1093 a 27; the *Margites* of 1140 a 15, 1448 b 30, 39; passages quoted or referred to:

Iliad i

l. 1, 180 a 22, 1415 a 16, 1456 b 16
l. 50, 1461 a 11
l. 82, 1379 a 5
l. 255, 1362 b 36
l. 356, 1378 b 33
l. 499, 397 b 27
l. 503, 1124 b 16

Iliad ii

l. 160, 1363 a 6
l. 196, 1379 a 4
l. 204, 1076 a 4, 1292 a 13
l. 298, 1363 a 7
l. 372, 1287 b 14
l. 391-3 (?), 1116 a 34, 35
l. 391-3, 1285 a 18
l. 403, 575 b 5, 6
l. 671-3, 1414 a 2, 3

Iliad iii

l. 24, 1118 a 23
l. 156-60, 1109 b 10

Iliad iv

l. 126, 1411 b 35

Iliad v

l. 75, 890 b 9

Iliad vi

l. 200-2, 953 a 23-25
l. 236, 1136 b 10
l. 442, 840 b 18

Iliad vii

l. 64, 934 a 14
l. 297, 840 b 18
l. 315, 575 b 5, 6

Iliad viii

l. 21, 700 a 1-3
l. 83, 84, 785 a 16, 17
l. 148, 149, 1116 a 25, 26

Iliad ix

l. 63, 1253 a 6
l. 202, 1461 a 14
l. 319, 1267 a 2
l. 385, 1413 a 31

l. 388-90, 1413 a 32-34
l. 526, 1410 a 29
l. 539, 578 b 1-3
l. 592-4, 1365 a 12-15
l. 648, 1278 a 37, 1378 b 33

Iliad x

l. 11-13, 1461 a 18
l. 152, 1461 a 2
l. 224, 1155 a 15, 1287 b 13
l. 251, 1461 a 26
l. 457, 673 a 15-17

Iliad xi

l. 11, 1116 b 27
l. 542, 1387 a 34
l. 553, 629 b 22
l. 574, 1412 a 1

Iliad xii

l. 243, 1395 a 14

Iliad xiii

l. 546, 513 b 26-28
l. 587, 1411 b 34
l. 799, 1412 a 8

Iliad xiv

l. 105, 840 b 18
l. 151, 1116 b 27
l. 201, 983 b 30, 1091 b 6
l. 214, 1149 b 18, 19
l. 217, 1149 b 18, 19
l. 246, 983 b 30
l. 291, 615 b 9-11

Iliad xv

l. 192, 400 a 19
l. 348-51 (?), 1116 a 34, 35
l. 542, 1412 a 2

Iliad xvi

l. 59, 1278 a 37
l. 529, 1116 b 27

Iliad xvii

l. 265, 1458 b 31
l. 663, 629 b 22

Iliad xviii

l. 109, 1370 b 12, 1378 b 6
l. 122, 840 b 18
l. 309, 1395 a 16
l. 376, 1353 b 37
l. 489, 1461 a 20

Iliad xx

l. 74, 519 a 19
l. 234, 1461 a 30
l. 267, 1461 a 33

Iliad xxi

l. 592, 1461 a 28

Homicide, 832 a 18, 846 b 28, 1267 b
37, 1274 b 24, 1275 b 11
Homoeomerous substances, 304 a 26,
486 a 1; of Anaxagoras 187 a 25; even
mixed bodies may be 302 b 16; homoeomerous bodies regarded by Anaxagoras as elements 314 a 20
Homoeoteleuton, 1410 b 1
Homogeneous parts (ὁμοιομερῆ), 203 a
21, 205 a 13, 212 b 5, 307 b 4, 308 b 9,
23, 384 b 31, 388 a 10-389 a 24, 486 a
5, 487 a 2, 489 a 27, 640 b 20, 650 b
13-655 b 27, 722 a 18, b 32, 734 b 27,
741 b 14; Anaxagoras' view of 188 a
13; homogeneous natural bodies 385
a 9; composed of the elements 389 b
22-390 b 21; sensation can occur only
in 646 b 6, 15, 647 a 23; relation to
heterogeneous parts 646 b 32, 724 b
25, 740 a 19; formed by heat and cold
743 a 5
Homophony, less pleasing than antiphony 921 a 7-30
'Honest Wife,' the celebrated mare in
Pharsalus 586 a 14, 1262 a 24
Honey, 383 a 5, 384 a 15, 385 b 2, 388 b
10, 23, 553 b 20-554 b 21, 832 a 6, 890
b 25, 928 a 5-10; differences in 485 b
26; how made by bees 623 b 4-627 b
22; much produced in fine weather
760 b 2-7; of Cappadocia 831 b 22; of
Trapezus 831 b 24-26; of Lydia 831 b
27-29; of Thrace 831 b 30-34
Honour (τιμή), 1107 b 22-27, 1116 a 28,
1130 b 2, 1159 a 16-25, 1165 a 24-30,
1183 b 23, 1192 a 21-33, 1195 b 15,

1200 a 17-29, 1201 a 37, 1202 a 30, 39, b 6, 1207 b 31, 1214 b 8, 1233 a 5, 1242 b 20, 1244 a 15, 1248 b 28, 1250 a 15, 28, b 35, 1251 b 17, 1358 b 28, 1362 b 21, 1371 a 7, 14; as the good for man 1095 b 22-1096 a 3; the end of virtue 1115 b 13, 1163 b 3; virtues concerned with 1123 a 33-1125 b 25; incontinence in respect of 1145 b 20, 1148 b 14; an external good 1202 a 30-39; two kinds of 1232 b 17-22; four states with regard to 1232 b 27-36; most people desire gain rather than honour 1318 b 16; a constituent of happiness 1360 b 24, 1361 a 27-b 2; noble acts are done simply for the reward of honour 1366 b 35; a topic of persuasion 1421 b 24, 1422 a 15, 16, 1423 b 6, 1425 b 40, 1427 a 26, b 40, 1430 a 28, 1436 a 14, 1438 b 20, 1439 a 12

Hoofs, 517 a 6-34, 655 b 7, 743 a 15, 797 b 19; of quadrupeds 690 a 4-28; formation of 745 a 1; swine with solid hoofs 835 a 35; contain gelatinous matter 935 b 39

Hoopoe, 633 a 18; habits of 488 b 2, 615 a 15, 616 a 34; has no nest 559 a 8

Hopelessness, 1251 b 25

Hoplosmios, 673 a 19

Horizon, 363 a 27; changes with change in our position 365 a 29

Horn, sounds of 802 a 17-b 18

Horn, the province, wandering fish in 835 b 5

Horned-beetle, antennae of 532 a 27

Hornet, anthrena, 553 b 10, 623 b 11, 624 b 25, 625 a 2; generation of 551 a 29, 554 b 22-555 a 11, 761 a 2; habits of 622 b 21, 628 b 31-629 a 27

Horns, 517 a 6-29, 655 b 7, 743 a 15; solidified by refrigeration 383 a 32; softened by heat 384 b 1, 385 b 12, 388 b 31; earth predominates in 389 a 11; of animals 499 b 15-500 a 13; nature and function of 662 b 23-664 a 13; found only in viviparous animals 662 b 24; found on most cloven-hoofed animals 662 b 35; colours of 797 b 20; as musical instruments 801 b 10, 802 a 17-b 13, 803 a 33, 804 a 38

Horse, 488 a 24, 491 a 1, 518 a 9, 626 a 22, 846 b 35; eyes of 492 a 7; hair of 498 b 31, 658 a 30, 780 b 5, 797 a 35, 798 a 6, b 7, 898 a 32; hoof of 499 b 11; mammae of 500 a 32, 521 b 22, 688 b 22, 33; genitals of 500 a 34; teeth of 501 a 18, b 2, 14-19, 576 a 7-16; heart of 506 a 9, 666 b 18; has no gall-bladder 506 a 22, 676 b 27; womb of 510 b 17; dreaming of 536 b 29; neigh of 545 a 7, 800 a 25; breeding of 545 b 10-20, 575 b 2-577 a 17, 747 b 2, 771 a 20; copulation of 572 a 9-b 17; drinking of 595 a 9, 605 a 10; diet of 595 b 23-30; diseases of 604 a 22-605 a 2; habits of 605 a 8-15, 609 b 14, 611 a 9-14; the king of Scythia's mare 631 a 1; wild horse 643 b 7, 895 b 26; tail of 658 a 33; spleen of 674 a 4; stomach of 674 a 27; growth of 686 b 15; movement of 712 a 34, b 7; viviparous externally and internally 718 b 30; women and mares only animals that admit male during gestation 773 b 27; length of gestation 777 b 14, 891 b 28; colour of eye 779 b 3, 892 a 1; wooden horse of Troy 840 a 31; excrement of 897 b 34-898 a 3; monstrous births in 898 a 11; keeping of horses is an indication of wealth 1289 b 35; fable of horse and stag 1393 b 8-22. Cf. Riding

Horsefly, myops, 552 a 30; sting of 490 a 20, 528 b 31, 532 a 10; diet of 596 b 13

Horse-mackerel, habits of 610 b 4

Horseman-ant, 606 a 5

Horseman-crab, 525 b 8

Horse-parsley, 923 a 34, b 8

Hot, 987 a 1; defined as that which associates things of the same kind 329 b 27; an active quality 378 b 12; ambiguous 648 a 20-649 b 8; hot climate promotes brutishness 909 a 13-17. Cf. Heat

Household, 1253 a 39-1260 b 23, 1278 b 32-40; household justice 1134 b 17, 1138 b 7; earlier and more necessary than city 1162 a 17; rule of a household is a monarchy 1180 b 5, 1255 b 18, 1259 a 40; the source of friendship, political organization, and justice 1242 a 27-b 2; three parts of 1253 b 1-14, 1259 a 37; the subject of economics 1343 a 2, 9; component parts of 1343 a 17; position of the wife in 1343 b 8-1344 a 7, 1345 a 6. Cf. Family

Householder, 1252 a 8, 11

Huckle-bone, 499 b 22, 26, 690 a 11-28

Humble-bees, 623 b 13; nest of 555 a 12-18; habits of 629 a 28-b 4

Humility, littleness of soul, meanness of spirit, poor-spirited, 1107 b 23, 1123 b 10, 24, 1125 a 16-27, 33, 1192 a 21, 1221 a 10, 33, 1233 a 16, 1250 a 2, 27, 1251 b 17-25, 1366 b 17; physiognomic signs of 808 a 30-32

Humour 673 a 34

Hunchback crab, cyphae, 525 b 2, 18, 29, 549 b 12

Hunger, not felt immediately after exercise 884 a 1-5; felt in winter rather than summer 887 b 38-888 a 21; can be tolerated easier than thirst 949 b 26-36

Hunter, 1256 b 3

Hunter-wasp. See Ichneumon

Hunting, art of acquiring slaves is a species of hunting or war 1255 b 37-40, 1333 b 38; a species of war 1255 b 38, 1256 b 23, 1324 b 39; a natural means of acquiring wealth 1256 b 2

Hurricane, 366 b 33, 370 b 8; commonest in autumn 365 a 2; moves downwards 369 a 19; never a hurricane when there is snow 371 a 4

Husbandman, 1256 b 2, 1262 a 40, 1381 a 23; makes best kind of democracy 1292 b 25, 1296 b 29, 1318 b 9, 1319 a 6-18; not to be citizen 1329 a 25, 1330 a 26; not to enter freemen's agora 1331 a 34

Husbandry. See Agriculture

Hybrids, 738 b 27-34, 746 a 29-b 12

Hybris, habits of 615 b 12

Hyena, glanus, 594 a 21-b 4; reproduction of 579 b 15-29, 757 a 2-13; heart of 667 a 21; in Arabia 845 a 24-27

Hygiaenon, 1416 a 28

Hymns, 1448 b 27

Hypanis River, 552 b 18

Hypate, 843 b 16, 918 a 19-21, 42, b 3-6, 919 b 1-19, 920 a 30, 921 a 10, 21, 922 b 4; easy to sing 917 b 35-39; relation of hypate and nete 921 b 14-38

Hypera, generation of 551 b 6

Hyperbole, a form of metaphor 1413 a 18-b 2; used in forming maxims 1430 b 9, 15, 18

Hyperboreans, 580 a 18

Hypochondrium, 493 a 20, 496 b 13

Hypodorian mode, unsuitable for tragedy 920 a 8-10, 922 b 10-27. Cf. Modes of music

Hypoglutis, 493 b 9

Hypolais. See Lark

Hypophrygian mode, unsuitable for chorus in tragedy 920 a 8-10, 922 b 10-27. Cf. Modes of music

Hypothesis, 119 b 35, 281 b 5, 1005 b 16, 1151 a 17; hypothetical reasoning 40 b 25, 41 a 22, 50 a 16, 72 b 13-15, 92 a 6-33, 108 b 8; rule of hypothetical reasoning 53 b 12, 57 b 1; defined 72 a 20-24; distinction between hypothesis and illegitimate postulate 76 b 23-77 a 4

Hypozoma, 532 b 16, 535 b 8, 659 b 16, 717 a 2, 718 b 2, 719 a 7, 739 b 6, 741 b 28, 749 a 30, 750 b 13, 751 a 5, 756 b 30, 757 a 20, 763 a 18

Hyrcanian Sea (Atlantic), 354 a 3, 393 b 24

Hystera, delphys, 510 b 14

I

Iambics, 1404 a 30, 1406 b 4, 1408 b 34, 1409 b 9, 1411 a 19, 1448 b 31, 33, 1449 a 5, 22, 1451 b 15, 1458 b 19, 1459 a 9, 11; most speakable of metres 1449 a 24; a metre of movement 1459 b 38

Iapygia, 838 a 28-34, 1303 a 5, 1329 b 21

Iapygian stone, 838 a 34-b 3

Iapyx (N.W. wind), 363 b 25, 364 a 18, b 4, 20, 22, 29, 365 a 2, 394 b 25, 31, 973 b 14-17; called Scylletinus at Tarentum 973 b 14; sometimes called Pharangites 973 b 16; sometimes called Argestes 973 b 17

Iberia, Iberians, 393 b 18, 748 a 26, 833 b 17, 837 a 9, 31, b 7, 844 a 6, 1324 b 18; silver in 837 a 24-29

Ibis, 617 b 28; copulation of 756 b 15

Icadius, 1461 b 8

Icarius, 1461 b 3, 8

Icarus, 836 b 10

Ice, 348 a 1, 32, b 35, 362 a 5, 385 a 32, b 7, 386 a 10, 387 a 19, 388 b 11; described 394 a 25

Ichneumon, hunter-wasp, 580 a 23; generation of 552 b 27-553 a 11; habits of 609 a 5, 612 a 17

Ichnussa, 838 b 22

Ichor, 521 a 13, 32, 838 a 30

Ida, Mount, 1401 b 22

Idea. *See* Form (Plato)

Ideal, Ideal Figures 968 a 10; Ideal Lines 969 a 18

Idrieus, 1406 b 28

Idyreus. *See* Meses

Ierne Isles, 393 b 13, 16

Ignorance (ἄγνοια), 1052 a 2, 1113 b 30, 1114 b 4, 1151 b 12, 1205 b 16, 1212 a 39, 1226 a 26, 1246 a 34, b 2, 21-30, 251 a 2; defined as error produced by inference 79 b 24; defined as negation of knowledge 81 a 37-b 9, 147 b 29-34; actions due to 1110 a 1, b 18-1111 a 22, 1113 b 24, 1136 a 7, 1144 a 15, 1145 b 27, 1217 a 4, 1221 b 24, 1225 b 5-15, 1226 b 32; actions done in 1110 b 24-27, 1135 a 24-34, 1136 a 5-8, 1195 a 23-b 4; ignorance of danger is not courage 1117 a 23-27, 1229 a 17, 1230 a 31. Cf. Error

Ignoratio elenchi, one of the seven fallacious refutations independent of language 166 b 24; all fallacies dependent on and independent of language can be reduced to 168 a 17-169 a 22; solution of fallacy of 181 a 1-14

Ileus, 1205 a 23

ILIAD, mentioned 92 b 32, 93 b 37, 180 a 21, 222 a 22, 1023 a 33, 1030 a 8, b 9, 1045 a 12, 1448 b 39, 1451 a 29, 1454 b 2, 1456 a 13, 1457 a 29, 1459 b 2, 14, 1462 b 3, 8. Cf. Homer

Ilissus River, 834 a 19

Illas, 617 a 22

Illiberality, meanness, 1107 b 9, 1108 b 22, 1119 b 29, 1121 a 11, b 13-1122 a 16, 1130 a 19, 1186 b 14, 21, 1192 a 1, 4, 9, 1221 a 5, 1231 b 30, 1250 a 2, 25, 1251 b 4-16, 1366 b 16; physiognomic

signs of 809 a 23, 811 a 5, 813 a 1; species of 1232 a 10-17

Illness, in illness whole body is deficient in natural heat 784 b 27; effect on voice 901 a 30-34

Illusions, 460 b 9-27, 461 b 8

Illyria, Illyrians, 499 b 12, 606 b 4, 832 a 6, 1461 a 3; fertility of the animals of 842 b 28-32; salt of 844 b 9-23

Image (εἴδωλον, φάντασμα), 431 b 2, 7, 438 a 12, 461 a 15, 464 a 5, 702 a 6, 990 b 15, 1079 a 12, 1378 b 9; contains no matter 425 b 25, 432 a 9; soul never thinks without image 431 a 16. Cf. Appearance

Imagination (φαντασία), 403 a 8, 415 a 10, 433 a 20, 26; nature of 427 b 27-429 a 9, 432 a 9; the imaginative part of the soul 432 b 1; a kind of thinking? 433 a 10; calculative or sensitive 433 b 29; does not involve opinion 434 a 10; a faculty of judgment 700 b 20; a cause of desire 701 a 36; has same effect as object imagined 701 b 19; depends on conception and sense-perception 702 a 19; not mistress of sleep or breathing 703 b 11; a feeble sort of sensation 1370 a 28

Imbecility, physiognomic signs of 811 b 24

Imitation, 1449 b 10, 24, 1451 a 30-33, 1453 b 13, 1454 a 27, b 8, 1460 b 8; of parents by offspring 894 a 30-37; in music 918 b 17; actors are imitators 918 b 28; Pythagorean 987 b 12; in painting 1190 a 31, 32; modes of 1447 a 14-16; distinguishing features of imitative poetry: (1) means 1447 a 19-b 29, (2) objects 1448 a 1-18, (3) manner of imitation 1448 a 19-b 3; as a cause of poetry 1448 b 4-23; natural to man 1448 b 6, 20; tragedy imitates life, not persons 1450 a 16, b 3, 24, 1452 a 1, 1459 a 15; the epic is a higher form of imitation than the tragedy 1461 b 26-1462 b 15

Immortality, 119 b 36, 145 b 22, 1177 b 33, 1183 b 3, 6, 1189 a 7, 1225 b 33; and God 122 b 12, 38, 128 b 19; an accidental feature of life 126 b 36; achieved through the species 415 b 1-7; only rational part of the soul is

An Index to Aristotle

immortal 430 a 23, 1070 a 26; impossible 1111 b 22

Immovable, unmoved (ἀκίνητος), kinds of 226 b 10-16; First Mover must be unmoved 258 b 12, 260 a 3; must be something immovable within the animal 698 b 13

Impetuosity, 1150 b 19

Impiety, defined 1251 a 31

Imports, 1345 b 21; import duty in Babylon 1352 b 26-32

Impossibility, contradictory of propositions expressing 22 a 6; meanings of impossible 280 b 13, 281 a 2-28, 699 b 18-30, 1019 b 22; relation to falsity 281 b 3-25, 1047 b 13; immortality an impossibility 1111 b 22. Cf. Possibility, *Reductio ad impossibile*

Impression, 386 a 18-28, 1203 b 5; in perception 450 a 31, b 16

Impressiveness of rhetorical style, 1407 b 26-1408 a 9

Improbable, in the epic 1460 a 13, 1461 b 13, 14

Impudence, effrontery, physiognomic signs of 805 b 3, 807 b 28-33, 809 a 22, 810 a 20, 33, 811 a 36, 812 a 8, b 9, 19, 22

Impulse, 1188 b 25, 1189 a 30, 1191 a 22, 1194 a 27, 1198 a 7-9, 1202 b 22, 1203 a 33, 1207 b 4, 1213 b 17; if no activity, then no impulse 1185 a 28-35; three forms of: (1) appetite, (2) passion, (3) wish 1187 b 37, 1188 a 24, 1223 a 27, 1247 b 20; not same as purpose 1189 a 1-4; impulse to the right 1200 a 1, 5, 1206 b 20, 24, 1207 a 36; rational and irrational 1247 b 19

In, 1023 a 24; eight possible meanings of 210 a 15-24; how a thing can be in itself 210 a 25-b 30

Inachus, 350 b 17

Inanimate things, problems connected with 913 a 19-915 b 35

Incense, 1118 a 11

Inconcoction, due to cold 379 b 13, 380 a 6; its species 379 b 13, 380 a 6

Incontinence, licentiousness (ἀκρασία), 1095 a 9, 1102 b 15, 1119 b 32, 1136 a 32, 1142 b 17, 1145 a 15-1152 a 35, 1166 b 8, 1168 b 34, 1200 b 6, 20-1204 a 18, 1206 a 39, 1223 a 37, 1224 b 19, 1229 b 37, 1231 b 3, 1237 a 7, 1240 b 14, 1246 b 12, 1250 a 1, 22, 1251 a 2, 23-29, 1366 b 15, 1383 b 23; not the giving away to pleasure, but rather to a certain kind of pleasure 146 b 28; used only of touch and taste 949 b 6-11, 37-950 a 17; men called incontinent only of desires 949 b 12-19; with regard to appetite 1111 b 13, 1149 a 24-1150 a 7, 1223 b 8, 19; with regard to anger 1145 b 20, 1148 b 14, 1149 a 4, 24-1150 a 7, 1202 b 10-28, 1223 b 18; with regard to honour 1145 b 20, 1148 b 14; with regard to gain 1145 b 20, 1148 b 14; how possible to behave incontinently with knowledge 1146 b 6-1147 b 19; knowledge of the incontinent man 1146 b 30-1147 a 18, 1201 b 9-1202 a 7; morbid forms of 1148 b 15-30, 1149 b 8-13, 1202 a 19-29; and softness 1150 a 14, 1202 b 34-38; self-indulgence is worse than incontinence 1150 a 30, b 29-1151 a 28; two species of 1150 b 19-28, 1203 a 30-b 11; and intemperance 1152 a 4-6, 1202 b 39-1203 a 29, b 24-1204 a 4; of Spartan women 1269 b 13-1270 a 14

Increase, magnification (αὔξη, αὔξησις), 206 b 28, 261 a 35, 284 b 28, 310 b 20, 465 b 31, 1016 b 11, 1088 a 32; as movement 15 a 13, 211 a 15, 226 a 31; infinity of 207 b 28; the limit of 241 b 34; presupposes alteration 260 a 30; does not admit of continuity 265 a 2-12; a body increases through contact with other bodies 270 a 23. Cf. Growth

Indefinite, indefinite noun 16 a 32, 19 b 8; indefinite verb 16 b 14, 19 b 10; indefinite premiss defined 24 a 19, 26 a 28; proof from indefinite nature of particular statement 26 b 14, 27 b 20, 28, 28 b 28, 35 b 11; may mean the possible 32 b 10, 19

Independence. See Self-sufficiency

India, 116 a 38, 167 a 8, 298 a 12, 362 b 22, 499 b 18, 501 a 25, 571 b 33, 597 b 27, 606 a 7, 607 a 33, 610 a 19, 834 a 3, 1189 a 21, 1226 a 29, 1332 b 25; lead of 835 a 8; wandering fish in 835 b 5; wild dogs of 895 b 25

Indian copper, 834 a 1-6

Indian Gulf, 393 b 2

Indignation, 1386 b 9-1387 b 20; defined as pain caused by the sight of undeserved good fortune 1387 a 9; used in rhetoric 1395 a 8, 1401 b 3, 1417 a 12, 1419 b 26; how aroused 1440 a 32-34, 1443 b 17. Cf. Righteous indignation

Individual (καθ' ἕκαστον, ἄτομον), 1017 b 25, 1030 a 5, 1070 a 10; never predicable of a subject 1 b 6; and substance 2 a 12-3 b 22; primary substance signifies individual 2 a 12, 3 b 10-22, 43 a 27; defined 17 a 39, 110 a 2; essence of things is in the individual 731 b 33, 742 b 34; actions concerned with the individual 981 a 17; is there anything apart from individuals? 995 b 32-39, 999 a 24-b 23; are first principles individual? 996 a 1, 999 b 24-1000 a 4, 1003 a 5-17, 1060 b 29, 1071 a 20, 1086 b 13-1087 a 25; prior in perception 1018 b 33; individuals are indefinable 1039 b 20-1040 b 4

Indivisible (ἄτομος, ἀδιαίρετος), 241 a 26, 448 b 14, 449 a 27, 999 a 2, 1016 a 19, 1052 a 15-1053 b 8; indivisibles have no parts 231 b 3; a continuous thing not composed of indivisible parts 232 a 24; indivisible bodies 314 a 21, 315 b 6-15, 325 a 23-b 5, 13-19, 34-326 b 6; no indivisible magnitudes 315 b 24-317 a 17, 440 a 27, 445 b 9, 448 b 14, 449 a 20, 1083 b 13; indivisible planes 315 b 30-316 a 4, 325 b 25-34, 326 a 22, 329 a 14-24; indivisible species 998 b 29, 1058 a 18

Indivisible lines, 299 a 10, 992 a 22, 1084 b 1; arguments for 968 a 1-b 20; the arguments answered 968 b 1-969 b 25; criticism of 969 b 26-970 a 33; impossible consequences of the theory 970 b 1-972 b 31

Induction (ἐπαγωγή), 68 b 8-37, 69 a 17, 72 b 30, 77 b 34, 90 b 14, 122 a 19, 252 a 25, 992 b 34, 1078 b 28, 1098 b 3, 1139 b 27, 1182 b 18, 1219 a 1, 1220 a 28, 1248 b 25, 1394 a 12; inductive inference 42 a 3; a form of dialectical reasoning 71 a 5; develops from particulars 71 b 1, 81 b 3, 105 a 13, 156

a 5, 1139 b 28; and demonstration 91 b 34; and definition 92 a 37-b 1; primary premiss known by induction 100 b 4; as a means of proving the division of predicables 103 b 3; compared to deduction 105 a 17; most useful against the crowd 105 a 17, 156 a 4-7, 157 a 21; reveals that things existing by nature are in motion 185 a 13; can prove existence of changes 224 b 30; reveals final cause 646 a 28; example is a rhetorical induction 1356 b 1-25, 1357 b 25, 1393 a 25; proofs are made either by syllogisms or inductions 1356 b 8; as a line of argument 1398 a 32-b 18

Indulgence, 1251 b 33

Indus, 350 a 26, 398 a 28, 34

Ines, 515 b 28

Infimae species (ἄτομα εἴδη), 96 b 16, 22, 24, 97 b 31, 414 b 27, 1016 a 29, 1018 b 5, 1059 b 27

Infinite (ἄπειρος, ἀόριστος), 440 b 24, 445 b 27; unknowable qua infinite 187 b 7, 994 b 22, 999 a 27; continuous defined as that which is divisible to infinity 200 b 18; the physicists regard infinite as attribute of a substance 203 a 17; cannot have a source 203 b 7, 742 b 20; five reasons for believing in the existence of the infinite 203 b 15-24; problems of asserting or denying its existence 203 b 30-207 a 31; three senses of term: (1) infinite in respect of addition, (2) division, or (3) both 204 a 1-8, 206 a 15, 25; criticism of Pythagorean and Platonic belief in a separately existing infinite 204 a 9-206 a 8; defined as what is boundlessly extended 204 b 21; exists only potentially and by reduction 206 a 15-b 32, 207 b 12; defined as a quantity such that we can always take a part outside what has been already taken 207 a 8; infinity consists in a process of coming to be 207 b 14; a cause in the sense of matter 207 b 36; its essence is privation 207 b 36; refutation of arguments for an actual infinite 208 a 5-24; relation of finite and infinite space and time 233 a 22-b 15, 237 b 23-238 b 22, 239 b 5-240 b 8; two senses of: (1) in divisibility and (2) in extremities 233 a 25; not composed of finite parts 238 a 13; infinite series 256 a 28; no body can be infinite 271 b 1-276 a 17, 699 b 28, 1073 a 10; infinite weight impossible 273 b 27-274 a 18; cannot move in a circle nor in straight line 275 b 13-25; Leucippus and Democritus think elements are infinite in number 303 a 5; things are infinite only potentially 318 a 21; unending and imperfect 715 b 16; Anaxagoras thinks principles are infinite in number 984 a 13; made out of great and small 987 b 26; cannot be an infinity of causes 994 a 1-b 30, 1074 a 29; no actual infinite 994 b 26, 1066 a 35-1067 a 38; by addition 994 b 30; how potential 1048 b 9; has no separate existence 1048 b 14; meanings of 1066 a 35-39; is number infinite? 1083 b 37-1085 a 2

Inflammable, 387 b 18-32

Inflections (πτώσεις), 119 a 37, 154 a 12, 172 b 26-174 a 11; as tests of ambiguity 106 b 29-107 a 2; as tests of accidents 114 a 26-b 24; as tests of genus 124 a 10-14; as tests of property 136 b 15-32; as tests of definition 148 a 10-13, 153 b 25-35; as tests of sameness 151 b 28-33

Inirascibility, lack of feeling, 1108 a 9, 1126 a 3-8, 1220 b 38, 1221 a 17

Injurious (βλαβερόν), defined 147 a 35; an object of avoidance 1104 b 32

Injustice, unjust (ἀδικία), 123 b 16, 135 b 12, 1129 a 2-1130 b 20, 1134 a 32, 1136 b 25-1137 a 4, 1223 a 36, b 15, 32, 1232 a 14, 1234 a 30, 1243 b 37, 1246 a 37, b 4, 31, 1248 b 31, 1250 a 2, 23, 1251 a 30-b 3, 1366 b 10, 1423 a 34; a vice of the soul 153 b 9; problems connected with justice and injustice 950 a 21-953 a 9; in respect of money 950 a 21-27, b 23-32; has no mean 1107 a 19; defined 1129 a 9, 34; can one treat oneself unjustly? 1134 b 12, 1136 b 1, 15-24, 1138 a 4-28, b 5-13; being unjustly treated is not voluntary 1136 a 10-b 14; acting unjustly is worse than suffering injustice 1138 a 28-b 5; does not imply wisdom 1199

a 19-b 9; can injustice be done to a bad man? 1199 b 10-35; man only animal that has sense of injustice 1253 a 15. Cf. Justice

Ink, 794 a 20; of molluscs 678 b 36-679 a 32

Inquiry, one of the genera of oratory 1421 b 9, 1430 a 26, 1441 b 31; methods of 1427 b 13-29, 1445 a 30-b 24

Insects, 475 a 1-b 4, 523 b 12-20, 531 b 20-532 b 18, 605 b 6-21; some live on when divided 411 b 20, 413 b 20, 468 a 25, 471 b 21, 531 b 30-532 a 4, 673 a 32, 707 a 28; do not possess organs 467 a 23; defined 487 a 34; sensation of 534 b 13-535 a 25, 682 a 2-9; have no voice or language 535 b 4; do not respire 535 b 7; sleep of 537 b 6; copulation of 542 a 1-17, b 29, 721 a 3-26, 729 b 25, 731 a 17; generation of 550 b 22-552 b 26, 758 a 26-759 a 6, 763 a 9; death of 553 a 12; food of 596 b 10-19; hibernation of 599 a 20-29; sloughing of 601 a 2-9; habits of 622 b 20-629 b 4; body of 654 a 26-31, 682 b 20-28; eyes of 657 b 38; perceive odours through the hypozoma 658 b 16; tongue of 661 a 15-28, 678 b 15; have no viscera 678 a 31; organs of nutrition in 682 a 10-29; small eaters 682 a 22; why they have many feet 682 a 39; wings of 682 b 5-19, 710 a 16, 713 a 11; sting of 682 b 29-683 a 26; legs of 683 a 27-b 3; flying of 710 a 2-22; some reproduce by spontaneous generation 715 b 6; scolex of 733 a 25-33, b 13, 758 b 7-37; eggs of 733 a 29, 758 b 10-15

Insensibility to pleasure, 1104 a 25, 1107 b 7, 1108 b 21, 1109 a 3, 1119 a 6, 1186 b 10, 1191 a 38, 1221 a 2, 22, 1222 a 3, 1230 b 14, 1231 a 26

Insolence, 1378 b 23-1379 a 8, 29; physiognomic signs of 808 b 36, 813 a 32

Intellect, 1183 b 22, 1196 b 37, 1248 a 29; deals with first principles of things 1197 a 20-29; rules the appetites 1254 b 4

Intellectual virtue. See Virtue, intellectual

Intelligence, understanding (διάνοια), 198 a 11, 1103 a 5, 1142 b 34-1143 a

1251 a 3-10; physiognomic signs of 806 b 32, 807 a 5, 811 a 31, 812 a 26

Iris, colours of 796 b 25

Iron, 378 a 28, 383 a 33, 384 b 15, 385 b 12, 386 b 10, 388 a 14, 389 a 11, 701 b 8, 837 b 32; Chalybian and Amisenian 833 b 23-32; as material for surgical instruments 863 a 25-30; coinage of iron at Clazomenae 1348 b 26

Irony. *See* Mock-modesty

Irrational element in soul, 1102 a 28, b 13, 29, 1138 b 9, 1139 a 5, 1168 b 21, 1172 b 10, 1185 b 1-13, 1219 b 26-1220 a 2, b 7, 1221 b 27-31, 1246 b 13, 20-23, 1260 a 7, 1334 b 19; irrational passions 1111 b 1; irrational creatures 1111 b 12; courage and temperance are virtues of irrational parts 1117 b 24; ought to be controlled by rational principle 1254 b 5, 1260 a 6, 1333 a 18

Is, meanings of 89 b 33, 185 a 21, 410 a 13, 979 a 35-b 19, 1003 a 33-b 18, 1030 a 18-26, 1042 b 25, 1061 a 7-9, 1069 b 16; 'what just is' 186 a 33-187 a 8; as many types of motion or change as there are meanings of 'is' 201 a 8; may refer to potentiality or actuality 206 a 14; the infinite 'is' 206 a 21. Cf. Being

Ischium, all birds have an ischium 695 a 1-16

Islands, 393 a 9-15

Islands of the Blest, 1334 a 31

Ismenias, 1398 b 2

Ismenium, temple of Ismenian Apollo at Thebes, 843 b 22

Isocrates, 1368 a 20, 1392 b 11, 1399 a 2, 5, b 9, 1408 b 15, 1411 a 30, 1412 b 6, 1414 b 27, 33, 1418 b 27; referred to 1181 a 14

Isosceles triangle, proof that angles at base are equal 41 b 14

Issus, Gulf of, 973 a 17

Ister. *See* Danube

Isthmian Games, 1406 a 21

Istria, 839 a 34

Istros, 845 b 9; revolution at 1305 b 5

Istrus River. *See* Danube

Italus, king of Oenotria, 1329 b 9-18

Italy, 367 a 7, 607 a 26, 632 b 26, 834 b 4, 835 b 35, 837 a 8, 838 a 5, 33, 839

a 12, 27, 840 a 3, 28, 843 a 6, 845 b 5, 973 b 20, 1274 a 25; origin of its name 1329 b 8-18

Iteration, 1428 a 8, 1433 b 29-1434 a 17, 1436 a 20, 1439 a 22, 29, b 11, 1440 a 24, 1441 b 1, 1444 b 22-34, 1445 b 21; defined as a means of briefly reminding one's hearers 1433 b 29

Ithaca, no hares in 606 a 5

Iulus, 523 b 18

Ivy, 831 a 2; blossoms are same colour as fruit 796 b 10

Ixion, 284 a 35

Ixions, 1455 b 34

J

Jackal, generation of 742 a 9; development of young at birth 774 b 17

Jackdaw, 617 b 16, 1155 a 35, 1208 b 9, 1371 b 16; oesophagus of 509 a 1; copulation of 756 b 23; habits of 841 b 29-842 a 4

Jailorship, 1322 a 21

Jason, 1277 a 23, 1400 b 12; journey of 839 b 14-840 a 6

Jason of Thessaly, 1373 a 26

Jaws, 492 b 22, 745 b 31; movement of 691 a 28-b 17; as a physiognomic sign 807 b 24

Jay, habits of 615 b 19, 744 b 29; nest of 616 a 2

Jealousy. *See* Envy

Jennet, 491 a 2

Jests, 1372 a 1; in oratory 1419 b 3-8

Jocasta, 1417 b 18

Joint, in plants 820 a 19; point is not an indivisible joint 972 b 25-31

Journey, unfamiliar journey seems longer 883 b 2-13, 955 b 9-21

Judge, 1132 a 7-30, 1268 b 7, 1358 b 1, 1391 b 12, 18; not to hold office for life 1270 b 39; modes of appointing judges 1300 b 28-1301 a 9; those who inflict penalties are not to execute them 1321 b 40-1322 a 18; is often perverted 1354 a 25; should decide only as few things as possible 1354 a 32-b 22

Judgement (δόξα), 1143 a 19-b 16; varieties of 427 b 25; faculties of 700 b 20. Cf. Opinion

Judicial element in the state, 1298 a 3, 1300 b 13-1301 a 15

Jugglers, 1346 b 22

Juli, 682 a 4; body and feet of 682 b 2-4

Jupiter, 343 b 30, 1073 b 35, 1074 a 7

Jury, 950 b 5-8

Justice (δίκαιον, δίκη), 106 a 4-8, 114 b 2, 117 a 21, 401 b 27, 1105 a 18, 30, b 5-12, 1108 b 7, 1120 a 20, 1129 a 2-1138 b 14, 1182 a 14, 1185 b 8, 1193 b 1-1196 b 3, 1216 b 4, 23, 1218 a 9, 18, 1221 a 4, 23, 1234 a 32, 1242 a 30, 1243 a 34, 1246 a 36, 1248 b 22, 1249 b 28, 1250 a 11, b 16-24, 1255 a 22, 1277 b 16, 1323 a 28, b 34, 1334 a 25, 1358 b 25, 1362 b 13, 28, 1365 b 6, 1366 b 1, 6, 9, 1375 b 4, 1447 b 5; a species of virtue 109 a 35-b 1, 121 b 26, 123 b 15, 127 b 20; desire justice in friends for its own sake, in enemies so they will not harm us 116 a 36; more desirable than strength 116 b 37; incorrectly defined as the ability to distribute what is equal 145 b 35; not to be defined as temperance and courage 150 a 4; approved most of all in the poor 949 b 20-25; problems connected with 950 a 21-953 a 9; become just by associating with just men 951 a 3-10; become just by doing just acts 1103 b 1, 15; defined 1129 a 6, 33, 1194 a 26, 27, 1421 b 37, 1447 b 1, 2; as the lawful (universal justice) 1129 a 32-1130 b 15, 1193 b 3-32; thought to be the greatest of virtues 1129 b 25-1130 a 12; as the fair (particular justice) 1130 b 8-1132 b 20, 1193 b 33-1194 a 18; commercial justice 1132 b 22-1134 a 15; political justice 1134 a 26-b 7, 19-1135 a 4, 1194 b 5-29, 1259 b 21-1260 a 20, 1277 b 16-29; household justice 1134 b 8-17, 1138 b 8, 1242 b 2; two kinds of: unwritten and legal 1134 b 18, 1135 a 3, 1162 b 21; as involving choice 1135 a 15-1138 b 14; all just action is voluntary 1136 a 13-b 14, 1195 a 14-1196 a 25; can a man be unjust to himself? 1136 a 34, 1138 a 4-27, 1195 b 35-

1196 a 33; not easy 1137 a 6; equality on basis of merit 1158 b 31; and friendship 1159 b 25-1162 a 33, 1211 a 6-15, 1241 b 11-1242 b 1; retaliatory justice 1194 a 29-b 2; economic justice 1194 b 20; natural and legal justice compared 1194 b 30-1195 a 7; just man will not become all things to all men 1199 a 14-18; man only animal that has sense of justice 1253 a 15; the bond of men in states 1253 a 37; as goodwill 1255 a 17; as equality 1280 a 8-31, 1282 b 15-1284 b 34, 1301 b 36, 1332 b 27; according to the democrats and oligarchs 1318 a 20; no government can stand that is not founded on justice 1332 b 27; a topic of persuasion 1421 b 24, 36-1422 a 1, 28-42, 1425 b 40, 1436 a 14, 1439 a 10, 37. Cf. Injustice

K

Keen, ambiguous 780 b 14

Keraiae, 499 b 29

Kestrel, 594 a 2; stomach of 509 a 6; eggs of 558 b 28, 559 a 25; most fertile bird 750 a 7

Kidneys, 496 b 34, 506 b 24-31, 670 b 23-30; veins of 514 b 16; left is fatter than right 520 a 29; nature and function of 671 a 27-672 a 8; have sensation in sexual intercourse 876 b 20. Cf. Bladder

Kindness, 1250 b 33, 1385 a 14-b 10; a cause of friendship 1381 b 35; defined 1385 a 18

King, 1159 a 1, 1252 a 8, 12, 14, 1259 b 14, 1322 b 29; must be self-sufficient 1160 b 2-11; friendship between king and subjects 1161 a 10-19; some say the gods have a king 1252 b 24, 1259 b 13; advantage or disadvantage to states? 1271 a 19; needs a special education 1277 a 17; may exercise compulsion 1284 b 14; superior to citizens 1284 b 25-34, 1288 a 15-33; guarded by citizens 1285 a 26, 1311 a 7; should king have a military guard? 1286 b 27-40; kings are selected by the better classes 1310 b 9; aims at honour 1311 a 4; not superior to subjects 1332 b 23. Cf. Monarchy

Kingfisher. *See* Halcyon

Kite 594 a 2, 842 a 35; spleen of 506 a 16, 670 a 33; gall-bladder of 506 b 23; eggs of 563 a 30; diet of 592 b 1; hibernation of 600 a 16; habits of 609 a 20, 610 a 11, 842 a 35; stomach of 670 a 34

Knee, 494 a 18; flexion of 698 b 4, 709 a 3, 712 a 17; fatigue in 882 b 25-36, 883 a 29-b 2

Knee-cap, 494 a 5

Knights. *See* Cavalry

Knock-knees, 808 a 13, 809 b 9, 810 a 34

Knot in wood, 819 a 14; a kind of root 850 a 1

Knowledge (ἐπιστήμη), 121 a 1, 132 b 10-13, 147 a 17, 151 b 1, 247 b 10, 428 a 17, 465 a 23, 1202 a 3, 1206 a 6-8, 1220 b 27; its relation to its object 7 b 27-34; three senses of 67 b 4; instruction proceeds from pre-existent knowledge 71 a 1-10; two kinds of pre-existent knowledge 71 a 11-b 8; nature of scientific knowledge 71 b 9-73 a 20, 1139 b 18-35, 1140 a 33, b 31, 1196 b 39, 1197 a 21, 1371 b 27; not all knowledge is demonstrable 72 b 19, 84 a 30, 1140 a 33; truth gained by demonstrative knowledge is necessary truth 73 a 22, 74 b 5-75 a 38; demonstrative knowledge obtained through necessary middle term 75 a 13; knowledge of the fact compared with knowledge of the reasoned fact 78 a 22-79 a 15; and sense perception 87 b 28-88 a 17, 441 b 23, 1142 a 27; compared to opinion 88 b 30-89 b 9, 121 a 21-25, 1145 b 35, 1146 b 24; defined 89 a 34, 146 b 5; nature of pre-existent knowledge 89 b 31-35; and intuition 99 b 15-100 b 17; knowledge and sensation 105 a 28, 108 a 4, 125 a 33, 156 b 11-14; disposition is the genus of knowledge 111 a 23, 145 a 36; distinction between potentiality and actuality of 114 b 34, 1225 b 12; self-knowledge 125 a 39; meanings of 'the knowledge of' 130 a 20-22; kinds of:

(1) Speculative, (2) Practical, (3) Productive 145 a 16, 157 a 10, 982 a 1, 993 b 21, 1025 b 19-27, 1026 b 5, 1046 b 3, 1064 a 17, 1103 b 27, 1139 a 27, b 16, 1216 b 11; scientific knowledge attained through acquaintance with principles, conditions, or elements of an inquiry 184 a 10; do not think we have knowledge until we grasp the primary cause 194 b 19, 983 a 25, 993 b 23, 994 b 29, 1025 b 6; all kinds to be honoured and prized 402 a 1; apprehends universals 417 b 23, 1180 b 15, 22; actual knowledge identical with object 430 a 20, 431 a 1-b 19, 1072 b 19-21; acquired only through intelligence or sense-perception 458 b 2; scientific and general knowledge 639 a 1-4; possession of knowledge does not alter the body 806 a 17; desired by all 980 a 21; sight gives more knowledge than any other sense 980 a 27; have knowledge of a thing only when know its essence 1031 b 7; called measure of things 1053 a 32; meaning of the term 1097 a 15; nothing is stronger than knowledge 1145 b 33; two senses of having knowledge 1146 b 30-34, 1201 b 11, 1225 b 12; acting against knowledge 1147 a 2; bad kinds of 1153 b 9; most permanent and constraining of all things 1200 b 37; a good thing 1205 a 29-33; men do not always use the knowledge they have 1264 a 5. Cf. Demonstration, Reason, Science

Knuckle, 493 b 28

Knuckle-beetle. *See* Sphondyle

Knuckle-bones, 1371 a 2

Koriskos. *See* Coriscus

L

Labrax, *See* Basse

Labyrinth, 499 b 26

Lacedaemon. *See* Sparta

Lachesis, the Fate dealing with the future 401 b 20

Lacinium, 838 a 17

magistrates should administer the state 1289 a 18; defined as the common consent of the community 1318 a 28-b 5, 1420 a 26, 1422 a 2, 1424 a 10; law is order 1326 a 30; ought to define all the points it can 1354 a 32-b 22; particular and universal 1368 b 8, 9, 1373 b 2-17; a form of persuasion 1375 a 22-b 25; written and unwritten 1373 b 5, 1374 a 19-b 22, 1375 a 16, 17, b 7, 1422 a 1, 1446 a 24; a subject of deliberative oratory 1423 a 24, 1424 a 9-b 27

Law Courts, varieties of 1300 b 13-1301 a 15; the rich should attend 1320 a 27. Cf. Areopagus, Council of

LAW of Theodectes, 1398 b 5, 1399 b 1

Lawful, a topic of persuasion 1421 b 24, 1422 a 2, 3, b 1-24, 1425 b 40, 1436 a 14, 1439 a 11, 28, 37

LAWS of Plato, 1072 a 2, 1098 b 12, 1111 a 24, 1180 a 5, 1260 b 5, 1266 b 5, 1271 b 1, 1330 b 32, 1336 a 34; criticism of the state in 1264 b 26-1266 a 30

Laziness, lethargy, 1166 b 10; physiognomic signs of 811 a 29, b 5, 10, 20, 31, 813 b 10

Lead, 385 a 33, 389 a 9, 834 a 8, 889 a 13; of India 835 a 8; white lead 978 a 10; mines at Laurium 1353 a 16

Leaves, cause of shedding of 783 b 14-25, 828 a 32-40; as dyes 794 a 19; colours of 797 a 15-30, 799 a 11, 818 a 15, b 9, 819 a 38, b 12, 821 b 25, 825 a 16, b 8; production of 827 a 7-b 6

Lebadia, 395 b 29, 606 a 1

Lecherousness, 1231 a 19

Lectum, 547 a 5

Leech, movement of 709 a 28

Leek, 551 b 20; effect on voice 903 b 27-29; cannot endure salt water 923 a 6-8

Leekbane, prasocuris, 551 b 20

Left. See Right-left

Leg, 491 a 29, 494 a 3, 709 a 1-9, 884 a 16-21; flexion of 687 b 25-688 a 12, 704 a 20, 711 a 8-713 b 22; why animals have an even number of legs 708 a 22-b 19; as a physiognomic sign 807 b 9, 21, 24, 26, 808 a 12, 30, 810 a 29-37, 814 b 6; acute angle made by

legs upon rising from sitting position 857 b 22-858 a 2; fatigue in legs 883 b 13-25

Legislation, legislative, 1141 b 25; needed to attain happiness 1179 a 33-1181 b 23; best legislators are from middle class 1296 a 18

Leguminous plants, 522 b 33, 750 a 24, 752 a 22

Leisure, 1177 b 4, 1198 b 15-20, 1326 b 32; in well-ordered state citizens must have leisure 1269 a 34, 1273 a 32-b 7; necessary for development of virtue 1329 a 1; citizens must know the right use of 1333 a 33-1334 a 11, 1337 b 23-1338 b 8, 1339 a 26; philosophy needed for 1334 a 24; music valuable for the proper enjoyment of 1337 b 28-1338 b 8; the first principle of all action 1337 b 32; gives pleasure, happiness, and enjoyment of life 1338 a 2. Cf. Amusement, Relaxation

Lemnos, 522 a 13

Lentil-soup, 936 b 23

Leodamas, 1364 a 18, 1400 a 31

Leontini, 520 b 1, 1275 b 27, 1310 b 30; oligarchy in Sicily 1316 a 37

Leopard, pard, 580 a 24, 606 b 16; temper of 488 a 28; feet of 499 b 8; mammae of 500 a 28; teeth of 501 a 17; habits of 608 a 33, 612 a 7-16; heart of 667 a 21; toes of 688 a 4-12; varicoloured 785 b 25; exhibits the female type 809 b 37-810 a 13; hunting of 831 a 3-10; never tame 895 b 26; odour of 907 b 35

Leopard's bane, 831 a 3-10

Leophanes, 765 a 25

Leprosy, 887 a 34, 891 a 26-b 3, 894 b 6-11; causes hair to become white 784 a 27, 797 b 14, 891 b 1, 894 b 6; found only in man 894 a 38-b 5

Leptines, 1411 a 4

Lesbian moulding, 1137 b 30

Lesbos, 393 a 13, 621 b 22, 763 b 2, 946 b 35, 947 a 4, 973 a 9, b 22, 1284 a 40

Lethargy. See Laziness

Leto, 580 a 18; temple of 1214 a 3

Letter, 1456 b 21-34

Leucadian, 808 a 32

Leucas, Island of, 1266 b 23

An Index to Aristotle

Leucippus, 213 a 34, 1072 a 7; whole exists as parts separated by void 275 b 30; elements in perpetual movement 300 b 9; infinite number of elements 303 a 3-b 8, 314 a 18; distinguishes between coming to be and alteration 314 a 12; makes careful study of coming to be 315 a 34-b 15; primary reals are indivisible bodies 315 b 30, 325 b 27; on the void 325 a 2, 23-b 5, 25; 'Arguments of Leucippus' 980 a 7; the full and the empty as elements 985 b 5-19; assumes eternal actuality 1071 b 32; referred to 1084 b 27

Leuconotus (S.S.W. wind), reason for its name 973 b 10, 11

Leucosia the Siren, 839 a 34

Leucothes, 1400 b 7; temple of 1349 b 34

Leuctra, the battle of, 1429 b 15

Lever, 255 a 22, 847 b 10-16, 853 a 9-854 a 15; raises great weights 850 a 30-b 9

Libanus 973 a 15

Liberality, generosity, 1099 a 19, 1103 a 6, 1107 b 8, 20, 1108 b 22, 1115 a 20, 1119 b 22-1122 b 18, 1125 b 2, 1151 b 7, 1158 a 20, 1186 b 14, 21, 1191 b 39-1192 a 20, 1221 a 5, 1231 b 27-1232 a 17, 24, 1249 b 28, 1250 a 13, b 25-33, 1251 b 13, 1265 a 33, 1326 b 32, 1366 b 1, 7, 16; physiognomic signs of 809 b 35, 811 a 2, 812 b 23, 36; lost in communism 1263 b 11

Liberty, freedom, the characteristic feature of democracy 1280 a 5, 1291 b 35, 1294 a 12, 1317 a 40-b 17, 1319 b 30, 1366 a 4; extreme democracies have a false idea of liberty 1310 a 25-36; as a reward for slaves 1330 a 33

Libonotus, Libophoenix, 394 b 34

Libya, 350 b 10, 352 b 31, 358 b 3, 363 a 6, 393 b 31, 606 a 7, 18, b 14, 607 a 21, 615 b 4, 746 b 8, 844 a 5, 906 b 18, 973 b 12, 1010 b 11, 1345 a 4; the serpents of 606 b 9; animals grow to large size in 655 a 9; Libyan ostrich 658 a 13, 695 a 17, 697 b 14, 749 b 17; salt in 844 a 7-16; mad-vine of 846 b 1; sheep of 896 a 26; water of 933 b 34-40; south winds of 942 a 7, 945 b 35-946 a 3; community of wives in 1262

a 19; sayings of 1345 a 2, 4; fables from 1393 a 30

Libyus, habits of 609 a 19

Lice, 537 a 5, 556 b 23-557 a 31, 602 b 29, 924 a 9; copulation of 539 b 12; louse-disease 861 a 10-19

Licentiousness. *See* Incontinence

Lichanos, 919 a 16

Lichen, 791 b 26, 792 a 2

Licymnius, 1405 b 7, 1413 b 14; the *Art of Rhetoric* of 1414 b 18

Life (ζωή, βίος), 415 a 25, 778 b 32, 1170 a 18; life of virtue and enjoyment 102 b 17; not genus of immortality 126 b 35; ambiguous 148 a 27-38; Xenocrates' proof that the happy life is the good life 152 a 7, 26; 'human life is a circle' 223 b 24, 916 a 18-39; respiration the characteristic mark of 404 a 10, 467 b 12, 480 b 12; derivation of ζῆν 405 b 28; implies self-nutrition and growth 412 a 15, 479 a 30; as implying thinking, perception, or movement 413 a 24; longevity and shortness of 464 b 19-467 b 9, 777 b 6; presupposes humidity and warmth 466 a 20, 469 b 8, 489 a 20; and warmth 469 b 6, 474 a 25, b 10; in plants and animals 815 a 1, 816 a 22-b 22; excess and cold are fatal to 861 a 20-32; three types: (1) enjoyment, (2) honour, (3) contemplation 1095 b 18, 1215 a 32-b 1, 1216 a 27-29; an activity 1098 a 6, 1100 b 33, 1175 a 11, 1254 a 7; according to reason 1177 b 30, 1178 a 7, 1180 a 18; most people regard happy life as the fortunate life 1206 b 32; all men cling to life 1215 b 15-1216 a 25, 1244 b 27, 1278 b 29; of a plant 1216 a 3-6; consists of perception and knowledge 1244 b 21-25; prefer social life 1245 a 11-27; of action 1265 a 25, 1324 a 5-1325 b 32; poets measure life by periods of seven years 1335 b 34, 1336 b 40; of slaves 1344 a 35

Ligeria the Siren, 839 a 34

Light (ἐλαφρόν), contrary of heavy 106 a 18, 201 a 8, 255 b 9, 703 a 27; natural locomotion of light objects is upward 205 b 27, 212 a 25, 269 b 20; rare 217 b 18, 260 b 11; heavy the privative, light the positive, term 286 a 26; not applicable to the primary body 286 a 26; examination of the theories of heaviness and lightness 308 a 34-310 a 13; may be absolute or relative 307 b 28-308 a 33, 311 a 16-312 a 22. Cf. Heavy

Light (φῶς), 146 a 15, 342 b 6, 15, 367 b 22, 374 a 27, 438 a 29; a species of fire 134 b 28; travels faster than sound 395 a 16; defined as the presence of fire or something resembling fire 418 b 16, 439 a 17; defined as the actuality of what is transparent 419 a 11; mind compared to light 430 a 17; quenching of light 437 b 17; not a movement 446 b 28; efficient cause of seeing 447 a 12; the colour of fire 791 b 7; does not penetrate dense objects 904 b 15-21, 905 a 35-b 23, 939 a 10-16

Light-bearing star, 392 a 27, 399 a 8

Lightning, 364 b 30; cause of 369 b 5-11, 370 a 25-32, 395 a 14; Empedocles' theory of 369 b 12; Anaxagoras' theory of 369 b 14-24; Cleidemus' theory of 370 a 10-22; perceived before thunder 395 a 16; types of 395 a 25-29

Liguria, 351 a 16, 368 b 31, 837 b 9; slingers of 837 b 16-19; women of 837 b 20-24; river of 837 b 25-27

Ligyans, seven-ribbed 493 b 15

Like, 124 a 15-20, 136 b 33-137 a 7, 138 b 22-27, 152 a 2, 1000 b 6; meanings of 1018 a 15-19, 1021 a 11, 1054 b 3-12. Cf. Analogy, Metaphor

Lily, 926 a 2

Lime, 383 b 8; consists of earth 389 a 28

Limit, termination, end (πέρας), 74 b 1, 185 b 18, 209 a 9, 218 a 23, 976 a 11, 977 b 17-978 b 14, 1002 b 10, 1023 a 34, 1357 b 9; change has a limit but no beginning 236 a 7-b 19; limit and starting-point coincide in a circle 264 b 27; sensible qualities are limited in species 445 b 22, 446 a 19; necessary to organic movement 700 b 14; of Being 975 b 37; meanings of 1022 a 4-13; the limits of bodies: (1) surface, (2) line, (3) point, (4) unit 1028 b 17 (Cf. 193 b 32); end is the limit of the means 1256 b 35, 1257 b 27; defined 1450 b 29

Limnostrea, lagoon oyster, 547 b 12; 'eggs' of 763 b 11

Limpet, 528 a 1, 14, 530 a 18, 547 b 22, 548 a 27, 590 a 34; motion of 528 b 1; mecon of 529 a 32, 680 a 23; the wild limpet or 'sea-ear' 529 b 15; mouth of 530 b 21; shell of 679 b 27

Line (γραμμή), 5 a 19, 193 b 24, 222 a 16, 231 b 9, 299 b 26, 409 a 5, 709 a 7, 917 b 25, 997 a 27, 1016 b 26, 1017 b 7, 20, 1036 b 13, 1043 a 34, 1052 b 33, 1060 b 12-19, 1090 b 6; can be divided indefinitely 5 a 1, 220 a 30, 233 b 16; indivisible lines 121 b 19, 206 a 18, 299 a 13, 968 a 1-972 b 31, 992 a 22, 1084 b 1; point is prior to line 141 b 15-22; criticism of definition of line as length without breadth 143 b 11-20; a limit of a body 193 b 32, 1028 b 17; perceptible lines 194 a 10, 998 a 1; cannot be composed of points 215 b 19, 231 a 25, 241 a 14, 970 b 1-972 b 31, 968 a 18-21, b 25-969 a 2, 1001 b 18; intermediate between points 231 b 9; no infinite straight line 265 a 18; divisible only one way 268 a 8; defined as limited length 272 b 18, 1020 a 13; 'line of life' 896 a 38-b 4, 964 a 33-38; commensurate lines 969 b 6-11, 970 a 3; a magnitude 971 a 20; is a line a substance? 996 a 13-17, 1001 b 26-1002 b 11, 1028 b 17; neither comes to be nor perishes 1002 a 32. Cf. Point

Lion, 594 b 17-28, 606 b 14, 612 a 9, 810 b 5, 950 a 12; temper of 488 b 17, 571 b 28, 629 b 8-630 a 8; neck of 497 b 17, 686 a 22; walk of 498 b 7; hair of 498 b 28, 658 a 31, 809 b 24; feet of 499 b 8; toes of 499 b 24, 688 a 4-12; mammae of 500 a 29, 688 a 36-b 4; genitals of 500 b 15, 16; teeth of 501 a 16, 507 b 16, 788 b 17; mouth of 502 a 7; stomach of 507 b 17, 21, 674 a 26; bones of 516 b 8, 521 b 12, 652 a 1, 655 a 15; claws of 517 a 34; copulation of 539 b 23; reproduction of 579 a 31-b 14, 742 a 9, 892 b 2; habits of 610 a 14; urination of 689 a 34; sterility in 750 a 32, 760 b 23; development of young at birth 774 b 15; tawny in colour 785 b 18; courage of

805 b 25, 806 b 9, 812 a 16, b 6; exhibits the male type 809 b 15-36; never tame 895 b 26

Lion-killer, 845 a 28-34

Lipara, Island of, 367 a 7, 395 b 21, 832 b 31-33; fire in 833 a 13, 16; tomb of 838 b 30-839 a 11

Lips, 492 b 25; purpose of 659 b 28-660 a 13; as a physiognomic sign 808 a 33, 811 a 19-28; lip hangs down when one is angry 948 b 4; tickling on 965 a 19-22

Lips (S.W. wind), 363 b 18, 364 a 16, b 3, 19, 24, 394 b 27, 945 a 23; rain comes if Lips blows at time of equinox 942 b 25-943 a 4; reason for its name 973 b 12

Liquid ($\dot{v}\gamma\rho\acute{o}v$), 388 a 27-b 14, 780 b 11, 784 b 11; a body adaptable to every shape 130 b 36; the most combinable of all bodies 328 b 3; is aerated 755 a 19; contained in a fine membrane 758 b 4; more plastic than water but not more material 761 b 1. Cf. Moisture

Lisping, 801 b 7, 902 b 22-29, 903 b 23-26. Cf. Speech, Voice

Literary study, problems connected with 916 b 1-917 b 17

LITTLE ILIAD, 1459 b 2, 5

Liver, 496 b 16, 30, 507 a 12-18, 586 b 18, 677 a 20; has no air-duct 484 a 12; found in all blooded animals 506 a 12; why not the primary organ of sensation 666 a 25-32; nature and function of 669 b 13-670 b 33, 673 b 18-32. Cf. Bile, Gall-bladder

Lizard, 488 a 23, 503 b 5; legs of 489 b 22, 498 a 14, 713 a 17, b 19; scales of 504 a 28; spleen of 506 a 20; stomach and intestines of 508 a 5; testicles of 509 b 7, 716 b 25; womb of 510 b 35; generation of 558 a 15; diet of 594 a 4-24; hibernation of 599 a 31; sloughing of 600 b 23, 835 a 28, 29; in Arabia 606 b 7; habits of 609 b 20, 831 b 6; tongue of 660 b 7, 691 a 5; lung of 669 a 29; eggs of 732 b 4; star-lizard 845 b 5-7

Loaves, whiter when cold 927 a 27-34; salt makes loaves weigh less 927 a 35-b 5; do not cohere when cold 927 b

6-14; twice-baked loaves 928 a 11-32. Cf. Bread

Lobe of ear, 492 a 15

Lobster, astacus, 490 b 11, 525 a 32, 526 a 12-b 18; copulation of 541 b 19-25; habitat of 549 b 14; sloughing of 601 a 10; when edible 607 b 3; claws of 684 a 33

Locomotion ($\phi o\rho\acute{a}$), 122 a 23, b 27, 211 a 14, 219 b 29, 226 a 33, 436 b 18, 1174 a 30; the primary motion 208 a 32, 243 a 12, 260 a 20-261 a 27; each element has a natural locomotion 214 b 14; always involves space 238 b 23; not always between contraries 241 b 2; four kinds of: (1) pulling, (2) pushing, (3) carrying, (4) twirling 243 a 16-245 a 18; only motion possible for eternal beings 260 b 30; the only continuous motion 261 a 28-b 26; circular motion is the primary locomotion 265 a 13-266 a 9; and the problem of projectiles 266 b 27-267 a 21; all natural bodies and magnitudes capable of 268 b 15; belongs only to isolated bodies 310 b 33; a species of movement 406 a 12; faculty of the soul 414 a 30, 415 a 14-416 b 31; not found in all living things 415 b 23; defined as movement in place 704 a 4; originals are thrusts and pulls 704 b 22 (Cf. 793 a 22); belongs only to animals that make their change of place by means of two or four points in their structure 707 a 19

Locri, Locrians, 847 b 7, 1266 b 19, 1395 a 1; received laws from Zaleucus 1274 a 23; revolution at 1307 a 38

Locust, attelabus, 550 b 34; generation of 556 a 8-13, 721 a 5; habits of 612 a 33; legs of 683 a 34; copulation of 721 a 24; voice of 804 a 22; the scorpion-fighter 844 b 24-31

Logic ($\dot{a}\nu\alpha\lambda\upsilon\tau\iota\kappa\acute{o}\nu$), 1005 b 3, 1359 b 10

Loins, 493 b 13; as a physiognomic sign 807 b 10, 24

'Long ago,' defined 222 b 14

Longevity, 464 b 19-467 b 9; cause of 777 b 6; those who have spongy teeth are not long-lived 896 a 30-36, 963 b 18-22; those who have cut across hand are long-lived 896 a 38-b 4, 964

94

a 33-38; effect of climate on 909 b 1-8, 25-36

Longing, 1105 b 22

Loquacity, 1277 b 22; physiognomic signs of 806 b 19-21, 808 b 8, 810 a 31, b 16

Loss, 1221 a 4, 23

Lot, used in democracies 1273 a 18, 1274 a 4, 1294 b 7, 1317 b 21, 1318 a 2, 1424 a 13; modes of 1300 a 19-b 4

Louse-disease, 557 a 2

Love (ἔρως, ἀγαπᾶν, φιλία, φιλότης), 1116 a 13, 1171 b 30, 1237 a 22-b 7, 1238 b 26-39; more dependent on friendship than on sexual intercourse 68 b 3; should parents be loved not a proper dialectical question 105 a 3-7; ambiguous term 106 b 2; not defined as desire for intercourse 146 a 10, 152 b 8; objects of: (1) good, (2) pleasant, (3) useful 1155 b 17-1156 a 5, 1235 b 13-1236 a 15; a feeling 1157 b 28-37; an excess of feeling 1158 a 11; loving is more like friendship than being loved 1159 a 13-b 23, 1239 a 31-b 2; an excess of friendship 1171 a 11; Parmenides on 984 b 24, 988 a 33; distinction between the lovable and what is to be loved 1208 b 36-1209 a 3; better to love than to be loved 1210 b 3-13; warlike races approve of male loves 1269 b 26; 'Caunian love' 1402 b 2

Love and Strife (Empedocles), 250 a 27, 252 a 7, 26, 265 b 20, 295 a 30, 300 b 29, 301 a 16, 314 a 17, 315 a 7, 17, 333 b 12-334 a 9, 985 a 1-9, 22-30, 988 a 33, 994 a 7, 996 a 8, 1000 b 12, 1004 b 33, 1072 a 6

Love-potion, philtre, 1188 b 32-38, 1225 b 4

Low spirits, physiognomic signs of 808 a 8-11

Lucanians, 838 a 12

Lucerne. See Median grass

Luck. See Chance

Lumbering, 1258 b 31

Lungs, 470 b 12, 481 a 30, b 13, 496 b 1-10, 734 a 18, 801 a 13; designed for refrigeration 475 b 18, 476 a 8, 732 b 33-733 a 4; nature and function of 478 a 11-14, 668 b 33-669 b 25; origin

of innate breath 482 a 34; found in all blooded animals 506 a 11; relation to sound 800 a 31-b 19, 803 a 13, 804 b 13-26

Lunules, 69 a 33

Lusi, mice of 842 b 8

Luxuriousness, 1221 a 9, 29

Lyceum, 219 b 21, 1385 a 28

Lycia, 548 b 19, 606 a 16; burning ground of 842 b 26; Lycians wear their hair long 1348 a 28

Lycoleon, 1411 b 6

Lycophron, the Sophist, 174 b 33, 1405 b 35, 1406 a 8, 1410 a 17; omits 'is' for fear of making the one to be many 185 b 31; knowledge is a communion of knowing with the soul 1045 b 10; his conception of law 1280 b 11

Lycormas River, lance-herb of the 847 a 1

Lyctians, 1271 b 27

Lycurgas, 1270 a 2, 1274 a 29, 1398 b 18; author of the Spartan constitution 1271 b 25, 1273 b 34; a member of the middle class 1296 a 20

Lydia, 617 b 19; honey of 831 b 27-29; fire in 833 a 20; mines in 834 a 23-31

Lydian harp, 1341 a 40

Lydian mode, best suited to children 1342 b 30. Cf. Modes of Music

Lydian War, 1290 b 17

Lye, 359 b 7, 378 a 25, 791 a 8, 794 a 22, 863 b 17, 887 b 7, 966 b 28; makes water bitter 357 b 1; contains heat potentially 358 b 9; thickened by cold 384 a 13, 389 a 12, 27

Lygdamis, tyrant of Naxos, 1305 a 40; his scheme for raising money 1346 b 7-12

Lymph, 489 a 23, 511 b 3, 515 b 29, 891 a 18

Lynceus of Theodectes, 1452 a 28, 1455 b 29

Lyncus, 359 b 17

Lynkeus, 328 a 15

Lynx, toes of 499 b 24; genitals of 500 b 15, 16; copulation of 539 b 23; urination of 689 a 34; urine of 835 b 30

Lyra. See Gurnard

Lyre, 801 b 18, 1332 a 27, 1341 a 41; as accompaniment to song 918 a 22-28,

922 a 1-20, b 16; Phoenician lyre 918 b 8; 'chordless lyre' 1413 a 1; lyre-playing 1447 a 15, 25, 1448 a 9

Lyrnatians, 973 a 8

Lysander, 97 b 21, 176 b 5, 953 a 19, 1301 b 16, 1306 b 33

Lysias, quoted 1399 b 16, 1420 a 8

Lysithidas, 1422 b 22

M

Macalla, 840 a 18

Macedonia, 596 a 3, 833 b 19, 842 b 18, 954 b 32, 1310 b 40, 1324 b 16, 1350 a 16, 1351 b 36; mines in 833 a 29-31; pigs in 835 a 34

Mackerel, spawning of 543 a 2, 571 a 12; diet of 591 b 17; migration of 597 a 22, 599 a 1, 610 b 7

Madness, 10 a 1, 831 b 25, 846 b 27, 957 a 2, 1149 a 12, 1390 b 27, 1455 b 14; insane man of Abydos 832 b 18-22; insane man of Tarentum 832 b 23-26; of Demaratus 847 b 7-10; due to black bile 860 b 23; poet must have a touch of madness 1455 a 33. Cf. Mania

Maeander River, 1289 b 40; stone of 846 b 26-28

Maedica, 630 a 19, 830 a 6, 841 a 29; bison of 500 a 1

Maemacterion, 566 a 19, 578 b 13, 597 a 24

Maenis, sprat, 569 b 28, 607 b 22; generation of 570 b 29; when edible 607 b 9; habits of 610 b 4

Maeotis, Lake of, 350 a 25, 353 a 1, 354 a 14, 393 a 33, b 7; wolves of 620 b 6

Magadizing, 919 a 1, 921 a 13, 29

Mageric school, 1046 b 28

Maggots, 614 b 2; found inside the head of deer 506 a 27

Magi, 1091 b 11

Magistrates, oligarchical mode of appointing 1266 a 10-19, 1298 a 34-b 5; elected by wealth in oligarchy 1266 a 13, 1273 a 25, 1299 b 25; taken from those that bear arms 1268 a 22, 1297 b 13; elected by merit in aristocracy 1273 a 26, 1299 b 24; elected by lot in democracy 1274 a 4, 1317 b 21, 1318 a 2; in democracy 1298 a 15-33, 1299 b 26-1300 a 5, 1317 b 17-1318 a 10, 1424 a 13-21; in oligarchy 1298 a 34-b 4, 1299 b 25-38, 1320 b 7-16, 1321 a 26-b 1, 1424 b 1; in aristocracy 1298 b 6, 1300 a 5, 1323 a 8; in polity 1298 b 39; elected from the free in democracy 1299 b 26

Magistrates, types of, Accountants 1322 b 11; Archons 1287 a 7, 1301 b 25, 1322 b 29, 1449 b 2; Auditors 1322 b 11, 26; Corn Measurers 1299 a 23; Council of One Hundred 1273 a 15; Counsellors 1299 b 38, 1322 b 17, 1323 a 8; Directors of Education 1336 a 30, 40; Directors of Gymnastics 1323 a 1; Eleven at Athens 1322 a 20; in charge of fountains 1321 b 26; Four Hundred at Athens 1304 b 12, 1305 b 26, 1419 a 28; Guardians of Children 1299 b 19, 1300 a 4, 1322 b 39; Guardians of Citizens 1305 b 29; Guardians of Laws 1287 a 21, 1298 b 28, 1322 b 39, 1323 a 8; Guardians of Shrines 1322 b 25; Guardians of Women 1299 b 19, 1300 a 4, 1322 b 38; Inspectors of the Woods 1321 b 29, 1331 b 15; Magistracy of the One Hundred Four at Carthage 1272 b 35; Magistracy of the Five 1273 a 12; Prytanis at Miletus 1305 a 17, 1322 b 29; Phylarchs at Epidamnus 1301 b 22; Presidents 1321 b 39; Receivers 1321 b 34; Recorders 1321 b 39, 1331 b 6; Revenue Officers 1300 b 9; Scrutineers 1322 b 11; Superintendents of Dionysiac contests 1323 a 1; Superintendents of Public Worship 1322 b 24; Superintendents of Walls 1321 b 26, 1322 a 36; Treasurers 1321 b 34; Treasurers of Sacred Revenue 1322 b 25; Thirty at Athens 1305 b 26, 1400 a 18, 33; Wardens of the Agora 1299 b 17, 1300 b 12, 1322 a 14, b 33, 1331 b 9; Wardens of the City 1321 b 23, 1322 a 13, 1331 b 10; Wardens of the Country 1321 b 29, 1322 b 33, 1331 b 15; Wardens of the Harbour 1321 b 26, 1322 b 23

Magnanimity, pride, greatness of soul, greatness of spirit (μεγαλοψυχία,

96

μεγαλόψυχος), 1107 b 22, 1123 a 33-
1125 a 35, 1183 a 1, 1192 a 21-36, 1221
a 10, 1231 a 22, 1232 a 18-1233 a 30, b
24-38, 1249 b 29, 1250 a 14, b 34-42,
1362 b 13, 1366 b 1, 17; physiognomic
signs of 811 a 15, 20, 32, 37, b 27, 34,
813 a 14; a sort of crown of the virtues 1124 a 1

Magnes, 1448 a 33

Magnesia, 1269 b 7; sheep of 896 a 26;
hot waters at 937 b 7-21; cavalry of
1289 b 39

Magnet, 267 a 2

Magnification. *See* Increase

Magnificence, magnificent, 1107 b 24,
1122 a 19-1123 a 32, 1125 b 3, 1192 a
37-b 17, 1221 a 11, 1233 a 31-b 15,
1362 b 13, 1366 b 1, 18, 1414 a 19

Magnitude, atomic magnitudes 187 a 3,
188 a 12; mathematical magnitudes
203 b 25, 445 b 15; infinite by division
206 a 16, 267 b 21, 268 a 28; continuous 219 a 11, 233 a 11, 239 a 21; complete in three directions 268 a 9;
straight and circular lines are the two
simple magnitudes 268 b 19; minimum magnitude impossible 271 b 10;
no indivisible magnitudes 315 a 26-
317 a 13, 440 a 27, 445 b 9, 448 b 14,
449 a 20; Zeno's proof of existence of
simple magnitudes 968 a 18-21; composition of points constitutes no magnitude 971 a 21-25

Magydum, 973 a 6

Maia. *See* Granny-crab

Major term, 99 a 4, 28; defined 26 a 22,
b 37, 28 a 13; wider than middle term
77 a 19. Cf. Middle term

Malacostraca. *See* Crustacea

Male, has more warmth than female
466 b 16, 648 a 32, 748 b 32; male animals generally the longer-lived 467 a
31-34, 538 a 22-32, 896 a 34; teeth of
501 b 20-23, 538 b 15-24, 963 b 20; oc-
casionally produces milk 522 a 12;
larger than female 538 a 23, 727 a 19,
806 b 33, 891 b 21-24, 894 b 27; upper
parts of male stronger than those in
female 538 b 2-6; voice of female is
sharper-toned than the male 538 b 12,
544 b 33; often only male has organs
of defense and offense 538 b 15-24;

temperamental differences of male
and female 608 a 22-b 25, 661 b 33,
809 a 26-810 a 13, 814 a 9; superior to
female 648 a 12, 814 a 9, 951 a 12,
1254 b 14; has more sutures in skull
than female 653 b 1, 896 a 35; bones
of male harder than those of female
655 a 13; jejunum in males and females 676 a 4; contains the efficient
cause of generation 716 a 7, 729 a 10,
34-730 b 32, 738 b 20-27, 740 b 25,
763 b 30, 764 b 12; defined as animal
that generates in another 716 a 14,
817 a 4; differences of blood-vessels in
male and female 727 a 16; not all
males have generative secretion 738
b 19; necessary in generation 741 a 6-
b 24, 1252 a 27; imparts the sensitive
soul 741 b 5; perfects eggs both in
birds and fish 757 a 32; nutritive faculty of soul found in both male and
female 757 b 17; principle of 762 b 11,
766 a 22-b 26; defined as that which
can concoct blood into semen 765 b
10; passes urine without effort 892 b
36-893 a 2; male and female are contrary yet not different in species 1058
a 29-b 26; a common life is natural to
male and female 1162 a 17, 1252 a
28, 1343 b 8-1344 a 7; more fitted to
rule than the female 1254 b 14, 1259
b 2. Cf. Female, Sex

Malea, Cape, 548 b 26

Malians, chose magistrates from those
in military service 1297 b 14-16

Malice, 1192 b 18, 27

Malignity, 1251 b 2

Malleable, 378 a 27, 385 a 16, b 10, 386
b 18-25

Mallow, 819 b 16

Mallus, 973 a 2, 12

Mammae, 493 a 12, 582 a 5-15, 711 b 31,
725 b 3, 776 b 20; of animals 500 a 14-
32; found only in viviparous animals
504 b 19, 692 a 11; of vivipara 688 a
19-b 34

Man (ἄνθρωπος), by nature a civilized
animal 128 b 17, 132 a 8; defined as
an animal capable of acquiring
knowledge 130 b 8, 132 a 20, 133 a
21, 134 a 15, 140 a 36; has a tripartite
soul 133 a 30; defined as an animal

that walks on two feet 133 b 8, 136 b 20, 140 b 33; begotten by 193 b 12, 198 a 26, 202 a 11, 1070 a 28; begotten by man and by the sun 194 b 14; only animal capable of deliberation 433 a 12, 488 b 24, 641 b 8, 1332 b 5, 1421 a 11; both gregarious and solitary 488 a 7, 9; a tame animal 488 a 27; species is simple in 490 b 17; anatomy of 491 a 20-497 b 1; only animal unable to move ears 492 a 31; sense of taste is highly refined in 494 b 18, 660 a 20; inner parts largely unknown 494 b 23; has largest brain in proportion to his size 494 b 28, 653 a 29, 658 b 8, 744 a 28; only animal that can learn to use both hands equally 497 b 32, 706 a 20; hair of 498 b 16, 893 a 17-b 9; genitals of 500 a 33, 509 b 15, 716 b 30; growth of 500 b 26-34; teeth of 501 b 2, 661 b 7-15; has a small mouth 502 a 7; a genus 505 b 28; position of heart in 507 a 1, 665 b 21, 666 b 7; stomach of 507 b 17, 21, 674 a 26; womb of 510 b 17; skull of 516 a 18, 653 b 1; nails of 517 a 33, 687 b 22-24; has most delicate skin of all animals 517 b 27, 781 b 22; has finest and purest blood 521 a 3; emits more semen than any other animal in relation to size 523 a 15, 728 b 15, 776 b 26, 877 a 18; indications of maturity in 544 b 22-27; age of maturity of 545 b 27; reproduction of 581 a 9-588 a 12, 737 b 26-739 b 33, 892 b 2; development of voice of 581 a 17-b 11, 905 a 31-34; generated from man 640 a 26, 735 a 22; differences between men and women 648 a 30-32, 775 a 5-b 24; only animal that stands erect 653 a 32, 656 a 13, 662 b 22, 669 b 6, 686 a 28, 689 b 12, 690 a 29, 710 b 11; has most varied heterogeneous parts of all animals 656 a 6; partakes of the divine 656 a 8, 686 a 29; in man the natural parts hold the natural position 656 a 13; head of man has no flesh 656 a 14, b 8-13; only hairy animal that has eyelashes on both lids 658 a 15; front of body more hairy than back 658 a 17, 896 b 29-39; why man has more hair on

head than any other animal 658 b 2-7; lips of man serve to protect teeth and aid in speech 659 b 32-660 a 10; has softest flesh of all animals 660 a 13; has most delicate sense of touch 660 a 13; tongue of man is softest, widest, and freest of all animals 660 a 18; face of 662 b 20; only animal that looks directly in front 662 b 23; only heart of man subject to palpitation 669 a 19; kidneys of 671 b 7; the only animal that laughs 673 a 8, 28; spleen of 674 a 3; some have gall-bladder, some do not 676 b 31; trunk of 686 b 5-21; most intelligent of animals 686 b 24, 687 a 7, 19, 744 a 30; hands of 687 a 5-b 21, 690 a 33; refutation of those who think man defenseless 687 a 23-b 7; fingers of 687 b 7-21; thumb of 687 b 12-18; breast of man broad, of quadrupeds narrow 688 a 13-18; mammae of 688 a 20-28; buttocks of 689 b 6, 15-690 a 3; legs of 689 b 8, 21, 710 b 11, 711 b 7-34, 895 a 20-30; toes of 690 a 8; has largest foot of all animals in proportion to size of body 690 a 28; the most natural animal 706 a 19, b 10; walking of 707 b 18, 709 b 26; form of man does not permit of wings 711 a 4; must hold breath before emitting semen 718 a 4; viviparous externally and internally 718 b 30; man is more languid after sexual intercourse than any other animal 725 b 18, 877 a 16-22, 879 a 4-10; most naked of animals 745 b 17; has least amount of earthy residue of all animals 745 b 18; origin of 762 b 28-763 a 23; 'earth-born' men 762 b 30, 1269 a 7, 1454 b 23; monstrosities in 770 b 35, 898 a 10; only animal in which the period of gestation is irregular 772 b 7; colour of eye of 779 a 34; only animal in which hair turns grey 780 b 5, 891 b 1, 898 a 31-37 (Cf. 797 a 35); man's sense-perception at a distance is poor, but in respect of quality it is keen 781 b 17; cause of baldness in men 783 b 9-784 a 22; physiognomic signs in 810 a 14-814 b 9; naturally hotter and moister than other animals 877 a 20;

thick-haired men are lustful 880 a 35-b 7, 893 b 10-16; only animal in which blood flows from nostrils 891 a 13-18; only animal that has white leprosy 891 a 35, 894 a 38-b 5; has smaller distance between eyes in proportion to size than any other animal 892 b 4-14, 960 a 14; only animal that emits semen during sleep 892 b 15-18; sneezes more than other animals 892 b 22-32, 897 a 1-b 13, 962 b 8-18; has no mane 893 b 17-19; utters many voices 895 a 5, 6; has many forms of speech 895 a 7-14; only animal that suffers from gall-stones 895 a 36-b 11; only animal apt to hesitate in speech 895 b 15-19, 905 a 20-23; has large navel 896 a 12-19; porous teeth a sign of short life 896 a 30-36; signs of length of life 896 a 30-b 4; squints more than any other animal 896 b 5, 6; more liable to suffer from epilepsy than any other animal 896 b 6, 960 a 10, 17; affected more by smoke than any other animal 896 b 8, 9; suffers more from running at the nose than any other animal 897 a 2; takes more moist than dry nourishment 897 b 19-22; excrement of 897 b 34-898 a 3; has hard frame 898 a 4-8; head of man is more hairy than rest of body 898 a 20-30; only animal that has speech 899 a 2, 1253 a 9; most unjust of all animals 950 b 33-35; has most practical wisdom of all animals 955 b 4-8; why should man be obeyed more than any other animal 956 a 12-14; usually lives by intelligence 956 b 33-35; more liable to distortion of vision than any other animal 960 a 8-20; lives by art and reasoning as well as by appearances and memories 980 b 25; compound of soul and body taken universally 1037 a 5; by nature a political animal 1097 b 11, 1162 a 17, 1169 b 18, 1242 a 22-27, 1245 a 11-27, 1253 a 2, 30, 1278 b 20; function of 1097 b 25-1098 a 20; a moving principle 1113 b 17; not the best thing in the world 1141 a 22, b 1; naturally inclined to form couples 1162 a 17, 1252 a 28, 1343 b 8-1344 a 7; only ani-mal that possesses happiness 1178 b 24, 1421 a 13; man alone originates actions 1222 b 18-20; only animal that has power of choice 1226 b 22; has natural desire to propagate self 1252 a 29; only animal that has sense of good and evil 1253 a 15; can be best or worst of animals 1253 a 32-36; most men tend to be bad 1263 b 22, 1382 b 4; time of generation 1335 a 9; rules for copulation in man 1344 a 13; characters of young men, middle-aged men, and elderly men 1388 b 31-1390 b 11; the most imitative animal 1448 b 8

Mandragora, 456 b 31

Mandrobulus, 174 b 27

Mane, 830 a 11; of lion 809 b 24; why man has no 893 b 17-19

Mania, 808 b 22-27; physiognomic signs of 812 a 21. Cf. Madness

Mantias, the orator, 1398 b 2

Mantinea, battle of 1304 a 26; democracy at 1318 b 25

Mantle of Alcimenes, 838 a 15-27

Many, 1075 a 33, 1087 b 16; Melissus' view of 974 a 18-b 7; meanings of 1017 a 4-6; opposition of the one and the many 1054 a 20-29, 1056 b 3-1057 a 17

Many questions, Fallacy of, 169 a 6-18, b 14-17, 175 b 40, one of the seven fallacious refutations independent of language 166 b 28; examples of 167 b 38-168 a 16; solution of 181 a 36-b 24

Maracus the Syracusan, 954 a 38

Marathon, 569 b 13, 1396 a 13

Marble, Parian marble 844 a 15

Mare, 611 a 11; milk of 522 a 28; wantonness of 572 a 8; deficient in catamenia 748 a 21; women and mares only animals that admit male during gestation 773 b 27; uterus of women and mares is large 773 b 28. Cf. Horse

Margites of Homer, 1141 a 14, 1448 b 30, 39

Maricus, 833 a 27

Marieus, 833 a 28. Cf. Fire-stone

Marinus, gestation of 570 a 31; blindness in 602 a 1

Marjoram, 818 b 38, 820 a 35, 831 a 27, 925 a 29, 39; medicinal qualities of 612 a 24-34; sweetens wine 926 b 32-927 a 2

Marriage, often causes quarrels which bring about revolutions 1303 b 39-1304 a 17, 1306 a 33-39; regulations in ideal state 1334 b 28-1336 a 2; is natural 1343 b 8-1344 a 7; rules for 1344 a 8-22; of slaves 1344 b 18

Marrow, 140 a 5, 487 a 3, 516 b 8, 521 b 4-16, 651 b 20-652 a 23; hot in natural state 389 b 9, 652 a 28; regarded by some as originator of motion 484 b 16; homogeneous 647 b 13; some think brain composed of 652 a 25

Mars, eclipsed by moon 292 a 5

Marseus. *See* Apeliotes

Marsh, 909 a 35; 'bellowings' of 937 b 37-938 a 16

Marsh-fishes, spawning of 568 a 11

Marsus, 973 a 20

Marten, polecat, 831 b 1-4; genitals of 500 b 24; habits of 612 b 10-17; heart of 667 a 21

Martichoras, 501 a 25-b 1

Marvelous, the, 1452 a 4, 1460 a 12-18; required in tragedy 1460 a 12

Mask, 1449 a 36, b 4; tragic masks 958 a 17

Massalia, 837 a 29; revolution at 1305 b 5; oligarchy at 1321 a 31

Massilian Lake, 837 b 8-15

Master, 1252 a 8, 10, 1259 a 37; the rule of 1160 b 29, 1161 b 1-10, 1253 b 18-22, 1255 b 16-40, 1260 a 9, 40, 1278 b 30-36; and slave have same interest 1252 a 34, 1278 b 34; slave is a part of the master 1255 b 11; treatment of slaves 1269 b 9, 1344 a 23-b 22; should superintend everything personally 1344 b 35-1345 a 10; should rise early and retire late 1345 a 11-17. Cf. Slavery, Slaves

Mathematics, 431 b 16, 868 b 4, 869 b 9, 968 b 5, 1061 a 29-b 32, 1142 a 18, 1151 a 17, 1222 b 24; instruction in mathematics depends on previous knowledge 71 a 3; formal fallacy not common in mathematics 77 b 27; takes definitions, not accidents for its premisses 78 a 12; is concerned with

forms 79 a 8, 81 b 4; mathematician compared with the physicist 193 b 22-194 b 15; its subject matter 193 b 23; necessity in 200 a 15-24; does not need the infinite 207 b 29; objects of 208 b 23, 989 b 32, 1028 b 20, 1036 a 4, 1083 a 23, 1090 b 26, 1094 b 26, 1112 b 22; has no minimum 271 b 10; and astronomy 291 b 9, 297 a 4, 298 a 16; deals with abstract objects 299 a 16; its principles are finite 302 b 31; the most accurate science 306 a 28; no mathematical entity is moved 698 a 26; demonstrates how phenomena come to pass 847 a 28; problems connected with mathematical theory 910 b 11-913 a 16; why founded in Egypt 981 b 23; Pythagoreans were first to take up mathematics 985 b 24; identified with philosophy by some 992 a 33, 1004 a 8; mathematical accuracy not always required 995 a 15; are mathematical objects substances? 996 a 13-17, 1001 b 26-1002 b 32, 1042 a 11, 1059 b 12, 1060 a 36-b 19, 1069 a 36, 1076 a 20; a theoretical science 1026 a 6-33, 1064 a 31, b 2; mathematical objects cannot exist as distinct substances 1076 a 17-1078 b 5; mathematical discourses depict no character 1417 a 18. Cf. Arithmetic, Geometry, Number, Science

Matter (ὕλη), 200 a 14, b 8, 210 a 20, 213 a 6, 217 a 22, 319 a 29-b 4, 320 b 14-25, 332 a 35, 412 b 8, 983 b 7-984 a 17, 1015 a 7, 1017 a 5, 1058 b 6; of the nature of a 'this' 190 b 23, 191 a 10; as substratum 192 a 32, 983 a 30, 988 a 12, 992 b 1, 1022 a 18, 1024 b 8, 1042 a 26, b 9, 1070 a 11; art requires knowledge of both form and matter 194 a 22-27; a relative term 194 b 8; has no form 207 a 22-36; place is neither matter nor form 209 a 2-210 a 13, 212 a 1; not separable from the thing 214 a 13; form and matter as proof that there is only one heaven 277 b 26-278 b 9; does not have the power to act 324 b 18, 335 b 30; prime matter (πρώτη ὕλη), 328 b 26-329 a 5, 24-35, 390 a 5, 1049 a 25; ratio of active powers to 378 b 33; other elements are matter relatively to fire 379 a 16; passive qualities are matter of a thing 380 a 8; earth and water are the matter of all bodies 382 a 7; dry and moist are matter 389 a 30; 'matter is potentiality' 412 a 10, 414 a 16; involves contrariety 465 b 11, 30; cannot easily be brought under control 778 a 8; as a principle 983 b 7, 986 a 17; as substance 1028 b 33-1029 b 12, 1042 a 26, 1043 a 33-b 8, 1049 a 36, 1077 a 35; defined 1029 a 20; change implies matter 1032 a 15-24, 1042 a 34, 1069 b 3-34; only combination of form and matter come to be 1033 a 24-1034 a 8; unknowable in itself 1036 a 9; all sensible substances have matter 1042 a 26; only things subject to generation and change have matter 1044 b 21-28; relations to its contrary states 1044 b 29-1045 a 5; proximate matter same as form 1045 b 18; things that have no matter are unities 1045 b 23; neither matter nor form comes to be 1069 b 35-1070 a 3; all contraries have matter 1075 b 22, 1087 b 1

Mausolus, tyrant of Caria, 1348 a 18; his methods of raising money 1348 a 5-17

Maxims, 176 b 19, 1428 a 20, 1430 a 40-b 29, 1431 a 36-43, b 26, 1432 b 26, 1433 a 25, 1434 a 36, 1439 a 4, 19, 35, 1440 a 23, 1441 a 19, 39, 1442 b 38, 1443 a 2; defined 1394 a 22-b 7, 1430 a 40; four kinds of 1394 b 8-25; uses of 1394 b 26-1395 a 34; advantages of 1395 b 1-18; as arguments 1418 a 17-21, b 34-38. Cf. Proverbs

Mead, 872 b 26, 874 b 11

Mean (μεσότης), 847 b 28, 1103 b 27-1104 b 3, 1227 a 37, 1239 b 30, 1309 b 18; true and rational position lies in the mean 652 b 19; not always a mean 1055 b 23; moral virtue defined as a disposition to choose the mean 1105 b 19-1108 b 10, 1220 b 21-1221 b 3; not every act or passion admits of 1107 a 7-26, 1221 b 18-26; has no excess nor deficiency 1107 a 26; sometimes more opposed to one extreme than to the other 1109 a 1-19, 1222 a

23-b 4, 1234 b 6-14; hard to attain, grasped by perception 1109 a 20-b 26; virtue is a mean 1133 b 33, 1295 a 37; opposition between mean and extremes 1186 b 4-33; hard to determine 1186 b 33-1187 a 4; a principle upon which education ought to be built 1342 b 34; in style of oratory 1414 a 18-25; in narration 1416 b 30-1417 a 2

Meaning, not to have one meaning is to have no meaning 1006 b 8

Meanness. See Illiberality

Means, end more desirable than means 116 b 23; wish relates to the end, choice to the means 1111 b 27, 1113 b 3; deliberate about means, not about end 1112 b 12, 34; practical wisdom determines the end, virtue the means 1145 a 5; end is the limit of the means 1256 b 35, 1257 b 27; means and end may agree or disagree 1331 b 29

Measles, in pigs 603 b 17

Measure, 1087 b 33-1088 a 14; man as measure of things (Protagoras) 1009 a 6-14, 1053 a 35, 1062 b 13, 1063 a 4; the one as measure 1052 b 1-1053 b 8; always homogeneous with thing measured 1053 a 24

Mechanics, 76 a 24, 78 b 39, the problems of 847 a 20-29

Mecon, 529 a 10, 30, 531 a 17, 547 a 16, 587 a 31, 679 b 11, 680 a 20

Medea, 839 b 19, 1453 b 28

MEDEA of Carcinus, 1400 b 10

MEDEA of Euripides, 1454 b 2, 1461 b 21

Medes, 1284 b 2; the Median kings not taught music 1339 a 35

Media, 552 b 9, 832 a 26; fire in 833 a 1-6

Median grass, lucerne, 627 b 17; quenches milk 522 b 26

Mediannus tree, bark of 820 a 19

Medicine (ἰατρική), 77 a 41, 79 a 14, 116 a 18, 143 a 2-5, 149 b 6-20, 1094 a 8, 1102 a 20, 1104 a 9, 1141 a 32, 1143 a 2, 1180 b 27, 1218 b 2, 1258 a 28; defined as the science of producing health and dieting 110 b 19; not well defined as knowledge of what makes for health in animals and men 141 a

18; medicinal plants 821 b 34, 826 b 2; problems connected with 859 a 1-866 b 6; no limit to its end 1257 b 25; aims at health 1258 a 12; changes in 1268 b 36

Medicine (φάρμακα), a good thing to take only when ill 115 b 27; not given immediately after exercise 883 b 33-36

Mediterranean Sea, 354 a 12

Medium, smelling, hearing, and seeing operate through external medium 436 b 18

Medius, 618 b 14

Megacles, assassin of the Penthilidae 1311 b 27

Megalopolis, burning ground of 842 b 26

Megara, Megarians, 1008 b 14, 1123 a 24, 1236 a 37, 1242 b 25, 1280 b 13, 1300 a 17, 1357 b 33, 1448 a 32; revolution at 1302 b 31, 1304 b 35-39, 1305 a 24

Megaric school, 1046 b 28

Megarid, 973 b 19

Melancholic, atrabilious, 878 b 38, 916 b 6, 917 a 22, 1203 b 2; effect of wine upon 873 a 32; affected by sleeplessness 874 b 18, 957 a 33; particularly inclined for sexual intercourse 880 a 30-34; hesitate in their speech 903 b 19-26; characteristics of 953 a 10-955 a 40

Melancraera, 838 a 11

Melanippe, 1454 a 31

Melanippides, 1409 b 27

Melanopus, 1374 b 27

Melanurus, diet of 591 a 15

Meleagar, 1365 a 12, 1379 b 15, 1453 a 21

MELEAGER of Antiphon, 1379 b 15, 1399 b 25

Meletus, 1419 a 8

Melis, disease of asses 605 a 16-22

Melissus, 214 a 28, 974 a 1-b 8, 979 b 22, 986 b 20, 27; Being is one 104 b 22; the universe is eternal 167 b 14, 168 b 35-40, 181 a 28; first principle of nature is a motionless one 184 b 17; criticism of 185 a 9, 974 b 9-977 a 11; refutation of Parmenides' and Melissus' conception of the oneness of Being 185 a 20-187 a 10; Being is infi-

nite 185 a 33, b 18; whole as infinite 207 a 16; the All is immovable 213 b 12; denial of generation 298 b 17; his view of the void 976 b 12-18

Melody, 1447 b 25, 1449 b 32, 35, 1450 a 14, b 16

Melon, cultivation of 926 b 4-15

Melos, Island of, 831 b 20, 833 b 4, 5

Melotontha, body and wings of 682 b 12

Melting, 383 a 26-b 17, 385 a 27-b 1, 12-26, 388 b 32-389 a 21

Membrane, 511 b 8, 519 a 30-b 25, 739 b 27; encloses the viscera 673 b 3-12; forms on compounds of solid and fluid when cooling 677 b 23, 678 a 4, 682 b 19; around brain 744 a 11; around embryo 746 a 18; in egg 752 b 10, 753 b 22, 758 b 4

Memnon, his schemes for raising money 1351 b 1-18

Memory (μνήμη), 163 b 30, 449 b 8-453 b 11, 456 a 27, 702 a 5, 1185 b 6, 1250 a 35; developed from sense perception 99 b 36, 100 a 3-5, 980 a 29; applies only to the past 111 b 30, 449 b 15; not defined as the abiding of knowledge 125 b 7; an activity, never a state 125 b 18; not same as recollection 449 b 3-8, 453 a 5-14; defined 449 b 25; organ of 450 a 14, 451 a 16; possessed by some animals 450 a 15, 453 a 8, 488 b 25; why old and young have poor memories 450 a 26-b 12, 453 b 6; physiognomic signs of a good memory 808 b 9; animals that have memory are more intelligent 980 b 21; produces experience in man 980 b 28; the blind have better memories 1248 b 2; old age lives by memory 1390 a 6

Memphis, 352 a 1, 945 a 22

Mende, methods of raising money at 1350 a 6-15

Menelaus, 1454 a 29, 1461 b 21

MENEXENUS of Plato, referred to 1367 b 8, 1415 b 31

MENO of Plato, 67 a 22, 71 a 29, 1260 a 22, 27

Menstruation, catamenia, 572 b 28-573 a 26, 582 a 33-583 a 13, 585 b 2, 727 a 2-729 a 33, 738 a 9-739 b 33, 891 a 31, 895 a 34, 896 a 29; most copious in women 521 a 27, 727 a 22, 728 b 14; Parmenides regards menstruation as a sign that women are hotter than men 648 a 30; the flow is a kind of fluid and residual matter 689 a 10; defined as semen in need of working up 728 a 26, b 23, 737 a 28; when begins in women 728 b 32; catamenia and milk are of same nature 739 b 25; birds discharge no catamenia 750 b 5; sign of coolness rather than heat 765 b 18-766 a 5; time of occurrence 767 a 2-8; does not occur in women while nursing children 777 a 13

Mentor, 1197 b 22; his trickery against Hermeias 1351 a 33-38

Mentoric district, 839 a 34

Mercenaries, guard tyrant 1285 a 26, 1311 a 7; admitted to citizenship at Syracuse at one time 1303 b 1; payment of 1347 b 20-30, 1353 b 8-19

Mercury, 342 b 33, 1073 b 31

Merlin, 620 a 18; habits of 609 b 8, 31

Merope, 1111 a 12, 1454 a 6

Merops, habits of 515 b 25, 626 a 8; nesting of 559 a 4

Merou, habitat of 598 a 10

Mese, 918 a 38, 919 a 11, 920 a 21, 31; used in tuning 919 a 14-28, 920 b 7-16; the middle note 919 b 20-22, 922 a 21-29

Mesentery, 495 b 32; found in all animals that have blood 676 b 11; nature and function of 677 b 36-678 a 26

Meses (N.N.E. wind), 363 b 30, 364 a 14, b 21, 29, 973 a 4-8; called Caunias at Rhodes 973 a 4; called Idyreus at Olbia 973 a 6

Mesopotamia, snakes of 845 b 9-11

Messapium, Mount, bison of 630 a 18

Messenian assembly, 1418 b 10

Messenians, 1269 b 4, 1270 a 3

Messenian speech, 1373 b 18, 1397 a 11

Messenian War, 1306 b 39

Messina, Straits of, 834 b 3, 840 a 2, 843 a 1-32, 932 a 6, 973 b 1

Metachoerum, a pig injured in the uterus 749 a 1

Metals, 'fossils' and metals are the two kinds of bodies that originate in the earth 378 a 20; have no rarity 822 a 31; metal ladles as a treatment of

bruises 890 b 7-27, 34-37. Cf. Copper, Gold, Iron, Silver

Metamorphosis, 758 b 28, 836 a 15; of birds 632 b 14-633 a 28

Metaphor, 97 b 37-39, 158 b 17, 1407 b 32, 1457 b 2, 7-1458 a 7, 32, b 13, 18, 1459 a 9, 13, b 36, 1460 b 12, 1461 a 31; must not be used in rendering genus 123 a 33-37; always obscure 139 b 34, based on resemblances 140 a 10; rules for use of 1404 b 32-1405 b 20; inappropriate metaphors 1406 b 5-19; similes compared with metaphors 1406 b 20-27, 1407 a 11-16, 1410 b 17-19, 1412 b 34-1413 a 13; enable us to get hold of new ideas 1410 b 13; the proportional metaphor 1411 a 1-b 20, 22, 1412 a 5; must be drawn from things related to the original thing 1410 b 32, 1412 a 10-17; give liveliness of style 1411 b 21-1413 b 2; defined 1457 b 7; makes language poetic 1458 a 22; mastery of metaphor is a sign of poetic genius 1459 a 5-7. Cf. Analogy, Like

Metaphysics, First Philosophy (σοφία), 89 b 8, 277 b 11

Metapontium, 840 a 28, 984 a 6, 1229 a 24

Meteor, 395 a 23

Meteorology, its subject matter 338 b 21-339 a 9

Method, of inquiry into the nature of virtue 1216 b 27-1217 a 17

Metre, 1408 b 21-1420 b 5, 1447 b 8, 16, 1456 b 38; a species of rhythm 1448 b 21; of epic and tragedy compared 1459 b 32-1460 a 4. Cf. Rhythm

Miccalus, 47 b 30

Midas, the fable of 1257 b 16

Middle, the limiting point 702 b 18; law of excluded middle 1011 b 23-1012 a 28

Middle class, virtue of 1295 a 25-1297 a 12; best state is composed of 1295 b 25-1296 a 21; small in ancient times 1297 b 27; a government composed of the middle class is closer to a democracy than to an oligarchy 1302 a 15

Middle term (μεσότης), 53 a 15-b 3, 59 b 2, 92 a 10, 98 a 24, 99 a 3, 25; defined 26 b 36; must be related to major and minor terms by predication 41 a 3; must be identical 44 b 41; location of middle term in the three figures 47 a 1; stated in both the premisses 47 a 39; no syllogism without 66 a 28; necessary and contingent 74 b 26-75 a 12, 76 a 5; extreme and middle terms must be derived from the same genus 75 b 10, 84 b 17; its dependence on the universal 77 a 8; as cause 78 b 4, 89 b 36-90 a 34, 93 a 8, 95 a 12; 'appropriate' middle term 80 b 18, 81 a 17; the four causes as middle terms 94 a 20-95 a 9; in causal inference 95 a 36-39. Cf. Cause, Demonstration, Fact, Predication

Midge. *See* Empis

Midget-bird, 592 b 23

Midriff. *See* Diaphragm

Migrant, gregarious 488 a 6

Mild-shell, 528 a 22

Miletus, 605 b 26, 1151 a 8, 1259 a 13, 1267 b 22, 1298 a 13, 1305 a 17

Military forces, four kinds of 1321 a 7

Milk, 521 b 17-523 a 12, 653 b 9-18, 776 a 15-777 a 31, 842 b 30, 929 a 31; found at times in the male 493 a 14; of women 585 a 29, 587 b 19-588 a 2; homogeneous 647 b 14; and rennet 676 a 11-16; of same nature as catamenia 739 b 25; amount of milk produced by different animals 891 b 4-12; food of young animals 1256 b 15; good food for human beings 1336 a 8

Milk-shelk, 528 a 22

Milky Way, cause and nature of 345 a 11-346 b 15; always unchanged 345 a 32; defined as a fringe attaching to the greatest circle, and due to the matter secreted 346 b 6

Millet, 551 a 16, 595 a 29

Millstone, 964 b 38

Milo, 1106 b 4

Miltiades, 1411 a 10

Mime, 1447 b 10

Mind (διάνοια), 452 b 11, 1217 b 30, 1240 b 34; soul and mind 404 a 31, b 2, 405 a 15, 408 b 18, 410 b 14, 413 b 25; Plato on mind 407 a 4; and intuition 415 a 12; acts purposively 415 b 16, 433 a 14; passive mind 429 a 10-

430 a 9; separable from body 429 b 4; active mind 430 a 10-25; compared to light 430 a 17; double operation of 430 a 26-b 30; practical mind 431 a 1-b 19; 'the form of forms' 432 a 1; aging of 1270 b 40; body should be trained before the mind 1338 b 6, 1339 a 7. Cf. Reason, Soul

Mines, in Macedonia 833 a 29-31; in Lydia 834 a 23-31; in Etruria 837 b 28-33; bitumen 842 b 16; salt 844 a 12; mining is an intermediate kind of acquisition of wealth 1258 b 32; art of mining 1343 a 27; lead mines at Laurium 1353 a 16

Minnow, phoxinus, 568 a 21; eggs of 567 a 30

Minor term, defined 26 a 23, b 38, 28 a 14. Cf. Middle Term

Minos, 836 a 30; the Cretan law-giver 1271 b 32, 1329 b 4, 24

Mint, 821 a 30; cooling effect of 923 a 9-12

Mirror, 915 b 30

Misanthropy, 1251 b 16

Mischievousness, physiognomic signs of 810 b 4, 30

Misreasonings (παραλογισμοί), start from premisses peculiar to the special sciences 101 a 6, 170 a 31-34; due to ignorance of force of names 165 a 15

Mist, 361 a 28, 367 b 17, 373 a 1, b 12, 374 a 7, 377 b 19, 394 a 20; distinguished from cloud 346 b 32, 369 a 15

Mistletoe, 716 a 1

Mithridates, his conspiracy against Ariobarzanes 1312 a 16

Mitylene, 973 a 11

Mitys, 624 a 14, 1452 a 7

Mixidemides, 1398 b 25

Mixolydian mode, 922 b 22; make men sad and grave 1340 b 1. Cf. Modes of Music

Mnaseas, a Phocian 1304 a 11

Mnasion, a Phocian 1304 a 11

Mnasitheus, 1462 a 8

Mock-modesty, self-depreciation, irony, understatement, 1108 a 23, 1124 b 30, 1127 a 22, b 23-31, 1186 a 25, 1193 a 32, 1221 a 6, 25, 1234 a 1, 1408 b 20, 1419 b 7, 1420 a 1, 1439 b 13, 1441 b 24, 1444 a 21, 36; defined 1434 a 18;

examples of 1434 a 19-31; its use in introduction of a speech 1436 b 22-28

Modality, 21 a 34-23 a 26; kinds of 25 a 1, 29 b 29, 32 a 15; modal syllogisms 29 b 29-40 b 16, 45 b 28-35; necessity 32 a 15, 34 a 5

Modes of music, 918 b 22, 1342 b 30; Hypodorian 920 a 8-10, 922 b 10-27; Hypophrygian 920 a 8-10, 922 b 10-27; Dorian 922 b 21, 1276 b 10, 1290 a 21; Phrygian 922 b 21, 1276 b 10, 1290 a 21; Mixolydian 922 b 22, 1340 b 1; effects of the various modes 1340 a 40-b 19, 1341 b 19-1342 b 34; Lydian 1342 b 30

Modesty. See Shame

Modon, a charm against wild beasts 846 a 33

Moerocles, 1411 a 16

Moisture (ὑγρόν), 397 a 22, 443 a 7, 466 a 22, 783 b 19; surrounding earth 346 b 27, 357 a 7; same places not always moist 352 b 18; drawn up by sun 357 b 20, 360 a 7; of air 374 a 24; passive quality 378 b 13; necessary for life 489 a 20, 703 b 23; and tone of voice 801 a 10-20, 804 a 20. Cf. Liquid

Mola uteri, 775 b 25-776 a 14

Mole, 488 a 21, 605 b 31; eyes of 425 a 11, 491 b 28, 533 a 1-15; none in Coronea 842 b 5, 6; of the Aetolians 847 b 4

Molluscs, cephalopods, 476 b 30, 487 b 16, 490 b 11, 523 b 2, 21-525 a 29, 706 b 2; bloodless 490 a 23; sensation of 534 b 13-535 a 25, 681 b 18-20; make no sound 535 b 13; sleep of 536 b 34-537 b 4, 5; sex in 537 b 26; copulation of 541 b 1-11, 544 a 1-6, 720 b 17-721 a 2, 755 b 32; generation of 549 b 30-550 b 21, 757 b 32-758 a 25; carnivorous 590 b 32; habits of 621 b 28-622 a 34; flesh of 654 a 10-25; teeth, mouth, and tongue of 661 a 14, 678 b 7; have no viscera 678 a 29; crop of 678 b 25-35; ink of 678 b 36-679 a 32; feet of 684 b 13-685 b 12; acetabula of 685 b 13-17; fin of 685 b 18-26; movement of 714 b 8-17; uterus of 717 a 4; eggs of 720 b 22, 727 b 4, 732 b 6, 733 a 22; have no distinction between upper and lower parts 741 b 34

Molossians, 1310 b 40; kingly power restricted among 1313 a 24

Moment. See Now

Momus, 663 a 36

Monarchy, royalty, kingship, 1160 a 31-36, b 24, 1241 b 29, 1265 b 36, 1266 a 6; rule of a household is a monarchy 1255 b 18, 1259 a 40; defined 1279 a 33, 1365 b 39; opposed to tyranny 1279 b 5, 1289 b 1, 1310 b 2; five forms of (1) Spartan, (2) the Barbarian, (3) Elective Dictatorship, (4) the Heroic, (5) Absolute Monarchy 1284 b 35-1288 b 5; first governments were monarchies 1286 b 8; should monarchy be hereditary? 1286 b 22-26; kind of people suited for 1287 b 37-1288 a 32; revolutions in 1310 a 39-1313 a 17; sphere of economics is a monarchy 1343 a 4; two forms of: kingship and tyranny 1366 a 2; final appeal is to reason 1420 a 22. Cf. King

Money (νόμισμα), 1127 b 13, 1250 b 25, 1251 b 8; forbidden in Balearic Islands 837 b 3-7; injustice in respect of 950 a 21-27, b 23-32; virtues concerned with 1119 b 22-1123 a 32; an intermediate set up by law 1133 a 18-b 29, 1194 a 19-25; origin of 1257 a 34; promotes unnatural acquiring of wealth 1257 b 1-1258 a 18; ways in which money has been made 1258 b 39-1259 a 36, 1346 a 33-1353 b 27; loved by most men 1263 b 4, 1364 b 1, 1389 a 14; money changing 1346 b 25. Cf. Usury, Wealth

Monkey, 502 b 25-27

Monopoly, as a means of acquiring wealth 1259 a 7-36

Monstrosity, 878 a 20, 898 a 9-19; cause of 769 b 11-770 a 8, 898 a 14-16; types of 770 a 9-771 a 17, 772 b 13-773 a 30; commoner in animals that produce many young 770 a 32

Moon, 392 a 30, 396 b 27, 398 b 9, 831 b 16; movements of 290 a 26, 291 b 35, 341 a 22, 778 a 4; perceive its spherical shape 291 b 19; Mars eclipsed by moon 292 a 5; earth causes eclipse of moon 297 b 30; effect on sea 396 a 26, 834 b 4; makes circuit in a month 399 a 7; said to be feminine 582 b 1; men in the moon 699 b 19; waning of 738 a 18; animals in the moon 761 b 21; a first principle 777 b 24; shape of 911 b 35-912 a 33

Mormyrus, spawning of 570 b 21

Moroseness, physiognomic signs of 807 a 5, 812 a 3, b 25

Mossynoeci, copper of 835 a 9-14

Moth, 605 b 14

Mother-urchins. See Echinometra

Motion, movement (κίνησις, φορά), 111 b 5, 1063 a 17-21, 1065 b 5-1066 a 34; six sorts of 15 a 13-b 16; Heraclitus' theory that all is in motion 104 b 22, 987 a 33; a kind of activity 125 b 17, 417 a 16, 431 a 6; Zeno's doctrine that there is no motion 160 b 8, 233 a 22-b 15, 239 b 5-240 b 8, 263 a 5-264 a 7, 272 a 29, 979 a 5-8; physical bodies in thought are separable from motion 193 b 34; belongs to class of things that are continuous 200 b 17, 228 a 20-b 12, 257 b 1, 1071 b 9-11, 1220 b 26; includes concepts of place, void, and time 200 b 20; as many types of motion as there are meanings of 'is' 201 a 8; defined as the fulfillment of what exists potentially as such 201 a 10, 202 a 7, 251 a 9, 1065 b 10; relation of the mover and the moved 202 a 12-b 29, 241 b 24-245 b 1, 254 b 8-256 a 3, 855 b 34-39, 858 a 24-b 4, 1071 b 34; infinite in virtue of the magnitude covered by the movement 207 b 23; in primary sense it is change of place 208 a 33, 336 a 18-23, 446 a 29, 1069 b 12, 26, 1071 b 11; void not necessary for 214 b 28-33; its relation to time 218 b 1-219 b 8, 234 b 21-235 b 5, 446 a 29; as perpetual succession 219 b 9; nature of the movement of which time is the number 223 a 29-b 12; the primary kind is locomotion 223 b 6, 243 a 12, 260 a 20-261 a 27; three kinds of: (1) quantitative, (2) qualitative, (3) local 225 b 8-226 b 9, 243 a 7, 260 a 27, 310 a 23, 1068 a 15; unity and diversity of 227 b 3-229 a 7; contrariety of 229 a 8-231 a 4; divisible in two ways: (1) in

respect of the time and (2) in respect of the movements of the parts of the moving thing 234 b 21-235 b 5; its relation to rest 238 b 23-239 b 4, 253 a 22-254 b 7, 426 a 5; requires that a thing have parts 240 b 8; must be a first mover 242 b 39; comparison of movements 248 a 10-249 b 26; proportion of movements 249 b 27-250 b 9; eternal 250 b 10-253 a 21, 259 b 32-260 a 19, 336 a 15, 338 a 18, 339 b 27, 1071 b 7, 32; natural and unnatural movements 254 b 12-256 a 2, 276 a 11, 406 a 25; requires three things: (1) mover, (2) moved, (3) instrument of motion 256 b 15, 266 a 13, 433 b 13; of circles 261 b 27-265 a 12, 337 a 1, 32, 847 b 20, 848 a 19, 851 b 35, 1071 b 11, 1072 a 21, 1073 a 32; soul thought by Plato to be cause of motion 265 b 33; simple movements are: (1) straight, (2) circular, (3) combination of the two 268 b 18; simple and compound 268 b 30, 302 b 6, 1053 a 9; no movement in absence of natural body 279 a 16; heaven moves the swiftest 287 a 26; movement of the heaven is regular 288 a 14-289 a 10; explanation of movements of elements 310 a 14-311 a 14; shape of bodies accounts for pace, but not the direction, of movement 313 a 14-b 24; of animals 398 b 30-35, 698 a 1-714 b 24, 875 a 25, 892 b 19; soul has no movement 405 b 32-407 b 25, 408 a 34-b 31, 410 b 17 (Cf. 123 a 15); direct and indirect 406 a 4-12; four species of: (1) locomotion, (2) alteration, (3) diminution, (4) growth 406 a 13; originated by soul and appetite 415 b 22, 432 a 14-434 a 22, 701 a 35, 702 a 35, 703 a 2; of projectiles 459 a 28; points of 490 a 27; why heart is material cause of movement 666 b 15, 703 a 6-b 2; commences from the right 671 b 30, 705 b 20, 30, 706 a 1, 5; origin of movement is the immovable 698 a 12, b 1; requires point of rest in a body and an external resisting fulcrum 698 b 8-699 a 12, 705 b 4-25; subordinate kinds of: (1) alteration, (2) growth, (3) generation, (4) decay 700 a 27-b 3; how soul moves body 700 b 4-701 a 6; why thought is sometimes followed by movement, sometimes not 701 a 7-b 33; minute movements are subconscious 701 b 38; involuntary movements 703 b 3-704 a 3; non-voluntary movements 703 b 3-704 a 3; originals of movements in place are thrusts and pulls 704 b 22 (Cf. 793 a 22); plants have no movement of themselves 706 b 6, 816 a 26, 817 b 23, 818 b 1, 822 b 2; nothing in nature has a movement backwards 706 b 30; in semen 734 b 23, 740 b 26, 765 b 13, 767 b 37, 768 a 13-b 37; physiognomic significance of 806 a 28, b 25, 37, 807 b 11, 26, 32, 808 a 6, 809 b 32, 813 a 3-20; some animals do not have movement 816 a 20; affects weight 853 b 18-24; body in motion easier to move than one at rest 858 a 3-12; body carried on by motion not its own 858 a 17-23; is all movement productive of heat? 884 b 11-21; of thought 968 a 25, 969 b 2; of Being 974 a 15, 976 b 12-977 a 11, 978 b 36; of the many 977 a 4, b 12; Not-being has no movement 977 b 10; of God and the One 978 b 37-979 a 8; every movement is incomplete 1048 b 28; of the planets 1073 a 13-1074 b 14; first causes of movement are the true causes 1222 b 20-23. Cf. Change, Circular motion, Locomotion, Mover, Prime Mover

Mould, decayed vapour 784 b 17, 22

Mountain-finch, 592 b 26

Mountains, hoar-frost not found on mountains 347 a 29; rivers flow from 350 a 4, 352 b 10

Mounting of a play, 1192 b 7

Mouse, 488 a 21, 698 b 16; have cotyledons in womb 511 a 31; generation of 580 b 10-581 a 5; drinking of 595 a 7; the white mouse 600 b 14; in Arabia 606 b 6; heart of 667 a 20; some have gall-bladder, some do not 676 b 31; of Gyaros 832 a 23; of Chalybia 832 a 24, 25; of Cyrene 832 b 1-3; amphibious mice 842 b 8, 9; habits of 845 b 8

Mouse-whale, hair of 519 a 24

Mouth, 502 a 5-8; compared to root of plant 468 a 10, 705 b 8; uses of 746 a 20; merely facilitates concoction 650 a 11; functions of 662 a 16-b 23, 691 b 13; problems concerning mouth and parts thereof 963 b 18-964 b 19; cold and hot breath from 964 a 10-18

Movement. See Motion

Mover, relation of the mover and the moved 202 a 12-b 29, 241 b 24-245 b 1, 254 b 8-256 a 3, 855 b 34-39, 858 a 24-b 4, 1071 b 34; movement always presupposes a mover 241 b 24-243 a 2; must be a first mover 242 b 39, 1049 b 26, 1071 b 3-1072 a 18; three kinds of: (1) causes locomotion, (2) alteration, (3) increase or decrease 243 a 10; first mover not moved by anything outside itself 255 a 4-257 a 31; first mover is unmoved 257 a 32-258 b 9, 259 b 20-31, 324 a 30, 434 b 33, 698 a 12, 700 b 37, 1012 b 31; two kinds 257 b 18; the first mover is eternal and one 258 b 10-259 b 19; first mover is indivisible and without magnitude 266 a 10-b 26, 267 b 18-26; first mover is at circumference of the world 267 b 6-8; may be either moved or unmoved 323 a 12-33; compared with the agent 324 a 24-b 13. Cf. Motion, Prime Mover

Moving principle. See Final cause

Mulberry, 606 b 15, 820 a 31, b 14, 41, 1413 a 21

Mule, 491 a 1, 3, 498 b 31, 728 b 12, 1033 b 33; a tame animal 488 a 27; hoof of 499 b 11; teeth of 501 b 3; has no gall-bladder 506 a 22, 676 b 27; menstruation of 573 a 15, 578 a 2; reproduction of 577 b 19-578 a 5; Athenian mule 577 b 30; the Syrian mule 580 b 1; diet of 595 b 23-30; spleen of 674 a 4; stomach of 674 a 27; sterile 746 b 12, 755 b 17; why sterile 747 a 24-749 a 5; in Cappadocia 835 b 1; has imperfect form 1034 b 4; mule-race 1405 b 24

Mullein, 602 b 31, 825 a 4

Mullet, gray, cestreus, 567 a 19; fins of 504 b 33, 696 a 5, 708 a 5; caeca of 508 b 18; hearing of 534 a 8; capture of 537 a 28, 541 a 20; breeding of 543 a 2, b 3, 12, 14; some of its species grow spontaneously from mud and sand 543 b 19; migration of 569 a 7; fry of 569 b 28; spawning of 570 b 17; diet of 591 a 13; habitat of 598 a 10, 601 b 20; blindness in 602 a 1; when edible 607 b 25, 621 b 21; habits of 610 b 12; swiftest of fishes 620 b 26; stomach of 675 a 12; sex in 741 b 1; scolex of 762 b 23

Mullet, red, trigle, caeca of 508 b 17; breeding of 543 a 6, 570 b 22, 621 b 2; diet of 591 a 12, 621 b 7; habitat of 591 b 20, 598 a 10; habits of 610 b 5

Muraena, smyraena, 505 a 15, 543 a 24; fins of 489 b 28, 504 b 34; gall-bladder of 506 b 17; egg of 517 b 8; breeding of 540 a 34, 543 a 20, 24; diet of 591 a 11; habitat of 598 a 14; hibernation of 599 b 6; body of 696 a 7

Murder, 951 b 2, 1262 a 27, 1269 a 2, 1275 b 10; of woman worse than of man 951 b 11-14; has no mean 1107 a 11

Murex, purple-shell, purpura, purple fish, 528 a 10, 529 a 7, 530 a 5, 25, 547 a 4-b 11, 568 a 9, 603 a 14; proboscis of 528 b 30, 532 a 9; capture of 535 a 7; breeding of 544 a 15, 761 b 31; spawning of 546 b 18-547 a 4; growth of 547 b 23; diet of 590 b 2; hibernation of 599 a 11; habits of 621 b 12; tongue of 661 a 22; shell of 679 b 14; operculum of 679 b 22; movement of 706 a 16; 'eggs' of 763 b 9; used in dyeing 794 a 21, 795 b 11-21, 797 a 5

Musaeus, 563 a 17, 843 b 5, 1339 b 22

Muses, 1406 a 24, 1415 a 16

Mushrooms, 819 a 31, 825 b 17

Music (μουσική), 1180 b 2, 1181 a 18, 1462 a 16; a kind of science 111 a 37, b 2, 128 a 31; harmony amid diversity 396 b 16; problems connected with 917 b 18-923 a 4; enjoy listening to familiar music 918 a 2-9, 921 a 31-39; has moral character 919 b 26-36, 920 a 3-7; why music delights man 920 b 29-921 a 6; many are a better judge of music than a single man 1281 b 8; a customary branch of education 1337 b 24, 1338 a 36; valuable for proper enjoyment of leisure 1337 b 28-1338 b 8; a moral discipline and a rational enjoyment 1339 a 11-1340 b 19; gives pleasure 1339 b 21, 1340 a 3, 15, b 16, 1341 a 15; children of ideal state must not become professional musicians 1340 b 20-1341 b 18; the musical instruments 1341 a 16-b 8; the various rhythms and modes 1341 b 19-1342 b 34, 1447 a 24; produced by melody and rhythm 1341 b 24; as a purgation 1341 b 32-1342 b 17. Cf. Modes of music, Rhythm

Mussel, 528 a 15, 22, 547 b 11, 614 b 28, 831 b 13; shell of 528 a 28, 683 b 15; bivalved 679 b 26; generation of 761 b 30; 'eggs' of 763 b 11

Must, 379 b 30, 380 b 32, 384 a 5, 385 b 2, 926 b 32

Mustard, 820 a 36

Mustelae, 832 b 2

Mute, 1456 b 26, 28, 1458 a 14

Mutilated (κολοβόν), meanings of 1024 a 11-28

Mycenae, 352 a 9

Mylassians, 1348 a 12

Mynniscus, 1461 b 34

Myops. See Horsefly

Myron, tyrant at Sicyon, 1316 a 31

Myrrh, 818 a 5, 906 a 25

Myrtle, 550 a 10, 627 a 8, 819 b 22, 820 a 31, 828 b 4, 931 a 7; myrtle berries seem sweeter when pressed 925 b 13-22; stones of myrtle berries 925 b 23-29; preserving of berry 926 a 33-b 3; foliage of tree 927 a 3-8

Myrtoan Sea, 393 a 30

Mysia, 973 a 11, 1353 b 8, 1405 a 29, 1460 a 31; bear in 845 a 17-23

Mysian prey, 1372 b 32

MYSIANS, THE, 1460 a 32

Mysteries, etymology of 1401 a 14, 15

Myth, 982 b 18, 1000 a 18; of Ocean and Tethys 983 b 30; about stars 1074 b 1-14

Mytilene, 1285 a 35, 1311 b 26, 1398 b 12; revolution at 1304 a 4-9

Mytis, 524 b 15, 526 b 32, 681 b 18-31

Myxon, smyxon, 570 b 1; breeding of 543 b 16

N

Nails, 487 a 7, 511 b 8, 517 a 6-34, 518 b 35, 743 a 15; of man 687 b 22-24; toe nails of man 690 b 9; formation of 745 a 1; as a physiognomic sign 810 a 21

Narce. *See* Torpedo-fish

Narcissus, bloom if hung up at summer solstice 925 a 19-25

Narration in oratory, 1354 b 17 1414 a 36, b 14, 1416 b 14-1417 b 20, 1438 a 3-b 12

Nasturtium, 925 a 30, 35

Natron, 383 b 12, 384 a 34, 385 a 31, b 23, 388 b 13, 389 a 18

Natural philosophy. *See* Physics

Nature (φύσις), 193 a 33, 261 b 25, 301 a 8, 452 a 28, 463 b 14, 472 a 2, 1032 a 24, 1043 b 22, 1044 a 9, 1112 a 25, 1114 a 24, 1133 a 31, 1202 a 20, 1205 a 1, 28-37, 1247 a 32, 1343 b 10; nothing by nature a noun or name 16 a 27; natural and necessary 32 b 5, 16; the natural affections 70 b 9; man is by nature a civilized animal 128 b 17, 132 a 8; in study of nature first task is to determine its first principles 184 a 15; in study of first principles of nature advance from generalities to particulars 184 a 16-b 14, 189 b 32; cause or source of being moved and of being at rest 192 b 11-23; two senses of: (1) as matter, (2) as form 193 a 28-b 22, 194 a 12, 199 a 31; always acts purposively 198 b 10-199 b 33, 271 a 34, 290 a 31, 415 b 16, 432 b 21, 434 a 30, 455 b 17, 471 b 26, 476 a 13, 477 b 19, 485 a 3-27, 641 b 12, 645 a 24, 661 b 24, 704 b 15, 708 a 10, 711 a 7, 18, 717 a 16, 738 b 1, 741 b 4, 744 a 38, 788 b 22, 1253 a 8, 1256 b 21, 1263 b 1; necessity in nature found in the matter 200 a 30-b 9; defined as a principle of motion and change 200 b 11; natural bodies 208 b 8; natural contrarieties 217 a 23; natural alterations 230 b 4; implies source of movement within thing itself 301 b 18; always brings the best to pass 336 b 27, 469 a 29, 658 a 23,

687 a 17, 704 b 16, 708 a 11, 711 a 19, 717 a 17, 738 b 1, 1099 b 22; as formal cause 379 b 25; art imitates nature 381 b 6; an intelligent agent 485 b 8, 731 a 24; always constant 485 b 14, 1247 a 32; final and material cause in 639 b 12-641 a 17; gives to one part what she subtracts from another 652 a 12, 655 a 27, 657 b 9, 658 a 35, 663 a 33, 644 a 2, 674 a 33, 684 a 16, 685 a 27, 689 b 14, 21, 714 a 16, 750 a 3, 760 b 27, 771 a 30, 777 a 16; often uses the results of necessity 658 b 6, 663 b 22, 677 a 16, 679 a 30; often uses one part of body for several purposes 658 b 30, 659 a 23, 660 a 2, 662 a 19, 683 a 1, 24, 688 a 24, 690 a 1, 3 (Cf. 691 b 26, 1252 b 3); gives to each animal only the appendages and organs it can use 661 b 30, 684 a 29, 687 a 14; never gives more than one adequate means of defense to an animal 663 a 18; places more honourable parts in more honourable position 665 b 20; passes from lifeless objects to animals in unbroken sequence 681 a 12, 26; never makes anything superfluous 691 b 4, 694 a 15, 695 b 19, 739 b 20, 744 a 37; makes the organ for the function, not the function for the organ 694 b 14; man is the most natural animal 706 a 19, b 10; nothing has natural movement backwards 706 b 30; does not like the infinite 715 b 15; acts like a modeler in clay 730 b 3; movement of 735 a 4; acts as a painter 743 b 22; compared to a good housekeeper 744 b 17; orderly 760 a 31; gives faculty and organ at same time 766 a 6-10; nothing can happen contrary to 770 b 11; workmanship of 781 b 23; what is done by violence is contrary to nature 788 b 27; uses breath to perform most of her operations 789 b 9; always follows same course 847 a 14; only one genus of being 1005 a 34; generation by 1033 a 24-1034 a 7, 1070 a 6, 1140 a 15; man by nature is a political animal 1097 b 11, 1162 a 17, 1169 b 18, 1242 a 22-27, 1245 a 11-27, 1253 a 2, 30, 1278 b 20; that which is by nature is hard to

change 1134 b 25, 1203 b 30; as cause 1143 b 9, 1148 b 31, 1206 b 39; a common life is natural to male and female 1162 a 17, 1252 a 28, 1343 b 8-1344 a 7; nothing that is by nature can be changed 1186 a 5; citizens tend to be equals by nature 1194 b 10, 30-1195 a 7, 1196 b 2, 1261 a 39, 1287 a 10-20; meanings of 1014 b 16-1015 a 19; does happiness come by nature? 1214 a 18; do not blame for what is due to 1223 a 11; makes a distinction between those who are to govern and those to be governed 1252 a 30, 1332 b 37 (Cf. 1254 a 19-1255 a 2); slavery is natural 1254 a 19-1255 b 15; male is naturally superior to female 1254 b 14, 1259 b 2; supplies food to all 1256 a 19-b 26, 1258 a 35; makes nothing incomplete 1256 b 21; an element in virtue 1332 a 39-b 11, 1334 b 8; the rational principle is the end of nature in man 1334 b 14; art and education fill up the deficiencies of 1337 a 2; natural and acquired 1365 a 28; a cause of action 1369 a 6, b 2-4; pleasant to move to a natural state of being 1370 a 3. Cf. Final Cause, Law, Necessity

Nauplia, 602 a 9

Nausicrates, 1416 a 10

Nautilus, argonaut, 622 b 5-19; habits of 525 a 20-28

Navel, 493 a 18, 586 a 31, 740 a 31, 808 b 3, 810 b 17, 898 a 37-b 2; navel-string 587 a 8; of birds 693 b 22-26; large in man 896 a 12-19

Naxos, 496 b 27, 677 a 2, 1346 b 7; wasps of 844 b 32-34; tyranny of Lygdamis at 1304 a 40

Necessity (ἀνάγκη), 198 b 11, 1025 a 18, 1027 b 8, 1112 a 32, 1140 a 36, 1223 a 1; difficulties of 18 b 5-36, 19 a 22-b 4; contradictory of propositions expressing 21 b 26, 22 a 3-6; in inference 24 b 20, 26 a 3, 47 a 33, 53 b 18, 57 a 40, 62 a 11; in conversion 25 a 6; conversion of necessary propositions 25 a 27-36; syllogisms with two necessary premisses 29 b 29-30 a 14; syllogisms with one pure and one necessary premiss 30 a 15-32 a 5; when

one premiss is necessary the conclusion is necessary 30 a 15, 32 a 7; and possibility 32 a 20, 28; nothing necessarily follows from the being of some one thing 34 a 18, 40 b 35; syllogisms with one contingent and one necessary premiss 35 b 23-36 b 25, 38 a 13-39 a 3, 40 a 4-b 16; two kinds: (1) in accord with natural tendency, (2) by constraint 94 b 40; absolute and hypothetical 119 b 35, 337 b 10-338 a 17, 639 b 25-640 a 12, 642 a 32, 1357 a 23-b 20; in mathematics and nature 199 b 34-200 b 9; God meant by the word 401 b 8; meaning of 455 b 26, 1006 b 32, 1015 a 20-b 15, 1026 b 28, 1064 b 34, 1072 b 10-13; distinction between necessity and final cause 663 b 14-23, 778 a 16-b 19, 789 b 12; and impossibility 699 b 20; demonstration is of necessary truths 1039 b 32; most people obey necessity rather than argument 1180 a 4; applies only to externals 1188 b 15-24; do not blame for what is due to 1223 a 11; and force 1224 a 14, b 1, 13; fosters invention 1329 b 27; a topic of persuasion 1421 b 26, 1422 a 20, 1439 a 12. Cf. Compulsion, Final Cause

Neck, 491 a 27, 493 a 5, 691 b 28; organs of 664 a 14-665 a 25; found only in animals that have a lung 664 a 20, 686 a 4; found in all vivipara 686 a 2; final cause of 686 a 19-24; as a physiognomic sign 807 b 14, 21, 26, 811 a 13-18

Nectar, 1001 a 12, 1205 b 15

Necydalus, 551 b 12

Negation (ἀπόφασις), 51 b 5-52 b 34, 978 b 18, 34; arises by combination of terms 2 a 5; 'opposite' as affirmation and negation 13 b 1-35; simple negation 17 a 8, 25; as a part of a contradiction 72 a 14, 1012 a 9; Forms of 990 b 13, 1079 a 10; and privation 1004 a 9-19, 1056 a 17, 29; negative proof (ἔλεγχος) 1006 a 18

Negligence, 1251 a 22, 27

Neleus River, 846 b 39

Nemean Games, 1018 b 18

Neocles, 956 a 12

Neoptolemus, 1146 a 19, 1151 b 18

Notus (S. wind), 361 a 22, 363 b 15, 23, 394 b 21, 32; attracts clouds 939 b 19, 945 a 39; blows after hoar-frost 940 b 8-15; blows less frequently than Boreas 941 a 27-30; blows as much on winter nights as on winter days 941 a 31-36; blows at time of the Dog-star 941 a 37-b 23, 944 a 4-9; causes evil odours 942 a 16-21; rainy when it is ending 942 a 29-33; when less strong brings clear weather 942 a 34-b 2; a rainy wind 943 a 5-27, 945 a 37-b 4; sea becomes blue when Notus blows 944 b 21-24; weak when it begins to blow 944 b 30-39, 945 a 26-36; in Egypt 945 a 19-25; reasons for its name 973 b 8, 9

Noun, 1404 b 27, 1456 b 22, 1457 a 11-13, 25; defined 16 a 19; simple and composite nouns 16 a 24; a symbol 16 a 28; cases of 16 b 1-5; Protagoras' classification of nouns into male, female, and inanimate 1407 b 7, 1458 a 8-16; simple and complex nouns 1457 a 32-36; kinds of 1457 b 1-1458 a 7

Now, present, moment (νῦν), its relation to time 218 a 6-29, 219 b 9; measures time in so far as time involves the before and after 219 b 12; the link and limit of time 220 a 4, 222 a 10-23, b 1, 6, 237 a 6-25; a moment is indivisible 233 b 33-234 b 9, 241 a 24, 262 a 30; a thing can be neither at rest or in motion at a moment 239 b 2; a kind of middle point 251 b 20; beginning and end of a time 971 a 17

Number, 150 a 24, 286 b 34, 969 a 14, 1076 a 20; a discrete quantity 4 b 23-31; the soul not a number 120 b 3, 123 a 12; always odd or even 120 b 4, 142 b 9, 978 b 35; its limit is the indivisible 207 b 8; two senses of 219 b 6, 223 a 24; smallest number in strict sense is two 220 a 27; the number three 268 a 15; Pythagorean view of 300 a 15; soul not a self-moving number 408 b 32-409 b 18 (Cf. 120 b 3-6, 123 a 11-14, 23-25); how perceived 425 a 19; as principles 985 b 26, 986 a 16, 987 a 19, b 24, 1036 b 12, 1076 a 31, 1090 a 23, 1092 b 16, 26; num-

ber ten said to comprise the whole nature of numbers 986 a 9, 1073 a 20, 1084 a 12, 32; the Forms as numbers 991 b 9-20, 1073 a 18, 1076 a 20, 1080 b 12, 23, 1081 a 1-1083 a 20, b 2, 1086 a 6, 1088 b 34, 1090 a 16, b 33, 1091 b 27; numbers as substance 1001 a 25, b 26, 1076 a 31, 1080 a 12-1086 a 18; attributes of 1004 b 10; a synthesis of units 1039 a 12, 1053 a 30; and definition 1043 b 34-1044 a 14; defined as plurality measured by one 1057 a 3; criticism of the theory of numbers 1087 a 28-1093 b 29; Plato's theory of number as the origin of change 1316 a 2-17

Numbness, cause of 886 a 10-14

Nuthatch, sitta, habits of 609 b 12, 616 b 21

Nutriment, 724 b 27, 731 a 6, 743 a 9, 765 b 30; may be used up in semen or fat 725 b 29-726 a 6, 736 b 27, 748 b 29, 750 a 21-34; two kinds of 744 b 32; used in producing young 749 b 30

Nutrition, nutritive (θρεπτικός), plants have power of self-nutrition 413 a 33; a faculty of the soul 414 a 30, 415 a 14-416 b 31, 736 a 36, 740 b 28, 745 b 24, 757 b 17, 815 b 29, 1102 a 33, b 12, 29, 1144 a 9, 1185 a 14-35, 1219 b 37-41; most primitive and widely distributed power of soul 415 a 23; soul is principal cause of 416 a 9-18; three factors of 416 b 20; nutritive soul possessed by all living beings 434 a 22, 816 b 13; and savour 436 b 17, 441 b 25, 443 b 22, 444 b 10; takes place better during sleep 455 a 1; does not require sense-perception 455 a 2; place of nutritive soul 468 a 21-b 15; of breath 481 a 1-482 a 27; two means of: respiration and digestive process 481 a 7; blood is universal and ultimate nutriment 481 a 12, 484 b 8; of sinews 484 a 17; of bones 484 a 23, 30; organs of nutrition necessary in all animals 678 b 5; of animals 797 b 22-799 a 18; of plants 815 b 29, 816 b 13, 817 b 15; cause of growth 815 b 34; nutritive principle derived from earth 817 a 25; life of nutrition 1098 a 1;

nutritive part of soul has no relation to happiness 1185 a 14-35, 1219 b 37-41

Nuts, why more easily cracked with nut-cracker than by blow 854 a 32-b 15; roasted nuts 930 b 15-19

Nut-tree, 819 b 20, 821 a 29

Nyctalopia, 780 a 16

Nympha, 551 b 2, 555 a 3, 758 b 32

Nymphia, in horses 604 b 10

Nyraeba, has no fins 504 b 33

Nysa, 391 a 21

Nyses, 350 b 11

O

Oak, 837 a 18

Oaths, sophistical proof that oath can be broken and kept at the same time 180 a 34-b 1; of ancient kings 1285 b 12; as a form of persuasion 1377 a 9-b 13; fourfold division of 1377 a 9; given under torture 1428 a 22; defined as an affirmation without proof accompanied by an invocation of the gods 1432 a 33; how to credit and discredit oaths 1432 a 33-b 10

Objection (ἔνστασις), 69 a 38-70 a 2, 73 a 33, 74 b 19, 157 a 38-b 2; defined 69 a 38; can always object to spoken word, not always to the inward discourse 76 b 27, 77 b 35; how to meet objections 134 a 3, 157 b 6, 9, 20-31; four kinds of: (1) solution of fallacy, (2) ad hominem, (3) objection to time allowed for discussion, (4) to questions asked 161 a 1-15; principal aim of dialectical training is readiness to object 164 b 3; used in rhetoric 1403 a 32, 33

Oboe, 800 b 24, 801 b 32-40, 802 a 8, 803 a 18; sound of 802 b 19-29; 'perfect' oboes 804 a 12

Obscurity (τὸ ἀσαφές), sources of 139 b 19-140 b 27; of rhetorical style 1407 b 21-25. Cf. Ambiguous terms, Equivocal

Obsequiousness, 1108 a 28, 1126 b 13, 1127 a 8, 1171 a 17, 1199 a 17; physiognomic signs of 812 a 1, 813 a 17

Occiput, 491 a 33

Ocean, the unity of 298 a 10; 'Oceanus' 347 a 6; the Ocean or Atlantic 393 a 17, b 2, 11, 29; Ocean and Tethys, the parents of creation 983 b 30; Ocean (Homer) 1091 b 6

Ochre, 378 a 23

Octave, accord in 918 b 7-12, 919 a 1-8, 920 a 28-37, 922 b 35-923 a 4; double octave 920 a 24-27, 921 b 1-13

Octopus, poulp, 490 a 1, 524 a 3-525 a 29, 534 a 25, 717 a 7; capture of 534 b 26; breeding of 541 b 1-11, 544 a 7-14, 720 b 33; generation of 549 b 32-550 a 9; diet of 591 a 1; when edible 607 b 6; habits of 621 b 30, 622 b 19; brain of 652 b 25; head of 654 a 23; ink of 679 a 8-32; feet of 685 a 14-b 12; fin of 685 b 18-26; uterus of 758 a 7

Odd, even and odd are the differentia of number 120 b 5, 123 a 11-13, 142 b 10; the Pythagorean conception 986 a 18, 990 a 9, 1091 a 23; an ambiguous term 1261 b 29

Odour, 492 b 14, 796 a 21, 802 a 13, 1231 a 7; smoke-like evaporation 438 b 24; nature of 442 b 27-445 b 1; based upon the sapid 443 a 8-20; elements have no odour 443 a 10; of palm trees 821 a 19; of plants 821 b 40; of honey 831 b 21; of unguents 832 a 4, 845 a 35; of copper 834 a 6; of an Italian lake 836 a 33; of violets at Enna 836 b 18; of ichor 838 a 31; of oil-well 841 a 16; of fire-stone 841 b 1; of persons after puberty 877 b 21-39, 879 a 22-26; problems connected with things of pleasant odour 906 a 22-907 b 19; things emit stronger odour when in motion 907 a 5-7, 909 a 8-10; perceived less in winter 907 a 8-12; smoke or vapour? 907 a 29-34; sweet-smelling plants promote flow of urine 907 b 4-13; unmixed wine has stronger odour than mixed 907 b 14-19; problems connected with unpleasant odours 907 b 21-909 a 10; unpleasant odours more so when hot 908 a 20-27; have upward tendency 908 a 25; 'the smell of fasting' 908 b 11-19; of armpit 908 b 20-23; of

mathematics 194 a 7; treatises on 913 a 27, 959 b 2

Opus, 576 b 26, 1287 a 9, 1462 a 8

Oration, 1459 a 12; three elements in speech making: (1) Thought-element 1393 a 22-1403 a 33, (2) Style 1403 b 6-1414 a 29, (3) Arrangement 1414 a 30-1420 b 4; speech-writers 1408 a 33; arrangement of 1414 a 30-1420 b 4; two parts of: statement and argument 1414 a 30-b 18, 1416 b 18; how to prolong a speech to the length desired 1434 b 1-27

Orator, 1305 a 13; shrewdness of 916 b 35-917 a 1; philosopher superior to orator 917 a 2-5, 956 b 6-10; attitude toward orators determined by habits of hearers 994 b 21-995 a 14; personal behavior of 1445 b 25-1446 a 36

Oratory, deliberative, political, or parliamentary, 1359 a 30-1366 a 22, 1393 a 12, 1421 b 7; writers on rhetoric give too much attention to forensic oratory, too little to political 1354 b 23-1355 a 3; urges us to do or not to do something 1358 b 8; concerned with the future 1358 b 14; end in view is the expedient or inexpedient 1358 b 22-25, 33-37; subjects of 1359 a 30-1360 b 3, 1423 a 13-1425 b 36, 1446 b 20; aim is utility 1362 a 18; enhanced by knowledge of the four types of government 1365 b 22-1366 a 22; effect of character of orator in 1377 b 24-1378 a 19; its style resembles scene-painting 1414 a 8; introductions to 1415 b 32-1416 a 2; narration in 1417 b 13-20; arguments in 1417 b 35-1418 b 38; persuasion and dissuasion in 1421 b 16-1423 a 12, 1439 b 14-1440 b 4. Cf. Deliberation

Oratory, epideictic, ceremonial, occasional, or declamatory, 1421 b 7; praises or censures somebody 1358 b 12; concerned with the present 1358 b 18; end in view is honour or dishonour 1358 b 28, 38-1359 a 5; concerned with virtue and vice 1366 a 23-1368 a 39; has most literary style 1414 a 17; narration in 1416 b 16-28; arguments in 1417 b 31-34, 1418 a 33-

37; eulogy and vituperation in 1425 b 37-1426 b 21, 1440 b 5-1441 b 29

Oratory, forensic, legal, or judicial, 1368 b 1-1377 b 12, 1421 b 7; writers on rhetoric give too much attention to forensic oratory, too little to political 1354 b 23-1355 a 3; attacks or defends somebody 1358 b 10; concerned with the past 1358 b 16; end in view is justice or injustice 1358 b 26, 32; proper style of 1414 a 10-15; introductions to 1415 a 8-b 31; narration in 1416 b 29-1417 b 12; arguments in 1417 b 22-30, 1418 a 2, 4, 22-32, b 7-23; accusation and defense in 1426 b 22-1427 b 11, 1441 b 30-1445 a 29

Orchomenus, 605 b 32, 926 b 5; cave in 838 b 4-12

Orcys, large-sized tunny, breeding of 543 b 5

Orderliness, 1250 b 11

Ordure, odour of 907 b 22

Orestes of Euripides, 1454 a 29, 1461 b 21

Orestes (of Euripides' *Orestes*), 1405 b 22, 1452 b 6, 1453 a 21, 38, b 23, 1454 b 32, 1455 a 6, 7, b 14

Orestes of Theodectes, 1401 a 35

Oreum, revolution at 1303 a 18

Oreus. *See* Antipheron

Organs, 412 b 13, 415 b 18; the parts of plants are organs 412 b 1; not possessed by insects 467 a 23; all organs are double 669 b 19; organs on the right side of the body are stronger than those on the left 671 b 31; one organ sometimes has several functions 690 a 1; made for the function, not the function for the organ 694 b 14; organs are needed for all functioning 716 a 25; shifting of places of 771 a 9; cases of double generative organs 772 b 27-34

Origanum, 534 b 22

Origin, study of origin gives clearest view of anything 1252 a 25

Oriole, 617 a 29; habits of 609 b 9, 616 b 11

Orion, 343 b 25, 361 b 24, 30, 859 a 22; days most changeable during period of 941 b 24-33

Ornithian winds, 395 a 4

Orpheus, 734 a 19

Orphic poems, 410 b 28

Orphus, sea-perch, growth of 543 b 2; hibernation of 599 b 6

Orpiment, 966 b 28

Orsodacna. *See* Budbane

Orthagoras, tyrant at Sicyon, 1315 b 13

Orthian songs, 920 b 20

Orus, 1351 b 19

Orynx, horns and hoofs of 499 b 19

Oryx, has a single horn 663 a 24

Osprey. *See* Sea-eagle

Ossa, 391 a 21

Ostensive proof, compared with *reductio ad impossibile* 29 a 31, 45 a 26, 62 b 29-63 b 20

Ostentation, 1192 a 37, b 2

Ostracism, 1284 a 3-b 34, 1288 a 26, 1308 b 20; at Athens and Argos 1302 b 18

Ostracoderms. *See* Testaceans

Ostrich, eggs of 616 b 4, 749 b 17; has eyelashes 658 a 13; hoof of 695 a 18, 697 b 23; part bird and part quadruped 697 b 14-26

Os uteri, 739 a 31; closed in some women 773 a 17. Cf. Uterus

Other, 1087 b 26; meanings of 1018 a 10-12, 1054 b 13-22; in species 1057 b 35-1058 b 26

Othrys, Mount, serpents on 846 b 10-17

Otter, 594 b 31; feet of 487 a 22

Outrage, a species of injustice 1251 a 30, 34

Ovaviviparous animals, 676 b 1-3

Oviparous animals, 475 b 22, 489 a 34, 490 b 21, 506 b 25, 510 b 34, 655 a 20, 669 a 35, 732 b 2, 739 b 33; lung of 470 b 16, 669 a 26; characteristics of 502 b 28-503 a 8; have no epiglottis 504 b 4; generation of 567 a 17-568 a 10, 730 a 18-23, 1256 b 12; eyes of 657 b 6-658 a 10, 691 a 21; less erect than viviparous animals 669 b 6; spleen of 670 b 12; have no kidneys 671 a 26-31; differences of viscera in 676 a 22-b 15; neck of 691 b 28; teeth of 691 a 10; ears of 691 a 14-20; have no mammae 692 a 11; tail of 692 a 18; uterus in 718 b 2, 719 b 17-27, 720 a 26; eggs of 718 b 5-16, 732 b 1-7, 752 b 33, 755 b 31

Oviposition, 733 a 31, 758 b 20

Ovum, 724 b 17. *See* Eggs

Owl, 592 b 9, 617 b 32; eyes of 504 a 27; spleen of 506 a 16; oesophagus of 509 a 3; caeca of 509 a 22; little horned owl 592 b 11, 617 b 31; horned owl 597 b 18, 617 b 31; capture of 597 b 25; hibernation of 600 a 27; habits of 609 a 8, 619 b 19; bird-catching with 609 a 15, 617 b 5. Cf. Night-raven

Owsel. *See* Blackbird

Oxus River, gold of 833 b 15

Oxylus, king of Elis, 1319 a 12

Oxymel, makes wine more pleasant 922 a 6

Oyster, 470 b 32, 487 a 26, 490 b 9, 523 b 12, 528 a 1, 23, 568 a 7, 654 a 3, 681 b 11; stationary 487 b 8; motionless 487 b 15; shell of 528 a 28; habitat of 547 b 20; when edible 607 b 3, 763 b 7; ovum of 680 b 7, 15, 23; spontaneous generation of 763 a 29-b 7

Ozolis, 525 a 19

P

Paches, captured Mytilene 1304 a 6

Paean, 1409 a 2-21

Paederasty, 1148 b 29

Paeonia, 499 b 12, 630 a 18, 846 b 30; bison of 500 a 1, 830 a 4; gold in 833 b 6-14; wild oxen of 842 b 33-35

Paesus, Lake of 935 b 34-936 a 4

Pagrean Mountains, 973 a 3

Pain (λύπη, ἀλγηδών), 125 b 29, 126 a 6-12, 145 b 2-14, 805 a 8, 1119 a 23, 1171 b 8, 1173 b 7-19, 1186 a 15, 1202 b 26, 1215 b 24, 1221 a 29, b 34, 1224 b 16, 1225 b 15, 1229 a 34-40, b 4, 15, 1231 b 6, 1250 b 15, 1385 b 13; poorly defined as violent disruption of parts that are naturally conjoined 145 b 2; causes change of temperature of body 702 a 4; insensibility to 808 b 38, 835 a 17-22; caused by being warmed too rapidly when chilled 888 b 39-889 a 9; the One is unaffected by 974 a 19; men seek the painless life 1104 b 32, 1152 b 16, 1153 a 27; relation to courage 1117 a 29-b 21; virtue may be determined by pleasure and pain 1185 b 34-37, 1204 a 29, 1206 a 20, 1222 a 1-14, b 10, 1227 b 2; all compulsory acts are painful 1188 a 3, 1206 a 14; all seek pleasure and avoid pain 1189 b 30-32, 1190 a 7; excess and defect are painful 1204 b 13, 1205 a 2; a passion 1220 b 13; friends share pain 1240 a 37. Cf. Pleasure

Painting, 1118 a 4, 1175 a 25, 1180 b 35, 1448 a 5, 1450 a 27, b 1, 1460 b 8; imitation in 1190 a 31, 32, 1371 b 6

Palamedes, 1413 b 25

Palate, 492 b 26

Palestine, 359 a 17

Palici, spring in 834 b 8-18

Palm of hand, 493 b 28, 33

Palm-island, 843 b 6-14

Palm tree, 610 a 22; seed of 821 a 7; propagation of 821 a 13-22; bark of 829 a 3

Palpitation, cause of 479 b 19, 480 a 14; involuntary 703 b 7

Pammenes, 1243 b 20

Pamphila, daughter of Plateus, 551 b 16

Pamphilus, a rhetorician, 1400 a 4

Pamphylia, 973 a 6; fire in 833 a 1-6

Pamphylian Sea, 393 a 29

Pan, 1401 a 17

Panaetius, tyrant at Leontini, 1310 b 30, 1316 a 37

Panathenaea, 712 a 34, 724 b 2

Pancratiast, 1361 b 26

Pancreas, 514 b 11

Pandosia in Iapygia, 838 a 33

Panegyric of Isocrates, 1408 b 16, 1418 a 32

Panegyrics, 1448 b 27

Pangaeus, Mount, 973 b 16

Pan-pipes, 919 b 8

Panspermia, 769 a 29, b 2

Pantheon, olive tree of 834 a 13-22

Panther. See Leopard

Panther's-bane, 612 a 7

Paphlagonia, fish in 835 b 24-27

Paradox, 174 b 16, 1399 a 22-25; to lead into paradox one of chief aims of dialectical reasoning 159 a 18; how to lead opponent into a paradox 172 a 29-173 a 30

Parallel, illustrative parallel 1393 a 30-b 8

Paralogism, 1460 a 21. Cf. Misreasonings

Paramese, 922 b 6

Paranete, 917 b 38, 918 a 37

Parasite, 557 a 28, 598 a 18, 599 b 26, 602 a 26, 826 b 32-41

Pard. See Leopard

Pardalus, habits of 617 b 6

Pardion, hair of 498 b 34

Parhelion, 912 b 27-913 a 4

Parhypate, voice wavers most when singing 917 b 30-34; difficult to sing 917 b 35-39

Parian marble, 844 a 15

Parians, 1398 b 10

Parian Sophists, 1421 a 32

Paris, Alexander, son of Priam, 1363 a 18, 1397 b 21, 1399 a 3, 1401 b 35, 1414 b 38; an essay on 1398 a 22, 1401 b 20

Parisosis, 1435 b 38-1436 a 4; defined 1410 a 23

Parmenides, 318 b 6, 984 b 2, 1009 b 22-24; problem of being 182 b 26, 191 b 37; first principle of nature is a motionless one 184 b 17; criticism of 185 a 9; refutation of Parmenides' and Melissus' conception of the oneness of Being 185 a 20-187 a 10; Being is finite 185 b 19; hot and cold as contrary principles 188 a 20; defined 'whole' as 'equally balanced from the middle' 207 a 17; denial of generation 298 b 17; two elementary bodies 330 b 14; said women were hotter than men 648 a 30; All as ungenerated but limited 976 a 6-10; God is limited 978 b 8; made love a principle 984 b 25, 988 a 33; universe as one entity 986 b 9-987 a 1; all things are one, all is being 1001 a 34; hot and cold 1004 b 32; no not-being 1089 a 3

Parmenon, the actor, 948 a 3

Parnassus, 350 a 20, 681 a 24

Parode, 1452 b 18, 21, 23

Parody, first written by Hegemon of Thasos 1448 a 13

Paromoeosis, 1436 a 5-13; defined 1410 a 24-36

Paron the Pythagorean, 222 b 18

Parrot, 597 b 27

Pelamys, gregarious 488 a 6; breeding of 543 a 2, b 3, 571 a 19; migration of 598 a 26; habits of 610 b 7

Pelasgians, 836 b 11

Peleus, 1071 a 22, 1418 a 35

PELEUS, 1456 a 2

Pelias, daughters of 1225 b 4

Pelican, migration of 597 a 9, b 30; habits of 614 b 28, 831 b 10-13

Peloponnese, Peloponnesus, Peloponnesians, 152 a 13, 351 a 2, 593 a 11, 618 b 15, 842 b 26, 1271 b 36, 1276 a 27, 1409 b 10, 13, 1429 b 14

Peloponnesian War, 1303 a 9

Pelorus, Promontory of, 840 b 25

Pelusium, 617 b 30

Pelvis, 493 a 22

Penduline titmouse, habits of 616 a 4

Penelope, 1417 a 14

Penelops, 593 b 23

Penestae, 1264 a 35, 1269 a 37, b 5

Penia, generation of 551 b 6

Penis, 493 a 25, 497 a 27, 500 b 20-25, 509 b 30, 510 b 28, 689 a 22-31, 716 a 32, 720 a 33; varies in different animals 717 b 14-25; erection of 879 a 11-21; erected by breath 953 b 35

Pennyroyal, bloom if hung up at summer solstice 925 a 19-25

Pentheus, 1400 b 24

Penthilidae of Mytilene, 1311 b 27

Penthilus, tyrant of Mytilene, 1311 b 29

Peparethus, 1398 a 33

Pepper, effect on stomach and bladder 864 b 12-18

Peraeas, diet of 591 a 23

Perception (αἰσθάνεσθαι), 50 a 1, 244 b 10, 716 a 31, 779 a 20, 1098 b 3, 1142 a 28, 1143 b 5, 1170 a 28-b 13, 1172 a 36, 1208 a 21-30, 1244 b 25; object is prior to the act of 7 b 35; when subject is destroyed perception ends but not the perceptibles 8 a 1-12; only means of grasping particulars 71 b 8; primary premises reached by sense-perception 78 a 35, 99 b 15-100 b 17; demonstration not possible through sense-perception 87 b 27-88 a 17; defined 99 b 35; a kind of judgment 111 a 16, 19; deals with particulars 189 a 7; error in 428 b 18-24, 1226 a 35-39; general faculty of perception

is one 426 b 8-29, 449 a 5-b 36; produced only through medium 435 a 16; a cause of desire 701 a 36; effect on heart 702 b 24; a kind of knowledge 731 a 33-b 7; animals differ from plants in having sense-perception 731 b 4, 741 a 10, 778 b 33; at a distance 781 b 6-12, 17; cause of the glorification of life 815 b 33; an effect produced on a sentient being 816 a 25; no mark of wisdom 982 a 12; called measure of things 1053 a 32; life defined by power of 1098 a 2, 1170 a 16; the mean is grasped by 1109 b 23; particulars are matters of perception 1113 a 1, 1147 a 27; perceptual knowledge 1147 b 17; perception that we perceive 1170 a 31

Perch, gills of 505 a 16; caeca of 508 b 16; spawn of 568 a 21; diet of 591 a 11; hibernation of 599 b 8

Percnopterus, 618 b 32

Perfume, burnt perfume less perceptible at a short distance 906 a 22-35, b 35-907 a 4, 24-28; stronger when burnt on ashes 907 a 13-19, 35-b 3; rose perfume 909 a 2

Perfumers, 1206 a 27

Pergamos in Lydia, 834 a 23

Periander, tyrant at Ambracia, 1304 a 33, 1311 a 40

Periander, tyrant of Corinth, 1284 a 27, 1311 a 20, 1313 a 37, 1315 b 25, 28, 1375 b 31

Pericarp, 722 a 15, 752 a 21

Pericles, 1140 b 8, 1274 a 8, 1365 a 31, 1390 b 31, 1407 a 1, 1411 a 2, 15, 1419 a 2

Perineum, 493 b 9

Perinthus, 773 a 27

Period, 1409 a 23-1410 b 5; defined 1409 a 35

Perioci, 1271 b 31, 40, 1272 a 18, 1327 b 11, 1329 a 26, 1330 a 30; well-behaved at Crete 1292 b 18; given citizenship at Argos 1303 a 7

Peripety, 1450 a 34, 1452 a 16, 22-b 10, 1455 b 34, 1456 a 19, 1459 b 11; defined 1452 a 22

Perishable, and imperishable differ in kind 1058 b 27-1059 a 14

An Index to Aristotle

Petitio principii, 41 b 8, 64 b 28-65 a 37, 161 b 11-16, 167 a 38, 169 b 14, 869 a 23, 1006 a 17, 20; defined 65 a 26; five types of 162 b 31-163 a 13; one of the seven fallacious refutations independent of language 166 b 25; solution of fallacy of 181 a 15-21

Pettiness. *See* Niggardliness

Peucetians, 836 a 4, 840 b 20

PHAEDO of Plato, 335 b 11, 355 b 32, 991 b 3, 1080 a 2

PHAEDRUS of Plato, 140 b 3, 1072 a 1, 1408 b 21

Phaethon, 345 a 16, 400 a 31, 836 b 2

Phalangium. *See* Venom-spider

Phalanx, 493 b 29

Phalaris, dictator of Himera, 1148 b 23, 1203 a 22, 1393 b 9-23

Phaleas of Chalcedon, criticism of his state 1266 a 38-1267 b 21; a legislator 1274 b 8-14

Phallic songs, 1449 a 12

Pharangites. *See* Iapyx

Pharnabazus, son of Pharnaces, 580 b 8

Pharnaces, father of Pharnabazus, 580 b 8

Pharos, 607 a 14, 1352 a 30

Pharsalus, 618 b 15; the Pharsalian mare 586 a 14, 1262 a 24; oligarchy at 1306 a 9-12

Pharynx, 492 b 27; necessary for voice 535 a 28

Phaselis, 973 a 8

Phasis, 350 a 27; cattle of 522 b 14

Phasis River, 846 a 29-32

Phayllus, wrote on the Epic Cycle 1417 a 15

Pheasant, lice on 557 a 12; eggs of 559 a 25; dust bath of 633 b 2

Phebol, an island, 393 b 17

Pheidon the Corinthian, 1265 b 12

Pheidon, tyrant of Argos, 1310 b 27

Phene, lämmergeier, 563 a 27, 592 b 5; habits of 619 b 22-620 a 13

Pheneus, 834 b 24

Pherecydes, a Syrian poet, 557 a 4, 1091 b 9

Phidias, 399 b 33, 846 a 19, 1141 a 10

Philaegides, the poet, 464 b 2

Philammon, 1413 a 13, 24

PHILEBUS of Plato, 1098 b 12, 1172 b 28, 1173 a 15, 29, b 7

Philemon, the actor, 1413 b 23

Philip, king of Macedonia, 1311 b 2, 1397 b 33

Philippi, mines in 833 a 29-31

Philippus, the comic dramatist, 406 b 18

PHILIPPUS of Isocrates, 1418 b 27

Philocrates, 1380 b 7

Philoctetes, 840 a 17, 1150 b 9, 1413 a 7, 1433 b 11

PHILOCTETES of Aeschylus, 1458 b 22, 1459 b 6

PHILOCTETES of Sophocles, 1146 a 20, 1151 b 18

Philolaus, 1225 a 32; gave laws to the Thebans 1274 a 32-b 4

Philomela, 1406 b 17

Philosopheme, defined as a demonstrative inference 162 a 15

Philosopher, 173 a 30, 1096 a 15, 1105 b 14, 1165 a 26, 1197 b 32, 1215 b 1, 1217 a 1-7; superior to the orator 917 a 2-5, 956 b 6-10; melancholic 953 a 10-955 a 40; must investigate all things 1004 a 34; most self-sufficient of all men 1177 b 1; Thales' proof that philosophers could be wealthy 1259 a 7-22; contemplative life is life for the philosopher 1324 a 28

Philosophy (σοφία), 391 b 8, 808 b 1, 1096 b 31, 1164 b 3, 1217 b 23, 1245 a 22; not defined as what produces happiness 149 b 33; a certain natural ability is necessary for the study of philosophy 163 b 10-16; first philosophy 194 b 15, 277 b 10, 1026 a 24; modesty in 291 b 27; divine and supernatural 391 a 2; deductive method of 807 a 9; begins in wonder 982 b 12-27; identified with mathematics by some 992 a 33; rightly called knowledge of the truth 993 b 19; treats of being *qua* being 1003 a 21-1005 a 17, 1060 b 31-1061 b 17; has many parts 1004 a 2-8, 1026 a 18; dialectic and sophistic 1004 b 18-26, 1061 b 8; must study primary axioms 1005 a 18-b 34, 1061 b 18-33; must study syllogism 1005 b 5; compounded of science and intellect 1197 a 23-29; a virtue 1197 b 3-11, 31; speculative philosophy 1214 a 14; the philosophic life 1216 a 28; the philosophic method 1216 b 39;

may discuss wealth-gaining 1258 b
10; must be thorough 1279 b 13-15;
philosophy needed for leisure 1334 a
24. Cf. Metaphysics, Wisdom

Philoxenus, 950 a 3, 1231 a 16, 1448 a
17; tried to compose his Mysians in
the Dorian mode 1342 b 10; his
scheme for raising money 1351 b 36-
1352 a 7; referred to 1118 a 32

PHINIDAE, 1455 a 10

Phlegm, 458 a 3, 463 a 13, 487 a 5, 511
b 10, 725 a 15, 824 b 19, 845 a 22, 860
a 25, 880 a 24, 891 a 12, 906 a 2, 908
b 15, 1044 a 18; not well defined as
undigested moisture that comes first
off food 140 b 8; cold 862 b 28; treatment of diseases caused by 865 a 31-
b 5, 878 b 14-16

Phlegraean Plain, 368 b 31

Phocaea, rivals at Phocaea deceived by
Aristotle, the Rhodian 1348 a 35-b 16

Phocis, Phocians, 69 a 2, 1398 a 2; revolution at 1304 a 11

Phocylides, quoted 1295 b 33

Phoenicia, Phoenice, Phoenicians, 364 a
3, 17, 525 b 7, 541 a 18, 603 a 1, 843
b 10, 844 a 11, 17, 24, 973 b 5

Phoenicias. See Eurus

PHOENISSAE, 1167 a 33

Pholidotes. See Tesselbates

Pholis, a nest-building fish 621 b 7

PHORCIDES, 1456 a 2

Phormis, a Sicilian poet, 1449 b 6

Phoxinus. See Minnow

Phoxus, tyrant at Chalcis, 1304 a 31

Phratries, 1241 b 26

Phreatto, Court of, 1300 b 28

Phrenes. See Diaphragm

Phrygia, 395 b 30, 522 a 28, 580 b 8, 617
b 19, 922 b 22, 973 a 25, b 15; cattle
there can move their horns 517 a 29

Phrygian ashes, 834 b 31

Phrygian mode, 922 b 21, 1276 b 10,
1290 a 21; inspires enthusiasm 1340 b
4, 1342 b 2-12. Cf. Modes of Music

Phrynichus, leader of the Four Hundred at Athens, 920 a 11-13, 1305 b 27

Phrynis, 993 b 17

PHTHIOTIDES, 1456 a 1

Phthisis, 860 b 1; those suffering from
phthisis apt to emit semen during

sleep 884 a 6-15; why infectious 887 a
22-39

Phycis, black goby, spawn of 567 b 20;
diet of 591 b 12; changes of colour in
607 b 18

Phycus, yellow substance carried into
the Hellespont by the Euxine 568 a 4

Phylarchs, magistrates at Epidamnus
1301 b 22

Phyle, 1429 b 9

Physician, 436 a 20, 463 a 4, 469 a 9,
1102 a 21, 1105 b 16, 1112 b 12, 1127
b 20, 1133 a 17, 1137 a 17, 1148 b 8,
1164 b 24, 1174 b 25, 1180 b 14, 1287
a 35, 1331 b 35, 1335 a 40; concerned
with health and disease 480 b 22-30;
continue treatment only till health is
restored 956 a 28-b 5; concerned with
individuals 1097 a 13; three kinds of
1282 a 3-5; in Egypt 1286 a 13; not to
coerce his patients 1324 b 30

Physics, natural philosophy, 251 a 9,
267 b 21, 441 b 2, 442 a 30, 995 a 18,
1025 b 19, 1216 b 12; first principle of
nature is a moving one 184 b 18; take
for granted that things existing by
nature are in motion 185 a 12; examination of the physicist's conception of Being 187 a 12-188 a 18; compared with mathematics 193 b 22-194
b 15; its subject matter consists of
things whose forms are separable but
which do not exist apart from matter
194 b 12; infinite as attribute of substance 203 a 17; deals with more concrete objects than the objects of mathematics 299 a 17; natural philosophers 436 a 17, 470 b 6, 472 a 2, 741
b 10, 742 a 17, 778 b 7, 986 b 14, 989
b 30, 990 a 3, 992 b 4, 1001 a 12, 1005
a 31, 1006 a 2, 1050 b 30, 1062 b 22,
1064 a 15, 1071 b 27, 1075 b 27, 1078
b 19, 1335 a 40; how far concerned
with the soul? 641 a 18-642 b 4; second philosophy 1005 b 1, 1037 a 16;
a theoretical science 1025 b 26-1026 a
33, 1064 b 2; studies things *qua* moving 1059 b 16, 1061 b 7, 28-32, 1064 a
30, 1069 b 1

Physiognomy, methods of 805 a 1-806 a
18, 807 a 3-30, 809 a 1-26, 814 a 6-b 9;
physiognomic signs 806 a 27-814 b 9;

physiognomic signs in man 810 a 14-814 b 9

Pieria, gold of 833 b 19-22

Piety, 1250 b 22

Pig, 674 a 27, 675 a 37, 774 b 20, 811 b 30, 812 b 28; hair of 498 b 27, 782 b 9, 893 a 3-16; feet of 499 b 12, 23; mammae of 500 a 27, 688 a 35, b 12; teeth of 501 b 4, 507 b 16, 538 b 21, 661 b 18, 663 a 8, 788 b 16; mouth of 502 a 8; some kinds have no gall-bladder 506 a 24; stomach of 507 b 17, 20, 508 a 8, 674 a 27, 675 a 27; testicles of 509 b 14, 716 b 30; womb of 510 b 17; brain of 520 a 27; bones of 521 b 15; breeding of 542 a 29, 545 a 28-b 4, 546 a 7-27, 572 a 7, 577 b 28; lice on 557 a 17; copulation of 572 b 23, 896 a 23; reproduction of 573 a 21-b 16, 771 a 23, 892 b 1, 894 b 13; habits of 580 b 24, 609 b 28; diet of 595 a 15-b 4, 621 a 1; diseases of 603 a 30-604 a 3; snoot of 662 a 14; has dull sensibility 667 a 10; spleen of 674 a 2; penis of 716 b 30; development of young at birth 774 b 17-23; in Macedonia 835 a 34; with solid hoofs 835 a 35; monstrous births in 898 a 12

Pigeon, gregarious 488 a 4; habits of 488 b 2; spleen of 506 a 16, 670 a 34; gall-bladder of 506 b 22; crop of 508 b 28; breeding of 544 a 30, b 8-12, 562 b 3-563 a 4; varieties of 544 b 1-8; generation of 558 b 12, 749 b 12; eggs of 558 b 23, 559 a 22, 560 b 22, 562 b 6, 749 b 18-26, 750 a 16, 774 b 31; wind-eggs in 559 b 27; copulation of 560 b 25-561 a 3, 756 b 23; brooding of 564 a 7; diet of 593 a 15; does not migrate 597 b 5; habits of 612 b 32-613 a 13, 620 a 25; bath of 633 b 4; eye of 657 b 11; stomach of 670 a 34; colour of 793 a 15. Cf. Rock-dove, Turtle-dove

Pillory, 1306 b 2

Pindar, quoted 1364 a 28, 1401 a 17, 18; referred to 1177 b 32 (?)

Pindarus, 1462 a 1

Pindus, 350 b 16

Pine tree, 818 b 36, 820 a 18, 32; seed of 821 a 6; bark of 829 a 3

Pinna, 528 a 24, 26, 547 b 15, 548 a 4, 588 b 15; incapable of motion 528 a 34; 'eggs' of 763 b 9

Pinna-guard, 547 b 16, 548 a 28

Pious, Race of the, 846 a 9-18

Pipe-fish, belone, gall-bladder of 506 b 9; breeding of 543 b 12, 567 b 22, 571 a 2, 755 a 33

Piper. See Cuckoo-fish

Piphinx, habits of 610 a 11

Piraeus, 177 b 13, 1267 b 23, 1401 a 27, 1411 a 14; inhabitants of the Piraeus are more democratic than people of Athens 1303 b 10

Pirates, 1405 a 26

Pitch, 382 b 16, 385 b 6, 387 b 22, 388 a 4, 818 b 36; burning of 791 b 23; spring of 842 b 16

Pitch of voice, 1403 b 30

Pitchwax, 624 a 17

Pithecusae, volcano in 833 a 15

Pittacus, 70 a 17, 1167 a 32, 1285 a 35, 1389 a 16, 1402 b 12; his laws in regard to drunkenness 1274 b 18-22

Pitthus, 1400 a 9

Pity (ἔλεος), 1105 b 22, 1109 b 32, 1111 a 1, 1354 a 16, 25, 1378 a 22, 1385 b 11-1386 b 8, 1404 a 15, 1419 b 26, 1439 b 17, 26-36, 1440 a 41, 1445 a 2, 1449 b 27; defined 1385 b 13; in tragedy 1452 a 2, b 1, 32, 35, 38, 1453 a 5, b 1, 12, 1456 a 38

Place (ποῦ, τόπος), 144 b 33, 146 b 30, 208 a 27-213 a 10, 226 b 22, 271 a 5, 273 a 12, 355 b 1-15, 706 b 3; examples of 2 a 1, 11 b 10; change of 15 a 13-b 16, 1042 a 34, 1069 b 13; the category of 103 b 23, 115 b 12, 146 b 20; a necessary condition of movement 200 b 20; natural place for each sensible body 205 a 10, 253 b 34, 276 a 12, 310 b 7; six kinds of 205 b 32, 208 b 13, 1067 a 29; existence of place obvious from fact of mutual replacement 208 b 1-8; each element has its proper place 208 b 10, 214 b 14, 330 b 30, 334 b 35, 335 a 20, 337 a 7-15; not dependent on things, though things are dependent on it 208 b 36; it is neither matter nor form 209 a 2-210 a 13; some things potentially in place, others actually 211 a

17-b 5, 212 b 4; cannot be the form 211 b 10-13; cannot be the interval between extremities 211 b 14-29; cannot be matter 211 b 30-212 a 2; defined as the innermost motionless boundary of what contains 212 a 1-31; proper or natural places 253 b 35, 276 a 12, 310 b 7; perceptible 275 b 11; intermediate place 277 b 23, 312 a 9; no place outside the heaven 279 a 12-b 3; and the void 309 b 26; and position 322 b 32-323 a 25; 'together in place' 1068 b 26; 'apart' 1068 b 27; 'touch' 1068 b 28; 'contrary in place' 1068 b 31; peculiar to individual things 1092 a 19

Plague, why contagious 859 b 15-20

Plaintiff, advantages of plaintiff in law court 951 b 26

Planes, 141 b 5-25, 286 b 27, 298 b 33, 971 a 9, 972 a 8, 30, 1028 b 26; analysis of bodies into planes refuted 299 a 1-300 a 19; resolution into planes as a theory of the generation of elements 306 a 1-18

Plane-tree, 820 b 41, 912 b 12

Planets, 342 b 28, 343 b 29, 344 a 36, 345 b 28, 346 a 2, 816 a 23; secondary revolution of 285 b 29, 291 b 1; do not twinkle 290 a 19; follow different courses 392 a 13; seven divisions 392 a 20-30; movement of 1073 a 13-1074 b 14. Cf. Heaven, Stars

Plangus, 610 a 11

Plank, longer it is the weaker it is 853 a 5-18; more difficult to carry if held at the end than if held in the middle 857 a 5-21; vibration in a long plank 857 a 22-33

Plants, 187 b 18, 190 b 4, 199 a 24, 261 a 16, 390 a 17, 410 b 23, 412 b 3, 732 a 1, 733 b 24, 738 b 35, 902 b 2, 1087 a 32, 1222 b 17; food of 335 a 11-14; composition of 384 b 31, 390 b 21; live on when divided 411 b 20, 413 b 18; have power of self-nutrition 413 a 33, 414 a 33, 415 a 2; have no sensation 424 a 33, 435 b 1, 454 a 16, 666 a 35, 731 b 4, 741 a 10, 778 b 33, 815 a 1-816 b 22; have longest life 466 a 10, 467 a 6-b 9; withering in 478 b 28; reproduction in 537 b 33, 539 a 16-20, 761 b 27, 827 a 3-5; how differ from animals 588 b 4-589 a 9, 666 a 35, 681 a 12, 26 (Cf. 686 b 34), 725 a 20, 779 a 4; concoction of 650 a 21, 678 a 11, 822 a 27-b 25, 825 a 30; discharge no waste residue 655 b 34, 681 a 34, 817 b 19, 908 a 6, 19; no great variety in heterogeneous parts 656 a 1; some grow independent of soil, some on other plants 681 a 22; upper and lower parts inverted 683 b 21, 686 b 32; roots of plants are equivalent of mouth and head of animals 686 b 35, 705 b 8, 706 b 5, 818 a 20, 741 a 4, 815 a 21, 816 b 23-818 a 3; 819 a 20; sex of 715 b 19, 731 a 2, 27, 741 a 4, 815 a 21, 816 b 23-818 a 3; some bear fruit, some do not 715 b 22, 723 b 11, 819 b 31; some have spontaneous generation 715 b 26, 762 b 19; seeds of 718 b 15, 722 a 12, 731 a 7; cuttings of 723 b 17; exhaustion in 750 a 30; embryo of 757 b 19; nourishment of 762 b 13; do not wake and sleep 779 a 2, 816 b 28, 817 b 20; shedding of leaves of 783 b 9-25; unctuous plants 783 b 20; colours of 794 b 12-797 a 32, 827 b 18-31, 828 a 40-829 a 35; have no movement of themselves 706 b 6, 816 a 26, 817 b 23, 818 b 1, 822 b 2; imperfect 816 b 6 (Cf. 817 a 21); do not have respiration 816 b 26; created for sake of animals 817 b 25; parts of 818 a 4-819 a 41; classification of 819 a 42-820 a 10; differences in 820 a 11-28; changes and variations in 821 a 27-b 26; three powers of 822 a 11; have motion in sense of attraction 822 b 2; effect of climate and locality on 824 b 36-825 a 39; conditions for growth of 824 b 36, 826 a 29, 38; do not grow in snow 825 a 2-21; water plants 825 a 40-826 a 19; rock plants 826 a 20-37; shapes of 827 b 32-828 a 31; effect of warm water on 898 a 8; sweet-smelling plants promote flow of urine 907 b 4-13, 924 b 18-27; parts which have no functional importance are round 915 a 25-33; increase in length more than in any other direction 916 a 12-17; some must be boiled to be edible 923 a 17-20; some must be roasted to be edible 923 a 21-24; edible and inedible 923 a 25-29; some live only till they produce seeds 923 a 30-b 9; watering of 924 b 15-17; stalks of 925 a 6; sprouting of 926 a 1-10; sweeter when watered with cold water 926 a 21-25; life of 1216 a 3-6; desire posterity 1252 a 29; exist for use of man 1256 b 16. Cf. Trees

Plateus, 551 b 16

Plato, 122 b 27, 140 a 4, 280 a 31, 401 b 24, 956 a 12, 1010 b 12, 1019 a 4, 1025 a 12, 1071 b 39, 1083 a 33, 1095 a 32, 1194 a 7, 1293 b 1, 1376 a 10, 1398 b 29, 1417 a 20; definition of soul 140 b 3; 'Great and Small' 187 a 18, 192 a 12, 203 a 15, 206 b 27, 987 b 21, 26, 988 a 26, 992 a 12, 998 b 10, 1055 b 30-1056 b 2, 1083 b 23, 1085 a 10, 1087 b 14; infinite as a self-subsistent substance 203 a 4, 5; criticism of Pythagorean and Platonic belief in a separately existing infinite 204 a 9-206 a 8; identifies matter and space 209 b 11, 34; time was created 251 b 16; soul thought by Plato to be cause of motion 265 b 33; limits his discussion of coming to be to elements 315 a 29-33; denies there is a void 325 b 33; three elementary bodies 330 b 17; theory of rivers and sea 355 b 32-356 a 33; his essay 'On Philosophy' 404 b 20; plants have sensation 815 a 22, b 15; melancholic 953 a 27; criticism of the Platonic philosophy 987 a 29-988 a 16, 990 a 33-993 a 10; constructs infinite out of great and small 987 b 25, 988 a 26; being and unity are substances 996 a 6, 1001 a 9; three kinds of substance: Forms, mathematical objects, and sensible bodies 1028 b 19; the one is a substance 1053 b 13; says Sophist spends time on non-being 1064 b 29; Forms for all natural objects 1070 a 18; assumes eternal actuality 1071 b 32; on education 1104 b 12; proves good to be pleasure 1172 b 29; on virtue 1182 a 24-29; soul has three parts 1249 a 32; criticism of the state in *The Republic* 1260 b 27-1264 b 25; criticism

of the state in *The Laws* 1264 b 26-1266 a 30; characteristics of Plato's constitution 1274 b 9-14; criticism of Plato's theory of revolutions 1316 a 2-b 27; Phaedrus 1408 b 21; references to:

Apology, 1419 a 8-12

Euthydemus, 74 b 25, 1097 a 26, 1098 b 12

Gorgias, 173 a 9

Hippias Minor, 1025 a 6

Laws, 1072 a 2, 1098 b 12, 1111 a 24, 1180 a 5, 1260 b 5, 1264 b 26-1266 a 30, b 5, 1271 b 1, 1330 b 32, 1336 a 34

Menexenus, 1367 b 8, 1415 b 31

Meno, 67 a 22, 71 a 29, 1260 a 22, 27

Phaedo, 335 b 11, 355 b 32, 991 b 3, 1080 a 2

Phaedrus, 140 b 3, 1072 a 1, 1408 b 21

Philebus, 1098 b 12, 1172 b 28, 1173 a 15, 29, b 7

Politicus, 1252 a 7, 1253 b 18, 1255 b 17, 1289 b 5

Protagoras, 1164 a 24

Republic, 992 a 33, 1075 b 20, 1130 a 3, 1260 b 27-1264 b 25, 1291 a 12, 1316 a 2, 1327 b 38, 1336 a 31, 1342 a 30, 1406 b 32

Sophistes, 1026 b 14, 1064 b 19, 1089 a 20

Symposium, 1262 b 12

Theaetetus, 76 b 25, 1010 b 12

Timaeus, 209 b 11, 34, 280 a 30, 293 b 32, 300 a 1, b 18, 306 b 19, 308 b 6, 315 b 32, 325 b 25, 329 a 13, 332 a 30, 1057 b 9, 1071 b 32, 1072 a 2, 1092 a 1

Cf. Form (Plato)

Platonists, 1096 a 11-1097 a 14; limit and unlimited 1004 b 33

Pleasant, 1156 b 23, 1154 b 16; an object of choice 1104 b 31; as an object of love 1155 b 18; activity of philosophical wisdom is the pleasantest activity 1177 a 24; two senses of: absolute and relative 1228 b 18; a topic of persuasion 1421 b 24, 1423 b 7, 1425 b 40, 1439 a 12, 37

Pleasantries, lively and taking sayings, 1410 b 6-1413 b 2

An Index to Aristotle

Pleasingly, how to speak, 1434 a 34-41, b 28-31, 1436 a 21

Pleasure (ἡδονή), 1148 a 22, 1151 b 22, 1172 a 18-1176 a 29, 1191 b 21, 1202 b 28, 1204 a 19-1206 a 35, 1216 a 27-37, 1245 a 37, 1250 a 9, 22, b 8, 14, 1251 a 18, 24-28, 1369 b 33-1372 a 2, 1448 b 18, 1453 a 36, b 11, 1459 a 21, 1462 b 13; ambiguous term 106 a 37-b 1; Prodicus' division of 112 b 23; makes good things more valuable 117 a 23; virtue better than pleasure 118 b 32; may be either objectionable or pleasant 119 b 6-10; as activity 146 b 16-19, 1175 b 24-1176 a 3; moral excellence concerned with bodily pleasures 247 a 8; where there is sensation there is pleasure 413 b 23, 414 b 3, 431 a 10; object of desire is the pleasant 661 a 8; a seeming good 700 b 29; has effect on temperature of body 702 a 1; as the good for man 1095 b 19-22, 1172 b 9-1173 a 13; a constituent of happiness 1098 b 24-29, 1214 a 31-b 5, 1215 a 33, 1323 b 1, 1338 a 6, 1339 b 20; a state of the soul 1099 a 8; virtue and vice concerned with pleasures and pains 1104 b 4-1105 a 17, 1220 a 39, 1221 b 27-1222 a 5, b 11, 1227 b 1-11; aimed at by all men and animals 1104 b 34, 1153 b 30, 1157 b 16, 1172 b 10, 1175 a 10-21, 1362 b 6; harder to fight pleasure than anger 1105 a 8; relation to courage 1117 a 29-b 21; of body and soul 1117 b 28; some are necessary, others are not 1150 a 16; views hostile to: (1) pleasure not a good, (2) pleasure not a chief good, (3) most pleasures bad 1152 b 1-1154 b 34, 1204 a 31-1206 a 35; necessarily a good 1153 b 4; no one thing is always pleasant 1154 b 20; found more in rest than in movement 1154 b 27; friendships of 1156 a 12, 32-b 5, 35, 1158 a 18, 29, 1162 a 25, b 13-16, 1164 a 7, 1165 b 2, 1167 a 12, 1169 b 26, 1170 b 28, 1209 a 4-b 37, 1236 a 37-b 1; Eudoxus' conception of 1172 b 9-1173 b 31; as wholly bad 1173 a 14-1174 a 12; complete at any moment 1174 a 13-b 14; never continuous 1174 b 3-9; each animal has its proper pleasure 1176 a 4-9; moral virtue determined by pleasure and pain 1185 b 33-37, 1186 a 35, 1204 a 29, 1206 a 20; all seek pleasure and avoid pain 1189 b 30-32, 1190 a 7; voluptuary seeks bodily pleasures 1215 b 3, 1216 a 17; bodily pleasures are not enough 1215 b 30-1216 a 10, 1258 a 5; temperance in 1230 b 25-1231 a 18; can friendship exist without pleasure? 1237 a 19; the absolute good is pleasant 1237 a 27; to love is to feel pleasure 1237 a 37; Plato deprives his guardians of pleasure 1264 b 16; given by music 1339 b 21, 1340 a 3, 15, b 16, 1341 a 15; a topic of persuasion 1421 b 25; 1423 a 10, b 7, 1425 b 40, 1427 b 40, 1435 a 12, 37; defined as that which causes joy 1422 a 17. Cf. Insensibility to pleasure, Pain

Plectrum, 516 b 1

Pleiads, 542 b 12, 543 a 15, 566 a 23, 592 a 7, 598 b 7, 599 a 28, b 11, 859 a 22, 861 a 20, 1093 a 13

Pleum, 840 a 14

Pleurisy, drunkards easily attacked by 871 a 1-7, b 33-872 a 2

Plexippus, 1379 b 14

Plot, fable, 1447 a 9, 1449 b 5, 8, 1450 a 14-39, 1453 b 4, 1454 a 12, 1455 a 22, b 8, 1456 a 8, 28, 1460 a 33, 1461 b 19; represents the action in a tragedy 1450 a 2; defined as the combination of incidents in the story 1450 a 4; the purpose of the tragedy 1450 a 23; arrangement and length of 1450 b 21-1451 a 15; unity of 1451 a 16-35; must depict the probable and the universal 1451 a 36-1452 a 11; simple or complex 1452 a 13-21, b 30, 1453 a 13, 1455 b 33, 1456 a 20, 1459 b 15; forms of plot to be avoided 1452 b 33-1453 a 7

Plum, 820 a 38

Pluto, 836 b 20

Pneumatic pressure, 586 a 16

Podagra, 575 b 8

Poecilis, habits of 609 a 7

Poetry, 953 a 11, 1342 b 4, 1371 b 6, 1403 b 25, 1405 a 32, 1406 a 13, b 2, 11, 1408 b 18, 1450 b 18, 1454 b 16;

An Index to Aristotle

many men are better judges of poetry than a single man 1281 b 8; the language of poetry 1404 a 28-b 4, 1458 a 18-1459 a 16, 1461 a 9-b 21; distinguished by: (1) means 1447 a 19-b 29, (2) objects 1448 a 1-18, (3) manner of imitation 1448 a 19-b 3; origin and development of 1448 b 4-1449 a 30; compared with history 1451 b 1-7; possibility and impossibility in poetry 1460 a 26-b 5, 1461 b 9-12; does not have the same kind of correctness as other arts 1460 b 14; error in 1460 b 15-1461 a 8; contradictions in 1461 b 15-18

Poets, 995 a 8, 1120 b 14, 1168 a 2, 1212 b 27; measure life in periods of seven years 1335 b 34, 1336 b 40; never show Zeus as playing or singing 1339 b 8; in drama actors count for more than poets 1403 b 33; the old poets 1409 a 26; must have a touch of madness 1455 a 33

Point (στιγμή, σημεῖον), 108 b 26, 193 b 24, 220 a 10, 231 a 9, 699 a 22, 992 a 19, 1085 b 28; defined as a unit having position 87 a 36, 88 a 33, 227 a 28, 409 a 6, 1044 a 8, 1069 a 12, 1084 b 26; defined as a beginning and end of a line 108 b 26, 971 a 18, 1090 b 5-13; prior to line 141 b 15-22; a limit of a body 193 b 32, 1028 b 17; not necessary that it have a place 209 a 11, 212 b 24, 320 b 1; impossible consequences of theory that line consists of points 215 b 18, 231 a 25, 241 a 14, 968 a 18-21, b 25-969 a 2, 970 b 1-972 b 31, 1001 b 18; has no magnitude, therefore indivisible 296 a 17, 299 b 7, 300 a 15, 316 a 25-34, 317 a 12, 407 a 12-15, 430 b 20, 702 b 32, 971 a 21-25, 1016 b 26 (Cf. 427 a 10); has no weight 299 a 30; the point is a division 430 b 20, 1060 b 19; is a point a substance? 996 a 13-17, 1001 b 26-1002 b 11, 1028 b 17; neither comes to be nor perishes 1002 a 32, 1044 b 22, 1174 b 12. Cf. Line

Poison, poisonous plants 831 a 3-10; of the Circaean Mountains 835 b 35-836 a 7; poisonous waters 836 a 30-34, 842 a 11-14; arrow-poison 837 a 13-23,

845 a 1-9; poisonous wasps 844 b 32-34; Scythian poison 845 a 1-9; poisonous snakes 845 a 1-14; poisonous tree 845 a 15; poisonous lizards 845 b 5-7; poisonous mice 845 b 7

Polecat. *See* Marten

Poles, 285 b 10, 293 b 31, 296 a 27, 391 b 24, 392 a 4, 699 a 23

Political economy, 1345 b 13; most varied and the easiest 1345 b 15; scope of 1346 a 5-7

Politicians, 1181 a 2; thought to be busybodies 1142 a 2

Politics, political science, 1130 b 28, 1145 a 11, 1181 a 24-29, b 24-28, 1182 b 16-1183 a 7, 1216 b 37, 1218 a 35, 1234 b 24, 1237 a 2, 1450 b 7, 1460 b 14; science of the good for man 1094 a 18-b 11; the master art 1094 a 24-28, 1182 b 1, 1218 b 10-14; requirements for student of 1095 a 1-12, b 6, 1102 a 22; end is action 1095 a 5, 1099 b 31; man is a political animal 1097 b 11, 1162 a 17, 1169 b 18, 1253 a 2, 30, 1278 b 20; more prized than medicine 1102 a 20; concerned with pleasures and pain 1105 a 11, 1152 b 1; political justice 1134 a 26, 29, b 13-19; political wisdom and practical wisdom compared 1141 b 23-1142 a 31; political friendship 1161 a 10-b 11, 1163 b 34, 1167 b 2, 1171 a 17; the highest science 1282 b 16; subjects to be studied by 1288 b 10-1298 a 25; aims at the good of the state 1324 a 20; compared with economics 1343 a 1-16

Politicus of Plato, 1252 a 7, 1253 b 18, 1255 b 17, 1289 b 5

Polity, constitutional government, 1160 a 35, 1279 a 37; rule of husband over wife is constitutional rule 1259 a 41; citizens rule and are ruled in turns 1259 b 5, 1261 a 30-b 10; composed of heavy-armed soldiers 1265 b 28, 1279 b 2; suitable for warlike people 1288 a 12; a compromise between democracy and oligarchy 1293 b 22-1294 b 39, 1298 a 34-b 11, 1307 a 5-23; used to be called democracy 1297 b 25; election in 1300 a 33-42; revolutions in 1303 a 2, 1306 b 6-16, 1307 a 5-33; preservation of 1308 a 35-b 10; works well in state with large country area 1319 a 33

Polium, 605 a 6

Poll-tax, 1346 a 4, 1348 a 33. Cf. Taxes

Polus, 981 a 4, 1400 b 21

Polybus, 1415 a 21; on the nature of veins 512 b 12-513 a 7

Polyclitus, 195 a 33, b 11, 1015 a 1, 1041 a 10

Polycrates, 1401 a 33, b 15; the Polycratean monuments at Samos 1313 b 24

Polycritus, wrote history of Sicily in verse 840 b 32

Polydamas, 1116 a 23, 1191 a 9, 1230 a 21

Polyeuctus, 1411 a 21

Polygnotus, 1340 a 37, 1448 a 6, 1450 a 27

Polyidus the Sophist, 1455 a 7, b 10

Polyneices, the burial of 1373 b 10

Polypus, changes colour of skin 832 b 15

Pomegranate, 820 a 30, b 41, 821 a 5, 36, 923 b 25; colour of fruit of 796 a 21, b 9, 799 a 10-14; blossom of 923 a 13-16

Pontus, 347 a 35, 348 b 35, 354 a 14, 367 a 1, 393 a 32, b 25, 554 b 8, 571 a 18, 596 b 31, 605 a 22, 606 a 20, 831 b 24, 835 a 15, 839 b 11, 1305 b 37, 1306 a 7; fish in 835 b 15-23; corn of 909 a 18-21; weather of 938 a 37-b 4

Pontus River, 841 a 30

Poor, the, should be well-treated 1267 b 9, 1297 b 7; always numerous 1279 b 38; degraded condition of 1295 b 5-25; will fight in war if fed 1297 b 11; may cause revolution 1302 b 34-1303 a 10; count equally with rich in a democracy 1318 a 7; the rich should help 1320 a 33-b 15. Cf. Poverty, Rich

Poor-spirited. See Humility

Poplar, 549 b 33, 726 a 7; black poplars in Crete 835 b 2, 836 b 4

Poppy, 456 b 31, 627 b 17; colour of blossoms and fruit 796 a 25, b 15

Population, must be limited for good government 1265 a 14, 40, 1270 a 29-b 6, 1326 a 5-b 25, 1327 a 16

Populonium, 837 b 33

Porcupine, spines of 490 b 30, 623 a 33; reproduction of 579 a 27; hibernation of 579 a 27, 600 a 28

Pordoselene, 605 b 29

Pores, 381 b 1, 385 a 29, b 20, 386 a 15, 387 a 2, 802 a 25, b 11; and perception 324 b 25-35, 325 b 1-11, 326 b 6-34; and colour 793 a 24-32, 794 a 25-b 10

Porphyrio, purple coot, stomach of 509 a 11; drinking of 595 a 12; tail of 710 a 13; legs of 710 a 15

Porpoise, 566 b 12, 598 b 2; mammae of 521 b 24

Poseideon, the month of December, 543 a 11, b 15, 570 a 33

Poseidon, 1455 b 18

Posidonia, 839 a 32

Posidonium, 973 a 17

Position (τὸ ποῦ), 103 b 22, 188 a 23, 254 b 24, 985 b 15, 1016 b 26, 1022 b 2, 1042 b 19, 1077 b 31; examples of 2 a 2, 11 b 10; some parts have position, some have not 5 a 15-37; six kinds of 205 b 32-206 a 8; lying down and other postures 885 b 15-886 a 20

Positives, 'opposite' as privatives to 12 a 26-13 a 37

Positive term, related to privative terms 52 a 15; prior to its privation 286 a 26

Possibility, 701 a 24, 1047 b 3-30; contradictory of propositions expressing 21 b 10-22; meanings of 22 a 15, 23 a 20-26, 25 a 37, b 15, 32 b 4-22, 33 a 3, 37 a 15; all premisses in mood of possibility are convertible 25 a 37, 32 a 30; defined 32 a 18; and necessity 32 a 20, 28; meaning of possible and impossible 281 a 2-28, 699 b 18-30; possible and impossible as a line of argument 1392 a 8-b 13; and impossibility in poetry 1460 a 26-b 5, 1461 b 9-12. Cf. Impossibility

Posterior (ὕστερος), meaning of 916 a 18-39, 1018 b 8-1019 a 14

Postulate (ὑπόθεσις), 1428 a 8, 1433 b 17-28, 1436 a 20; distinction between hypotheses and illegitimate postulate 76 b 23-77 a 4; defined as the demands which speakers make from their hearers 1433 b 17

Potameus. See Apeliotes

Potentiality, potency, power (δύναμις), 186 a 3, 191 b 28, 262 a 22-264 a 34, 417 a 9, 427 a 6, 429 b 8, 430 a 10-20, 445 b 30, 734 a 30, b 21, 735 a 10, 740 b 20, 741 b 15, 743 a 23, 1009 a 35, 1044 b 29-1045 a 5, b 28-1051 a 33, 1065 b 5-1066 a 34, 1071 a 5, b 23, 1103 a 27, 1170 a 17, 1363 b 31; senses of 22 b 36-23 a 18, 255 a 30-b 32, 417 a 26-33, b 30; all causes may be either potential or actual 195 b 4; as used in a definition of movement 201 b 10-202 b 22, 257 b 7; matter is potentiality 412 a 10, 414 a 16; potentiality and actuality in sensation 431 a 5, b 25; do elements exist potentially? 1002 b 33-1003 a 4; that which exists potentially is indeterminate 1007 b 28; meanings of 1019 a 15-1020 a 6; many so-called substances are potentialities 1040 b 5-15; actuality is prior to potentiality 1049 b 4-1051 a 3; geometrical truths found by actualization of potentialities 1051 a 22-23; and change 1069 b 16; good as a potency 1183 b 21-35. Cf. Actuality

Potidaea, 1396 a 20; Athenians at Potidaea levied property tax 1347 a 18-24

Pottery, 823 a 18; consists of earth alone 384 b 19; three elements in 822 a 16-24; potter's wheel 851 b 20

Poulp. See Octopus

Poultice, 863 a 6, 7, 864 b 32-35

Poverty, 1115 a 11, 17; why more commonly found among good than bad 950 b 9-22; brave man does not seek to escape 1116 a 12; friends are only refuge in 1155 a 11; the parent of revolution and crime 1265 b 12; a cause of civil troubles 1266 b 39; the poor are many in number 1291 b 10; a characteristic of democracy 1317 b 41; extreme poverty lowers the character of democracy 1320 a 34. Cf. Poor, Wealth

Power. See Potentiality

Poynx, habits of 617 a 8

Practicable, a topic of persuasion 1421 b 26, 1422 a 19, 1423 b 8, 1439 a 12

Praise, 1109 b 31, 1110 a 24, 33, 1120 a 16, 1127 b 17, 1178 b 16, 1183 b 27, 1185 b 9, 1195 b 15, 1197 a 18, 1219 b 14, 1358 b 12, 1367 b 21, 1374 a 22; confined to voluntary acts 1223 a 13

Prasocuris. See Leekbane

Pratys, 1413 a 7

Prawn. See Carid

Predetermination of future events, 19 a 7-22

Predication, 25 b 23, 26 a 17, 41 a 15, 48 a 41, 49 a 16, 968 a 3, 978 a 33; some things predicable of and not present in a subject 1 a 20; some things present in but not predicable of a subject 1 a 24; some things both predicable of and present in a subject 1 a 29; some things neither predicable of nor present in a subject 1 b 3; all predicable of the predicate is also predicable of the subject 1 b 11, 2 a 20; definition is never predicable 2 a 30; everything except primary substance predicable of or present in a primary substance 2 a 33, b 16; genus and species only predicates that convey a knowledge of primary substance 2 b 31; substances and differentia predicated univocally 3 a 33; primary substance not predicable of anything 3 a 36, 43 a 25; all predicated of predicate predicated also of subject 3 b 4; equality and inequality predicated of quantity 6 a 27; combinations of predicates 20 b 31-21 a 34; predicate and predicated 24 b 17; meanings of 32 b 25; natural and accidental 81 b 24, 82 a 20, 83 a 1-b 17; possibility of infinite series of 81 b 30-84 b 2; implies single subject and single attribute 83 a 22, b 18; predicates which do not signify substance must be predicates of some other subject 83 a 31; series of intermediate predications in a demonstration must terminate 83 b 39; the four predicables: (1) property, (2) definition, (3) genus, (4) accident 101 b 24, 37-103 a 5; fourfold division of predicables proven by induction and reasoning 103 b 1-19; relation of categories to the predicables 103 b 20-104 a 2; commonplace rules respecting predications 108 b 37-155 a 39. Cf. Category

Pregnancy, generally milk comes only in 522 a 1; signs of 583 b 29-585 b 5, 775 b 10; effect of seasons on 860 a 19-24; care of woman during 1335 b 12-19

Prejudice, calumny, 1354 a 16, 1382 a 2, 1415 a 27; ways of arousing and allaying 1416 a 3-b 13, 1445 b 16-22; how to meet 1436 b 30-1437 b 33, 1442 a 22-b 27

Prelude in music, 1414 b 20

Premiss (πρότασις), defined 24 a 16; universal 24 a 17; particular 24 a 18; indefinite 24 a 19; demonstrative 24 a 23; dialectical 24 a 25; a syllogism has two and only two premisses 42 a 33; universal affirmative premiss most difficult to establish, easiest to overthrow 43 a 1; rules for selecting 43 a 20-46 a 30; quantity of the premiss 47 b 15-39; rules for drawing true conclusions from false premisses 53 b 4-57 b 17; proper form of 71 b 4; nature of the premiss is of demonstrated knowledge 71 b 20; premisses of demonstrated knowledge must be primary 72 a 6, 100 a 28; primary premiss identified with basic truth 72 a 7; primary premisses are cause of knowledge 72 a 30; knowledge of immediate premiss is independent of demonstration 72 b 19; two premisses are smallest foundation for a conclusion 73 a 10; non-necessary premiss may give necessary conclusion 75 a 3; false premiss may give true conclusion 75 a 4, 78 a 8, 88 a 20; homogeneous with conclusion 84 b 1-4; identical in number with middle terms 84 b 21; none common to all sciences 88 a 18-b 29; basic premisses of demonstrations are definitions 90 b 24; apprehended only by intuition 99 b 15-100 b 17; necessary premisses defined as those through which the actual reasoning is constructed 155 b 20; the four non-necessary kinds 155 b 22; use of necessary premisses in dialectics 155 b 29-156 a 2; in dialectics a premiss is valid if it holds in several instances and if no objection is raised 157 b 2; dialectical premiss

must be able to be answered by 'yes' or 'no' 158 a 17; argument is bad if true conclusion is reached through false premisses 162 b 23; conclusion follows at once on conception of two premisses 701 a 11; of practical syllogism may be the good or possible 701 a 24; suppression of one of the premisses 701 a 25-39; universal and particular 1147 a 1, 1201 b 27. Cf. Demonstration, Knowledge, Principles, Syllogism

Prepuce, 518 a 2

Presbys, 609 a 17, 615 a 19. Cf. Wren

Present. See Now

Presently, just, defined 222 b 9

Prester, a large snake 843 a 33

Priam, 618 b 27, 1100 a 7, 1101 a 8, 1145 a 21, 1362 b 36, 1363 a 6, 1414 b 38, 1416 b 2

Pride. See Magnanimity

Priests, are not political officers 1299 a 18; duties of 1322 b 19-29, 1328 b 21; old men of warrior and councillor class to become 1329 a 27-33; common tables of 1331 b 5

Primary, 1034 b 9; all things are referred to that which is primary 1004 a 25; defined 1030 a 10; has no contrary 1075 b 22-24

Primas-tunny, hibernation of 599 b 18

Prime, two meanings of 96 a 36

Prime matter. See Matter

Prime Mover (πρῶτον κινοῦν), 1041 a 30; necessity of 242 b 39, 1049 b 26, 1071 b 3-1072 a 18; unmoved 255 a 4-258 b 9, 259 b 20-31, 324 a 30, 434 b 33, 698 a 12, 700 b 37, 1012 b 31; must be eternal and one 258 b 10-259 b 19; indivisible 266 a 10-b 26, 267 b 18-26; causes movement in virtue of its natural movement 300 b 22; must lie outside the universe 699 a 12-700 a 26; that nearer the first mover is prior 1018 b 20; operation of 1072 a 18-1073 a 12; nature of its thought 1074 b 15-1075 a 11. Cf. Motion, Mover

Principle, beginning, starting-point, basic truth (ἀρχή), 84 b 24, 85 b 15, 271 b 12, 732 a 15, 740 a 23, 747 a 20, 764 a 28, 983 b 7, 986 a 17, 987 a 4,

1039 b 30, 1098 b 1-8, 1140 a 34, 1187 a 30-b 18, 1203 a 15-29, 1207 b 15, 1222 b 16-1223 a 7; identified with primary premiss 72 a 7; basic truths of syllogism more vital to knowledge than is the conclusion 72 a 37; basic truths of inhering attributes are indemonstrable 76 a 17; basic truths of a genus are those elements in it the existence of which cannot be proved 76 a 31; common and peculiar 76 a 40-b 5; necessarily involved in demonstrations 84 a 31; all sciences cannot have the same basic truths 88 a 18-b 29; more numerous than conclusions 88 b 5; apprehended only by intuition 99 b 15-100 b 17, 1141 a 8; study of first principles gives scientific knowledge 184 a 10; in study of nature must first determine the first principles 184 a 16; one or many? 184 b 15-22, 302 b 27, 303 a 18, 984 a 13, 986 a 22; examination of the physicist's conception of 187 a 27-188 a 17; contraries are principles 188 a 18-189 a 10; two or three in number, cannot be one nor an infinite number 189 a 11-191 a 22, 404 b 30; of movement 268 b 16, 284 b 32, 285 a 29, b 7, 701 a 21, 732 a 4, 734 b 23, 735 a 25, 742 b 35, 1224 a 23, b 12; of geometrical figures 303 b 2; no sanguineous animal can move itself at more than four points 693 b 9, 695 b 24, 696 a 17, 707 a 20, 708 a 13, 711 a 5 (Cf. 707 b 9); of generation 724 b 15; of art 735 a 2; must not seek a first principle of all things 742 b 30-34; God is a first principle 983 a 8; a first principle is necessary 994 a 1-b 30; are first principles universal or individual? 996 a 1, 999 b 24-1000 a 4, 1003 a 5-17, 1060 b 20-30, 1069 a 26-30, 1071 a 20, 1086 b 13-1087 a 25; are principles of perishable and imperishable things the same? 996 a 3, 1000 a 5-1001 a 1, 1060 a 27-35; do principles exist potentially or actually? 996 a 10, 1002 b 33-1003 a 4; of being 1003 a 21-32, 1025 b 1-1026 a 32; meanings of 1012 b 34-1013 a 23, 1049 b 6; form, privation, matter 1069 b 34, 1070 b 19; one

in kind or in number? 1070 a 31-1071 b 2; theory of Forms treats contraries as first principles 1087 a 28-1090 a 1; relation between first principles and the good 1091 a 29-1092 a 21; arguments from and arguments to first principles 1095 a 30; the fact is the first principle 1098 b 2; first principles ought to be appropriate 1183 b 1-8; the end is a kind of 1190 a 24; philosophy deals with first principles 1197 a 24-29; the feelings are principles and guides to virtue 1206 b 18; defined 1450 b 27. Cf. Cause, Elements, Premiss

Prior (πρότερος), 989 a 15, 999 a 7, 1080 b 12; meanings of 14 a 26-b 23, 71 b 33-72 a 5, 260 b 15-261 a 27, 916 a 18-39, 1018 b 8-1019 a 14, 1028 a 31-b 7; is more intelligible than the posterior 141 b 6; nothing prior to itself 700 b 2; ambiguous 742 a 20; in definition 1018 b 31, 1028 a 32, 1038 b 27, 1049 b 12, 1054 a 28, 1077 b 1, 1078 a 9; in time 1028 a 32, 1038 b 27, 1049 b 12

Privation (στέρησις), 73 b 21, 201 a 5, b 34, 215 a 11, 1019 b 9, 1058 b 27, 1061 a 20, 1063 b 17; distinguished from privative 12 a 38; rules for testing the definition of 147 b 26-148 a 2; things come to be from 191 b 15; in its own nature is not-being 192 a 5; as a form 193 b 20; positive is prior to 286 a 26; and positive predication 318 b 16; and negation 1004 a 9-19, 1056 a 15-b 2; defined 1011 b 19, 1055 b 3-29; meanings of 1022 b 22-1023 a 6, 1046 a 31-35; a kind of contradiction 1055 b 3

Privatives, privative and positive terms refer to same subject 12 a 26-13 a 36; distinguished from privation 12 a 38; related to positive terms 52 a 15; admit of no subdivision 642 b 21

Probability (εἰκός), 1359 a 9, 1428 a 19, 1431 a 24, 1439 a 5, 1442 b 39, 1443 b 40; defined 70 a 4, 1357 a 35; signs and probabilities are the materials of enthymemes 1357 a 33; as a basis of an enthymeme 1402 b 14, 15, 22-1403 a 2; the nature of 1428 a 25-34; three kinds of 1428 a 35-b 11; methods of

must be true or false 18 a 28; has only one proper contradictory 20 b 3; proper contradictories of possible, contingent, impossible, and necessary propositions 21 a 35-22 a 13; relation between possible, impossible, contingent, and necessary propositions 22 a 14-23 a 26; universal affirmative 24 b 26; universal negative 24 b 30; particular affirmative 25 a 10; particular negative 25 a 12; all propositions except particular negative are convertible 53 a 8; immediate proposition defined 72 a 7; either part of an enunciation 72 a 8; dialectical proposition 72 a 9; demonstrative proposition 72 a 10; immediate negative propositions 79 a 33-b 22; the material of reasoning 101 b 15; difference between propositions and problems 101 b 28; dialectical proposition defined 104 a 3-37; securing of propositions is a source of argument 105 a 33; divisions of: (1) ethics, (2) natural philosophy, (3) logic 105 b 20; particular proposition is easier to establish than to overthrow 154 b 38; defined as a single statement about a single thing 169 a 8. Cf. Premiss

Propriety, 1109 a 17

Prose, 1361 a 35, 1447 a 29, 1448 a 11, 1450 b 15, 1451 b 1; language of prose and of poetry are distinct 1404 a 28-b 4; four possible faults of prose style: (1) misuse of compound words, (2) use of strange words, (3) long, unseasonable, or frequent epithets, (4) inappropriate metaphors 1405 b 34-1406 b 19; rhythm of 1408 b 22-1409 a 22

Proserpine 836 b 20

Prosperity. See Good fortune

Prosyllogism, 82 b 27, 86 b 23, 156 a 7; always has one more term than the number of premisses 42 b 7

Protagoras, 173 b 19, 998 a 3, 1007 b 22, 1047 a 6, 1164 a 25, 1402 a 25, 1456 b 16; refutation of 1009 a 6-1011 b 23, 1062 b 12-1063 b 35; 'man is the measure of all things' 1009 a 6-14, 1053 a 35, 1062 b 13, 1063 a 4; classifies

nouns into male, female, and inanimate 1407 b 7; referred to 999 b 3

PROTAGORAS of Plato, 1164 a 24

Protarchus, his remark about altar stones 197 b 8

Proverbs, 983 a 28, 1168 b 7, 1345 a 11-17, 1376 a 2; 'Well starred is he who has a noble soul' (Xenocrates) 112 a 38; 'To be a philosopher is better than to make money' 118 a 11; 'Always something fresh in Libya' 606 b 20; 'Have no fear of a cloud from the land . . .' 938 b 10, 947 a 7-9; 'Boreas blows not at night when once the third sun hath risen' 941 a 21; 'When the South wind begins and when Boreas ceases his blowing' 942 b 2, 945 a 8, 29; 'Drawing it to himself, as Caicias draws clouds' 943 a 33; 'Straightway the winter comes, if the South wind call to the North wind' 945 a 37; 'When Boreas findeth the mire, soon cometh the season of winter' 945 b 3; 'Experience made art, but inexperience luck' (Polus) 981 a 4; 'Bards tell many a lie' 983 a 3; 'Man is the measure of all things' (Protagoras) 1009 a 6-14, 1053 a 35, 1062 b 13, 1063 a 4; 'The rule of many is not good; one ruler let there be' (Homer) 1076 a 4; 'For one swallow does not make a summer, nor does one day' 1098 a 18; 'Time is a good discoverer or partner in such a work' 1098 a 23; 'The happy are no better off than the wretched for half their lives' 1102 b 8; 'It is harder to fight with pleasure than with anger' (Heraclitus) 1105 a 8; 'In justice is every virtue comprehended' 1129 b 29; 'When water chokes, what is one to wash it down with?' 1146 a 35; 'The Milesians are not without sense, but they do the things that senseless people do' (Demodocus) 1151 a 9; 'Change in all things is sweet' (Euripides) 1154 b 28, 1371 a 28; 'Like to like' 1155 a 34, 1235 a 9, 1371 b 16; 'Birds of a feather flock together' (literally 'Jackdaw sits by jackdaw') 1155 a 35, 1208 b 9, 1371 b 16; 'It is what opposes that helps' (Heraclitus)

1155 b 5; 'From different tones comes the fairest tune' 1155 b 6; 'Eaten salt together' 1156 b 27; 'Out of sight, out of mind' 1157 b 13; 'What friends have is common property' 1159 b 31, 1168 b 8, 1263 a 29; 'Two of an age take to each other' 1161 b 34; 'Let a man have his fixed reward' 1164 a 27; 'Friendship is equality' 1168 b 8; 'Charity begins at home' 1168 b 8; 'Where fortune is kind, what need of friends' 1169 b 8; 'Neither a man of many guests nor a man with none' 1170 b 22; 'Enough is my misfortune' 1171 b 18; 'Noble deeds from noble men' 1172 a 14; 'Asses would prefer sweepings to gold' 1176 a 7; 'Earth loves the shower, what time the plain is dry' 1208 b 17, 1210 a 14, 1235 a 16; 'My soul and his are one' 1211 a 32; 'What need of friends, when Heaven bestows the good?' 1212 b 28; 'How God ever draws like to like' 1235 a 9; 'None is a lover but one who ever loves' 1235 b 21; 'Glaucon, a helper is a friend so long as he fights' 1236 a 36; 'The Athenians no longer know the Megarians' 1236 a 37, 1242 b 25; 'Like is pleased with like' 1238 a 34; 'Bad adheres to bad with pleasure' 1238 a 34; 'Pleasure glues the bad to the bad' 1239 b 22; 'A fixed wage for a friend' 1242 b 34; 'A word is your just pay for a word, but a deed for him who has given deeds' 1244 a 10; 'Distant friends are a burden' 1245 b 24; 'The ox is the poor man's slave' 1252 b 12; 'Slave before slave, master before master' 1255 b 29; 'Silence is woman's glory' 1260 a 30; 'He who has never learned to obey cannot be a good commander' 1277 b 13; 'Well begun is half done' 1303 b 30; 'Potter hates Potter' (Hesiod) 1312 b 4, 1381 b 17, 1388 a 16; 'Nail knocks out nail' 1314 a 5; 'Cruel is the strife of brethren' (Euripides) 1328 a 16; 'They who love in excess also hate in excess' 1328 a 17; 'There is no leisure for slaves' 1354 b 21; 'Evils draw men together' 1362 b 39; 'Breaking the pitcher at the door' 1363 a 7; 'The best of things is water' (Pindar) 1364 a 27; 'Mate delights mate' 1371 b 16; 'Beast knows beast' 1371 b 16; 'Mysian prey' 1372 b 32; 'Wickedness needs but a pretext' 1373 a 3; 'Never show an old man kindness' 1376 a 5; 'Fool, who slayeth the father and leaveth his sons to avenge him' 1376 a 7, 1395 a 17; 'He would pick a corpse's pocket' 1383 b 25; 'Shame dwells in the eyes' 1384 a 33; 'Kin can even be jealous of their kin' (Aeschylus) 1388 a 7; 'Insolence is better avoided, lest the cicalas chirp on the ground' 1395 a 1, 1412 a 23; 'The War-God showeth no favour' 1395 a 15; 'An Attic neighbour' 1395 a 18; 'Buying the marsh with the salt' 1399 a 25; 'Fish need salt' 1400 a 12; 'Caunian love' 1402 b 2; defined as metaphors from one species to another 1413 a 14-17; 'The man who swallowed a poker' 1413 b 27. Cf. Maxims

Prudence. *See* Wisdom, practical

Prytanis, chief magistrate at Miletus 1305 a 17, 1322 b 29

Psammetichus, tyrant at Corinth 1315 b 25

Psen, fig-wasp, 557 b 26

Psetta. *See* Flat-fish

Psittacene, fire in 833 a 1-6

Psyche. *See* Butterfly

Psychrus River, 519 a 14

Pubes, 493 a 20; hair on 498 b 23, 797 b 31, 798 a 1

Pudenda, 725 b 5, 747 a 21, 749 a 31, 764 b 23

Pugnacity, 1419 b 26

Pulley, 851 b 19, 852 a 5, 16; why it can raise great weights 853 a 33-b 13

Pulse, function of the breath 482 b 29; originates in the heart 482 b 29-36; irregularity of 483 a 3; prior to other activities 483 a 15

Pulse (the vegetable), 522 a 19

Pumice-stone, 847 a 9, 886 b 11, 939 a 13, 964 b 38

Pumpkin, blossom of 923 a 13-16; grow large if buried 923 b 16-29; storing of 924 a 36-b 14

Punctuation, 1407 b 13, 1409 a 20

Puns, 1400 b 17-24, 1412 a 33-b 33

Pupa. *See* Chrysalis

Pupil of eye, 438 a 16, b 16, 491 b 21, 520 b 3

Puppet, movements of animals compared to those of puppets 701 b 1-32

Purgation, catharsis (κάθαρσις), 1449 b 27; purgative drugs 808 b 23; music as a catharsis 1341 b 32-1342 b 17

Purity, 1250 b 24

Purple, purple colour 792 a 17-29, 795 b 19, 796 b 25, 797 a 5; dealers in 849 b 36. Cf. Murex

Purple Coot. *See* Porphyrio

Purple-fish. *See* Murex

Purpose. *See* Choice, Final Cause

Purpura. *See* Murex

Purse-proud, 1221 a 35

Purse-tassels, 926 a 6

Purslane, stops inflammation of the gums 863 b 11-18, 887 b 1-9

Pus, corrupt blood tends to turn to 521 a 20

Putrefaction, 379 a 3-b 9, 389 b 8, 753 a 24, 763 a 28; defined 379 a 17; nothing comes into being by 762 a 15

Pycnon, 922 b 7

Pygmies, 597 a 6

Pyrallis, habits of 609 a 18

Pyramids of Egypt, 1313 b 21

Pyrene Mountains, 350 b 1

Pyriphlegethon, 839 a 23

Pyrrha, 621 b 12, 763 b 2, 973 b 23, 1024 a 37

Pyrrhaean Straits, 544 a 22, 548 a 10, 603 a 21, 22

Pyrrhus, 522 b 24, 595 b 18

Pythagoras, 1398 b 14; first to speak about virtue 1182 a 11

Pythagoreans, 94 b 33, 222 b 18, 285 a 11, b 26, 439 a 31, 996 a 6, 1036 b 18, 1078 b 22, 1080 b 16, 1091 a 14, 1344 a 10; infinite as a self-subsistent substance 203 a 4-9; identify infinite and the even 203 a 10; criticism of Pythagorean and Platonic belief in a separately existing infinite 204 a 9-206 a 8; the void exists 213 b 22; the number 'three' 268 a 12; attribute spatial oppositions to the heaven 284 b 7; 'harmony of the spheres' 290 b 12-291 a 29; fire has central position, not earth 293 a 20-b 15; some make all

nature out of numbers 300 a 16; theory of the nature of comets 342 b 30; on nature of milky way 345 a 14-24; view of soul 404 a 17, 407 b 23; think some animals are nourished by odours 445 a 16; think whole world is made of numbers 910 b 37; think numbers to be elements of all things 985 b 22-986 b 8; two principles of 986 a 22-26, 987 a 13-28; things exist by 'imitation' of numbers 987 b 12; criticism of 989 b 29-990 a 32; think being and unity are substances 996 a 6, 1001 a 9; think the one is a substance 1053 b 13; on beauty and goodness 1072 b 30-35; suppose numbers to have magnitude 1080 b 32, 1083 b 8-18; think things are number 1090 a 20-1091 a 22; on nature of the good 1096 b 5; on nature of evil 1106 b 28; conception of justice 1132 b 23, 1194 a 29; referred to 998 b 10, 1002 a 12, 1004 b 32, 1017 b 19, 1028 b 5, 1036 b 8, 1043 b 35, 1060 b 6, 1066 a 11, 1075 a 36, b 28, 1076 a 22, 1087 b 27, 1090 b 2

Pythian Games, 1018 b 18, 1460 a 31

Pythian oracle, 1331 a 27

Pythian priestess, 832 a 22

Pytho, assassin of Cotys 1311 b 20

Pythocles, advised the Athenians to fix the market price of lead 1353 a 15-18

Python, 1243 b 20

Pythopolis, wells in 834 a 34-b 2

Q

Qua, defined 1065 b 24

Quail, gall-bladder of 506 b 22; crop of 509 a 2, 13; call of 536 a 26; nesting of 559 a 1; migration of 597 a 23, b 5; habits of 613 b 6-614 a 34, 615 a 6; white quail 798 a 27; timidity of 806 b 12

Quality (ποιόν), 103 b 22, 146 b 20, 179 a 9, 185 a 34, 1063 a 27, 1083 a 11, 1220 b 14; examples of 1 b 28; subsists in things in varying degrees at different times 4 a 3, 10 b 26; substance admits contrary qualities 4 a

12, 6 a 1; statement and opinion incapable of admitting contrary qualities 4 b 12; defined 8 b 25, 226 a 26, 1068 b 17-19; as habit 8 b 27; as inborn capacity 9 a 15; as affections 9 a 27; as shape 10 a 11; one may be contrary of another 10 b 12; likeness and unlikeness its distinctive feature 11 a 17; genus of a quality must be a quality 121 a 8; differentia always signifies a quality 128 a 27, 144 a 19-21; the four elementary qualities 329 a 6-330 a 29; meanings of 1020 a 34-b 25; change of 1069 b 10

Quantity (ποσόν), 103 b 22, 146 b 20, 178 a 8, 179 a 9, 226 a 30, 1052 b 20, 1063 a 28, 1083 a 12; examples of 1 b 28; has no contrary 3 b 28, 5 b 11; either discrete or continuous 4 b 20; number a discrete quantity 4 b 31; speech a quantity 4 b 32; line a continuous quantity 5 a 1; space and time continuous quantities 5 a 6; some parts have position, some have not 5 a 15-37; has no variation of degree 6 a 19; equality and inequality predicated of 6 a 27; of premisses 47 b 15-40; determinate 955 b 17; meanings of 1020 a 7-33; change of 1069 b 10; in a tragedy 1452 b 16, 26

Quartan fever, 861 b 5, 866 a 31

Querulousness, physiognomic signs of 812 a 5, 813 a 17, 34

Question. See Interrogation

Quibbling, 1251 b 2

Quicker, two senses of 848 b 6-8

Quickness of sense, physiognomic signs of 811 a 6, b 33, 812 a 6

Quicksilver, 385 b 5, 406 b 19

Quick wit (ἀγχίνοια), 449 b 8; defined as faculty of hitting upon the middle term instantaneously 89 b 10-20

Quinsy, in dogs 604 a 4

Quoit-throwing, 1461 b 31

R

Rabies, in dogs 604 a 4; in camels 604 a 10

Racial characteristics, 805 a 26, 806 b 14-18, 812 a 13, b 31

Radish, 890 a 25, 908 b 3, 923 b 38; cultivation of 924 a 24-30

Rage. See Anger

Railing, physiognomic signs of 808 a 33, 811 a 28

Rain, 349 a 5, b 32, 358 a 28, 360 b 27, 365 b 10; cause of 346 b 16-347 a 13, 368 b 19, 370 b 12, 394 a 16, 28, 653 a 4-7; more rain in winter and at night 360 a 2; rainstorms 392 b 10, 394 a 16, 27-32; effect on fish 601 b 9-34; sound of 803 a 5

Rainbow, cause and nature of 371 b 26-372 a 9, 17-21, 373 a 33-375 b 15, 395 a 31-38, 906 b 7; moon rainbows 372 a 22-28; cannot be more than a semicircle 375 b 16-377 a 27; its supposed effect on trees 906 a 36-b 34

Rainbow-wrasse, habits of 610 b 6

Raphanus. See Cabbage

Rashness, audacity, 1104 a 22, 1108 b 19, 24, 1109 a 2, 8, 1115 b 30-34, 1151 b 8, 1186 b 7, 1220 b 39, 1228 b 2, 1383 a 13-b 11

Ratio (λόγος), 993 a 19, 1001 b 30, 1061 b 2, 1092 b 31; of division 969 a 3, 4; of musical scales 985 b 32, 1053 a 16, 1092 b 14; of numbers 991 b 14

Ratiocinative desire, 1139 b 4

Rational principle, reasoning, rule, rule of life, 1095 a 10, 1098 a 8, 1102 b 14-1103 a 2, 1119 b 11-18, 1140 a 10-b 33, 1169 a 4; an element in the soul 1098 a 2, 1102 a 28, 1119 b 15, 1138 b 8, 1139 a 5, 1182 a 20, 1185 b 1-13, 1208 a 11, 1219 b 26-1220 a 2, 1221 b 27-31, 1249 b 26, 30, 1250 a 3, 16, 1260 a 7, 1333 a 17, 1334 b 19; right rule 1103 b 33, 1138 b 34, 1144 b 27, 1147 b 2, 1151 a 2; virtues are rules 1144 b 28; ought to control the irrational element of the soul 1254 b 5, 1260 a 6, 1333 a 18; found only in part in slaves 1254 b 22, 1259 b 28; the master artificer 1260 a 18; may give way to passion 1312 b 29, 1315 a 29; an element in virtue 1332 a 39-b 11, 1334 b 8; not found in animals 1332 b 3; may be mistaken 1334 b 10; the end of nature 1334 b 14

Rattle, a good toy for children 1340 b 26-32. Cf. Archytas

Raven, 812 b 12; gall-bladder of 506 b 22; oesophagus of 509 a 2; change of colour in 519 a 6; eggs of 563 b 1; habits of 609 a 20, b 4, 32, 617 b 13, 618 b 9-18; copulation of 756 b 15; white ravens 785 b 35; colour of 799 a 20. Cf. Crow

Ravenswort, 837 a 20

Rawness, a species of inconcoction 379 b 12; defined 380 a 28-b 12

Ray, batos, 489 b 31, 746 b 6; gills of 505 a 4; copulation of 540 b 7; generation of 565 a 15-b 28, 566 a 33; hibernation of 599 b 28; habits of 620 b 30; body of 695 b 27; swimming of 696 a 26, 709 b 17; skin of 697 a 6. Cf. Aetos, Bos

Razor-fish, solen, 528 a 18, 22, 547 b 14, 548 a 5, 588 b 16; hearing in 535 a 14; shell of 683 b 17

Reading, keeps some awake but puts others to sleep 916 b 1-18, 917 a 18-b 2; a customary branch of education 1337 b 24

Ready wit, ready witted, 1108 a 24, 1127 b 34-1128 b 8, 1156 a 12, 1157 a 6, 1158 a 32, 1185 b 6, 1193 a 11-19, 1234 a 4-23

Realgar, 378 a 23; medicine for horses 604 b 27

Reality, fulfilment (ἐντελέχεια), 193 b 7, 200 b 26, 257 b 7, 1007 b 28, 1039 a 4; and matter 1038 b 6, 1078 a 31; and substance 1039 a 4, 1044 a 9; and actuality 1047 a 30, 1050 a 23. Cf. Actuality

Reason, thought, intuition (νοῦς, νόησις), 415 a 12, 736 b 29, 984 b 16, 993 b 10, 1025 b 22, 1036 a 6, 1070 a 27, 1074 b 16, 1168 b 35, 1180 a 22; reason cannot be established from false premisses 53 a 9, 57 a 40; the unit of demonstration 85 a 1, 88 a 17; intuitive reason 88 b 36, 1140 b 31-1141 a 7, 1143 a 35-b 14; the originative source of scientific knowledge 100 b 8-17, 1140 b 31-1141 a 7, 1150 a 5; reason in soul, like sight in eye 108 a 11; starting-point of art and nature 639 b 15; not involved in non-volun-

tary and involuntary movements 703 b 5, 17; that by which we know first principles 1140 b 31-1141 a 8, 1142 a 25; is the man himself 1169 a 2, 1178 a 4; contemplative reason 1177 a 13, b 19, 1178 a 22; the best thing in us 1177 a 20; life according to 1177 b 30, 1178 a 7, 1180 a 18; found in intellectual part of the soul 1182 a 18, 1196 b 14; man the only animal that has reason 1189 a 3, 1421 a 11; impulse must proceed from 1191 a 22; seeks the best 1199 a 11; judgement of 1199 a 13, 1202 a 12-1204 a 4; natural virtues are impulses to right apart from 1200 a 1-1206 b 29; as first principle 1203 a 15-1206 b 29; warns against bad action 1203 a 35, b 6; and mind 1207 a 4, 14; parts of the soul which partake of 1219 b 28, 1220 a 8-11, b 7, 1221 b 29; governs desire and the passions 1219 b 42; and desire 1224 a 24, 1225 a 3; age of 1224 a 27; and final cause 1227 b 12-19; bids one choose the noble 1229 a 2; springs from God 1248 a 27-29. Cf. Knowledge, Mind, Soul

Reason, faculty of (τὸ λογιστικόν), the seat of shame 126 a 8; the seat of wishing 126 a 13; the seat of ignorance 147 b 29-33

Reasoning, 172 a 35, 1201 a 19, 25, 1220 b 29; defined 100 a 25; varieties of: (1) demonstrable, (2) dialectical, (3) contentious, (4) false 100 a 25-b 24; as a means of proving the division of predicables 103 b 7; compared to induction 105 a 17, 153 a 8, 155 b 35, 164 a 13; needs universal premisses 164 a 10; a cause of action 1369 a 6, b 8-11. Cf. Demonstration

Reciprocal proof, defined 57 a 18; in the first figure 59 a 32. Cf. Circular proof

Reciprocity, 1132 b 22-1133 b 7; of correlatives 6 b 28-7 b 14

Recollection, 124 a 22, 451 a 7, 19-453 b 11, 465 a 22, 886 a 33-36, 887 a 6; not same as memory 449 b 3-8, 451 a 21, 453 a 5-14; cause of 451 b 10; how it differs from relearning 452 a 4-12; man alone has the faculty of 453 a 9; not under control of will 453 a 20

Recorders, Sacred Recorders, 1321 b 39, 1331 b 6

Rectangle, 910 b 11, 19, 970 a 4, 5

Rectum, 507 a 33

Red Sea, 342 b 24, 354 a 1, 466 b 22, 606 a 12; plants of 819 b 40

Redstart, 632 b 28

Reductio ad absurdum, 37 a 10, 35

Reductio ad impossibile, 27 a 15, 28 b 21, 29 b 6, 34 a 3, 36 a 22, 39 b 33, 40 b 27, 50 a 29-38, 65 a 40, b 10-20, 77 a 23, 162 b 7, 167 b 23, 170 a 2; rules for 45 a 23-b 10; in the three figures 61 a 18-62 b 28; its resemblance to conversion 61 a 21; compared with ostensive proof 62 b 29-63 b 20; its method 87 a 6-30; not wise to use it in dialectics 157 b 34-158 a 2. Cf. Impossibility

Reduction, by conversion 27 a 6, 28 a 19, 29 a 30; all syllogisms may be reduced to universal syllogisms in the first figure 29 b 1, 40 b 17; reduction of arguments to figures and moods of syllogism 46 b 40-50 b 4; cannot reduce hypothetical syllogisms 50 a 16-51 b 4; reduction of syllogisms of one figure into another 50 b 5-51 b 4; defined 69 a 20; and the infinite 206 b 13, 207 a 23, 208 a 21

Reed, 553 a 21, 568 a 25, 601 b 15, 621 b 1, 820 a 19

Reed-warbler, habits of 606 b 13-19

Reflection (ἀνάκλασις, εἴδωλον), 435 a 5, 464 b 9; haloes and rainbows are reflections 346 a 5, 372 a 18, 373 b 31, 374 a 8; some regard lightning as a reflection 370 a 23; and colours 791 a 15-b 2, 792 b 17, 793 b 31

Reflectiveness, physiognomic signs of 813 a 29

Refrigeration, 470 a 7, 26, 477 a 11-31, 478 a 28; things solidified by 388 b 13, 389 a 20; in fish 478 b 10, 669 a 2; by means of respiration 480 b 18, 482 a 16, 32, 483 b 6; a function of soul 482 b 22; body needs cooling 668 a 34-b 6. Cf. Respiration

Refutation (ἔλεγχος), 1414 b 15, 1428 a 20, 1431 a 6-22, b 2, 3, 1443 a 1; easier to refute than to establish 43 a 14; when possible 66 b 4-18; defined 66

b 11, 165 a 3, 171 a 3, 179 b 1, 1431 a 6; sometimes genuine, sometimes apparent 164 b 25; two styles: those dependent on language and those independent of language 165 b 23-168 a 16; by arguments which, though valid, are only apparently appropriate to the subject matter 169 b 17-174 b 40; sophistical refutation defined 170 a 12; infinite in number 170 a 20; solutions of 177 a 9-181 a 35; refutative enthymeme 1396 b 25-28, 1400 b 25-33, 1403 a 25-33, 1418 b 2; of enthymemes 1402 a 29-1403 a 16

Registration of citizens, 1297 a 23-28

Relation (πρός τι), 103 b 22, 142 a 28, 146 b 3, 1056 b 35, 1089 b 6; examples of 1 b 29; things of something else or related to something else 6 a 36; no substance is relative 8 a 12; use of the term 200 b 29; no motion in respect of 225 b 11; ideas of 990 b 24, 1079 a 12; meanings of 1020 b 26-1021 b 11; has no generation, destruction, or movement 1088 a 30

Relative terms, 181 b 26; some have contraries 6 b 15; some have variation of degree 6 b 20; all have correlatives 6 b 26, 7 a 21; as tests of accident 114 a 13-25, 119 a 37; genus of relative terms must also be relative 121 a 3-124 b 17; as tests of genus 124 b 15-125 b 14, 147 a 23-28; as tests of property 135 b 17-27; as tests of differentia 145 a 13-32, 146 a 21-31; rules for testing the definition of 146 a 37-147 a 11, 23-31, 149 b 4-23

Relaxation, amusement gives relaxation 1127 b 34, 1176 b 34, 1337 b 38, 1339 b 15; necessary element in life 1128 b 3, 1339 a 16. Cf. Amusement, Leisure

Rennet, 516 a 3, 522 b 2-12, 676 a 6-19, 835 b 33; its action on milk 729 a 12, 739 b 23, 772 a 25

Repentance, 1110 b 17, 22, 1111 a 20, 1150 a 22, b 30, 1166 a 28, b 24, 1211 b 2

Reptile. *See* Serpent, Snake, Viper

REPUBLIC of Plato, 992 a 33, 1075 b 20, 1130 a 3, 1291 a 12, 1316 a 2, 1327 b 38, 1336 a 31, 1342 a 32, 1406 b 32;

criticism of state in 1260 b 27-1264 b 25

Reserve. *See* Dignity

Resin, 818 a 4

Resonance, 899 b 18-900 a 2

Resources, a subject of deliberative oratory 1423 a 26, 1425 b 16-31; source of 1446 b 17-19

Respiration, 420 b 23, 470 b 6-480 b 30, 589 a 10-b 28, 964 a 10-24; not every animal breathes 78 a 23, 444 b 6, 470 b 10-27, 659 b 13, 816 b 27; two purposes of 444 a 25; not a method of nutrition 473 a 3; Aristogenes thinks growth of breath due to respiration 481 a 28; its purpose is refrigeration 482 a 32; requires external fulcrum 700 a 24; a non-voluntary movement 703 b 9; smells perceived through 747 a 22; plants do not have respiration 816 b 26; while running 882 b 1-22; movement of stomach in 964 a 39-b 4; nature of 964 b 5-19

Rest (ἠρεμία, ἠρέμησις), contrary of motion 15 b 1, 202 a 4, 226 b 15, 229 b 23-231 a 4, 251 a 26, 264 a 24; contrary of change of place 15 b 3; of an infinite body 205 a 16; all rest is in time 221 b 8; its relation to motion and time 238 b 23-239 b 4; some things are sometimes in motion, sometimes at rest 253 a 22-254 b 7; either constrained or natural 300 a 28; origin of movement is at rest 698 a 12, b 1; body in motion easier to move than one at rest 858 a 3-12; why object that is thrown comes to a standstill 858 a 13-16; defined 1068 b 25

Retaliation, 1194 a 29-b 2, 1373 a 10-27, 1378 b 26, 1382 b 10-12

Reticulum, 507 b 5

Revenue, 1359 b 25, 1396 a 10; officers of 1300 b 9; of state should be announced in assembly 1309 a 10-12; necessary for state 1328 b 11; six kinds of 1345 b 30-1346 a 4; sources of 1346 a 21-25

Revolutions, property is the question upon which revolutions turn 1266 a 37, b 14; preventatives of 1273 b 18, 1302 b 19-21, 1307 b 26-1310 a 38, 1313 a 18-1315 b 10, 1319 b 6-1321 a 4; problem of citizenship after a revolution 1275 b 34-1276 a 6; should old contracts be met after revolution? 1276 a 7-11; forms of 1301 b 6-19; chief cause of revolutions is inequality 1301 b 26, 1302 a 23-31; causes of 1302 a 17-1304 b 18; in oligarchies 1302 b 27, 1303 b 4-6, 1305 a 36-1306 b 21; in democracies 1302 b 28, 1303 a 11, b 7, 1304 b 19-1305 a 35; occasions of 1303 b 18-1304 b 18; may be effected by force or fraud 1304 b 8-17; in polities 1306 b 11, 1307 a 5; in aristocracies 1306 b 22-1307 b 25; in monarchies 1310 a 39-1313 a 17; in tyrannies 1310 a 39-1315 b 10; criticism of Plato's theory of 1316 a 2-b 27

Revolutions, at Abydos 1306 a 32; at Aegina 1306 a 4; at Ambracia 1303 a 22-24, 1304 a 32; at Amphipolis 1303 b 3, 1306 a 2; at Antissa 1303 a 34; at Apollonia 1303 a 38; at Argos 1303 a 7; at Athens 1303 a 8, 1305 a 23, b 26; at Byzantium 1303 a 33; at Chalcis 1304 a 30; at Chios 1306 b 6; at Clazomenae 1303 b 8; at Cnidos 1305 b 12-18, 1306 b 6; at Colophon 1303 b 9; at Corinth 1306 a 24; at Cos 1304 a 26; at Cyme 1305 a 1; at Cyrene 1319 b 16; at Delphi 1303 b 39-1304 a 4; at Elis 1306 a 16-20; at Epidamnus 1301 b 21, 1304 a 14-17; at Eretria 1306 a 35; at Erythrae 1305 b 19-21; at Heraclea 1304 b 32, 1305 b 5, 37, 1306 a 37; at Heraea 1303 a 15; at Hestiaea 1303 b 32-38; at Istros 1305 b 5; at Lacedaemon 1306 b 29-1307 a 4; at Larissa 1305 b 28, 1306 a 31; at Locri 1307 a 38; at Massalia 1305 b 5; at Megara 1302 b 31, 1304 b 35-39, 1305 a 24; at Mytilene 1304 a 4-9; at Oreum 1303 a 18; at Phocis 1304 a 11; at Rhodes 1302 b 23, 33, 1304 b 27-31; at Sparta 1301 b 19; at Sybaris 1303 a 30; at Syracuse 1302 b 33, 1303 a 39, b 20-26, 1304 a 27, 1306 a 2; at Tarentum 1303 a 3; at Thebes 1302 b 29, 1306 a 37; at Thurii 1303 a 32, 1307 a 28, b 6-18

Rhadamanthus, 1132 b 26, 1413 b 25

Rhapsody, 1447 b 22

moist 351 a 20; Plato's theory of rivers 355 b 32-356 a 33

River worms, develop into gadfly 487 b 5

Road, 1352 b 26; the royal roads 1348 a 24, 1353 a 25

Robin, erithacus, 592 b 23, 632 b 28

Rock-crab, diet of 590 b 11

Rock-dove, 544 b 2; diet of 593 a 16; migration of 597 b 3. Cf. Pigeon

Rock-fishes, breeding of 543 a 4; diet of 548 b 16, 591 b 13; habitat of 598 a 11; hibernation of 599 b 7, 28

Rock-plants, 826 b 20-35

'Rods,' cause and nature of 372 a 10-21, 377 a 29-378 b 6

Roe, has no gall-bladder 506 a 22, 676 b 27; blood of 515 b 33, 520 b 24, 650 b 15

Roguery, 1221 a 12, 37; physiognomic signs of 812 a 16, 814 a 1. Cf. Villainy

Rollers, heavy objects easier moved on rollers than on carts 852 a 30-38

Rook, 774 b 28

Root, roots of plants are equivalent of mouth and head of animals 686 b 35, 705 b 8, 818 a 20, 819 a 20, 820 a 24, b 31, 821 a 12, b 9, 826 b 34; superior part of plants 705 b 7; as dyes 794 a 18; aromatic roots 820 b 26

Rose, 924 a 4, 1118 a 11; colour of petals 796 a 21; scent of 845 b 2, 907 a 20-23, 950 a 17; smells sweeter when centers are rough 907 a 20-23; rose perfume 909 a 2

Rosian Mountains, 973 a 19

Rosus, 973 a 18

Rot, in sheep 672 a 28-b 8

Rotation. See Circle, Circular motion

Round, why pebbles are round 852 b 29-853 a 4; the most beautiful form 915 a 35. Cf. Circle

Round-worm, 551 a 10

Rowing, mechanics of 850 b 10-27

Royal economy, 1345 b 12; most important and simplest 1345 b 14; departments of 1345 b 20-27

Royalty. See King, Monarchy, Tyranny

Rudder, 7 a 7-13; small rudder moves large ship 850 b 28-851 a 38

Ruddle, 378 a 23

Rue, 612 a 29, 819 b 11, 867 b 8; grafted on fig-tree 924 b 35-925 a 5; gives perspiration an evil odour 926 b 16-19; a remedy against the evil eye 926 b 20-31

Rule. See Rational principle

Rule, different kinds of 1252 a 7, 1253 b 18, 1254 b 2, 1255 b 16, 1259 a 37-b 16, 1260 a 9, 1277 b 9, 1325 a 27, 1333 a 3; nature makes distinction between ruler and ruled 1252 a 30, 1254 a 19-1255 a 2, 1332 b 37; better to rule over men than over beasts 1254 a 26; virtue of ruler and ruled 1259 b 33-1260 a 9; of master over slave and of state over citizens compared 1278 b 30-1279 a 21

Rumination 507 a 36, 632 a 33-b 11; of the Scarus 508 b 12, 591 b 23, 675 a 4; of camel 674 b 5; horned animals that have no front teeth in the upper jaw ruminate 675 a 5

Rump, 493 a 23

Running, 885 a 6-13; effect on the head 881 b 8-17; respiration while running 882 b 1-22; difference between walking and 882 b 23, 24, 883 b 37-40; apt to become chilled through running in winter 888 b 21-26; friction produces more flesh than running 966 b 10-17

Rust, 792 b 28; rustless iron 833 b 31; rustless copper 834 a 3

Ryades, runners, shoal-fish, breeding of 543 b 14, 570 b 22

S

Sacred enclosure, Byzantines sold their sacred enclosures 1346 b 13, 16

Sacred rites, a subject of deliberative oratory 1423 a 24, 29-1424 a 8; proper conduct of 1446 a 37-b 5

Saffron, 840 b 25-31

Sagacity, 1250 a 36

Sail of a ship, 851 b 6-14

Sailors, 1291 b 22, 1327 b 14, 1424 a 28; analogy of sailors and citizens 1276 b 20-34; support democracy 1321 a 14

Salamander, can walk through fire 552 b 15

Salamis, 569 b 12, 27, 956 a 20, 1375 b 30, 1396 a 13, 1411 a 33, 1459 a 25; victory of 1304 a 22

Salpe. *See* Saupe

Salt, 383 b 12, 384 a 34, 385 a 31, 388 b 13, 389 a 18, 596 a 18, 823 b 16, 1238 a 2; why the sea is salty 356 b 3-359 b 25, 824 a 4-b 2; a form of earth 441 b 4; more odorous than natron 443 a 14; why it does not grow 822 a 31-39; in Utica 844 a 7-16; of Illyria 844 b 9-23; as cure of disease 859 a 7; stops inflammation of the gums 863 b 11-18, 887 b 1-9; cures inflammation 889 b 19; makes a noise when thrown on fire 902 a 1-4, 904 a 4-15; makes bread lighter 927 a 35-b 6; melts quickly in salt water 934 a 1-12; rights over sale of 1346 b 22

Salt water, 923 a 6, 935 b 3-16; drunkards sensitive to 872 a 9-17, 873 b 38-874 a 4; problems connected with the sea and salt water 931 a 35-936 a 10; less cold than drinking water 932 a 39-b 8; more transparent than fresh water 932 b 9-15, 935 b 17-26; dries more quickly than fresh water 932 b 25-28; combustible 933 a 17-27, 935 a 5-8; drinkable after being heated 933 b 11-17; does not flow readily 933 b 21-33; melts salt more quickly than does fresh water 934 a 1-12; waters are saltier in regions facing the south wind 934 a 30; the salt comes to the surface in sweet wine 934 a 33-38; why salty element floats 934 a 39-b 3. Cf. Sea

Sambuca, a musical instrument 1341 a 41

Sameness (ταὐτόν), 169 b 4, 224 a 2, 995 b 20, 1021 a 11; kinds of: (1) numerical, (2) specific, (3) generic 103 a 6-39; discovery of the differences of things aids in reasoning about 108 a 38; commonplace rules governing predications of 151 b 26-153 a 5; meanings of 1017 b 26-1018 a 9, 1054 a 30-b 2; by accident 1037 b 6

Samos, Samians, 1248 a 40, 1303 a 36, 1347 b 16, 1350 b 4, 1384 b 33, 1393 b 24, 1407 a 1; Polycratean monuments at 1313 b 24

Sand, 698 b 16, 825 a 36, 833 b 24, 934 b 12; wrestlers train by crawling through sand 709 a 14; why found under sea 823 b 19-824 a 3; does not form in lakes as it does in sea and rivers 935 a 9-17

Sandpiper, trochilus, 593 b 12, 1236 b 9; habits of 612 a 20, 831 a 11-14

Sanguine, temper 806 b 3; complexion 807 b 32; sanguineness sometimes thought to be courage 1117 a 10-22

Sanguineous animals, do not always live the longest 466 a 5; have viscera 665 a 32; always have heart 665 b 10, 666 a 25; oneness of sensory soul 667 b 24; have hot nature 668 b 36; the more perfect animals 682 a 34; always have head 685 b 34, 690 b 18; never have more than four points for motion 693 b 9, 695 b 24, 696 a 17, 707 a 20, 708 a 13, 711 a 5 (Cf. 707 b 9); sexes of 715 a 20-29; genitals of 716 b 13-717 a 12; blood in 726 b 3; embryo in 731 a 15-20; infertile 732 b 9; heart of 742 b 36; larger not always the longer-lived 777 b 1. Cf. Animals

Saperdis, when edible 608 a 3

Sappho, 1367 a 11, 1398 b 12, 27

Sardanapallus, 1095 b 22, 1216 a 16; assassination of 1311 b 40

Sardinia, 218 a 25, 393 a 13, 838 b 13-29

Sardinian Sea, 354 a 22, 393 a 27

Sardis, 94 b 1

Sarginus, habits of 610 b 6

Sargue, sargus, spawning of 543 a 7, b 8, 16, 570 a 33; diet of 591 b 19

Satrap, 1345 b 25, 1351 b 36, 1352 a 8, 17, b 29, 1353 a 3

Satripic economy 1345 b 12, 28-1346 a 7

Saturn, 1073 b 35, 1074 a 7

Satyric, 1449 a 21, 23

Satyrism, a disease 768 b 35

Satyrium, 594 b 31

Satyrus of Clazomenae, 875 a 35-40, 1148 b 1

Saupe, salpe, hearing of 534 a 9; spawning of 543 a 8, b 8, 570 b 17; diet of 591 a 15, 621 b 6

Saurian, tongue of 508 a 23

Sauromatic sheep, 783 a 14

Savior Goddess, 1419 a 2

Saw, 200 a 10, 886 b 10

ent 185 a 31, 1069 a 25; Platonic Forms thought to be separable 1040 a 9, 1078 b 31, 1086 a 18-1087 a 25; objects of mathematics are not separable 1059 b 12

Sepes, on Mount Othrys 846 b 10-17

Sepia, cuttlefish, 489 b 34, 523 b 4, 524 a 27-525 a 13, 531 b 2, 607 b 6, 622 a 31; bloodless 489 a 32, 490 b 14; tentacles of 523 b 29; mytis of 524 b 16, 621 b 29; as bait 534 a 23; capture of 534 b 25, 608 b 18; generation of 541 b 1-16, 544 a 2, 549 b 6, 550 a 10-b 21, 567 b 6-11, 757 b 32-758 a 25; diet of 590 b 33; most cunning of molluscs 621 b 28; change of colour in 622 a 11; *os sepiae* of 654 a 21; ink of 679 a 5-32; feet of 685 a 14-b 12; fin of 685 b 18

Septic drug, 607 a 22

Sequence, one thing prior to another when their being cannot be reversed 14 a 30, b 12, 15 a 6; in propositions 22 a 14-23 a 26

Seriphos, frogs in 835 b 4

Serpent, snake, 488 a 23, 490 a 11, b 24, 690 b 15, 691 a 6, 835 a 28; oviparous except viper 76 b 1; temper of 488 b 16; movement of 489 b 29, 490 a 31, 707 b 6-708 a 21, 709 a 25, 710 a 1; horned serpent of Thebes 500 a 4; tongue of 504 a 14, 660 b 7-11; description of 505 b 5-24, 508 a 8-b 7; do not have testicles 509 b 4, 16-23, 717 a 19, 765 a 34; womb of 511 a 14-22; bones of 516 b 19, 655 a 21; sound of 536 a 6; female larger than male 538 a 27; copulation of 540 b 1-5, 717 b 34, 718 a 17-34; generation of 558 a 25-b 3, 571 a 30; blind snakes 567 b 25; diet of 594 a 4-24; hibernation of 599 a 31; sloughing of 600 b 23-34; in Libya 606 b 9; bite of 607 a 21-34; habits of 609 a 4, 24, b 28, 610 a 12, 612 a 29, b 3; gall-bladder of 676 b 23; ears of 691 a 13-18; eyelids of 691 a 21; 'neck' of 691 b 29; body of 692 a 2-8; has no mammae 692 a 10; swims in water 696 a 9; why limbless 708 a 9-21; spermatic ducts of 716 b 15; eggs of 732 b 4; monstrosities in snakes 770 a 24-28; of Thessaly 832 a

14-18; of Lacedaemon 832 a 19-22; of Cyprus 845 a 10-14; in Mesopotamia 845 b 9-11; of the Euphrates 845 b 12-16; sacred-snake of Thessaly 845 b 17-33; Sepes on Othrys 846 b 10-17. Cf. Asp, Viper

Serranus. *See* Channa

Serum, 487 a 3, 489 a 23, 651 a 17; homogeneous 647 b 13

Servility, 1221 a 8, 28

Ses. *See* Clothes-moth

Seseli shrub, 611 a 18

Sesostris, king of Egypt, 352 b 26, 1329 b 4, 24

Sestros, 1411 a 14

Seuthes the Thracian, 1312 a 14

Seven, Pythagorean use of the number 1093 a 13-19

Sex, differences between male and female 466 b 16, 467 a 31-34, 538 a 22-24, 544 b 33, 608 a 22-b 25, 648 a 12, 32 (Cf. 648 a 30), 653 b 1, 655 a 13, 661 b 33, 675 a 4, 727 a 26, 729 b 13, 748 b 32, 757 b 17, 765 b 17, 766 a 22-b 26, 806 b 33, 809 a 26-810 a 13, 814 a 9, 891 b 21-24, 894 b 27, 963 b 20; in animals 489 a 11, 537 b 22-538 b 24; in plants 715 b 19, 815 a 21, 816 b 23-818 a 3; sexes are separated in all animals that can move about 730 b 34; why the sexes are divided 731 b 18-732 a 24; causes of sex in the embryo 763 b 20-767 a 35; some animals have no female sex 816 a 18; why flesh has unpleasant odour when sexual powers are present 877 b 21-39. Cf. Female, Male

Sexual intercourse. *See* Copulation

Shabbiness, 1192 a 37, b 5

Shadows, 845 a 24-27; why black 791 a 13-20; increase and decrease of 911 a 14-b 2, 912 a 34-b 3; those thrown by moon longer than those thrown by sun 912 b 4-10; trembling of 913 a 5-16

Shame, modesty (αἰσχύνη), 126 a 6, 1108 a 31-35, 1115 a 13, 1116 a 28, 31, 1128 b 10-35, 1136 b 20, 1179 b 12, 1191 a 7, 13, 1193 a 1-10, 1220 b 12, 1221 a 1, 1229 a 39, 1230 a 17, 1233 b 26-29, 1234 a 32, 1250 b 11, 1383 b 12-1385 a 16; causes blushing 903 a 3,

Simplicity, sincerity, 1221 a 12, 37, 1233 b 38, 1234 a 33, 1250 b 42

Simultaneity, of correlatives 7 b 15; kinds of 14 b 23-15 a 13; in nature 15 a 8

Sincerity. See Simplicity, Truthfulness

Sinciput. See Bregma

Sinew, 484 a 14-b 8, 487 a 6, 511 b 8, 515 a 27-b 27, 743 a 18, b 5; homogeneous 385 a 8, 388 a 17, 390 b 5; tractile 386 b 11; earth predominates in 389 a 12; skin contains sinews 483 b 15; connects bones 483 b 31, 484 a 17, 787 b 19; found in the heart 484 a 17, 485 a 8; formation of 744 b 37

Sinon, 1459 b 7

Sinope, 973 a 25

Sinti, 841 a 29

Siphae, Lake, 504 b 32, 692 a 5, 708 a 5

Sipylus, Mount, 368 b 30; stone of 846 b 3-6

Siren, 623 b 12, 1230 b 36

Siren Islands, 839 a 27-34

Siritus in Italy, 1329 b 22

Sirrhas, 1311 b 12

Sistros, 846 a 35-38

Sisyphus, 1412 a 5, 1456 a 22

Sitta. See Nuthatch

Skate. See Ray

Skin, 487 a 6, 517 b 27-518 a 4, 938 b 15; homogeneous 388 a 17; contains veins, sinews, and air ducts 483 b 15; man has most delicate skin of all animals 517 b 27; formation of 743 b 7; nails, hair, horns, etc. formed out of skin 745 a 20; colour of 778 a 20, 785 b 15, 797 a 34, b 12, 18, 21, 798 b 21; as a physiognomic sign 806 a 30, b 5, 807 b 17, 808 a 18; darkens with age 890 a 19, 967 b 13-18; effect of hot water on 936 b 12, 937 a 10; why inflated skin floats 939 a 33-38; preservation of food in 939 b 12-14; running naked makes skin ruddy 966 b 34-967 a 10; sitting still in sun burns the skin 967 a 20-23. Cf. Complexion

Skull, 491 a 31-b 8, 516 a 15-22, 587 b 13, 896 a 31. Cf. Sutures of skull

Sky, clearer at night 938 b 5-13; colder when sky is clear 939 b 15-22, 33-940 a 2

Slavery, is natural 1254 a 19-1255 a 2 (Cf. 1253 b 21, 22); by law and by nature 1255 a 3-b 15, 1325 a 30

Slaves, 7 a 28, 1277 a 8, 1415 b 23; as rulers 838 a 1-4; rule of master over slave 1160 b 29, 1161 b 1-10; defined as animate property 1241 b 23, 1253 b 23-1254 a 17; and master have same interest 1252 a 34, 1278 b 34; difference between the slave and the female 1252 b 1-9; ought captives of war to be made slaves? 1255 a 3-b 3; art of acquiring slaves is a species of hunting or war 1255 b 37-40, 1333 b 38; capable of only an inferior virtue 1259 b 21-1260 b 7; has no deliberative faculty 1260 a 11; not allowed gymnastic exercises in Crete 1264 a 22; treatment of 1269 b 9, 1325 b 5, 1344 a 23-b 22; classes of 1277 a 38; cannot form a state 1280 a 32; dependent 1291 a 10; enjoy democracies and tyrannies 1313 b 33-38; liberty should be held out as a reward 1330 a 33, 1344 b 16; not good company for children 1336 a 41; two kinds of: overseer and worker 1344 a 25; sold at Mende to pay expenses of war 1350 a 13-15; insurance of 1352 b 33-1353 a 4. Cf. Master

Sleep, 102 a 23, 453 b 12-458 a 32, 1044 b 16, 1185 a 10, 1201 b 17-21, 1216 a 3-10; poorly defined as failure of sensation 145 b 1-4, 14-16; sleep and waking assume faculty of sense-perception 412 a 25, 454 a 16, b 28; sleep or waking not attributes of pure intelligence 454 a 12; can neither sleep nor wake all the time 454 a 19-b 23; an affection of common sense 454 a 22, b 10, 455 a 26, b 10, 456 b 9, 458 a 26; an inhibition of function 454 b 26; same affection is extended to all senses 455 a 11; distinguished from a swoon 455 b 6, 456 b 10; causes of 455 b 14-28, 456 b 18-458 a 32, 653 a 12-20, 816 b 33-39; no sense is active in sleep 459 a 1; in animals 536 b 24-537 b 21, 599 a 29, 894 a 22-29; of fish 537 a 13-b 21; a non-voluntary movement 703 b 9; of embryo and infant 778 b 20-779 a 27; plants do not sleep

22; women and children to be held in common 1261 a 5, 11, 14, b 19, 1262 a 33, b 6, 9, 1264 b 29; praise of his discourses 1265 a 10-12; on the people necessary for a state 1291 a 12; his treatment of revolutions in *The Republic* 1316 a 2-b 27; on musical modes 1342 a 32, b 24; used illustrative parallels 1393 b 4-8; the *Funeral Speech* of 1415 b 30

Socrates (anyone), 13 b 14, 17, 18, 22, 25, 30, 14 a 10, 17 b 28, 18 a 2, 20 a 25, 21 a 2, 43 a 35, 103 a 31, 160 b 27, 166 b 34, 228 a 3, 644 a 23, 767 b 25, 768 a 1, 7, 24, 29, 33, b 14, 981 a 9, 18, 983 b 13, 16, 991 a 25, 1003 a 10, 1004 b 2, 1007 b 5, 9, 14, 1017 a 32, 1018 a 2, 1024 b 31, 1032 a 7, 1033 b 24, 1034 a 7, 1035 b 31, 1037 a 7, b 6, 1038 b 28, 1040 b 2, 1055 b 35, 1070 a 12, 1074 a 35, 1079 b 30, 1356 b 30, 34, 1357 b 12, 1382 a 5

SOCRATES of Theodectes, 1399 a 8

Socrates the younger, 1036 b 25

Socratic Conversation, 1447 b 11

Soda, 834 a 32, 863 b 17, 887 b 7, 936 a 2

Soft, 382 a 12-23

Softening, by fire 385 b 7-12

Softness of character, 1116 a 14, 1145 a 35, b 9, 1147 b 23, 1148 a 12, 1150 a 31, b 2, 1251 a 14; physiognomic signs of 808 a 10, 810 a 19, 27, 35, b 2, 8, 11, 14, 27, 37, 811 a 13; and incontinence 1150 a 14, 1202 b 34-38

Soldiers, courage of citizen-soldiers 1116 a 16-b 2; heavy-armed soldiers 1265 b 28, 1279 b 3, 1297 b 22, 1321 a 12-19; Plato says soldiers should learn to use both hands 1274 b 13; necessary to state 1291 a 7-32, 1326 a 23, 1328 b 7, 1329 a 37; shepherds make good soldiers 1319 a 22; relation of different soldiers to different constitutions 1321 a 5-26; light-armed soldiers 1321 a 12-34; should be separated from the husbandmen 1329 b 1

Solecism, 165 b 20, 1407 b 18-21; how to produce solecism in an opponent 173 b 17-174 a 16; solution of arguments leading to 182 a 7-b 6

Solen. *See* Razor-fish

Solid, 141 b 5-22, 969 a 25, 970 b 32, 971 a 2, 972 a 8, b 10; hard to heat or chill but holds the affection for a long time 648 b 33, 658 b 9; ambiguous 649 b 9-22; the ideal solid 968 a 13

Solidification, 382 a 25; nature of 382 b 31-384 b 23; bodies that do not admit of 385 b 1-6; caused by heat or cold 649 a 29-35

Solitary life, 1097 b 10, 1099 b 4, 1157 b 22, 1169 b 17, 1170 a 5

Solon, 1100 a 11, 1219 b 7, 1256 b 32, 1266 b 17, 1273 b 34-1274 a 7, 15, 1281 b 32, 1375 b 33, 1398 b 17; his description of the happy man 1179 a 9-12; a member of the middle class 1296 a 19

Solstice, summer 343 a 15, b 1, 362 a 12, 31; winter 343 b 6, 362 a 22, 941 b 15; cause of 355 a 25; announced by bee and grasshopper 835 a 23-26; why deaths are likely to occur during the hundred days following each solstice, 862 b 7-10

Somnolence, physiognomic signs of 808 b 7, 811 b 18

Song, 1449 b 29, 1452 b 22, 1459 b 10

Soot, 967 b 5

Soothsayers, 954 a 37, 1346 b 22. Cf. Divination

Sophist, 996 a 32, 1004 b 17, 1026 b 15, 1164 a 31, 1181 a 1, 12-18, 1218 b 22, 1240 b 24, 1355 b 18, 20; denied the necessity of everything coming to be or being eternal 104 b 25; his art is the semblance of wisdom without the reality 165 a 22, 171 b 33; one who makes money from apparent but unreal wisdom 165 a 23, 171 b 28; defined 171 b 8; uses words of ambiguous meaning 1404 b 38; the Parian Sophists 1421 a 32

SOPHISTES of Plato, referred to 1026 b 14, 1064 b 19, 1089 a 20

Sophistry, 162 a 17, 856 a 33, 969 b 8, 1026 b 14, 1032 a 6, 1049 b 32; defined as a kind of art of money-making from apparent wisdom 171 b 28; appearance of wisdom without the reality 171 b 33, 1004 b 24; how to arrange the arguments and questions 174 a 17-b 40; and dialectic 183 b 2

(Cf. 1359 b 11), 1004 b 18-26, 1061 b 8

Sophocles, 400 b 25, 1015 a 31, 1146 a 19, 1151 b 18, 1373 b 9, 1374 b 36, 1375 a 34, 1400 b 17, 1409 b 9, 1415 a 20, 1416 a 14, 1419 a 27, 1448 a 25, 1453 b 31, 1454 b 8, 1455 a 18, 1456 a 27, 1460 b 33, 1462 b 2; added a third actor and scenery 1449 a 18. Cf. *Antigone, Electra, Iphigenia, Tereus, Teucer*

Sophron, 1447 b 10

Sores, effect of marshy districts on 861 a 33-39; treatment of 865 a 25-30; formed in some people by exertion 883 b 26-33; effect of climate on 909 a 35-40; caused by black bile 953 a 18, 954 a 26

Sosipolis, raised money by selling offerings to Dionysus 1347 a 25-31

Sosistratus, 1462 a 8

Soul, vital principle (ψυχή), 465 a 27, 483 b 11, 1036 a 1, 1046 a 36, 1143 a 16, 1144 a 2; discourse within the soul 76 b 25; growth of knowledge in the soul 99 b 15-100 b 17; more important than body 118 a 32, 731 b 29; its immortality questioned 119 b 36, 1070 a 26; may be that it possesses knowledge of itself 125 a 39, 402 a 10, 425 b 10-25; commands the body 128 b 18, 1254 b 3; has man a tripartite soul? 133 a 30, 432 a 24-b 8, 1249 a 32; not a self-moving number 140 b 3, 408 b 32-409 b 18 (Cf. 120 b 3-6); 'the self-mover' (Plato) 140 b 3; is time soul-dependent? 223 a 16-28; souls of children more restless than those of adults 248 a 1; thought by Plato to be cause of motion 265 b 33; principle of living beings 402 a 6, 415 b 8-28, 470 a 20, 641 a 18, 1035 b 14, 1043 a 25; inseparable from body 403 a 2-b 19; views of early thinkers 403 b 20-405 b 31; three marks universally ascribed to soul: (1) movement, (2) sensation, (3) incorporeality 405 b 12; supposed derivation of ψυχή 405 b 29; has no movement 405 b 32-407 b 25, 408 a 34-b 31; not a spatial magnitude 407 a 2-b 25, 467 b 14; not a harmony 407 b 27-408 a 33; not composed of

elements 409 b 19-411 a 6; not present in all things 411 a 7-23; unity of 411 a 24-b 30; defined as a substance in the sense of the form of a natural body 412 a 12-413 a 10; defined as an actuality or formulable essence of something that possesses a potentiality of having a soul 413 a 11-414 a 27; faculties of 414 a 28-415 a 13, 1144 a 9; principal cause of nutrition and growth 416 a 9-18; all things having souls are warm 416 b 29; never thinks without an image 431 a 16; of animals 432 a 15; parts of 432 a 29-b 4, 433 b 3; relations of the faculties of 434 a 22-435 b 25, 449 b 5, 450 a 16, 454 a 12, 467 b 17; breath is akin to 481 a 17, 483 a 26-35; respiration a function of 482 b 22; how far within the province of science? 641 a 18-642 b 4, 1026 a 5; is final cause of body 645 b 15; thought by some to be fire 652 b 8; how soul moves body 700 b 4-701 a 6; the original of movement 702 a 35, 703 a 2; resides in heart 703 a 2, b 38; not in every part 703 a 38; semen possesses soul potentially 735 a 8, 737 a 17; three kinds of 736 b 15; contributed by the male 738 b 27; in a sense all things are full of 762 a 21; influences body 805 a 3, 808 b 11-39, 1254 a 31-b 9; do plants have souls? 815 a 14, 31, b 29-34, 816 a 40, b 4-22; every animal has a soul 816 b 6; rational and irrational parts of 1098 a 2, 1102 a 28, b 13, 29, 1119 b 15, 1138 b 8, 1139 a 5, 1168 b 21, 1172 b 10, 1182 a 24-29, 1185 b 1-13, 1196 b 14, 1219 b 26-1220 a 2, 1221 b 27-31, 1250 b 37, 1260 a 7, 1333 a 17, 1334 b 19; function of man is activity of 1098 a 7-17; happiness is virtuous activity of 1098 a 17, b 30, 1099 b 26, 1102 a 5, 17, 1177 a 11, 1184 b 23-1185 a 13, 1204 a 28, 1219 a 35-b 25; divided into rational and irrational elements, latter into nutritive and desiderative 1102 a 27-1103 a 3; pleasures of 1117 b 28; calculative and scientific faculties in 1138 b 35-1139 a 16, 1196 b 12-33; eye of 1144 a 30; a single soul 1168 b 7; goods of 1184 b 2, 1218 b

32-34; nutritive part of soul has no relation to happiness 1185 a 14-35, 1219 b 37-41; feelings, capacities, and states in 1105 b 20, 1186 a 10-19, 1286 a 19; injustice within the soul 1196 a 26-28; divisions of rational part of 1196 b 11-33; three parts according to Plato 1249 a 32; virtue makes the soul good 1251 b 7; beauty of soul harder to see than beauty of body 1254 b 37; interests of body and soul are same 1255 b 9; more truly a part of animal than is the body 1291 a 25; body prior in generation to the soul 1334 b 20. Cf. Appetitive soul, Irrational element in soul, Nutrition, Rational principle, State of character

Sound, unheard if continuous 290 b 26; sound of thunder splits rocks 290 b 35; caused when a moving body is enclosed in an unmoved body 291 a 16; travels slower than light 395 a 16; medium of 419 a 25-29, b 18, 420 a 3-18; actual and potential 419 b 5; description of 419 b 20-24; defined as movement of what can rebound from a smooth surface when struck against it 420 a 21; acute and grave 420 a 27-b 4; sense of sound consists of air 438 b 20; species of sound are limited 445 b 22; differs from voice 535 a 27; produced by meeting of bodies 800 a 1-15; dim 800 a 14; misty 800 a 14; causes of differences in 800 a 17-801 a 20; hard 801 a 17, 802 b 30-803 b 1; heard only when strikes the ear 801 a 21-40; clearness in 801 b 23-802 a 7; rough 803 b 2-17; thin 803 b 18-804 a 8; thick 804 a 9-21; piping 804 a 22-32; cracked 804 a 33-b 8; aspirated 804 b 9; smooth 804 b 10; more audible at night 899 a 19-21, 903 a 7-25; sound is air set in motion 899 a 35, 902 b 13, 920 b 4; of weeping and laughter 900 a 20-31, b 7-14, 904 b 22-26; penetrates dense objects 904 b 15-21, 905 a 35-b 23

Source (ἀρχή), has many meanings 415 b 8-11; of soul 469 a 6

South winds, 361 a 22, 831 a 15-19, 942 a 5-15; dry south winds cause fever 862 a 17-25, 946 b 4-9; make men feel heavier and weaker 862 a 26-33, 945 a 13-17; do not blow at fixed period of year 940 a 35-b 7; of Libya 942 a 7, 945 b 35-946 a 3; and north winds are most frequent 944 a 36-b 2; cause overclouding when they blow strongly 944 b 25-29. Cf. Euronotus, Eurus, Leuconotus, Lips, Notus, Wind

Space (χώρα), 209 a 8; a continuous quantity 5 a 6; appears to admit of a contrary 6 a 11; Plato held that space and matter are identical 209 b 12; relation of finite and infinite space and time 233 a 22-b 15, 237 b 23-238 b 22, 239 b 5-240 b 8

Sparrow, 613 a 30; gall-bladder of 506 b 22; stomach of 509 a 8; caeca of 509 a 24; change of colour in 519 a 6; copulation of 539 b 33; diet of 592 b 17; bathing of 633 b 4; eggs of 774 b 28; white sparrows 785 b 35

Sparrow-hawk, hobby-hawk, 592 b 2, 620 a 20

Sparta, Spartans, 152 a 13, 176 b 6, 1102 a 12, 1112 a 28, 1117 a 27, 1124 b 17, 1127 b 28, 1145 a 28, 1167 a 32, 1180 a 25, 1263 a 35, 1264 a 11, 1275 b 9, 1293 b 17, 1316 a 35, 1324 b 8, 1334 a 41, 1341 a 32, 1367 b 10, 1398 b 13, 1411 a 4, 1415 b 31, 1419 a 31, 1422 a 41, 1423 a 2, 7, 1429 b 1, 11, 1434 a 1, 7, 1435 a 17, 1461 b 4, 6; serpents of 832 a 19-22; common meals at 1263 b 41, 1265 b 41, 1271 a 27-37, 1272 a 2, 15, 1294 b 27; Spartan citizens not allowed to engage in agriculture 1264 a 10; criticism of the Spartan constitution 1265 b 32-1266 a 1, 1269 a 29-1271 b 19, 1293 b 17, 1294 b 19-34, 1316 a 18, b 9, 1333 b 11; Helots often revolted 1269 a 37-b 12; warlike 1269 b 4, 1270 a 2; licentiousness of Spartan women 1269 b 13-1270 a 14, 1361 a 11, the Spartan monarchy 1271 a 40, 1285 a 2-13, b 34-1286 a 5, 1313 a 26; prohibits strangers 1272 b 17; law-courts at 1273 a 21, 1279 b 9; revolution at 1301 b 19, 1306 b 29-1307 a 4; tyrants put down 1312 b 8; take great pains with their children 1337 a 32; good judges of music 1339 b 2; gymnastic exercises carried to excess in Sparta 1338 b 9-38; fasted for a day and gave money they usually spent to the Samians 1347 b 16-19; free men have long hair at Sparta 1367 a 29

Sparus, caeca of 508 b 17

Spatangus, a species of urchins, 530 b 4

Species (εἶδος), 1023 b 24, 1024 b 8, 1038 a 6; and substance 2 a 14, 22; species nearer to primary substance than the genus 2 b 7; species is to genus as subject to predicate 2 b 19; no one species more truly substance than another 2 b 23; genus and species only predicates that convey a knowledge of primary substances 2 b 31; definition of species and genus applicable to primary substance 3 b 2; determines quality of substance 3 b 19; simultaneous 14 b 33; infimae species 96 b 16, 22, 24, 97 b 31, 414 b 27, 1018 b 5, 1059 b 27; as tests of ambiguity 107 b 34-37; take on name and definition of their genera 109 b 7; attributes that belong to the species belong also to genus 111 a 21-33; danger of placing a state and an activity in genus-species relationship 125 b 15-127 a 19; priority of species to genus and differentia 141 b 30; made up of differentia added to the genus 143 b 8; combination of differentia and matter 643 a 24; give names to individuals 816 a 14; change of species in plants 821 a 28-41; genera are starting-points of 998 b 8; same in species 999 a 3, 1016 b 32, 1018 b 7, 1049 b 18, 1058 a 18; other in species 1018 a 38, 1054 b 28, 1057 b 35-1058 b 26; male and female are contrary yet not different in species 1058 a 29-b 26. Cf. Definition, Differentia, Genus

Spectacle, 1449 b 32, 1450 a 14, b 17-20, 1456 a 2, 1459 b 10, 1462 a 17; may arouse fear and pity 1453 b 1, 9

Spectators, vulgarity of spectators lowers character of performers 1341 b 15; two kinds: the vulgar and the educated 1342 a 19

Speech, 488 b 33, 813 b 1, 1456 b 22, 1457 a 23-30; a quantity 4 b 32; lips designed for 659 b 33-660 a 12; consists of combinations of letters 660 a 4, 895 a 10; tongue designed for 660 a 14-28; in birds 660 a 29-b 3; teeth designed for 661 b 14, 15; slow speech a sign of good moral character 807 b 35; effect of drunkenness on 875 b 19-33; man has many forms of 895 a 7-14; man only animal that has speech 899 a 2, 1253 a 9; hesitation of 895 b 15-19, 902 b 16-29, 903 a 39-b 12, 19-26, 905 a 16-23, b 29-37; censorship of speech in the ideal state 1336 b 3-23. Cf. Voice

Speed, meanings of 1052 b 29

Spelt, tiphe, 603 b 26

Sperm, 487 a 4, 509 b 35, 521 b 19, 523 a 13-27; of birds 559 b 7. Cf. Semen

Speusippus, 1096 b 7, 1153 b 4, 1411 a 21; his conception of substance 1028 b 21; on beauty and goodness 1072 b 30-35; referred to 1069 a 36, 1075 a 34, b 37, 1076 a 21, 1080 b 14, 26, 1084 a 13, 1085 a 32, 1086 a 2, 29, 1087 b 6, 27, 1090 a 7, 25, b 17, 1091 a 34, b 23, 32, 1092 a 11-b 8, 1104 b 24 (?), 1172 a 28

Sphecons, 628 a 12

Sphere, 218 b 1, 240 a 29, 976 a 8, 978 b 9; spherical shape of stars 91 b 10, 290 a 8, b 1; the primary shape 286 b 10-33; spherical shape of universe 287 b 15, 290 b 1; two movements of: spinning and rolling 290 a 10; no harmony of the spheres 290 b 12-291 a 29; each has its own motion 293 a 11; spherical shape of earth 297 b 21; why spherical bodies are easily moved 851 b 15-852 a 13; is God spherical? 977 b 1-3, 19, 978 a 7-979 a 7; spheres of the stars 1073 a 13-1074 b 14. Cf. Circle

Sphinx, 208 a 32

Sphondyle, knuckle-beetle, 604 b 18; copulation of 542 a 12

Sphyraena, habits of 610 b 5

Spider, 140 a 4, 199 a 22, 27, 550 b 33, 623 b 15; diet of 488 a 17, 594 a 14; web of 542 a 13; generation of 553 a 8, 555 a 27-b 17, 721 a 5; habits of 609 a 29, 622 b 28-623 b 1; scolex of

State. *See* City

State of character, state of mind, state of soul (ἕξις), 1 b 27, 103 b 23, 193 a 25, 246 a 10, 1104 b 19, 1114 b 2, 1115 b 21, 1117 a 20, 1123 a 36, 1126 b 21, 1129 a 14-18, 1139 a 16, 1140 a 4-22, 1141 b 24, 1147 a 12, 1154 a 13, 1174 b 32, 1186 a 17-19, 1197 a 14, 1199 a 8, 1219 a 3-12, 31-35, 1221 b 35, 1231 a 36; danger of placing a state and an activity in genus-species relationship 125 b 15-19; rules for testing the definition of 147 a 12-22; and activity 1098 b 33, 1103 b 21, 1122 b 1, 1152 b 34, 1157 b 6, 1190 b 2, 1218 b 36; virtue is a state of character 1105 b 19-1106 a 12; and feeling 1128 b 11, 1157 b 29; in accord with practical wisdom 1144 b 25; natural state 1152 b 34, 1153 a 14; virtue is the best state 1185 a 37, 1191 a 39, b 28

Statement (ἑρμηνεία), its truth or falsity depends on facts 4 b 8; incapable of admitting contrary qualities 4 b 12; methods of 1428 a 10, 1435 a 4-32, 1436 a 22

Statesman, 1252 a 7, 12, 16; practices natural art of acquisition 1256 b 38; must discern the beginning of evil 1303 b 27, 1308 a 34; and the philosopher 1324 a 29

Stature, as a physiognomic sign 813 b 6-35; climate affects stature 909 b 15-24

Steel, how made 383 a 33

Steelyard, weighs great weights with a small counterpoise 853 b 25-854 a 15

Stentor, 1326 b 7

Stereometry, 78 b 38

Sterility, 746 b 12-747 a 23; why mules are sterile 747 a 24-749 a 5; in lions 750 a 32, 760 b 23

Stesichorus, 542 b 25, 1395 a 1, 1412 a 22; his fable about Phalaris 1393 b 9-23

Sthenelus, the poetry of 1458 a 21

Stilbon, 1398 b 2

Sting-ray, trygon, 489 b 31, 620 b 24; copulation of 540 b 8; generation of 565 b 27; habitat of 598 a 12; tail of 695 b 9; body of 695 b 27

Stock-dove, oenas, 544 b 6; eggs of 558 b 23

Stomach, 457 b 11, 495 b 24-34, 507 a 27-509 a 24; and nutrition 469 a 2; nature and functions of 674 a 9-675 a 30; effect of drugs on 863 b 29-864 b 27; cooled and dried by sexual intercourse 878 b 17-20; becomes thinner in those who take physical exercise 880 b 34-36, 882 a 13-28; area about stomach fattest 880 b 39-881 a 3; has power to melt food 936 a 26-31

Stone-curlew. *See* Charadrius

Stones, 197 b 10, 388 a 14, 443 a 16, 470 a 33, 793 a 20, 838 b 1; in bladder 519 b 19; in head of fish 601 b 30; stone-throwing engine 800 b 14; why stones do not grow 822 a 31-39; some stones float in water 823 a 41; burning stones of Thrace 833 a 25-28, 841 a 27-b 2; as charms 846 a 32-34, b 3-6; of Mount Sipylus 846 b 3-6; the Nile-stone 846 b 22-25; of the Maeander River 846 b 26-28; stone of madness 846 b 27, 847 a 5-7; changing stone on Mount Tmolus 847 a 8-11; moved by plants 902 b 2; why made round by sea 935 a 38-b 2; formed by hot water 937 a 12-19. Cf. Pebbles

Stork, 593 b 3; hibernation of 600 a 19; habits of 612 a 32, 615 b 24-32, 832 a 14-18

Strabax, 1399 b 2

Strangalides, 587 b 23

Strangury, 612 b 16, 783 a 21; cure for 831 b 1-4

Stratonicus, 1231 a 12

Strattis, 443 b 30

Strength of character, physiognomic signs of 810 a 16, 25, 30, 35, b 1, 8, 10, 14, 24, 25, 36, 811 a 11

Strigil, 145 a 24

Strike, soft-head, 617 b 1

Stromboids, spiral-shaped testaceans, 492 a 17, 528 a 11; anatomy of 528 b 18-529 a 25; mouth of 530 b 21

Strymonias. *See* Thracias

Strymon River, 350 b 17, 592 a 7, 597 a 10, 973 b 18

Stubbornness, 809 a 36, 1221 a 8, 28

Stupidity, physiognomic signs of 808 b 2, 811 b 30

Style in rhetoric, 1403 b 6-1414 a 29; prose style and poetical style are distinct 1404 a 28-b 4; four possible faults of: (1) misuse of compound words, (2) use of strange words, (3) long, unseasonable, or frequent epithets, (4) inappropriate metaphors 1405 b 34-1406 b 19; correctness of language is foundation of good style 1407 a 18-b 10; impressiveness of 1407 b 26-1408 a 9; appropriateness of 1408 a 10-b 21; periodic style 1409 a 23-1410 b 5; ways of achieving liveliness of style 1410 b 6-1413 b 2; each type of oratory has its own appropriate style 1413 b 3-1414 a 28

Styrax, 534 b 25

Styx, 983 b 33

Subject, 1 a 20, 2 a 12, 3 a 8; subject-genus 75 a 39-b 1, 76 a 12; as substratum 79 a 9, 81 b 28, 83 a 6-13; as reciprocating with predicate 82 a 15-20; an attribute is never a subject 83 b 22. Cf. Substratum

Submission to evils, hard, patient, 1221 a 9, 31

Substance (τόδε τι, οὐσία), 103 b 22, 108 b 23, 122 a 3-b 12, 186 b 4-187 a 10, 410 a 13, 20, 412 b 11, 988 b 28, 1007 a 20, 1028 a 6-1045 b 24, 1089 b 31, 1096 a 21, 1205 a 10; examples of 1 b 27; definition of primary substance 2 a 11, 1037 b 3; definition of secondary substance 2 a 14; everything except primary substance predicable of or present in a primary substance 2 a 33, 465 b 7; species nearer the primary substance than the genus 2 b 7; primary substance underlies everything else 2 b 16, 39; no one species more truly substance than another 2 b 23; no primary substance more truly substance than another 2 b 27; genus and species only predicates that convey a knowledge of primary substance 2 b 31; never present in a subject 3 a 6; predicated univocally 3 a 33; primary substance not predicable of anything 3 a 36; in secondary substance, species is predicated of individual, genus of species and individual 3 a 39; definition of species

and genus applicable to primary substance 3 b 2; primary substance signifies individual, secondary substance, class 3 b 10-23, 644 a 23; has no contrary 3 b 24, 225 b 10, 1068 a 11, 1087 b 2; no variation of degree 3 b 32; admits contrary qualities 4 a 12, 6 a 1; not relative 8 a 12; primary substances are actualities without potentiality 23 a 23; signifies a 'this somewhat' 73 b 7; predicates which do not signify substance must be predicates of some other subject 83 a 31; essentially definable 83 b 5; how prove substance by definition 92 a 34-b 38; how to obtain a definition of 96 a 20-97 b 40; that which reveals essence is not a property but a definition 135 a 12; as a source of fallacy 168 a 25, 169 a 34, 170 a 15; individual and being in the fullest sense belong to 169 a 35; only category that can exist apart 185 a 31, 1069 a 25; never a predicate 186 b 2; is it a third principle? 189 a 28-b 29; underlies all becoming 190 a 14, 33, 192 a 29; the physicists regard infinite as attribute of 203 a 17; does substance come to be? 317 b 21; perishable and imperishable 338 b 13-19; three meanings of: (1) form, (2) matter, (3) complex of both 412 a 7, 414 a 15; the actuality of a potentiality 415 b 14; Democritus was first to come near notion of 642 a 27; criticism of Plato's treatment of 990 b 23-991 a 7; are there non-sensible substances? 995 b 13-18, 997 a 34-998 a 19, 1059 a 38-b 21; who studies the attributes of substances? 995 b 19-27, 997 a 25-33, 1059 a 29-33; are unity and being substances or attributes? 996 a 5-8, 1001 a 4-b 25, 1060 a 36-b 19; that on which other things depend 1003 b 17; composed of contraries 1004 b 30; and accident 1007 a 30-b 18; meanings of 1017 b 10-25; immovable substance 1026 a 29, 1064 a 34; first in definition, in order of knowledge, and in time 1028 a 31-b 1; the denotation of 1028 b 8-32; word 'substance' is applied to four things: (1) essence, (2) universal,

(3) genus, (4) substratum 1028 b 33-1041 b 33; matter cannot be primary substance 1029 a 1-26; matter and form cannot be primary substance 1029 a 27-33; only substance is definable 1031 a 1; the starting-point of everything 1034 a 30, 1078 b 24; produced only from substance 1034 b 16-19; cannot consist of universals 1038 b 1-1039 a 23; cannot consist of substances 1038 b 24-1039 a 23; Platonic Ideas are not substances 1039 a 24-b 19; two kinds: concrete thing and the formula 1039 b 20; many things thought to be substances are only potencies 1040 b 5-15; substance as form 1041 a 6-b 34; a principle and a cause 1041 a 9; as actuality of sensible things 1042 b 9-1044 a 14; that in virtue of which other things exist 1045 b 30; no universal can be a substance 1053 b 17; cannot be demonstrated 1064 a 9; priority of 1069 a 17-29; early philosophers made it particulars, later philosophers made it universals 1069 a 26-29; three kinds of 1069 a 30-b 2, 1071 b 3; generated from another of the same kind 1070 a 4-30; three kinds: (1) matter, (2) the individual nature, (3) the resulting individual 1070 a 9-12; can exist apart 1070 b 37; necessity of an eternal unmovable substance 1071 b 3-1072 a 18; the first of existing things 1071 b 5; the number of eternal unmovable substances 1073 a 13-1074 b 14; a sort of principle 1222 b 16

Substratum (ὑποκείμενον), 83 a 6-14, 192 a 2, 984 a 22, 1016 a 19, 1017 b 24, 1024 b 11; a third somewhat, as substratum of contraries 189 a 35-b 29, 190 b 34, 191 a 4; and change 225 a 3-b 2; change of substratum is called altering 314 b 3; material cause of coming to be 319 a 19; of fire 649 a 21; as matter 983 a 30, 985 b 10, 992 b 1, 1022 a 18, 1038 b 7, 1070 a 11 (Cf. 1044 b 9); substance as substratum 1028 b 33-1029 a 33, 1043 a 26-32; defined 1028 b 35; a substratum for each category 1029 b 24; two meanings of 1038 b 4-7, 1049 a 27

Successive, 1005 a 11, 1085 a 4; defined 226 b 34-227 a 7, 231 a 23, 1068 b 32-1069 a 14; a property of things prior to definition 227 a 19

Suddenly, defined 222 b 15

Suet, 487 a 3, 511 b 9, 520 a 6-b 3; homogeneous 647 b 13; composition and purpose of 651 a 20-b 19

Suffering in tragedy, 1447 a 28, 1452 b 10-12, 1455 b 34, 1459 b 9, 15

Suffocation, 470 b 22, 475 b 2, 476 a 30; in mines 834 a 23-32

Suicide, 954 b 35-955 a 28, 1138 a 10; the way of the coward 1116 a 13, 1166 b 12; forbidden by law 1138 a 7

Sulkiness, 1251 a 4; physiognomic signs of 807 a 5, 808 a 17-19

Sulphur, 378 a 23, 826 a 2, 842 b 23; sacred 937 b 28

Summer, 349 b 8; hailstorms common in summer 348 a 18, b 27; due to sun's motion 361 a 13; illness is rarer but more fatal in winter than in summer 862 b 16-24; winds come from west in 942 b 3-12, 946 a 35-b 21; winds blow in summer in evening 946 a 35-b 21; body is colder to touch in summer than in winter 964 b 39-965 a 8

Sun, 142 b 1, 194 b 13, 392 a 29, 396 b 28, 778 a 4, 911 b 3-34, 946 b 2-21, 947 a 26-32; 'brightest star that moves over the earth' 131 b 27; its heat 289 a 32; appears to spin 290 a 15; eclipses of 291 b 23, 912 b 11-26; movements of 292 a 1, 398 b 6, 21; distance from earth 294 a 5; its annual movement is the efficient cause of coming to be and passing away 336 a 15-337 a 33; motion of sun is rapid and near, therefore heats earth 341 a 19-29; white not fiery in colour 341 a 37; warms the earth 341 b 7; larger than earth 345 b 2; gives rise to generation and destruction 346 b 22; not nourished by moisture 354 b 32-355 a 32; draws moisture from earth 357 b 20, 360 a 7; its effect upon winds 361 b 14-22, 944 a 25-35; mock suns 372 a 10-21, 377 a 29-378 b 6; called 'father' 716 a 18; colour of 791 a 3, 793 a 14; some colours rise only by mixture with rays of sun 792 a 10, b 23, 793 b 17, 794 b 28, 795 a 11, 799 b 4; effect on plants 817 a 26, 826 b 5-9, 36, 827 a 20, 32, 830 b 2; effect on the body 865 b 28-38; drunkards enjoy the sun 875 b 5-8, 34-38; unhealthy to walk naked in the sun 884 a 37-b 8; consumes outer surface of the earth 897 b 16; the source of movement 899 a 21; disturbs the air 903 a 8; shadows of 911 a 14-b 1, 912 a 34-b 20; shape of 912 a 27-33; hot things cool off in the sun 937 a 25-33; water heated by sun unfit for washing purposes 937 a 34-b 6; darkens flesh 966 b 20-24, 967 b 1-12, 23-27; bleaches wax and olive oil 966 b 20-24, 967 b 23-27; sitting still in sun burns the skin 967 a 20-23; why sun scorches 967 a 24-28

Sunrise, colours of 792 a 18; wind rises and falls at 944 a 25-30

Sunset, colours of 792 a 18; clear sunset sign of fine weather 941 a 1-19

Superfoetation, 773 a 32-774 b 4

Surgery, 1199 a 33

Susa, 398 a 14, 832 a 26, 838 a 24

Sutures of skull, 491 b 2, 515 b 14, 516 a 14, 658 b 3, 896 a 35; man has more than any other animal 653 b 1; ventilate the brain 653 b 2. Cf. Skull

Swallow, 199 a 26, 487 b 26, 626 a 8; gall-bladder of 506 b 22; eyes of 508 b 5, 563 a 13, 774 b 31; stomach of 509 a 8; change of colour in 519 a 6, 799 b 12; breeding of 544 a 26; nesting of 559 a 5, 563 a 13, 612 b 20-31; diet of 592 b 16; hibernation of 600 a 15; bath of 633 b 4; white swallows 798 a 27

Swan, 839 a 25; habits of 488 a 4, 10, 593 b 16, 610 a 1, 615 a 32-b 5; caeca of 509 a 22; migration of 597 b 30

Sweat. See Perspiration

Swift. See Apus

Swimming, easier to swim in sea than in river 933 a 9-13; affects bowels 935 b 27-33

'Swipe,' 857 a 34-b 8

Sword-fish, gills of 505 a 19; gall-bladder of 506 b 17; parasites in 602 a 27

Sybaris, 838 a 15, 27, 840 a 17; revolution at 1303 a 30

Sybaris River, 840 a 23, 846 b 34

Sybarite, 1216 a 16, 1303 a 32

Sycamore, 820 a 21

Syennessis, on the nature of veins 511 b 24-29

Syllable, 1456 b 21, 34-39, 1458 a 2

Syllogism (συλλογισμός), 413 a 16, 917 b 5, 1139 b 27, 1142 b 23, 1400 b 28-33; defined 24 b 18; perfect 24 b 23, 25 b 35, 26 b 29, 27 a 17, 28 a 4, 29 a 15, 30, 33 a 20, 22, b 20, 27, 35, 34 a 1, 40 b 18, 41 b 33; imperfect 24 b 24, 28 a 4, 29 a 15, 30, 33 b 29, 36 b 24, 40 b 15; valid 27 a 2, 28 a 17; must have one affirmative and one universal premiss 41 b 6, 7; must have three and only three terms 41 b 36; in syllogism one term must be related to another as whole to part 42 a 10; has two and only two premisses 42 a 33, 1201 b 25; every syllogism is necessary but not everything that is necessary is a syllogism 47 a 34; more than one conclusion from a universal syllogism 53 a 5; more than one conclusion from particular affirmative 53 a 6; only the stated conclusion from particular negative 53 a 7; a form of dialectical reasoning 71 a 5; ground of syllogism is the facts constituting its premisses 72 a 27; syllogistic questions 77 a 36-b 33; should be used in reasoning against dialecticians rather than against the crowd 157 a 20; when it is most incisive 182 b 38; practical and speculative syllogisms 701 a 10-39; philosophy must study syllogism 1005 b 5; primary syllogisms 1014 b 2; starts from 'what a thing is' 1034 a 31, 1078 b 24; proceeds from universals 1139 b 29; syllogisms concerning acts to be done 1144 a 31, 1147 a 1-b 19; business of dialectic is the study of syllogisms 1355 a 9, b 16; proofs are made either by syllogisms or inductions 1356 b 8; may be formed from previous syllogisms or from premisses not yet proved 1357 a 8-13; ordinary opinions of men are the materials 1402 a 33

Syme, 1414 a 2

Sympathy, of body and soul 808 b 11-27; problems connected with sympathetic action 886 a 24-887 b 9; friendships that arise from sympathy 1210 b 23; we are most sympathetic with ourselves 1210 b 37, 1211 a 21

Symphonic accompaniment, antiphonal accompaniment more pleasing than 918 b 30-33

Symplegades, 839 b 30

Symposium of Plato, 1262 b 12

Synagris, gills of 505 a 15; gall-bladder of 506 b 17

Synodon, dentex, diet of 591 a 11, b 5; habitat of 598 a 10; habits of 610 b 5

Synonyms, 1404 b 39

Syracuse, 559 b 3, 1255 b 23, 1259 a 30, 1286 b 39, 1310 b 31, 1313 b 27, 1316 a 34, 1349 a 14, 1384 b 16, 1429 b 16, 21, 1436 b 2, 1439 a 25; spring near 834 b 5-7; fount of Arethusa at 847 a 4; revolution at 1302 b 33, 1303 a 39, b 20-26, 1304 a 27, 1306 a 2; female detectives at 1313 b 14

Syria, 821 a 34, 843 b 10, 906 b 18, 908 a 14, 973 b 2, 1352 a 8; the Syrian mule 491 a 2, 577 b 24, 580 b 1; the Syrian lion 579 b 9; sheep of 606 a 14; asses in 831 a 23-25; lion-killer of 845 a 28-34; the Syrian Gates 973 a 18

Syriandus. See Apeliotes

Syrian Sea, 393 a 29

Syrophoenicia, 577 b 24

Syrtes, 393 a 25

T

Tact, 1128 a 18, 1171 b 4, 1250 a 36

Tactlessness, 1251 a 2

Tail, hair on tail is in relation to hair on body 658 a 33; of fish 684 a 3, 695 b 5-12, 714 b 7; found in most quadrupeds 689 b 3; diversity of 690 a 1; uses of 690 a 2; of birds 697 b 8-12, 710 a 2-24; of crayfish 713 b 30; insolence found in all animals with bushy tails 808 b 36

Talon, 710 a 27

Tamarisk, 820 a 8, 827 a 2

Tanais River, 350 a 25, 353 a 16, 393 b 25

Taprobane (Ceylon), 393 b 14

Tarandos. See Elk

Tarentum, 631 a 10, 836 a 6, 8, 840 a 6-16, 973 b 14, 1291 b 23, 1320 b 4; insane man of 832 b 23-26; revolution at 1303 a 3; colonized by the Partheniae 1306 b 32

Tares, 821 a 32

Tartarus, 356 a 1

Tartessus, 350 b 2; silver of 844 a 17-23

Taste (γεῦσις), 426 a 14, 447 a 7, 492 b 27, 532 b 33, 744 a 1, 1150 a 10, 1196 b 22, 1202 a 32, 1230 b 24, 38, 1231 a 14; medium is necessary 419 a 30-b 2; related to sense of smell 421 a 16-b 7, 443 a 8-20; nature and objects of 422 a 8-b 16, 440 b 26-442 b 26; a sort of touch 421 a 18, 422 a 8, 434 b 18, 439 a 1, 441 a 2, 656 b 37, 660 a 22; dulled by cold 443 b 15; highly refined in man 494 b 18, 660 a 20; in fish 533 a 31-33, 660 b 16-23; taste and touch are in immediate connection with the heart 656 a 30; double character of 656 b 38-657 a 2; found even in tongueless animals 691 a 2; incontinence of 949 b 6-11, 37-950 a 17; intemperance found only in taste and touch 1191 b 10, 21

Tastelessness. See Vulgarity

Taulantians, 832 a 6, 842 b 16

Taurus Mountains, 973 a 19

Taus, king of Egypt, 1353 a 20; his method of raising money 1350 b 33-1351 a 17

Taxes, 1271 b 13, 1314 b 14, 1320 a 20, b 3, 1397 a 25, 1425 b 26, 1446 b 18; multiplied by tyrants 1313 b 26; property-tax in democracies 1320 a 21; various kinds of 1345 b 29-1346 a 4; property-tax levied by the Athenians at Potidaea 1347 a 18-24; on cattle at Syracuse 1349 b 6-13; property-tax at Mende 1350 a 6-11; on corn in Egypt 1351 a 9. Cf. Poll-tax

Taygetus, Mount, 846 b 7-9

Teal, 593 b 16

Tears, hot and cold 959 b 20-30

Teeth, 198 b 24-37, 501 a 8-502 a 2; composed of bone 493 a 1, 516 a 25;

males have more teeth than females in case of men, sheep, goats, and swine 501 b 20, 963 b 20; more teeth the longer is the life 501 b 23; wisdom-teeth 501 b 24-29; of fish 505 a 28-31; of horses 576 a 4-16; cutting of 587 b 14; functions of 655 b 8, 661 a 34-662 b 23; formation and development of 745 a 19-b 15; differences of teeth in animals 788 b 3-789 b 20; purposes of 788 b 3; shedding of 788 b 10-789 b 2; set on edge 886 b 12; porous teeth a sign of short life 896 a 30-36, 963 b 18-22; of Ethiopians 898 b 12-19; effect of figs on 931 a 28-32; stronger than flesh yet more sensitive to cold 963 b 23-25; more sensitive to cold than to heat 963 b 26-32

Tegea, 1365 a 27, 1460 a 31

Telamon, 1387 a 34, 1416 b 2

Telecles, constitution of 1298 a 13

Telegonus, 1453 b 34

Telemachus, 1461 b 5

Telephus, 1405 a 28, 1453 a 21

Temper, 809 a 34-37; physiognomic signs of fierce temper 806 b 3, 808 a 2, 20-23, 37, 811 a 15, b 1. Cf. Good-tempered

Temperament, temperamental differences of male and female 608 a 22-b 25, 661 b 33, 809 a 26-810 a 13, 814 a 9; moist temperament 883 a 3-10; equable temperament 883 a 11-20; effect of locality on 909 a 13-910 b 8

Temperance (σωφροσύνη), 138 b 4, 1102 b 27, 1103 a 6, b 1, 1104 a 20-26, 33, b 6, 1105 a 18, 30, b 5-12, 1107 b 5, 1108 b 21, 1109 a 5, 18, 1117 b 23-1119 b 19, 1123 b 6, 1125 b 13, 1129 b 22, 1145 b 14, 1146 a 10, 1147 b 27, 1148 a 5, 13, 1149 a 22, b 30, 1150 a 11, 1151 a 19, 1168 b 26, 1177 a 32, 1178 a 32, 1179 b 33, 1185 b 8, 1186 b 8, 1191 a 37-b 22, 1192 a 18, 1201 a 10-16, 1220 b 19, 1221 a 2, 1230 a 37-1231 b 3, 1234 a 32, 1249 b 27, 1250 a 8, b 7-11, 1265 a 33, 1267 a 10, 1277 b 16, 20, 1323 a 28, b 29, 1326 b 32, 1334 a 24, 1362 b 13, 1364 b 36, 1366 b 1, 14, 1369 a 21, 1381 a 24; young are more troubled by their passions than are the elders 117 a 34; not defined as a harmony 123 a 34, 139 b 33; natural virtue of the faculty of desire 136 b 10-14; problems connected with continence and temperance 949 a 23-950 a 19; men become ill when change their mode of life 949 a 23-b 5; approve most of temperance in the young and wealthy 949 b 20-25; has no excess nor deficiency 1107 a 22; limited to sense of touch 1117 b 23-1118 b 7, 1191 b 10, 21, 1230 b 21-1231 a 25; harmony of the appetitive and rational principles 1119 b 16; etymology of σωφροσύνη 1140 b 12; contrary to self-indulgence 1151 b 31; and continence 1151 b 32-1152 a 3, 1203 b 12-23; temperate man avoids certain pleasures 1152 b 15, 1153 a 27-35; different in men and women 1260 a 21; lost in communism 1263 b 9; in a state 1334 a 20

Temperature, anything painful or pleasing is accompanied by a change in temperature of body 701 b 35-702 a 7; change in temperature as cause of movements 703 b 15

Temples of the head, 798 a 22; as a physiognomic sign 808 b 7, 812 a 29, b 27

Ten, said to be the whole nature of numbers 986 a 9, 1073 a 20, 1084 a 12, 32

Tenedos, 1291 b 25, 1375 b 31, 1401 b 18

Tenos, 845 b 22; fire-bowl in 832 b 27

Tenthredo, ground-wasp, 623 b 11, 629 a 31

Teos, 973 a 21, 1403 b 26

Terebinth, 820 b 41

Teredo, 605 b 16

Tereus of Sophocles, 1454 b 37

Term (ὅρος), defined 24 b 16; major, minor, and middle in first figure 25 b 35, 26 a 22; major, minor, and middle in second figure 26 b 36; major, minor, and middle in third figure 28 a 12, b 1; syllogism must have three and only three terms 41 b 36; in syllogism one term must be related to another as whole to part 42 a 10; importance of setting out terms well 48 a 1-28; cannot always set out the terms in a single word 48 a 30; terms may be related in various ways 48 a 40-49 a 5; rules for setting out the terms when they are qualified or conditioned 49 a 11-b 2; the simpler terms are to be preferred 49 b 3-9; use of the definite article in terms 49 b 10-14; definition to be substituted for terms 110 a 5; unfamiliar terms to be changed to more familiar 111 a 8

Termination. *See* Limit

Terpander, 920 a 17

Tesselbates, pholidotes, 490 b 22, 492 a 26, 508 a 11, 517 b 15, 594 a 4; hibernation of 599 a 31, 600 b 18-34

Testaceans, ostracoderms, 523 b 9, 527 b 34-531 b 19; have no eyes 491 b 27; sensation of 534 b 13-535 a 25, 681 b 32-682 a 1; breeding of 544 a 17, 720 b 6; generation of 546 b 15-549 a 13, 761 a 12-763 b 16; resemble vegetables 588 b 17; shell of 654 a 1-8; tongue of 661 a 17, 22, 678 b 13-33; have no viscera 678 a 31; mecon of 679 b 11, 680 a 22; have numerous genera and species 679 b 15; cannot endure extremes in temperature 680 a 29; body of 683 b 4-24; head of 863 b 18; have shell on the right side 706 a 13; spiral-shaped testaceans have front and back identically situated 706 b 2; have no sex 715 b 18, 731 b 8-14; analogous to plants 761 a 15-32

Testicles, 493 a 33, 497 a 28, 500 b 4, 509 a 31-510 b 5, 716 a 32; vary in different animals 716 b 13-32; final cause is the steadying of the spermatic secretion 717 a 13-b 13; position of 719 b 1-17, 720 a 30; male from right testicle, female from left 763 b 34

Testimony, witness, 1375 a 24, b 26-1376 a 32, 1446 a 24; given under torture 1428 a 22, 1432 a 12-32, 1442 b 37, 1443 b 28; defined as a confession made voluntarily by one who knows 1431 b 20; how to support 1431 b 24-33; how to refute 1431 b 34-1432 a 2; how to disguise 1432 a 3-11. Cf. Evidence

Tetanus, in horses 604 b 4

Tethya. *See* Ascidians

Tethys, 983 b 30

Tetrameters, 1404 a 31, 1408 b 38, 1449 a 22

Tetrix, nesting of 559 a 2, 14

Tettigonium. *See* Cicadelle

Tettix. *See* Cicada

TEUCER of Sophocles, 1398 a 4, 1416 b 1

Teumessus, 1408 a 3

Thales, 1141 b 4; earth rests on water 294 a 28; view of soul 405 a 20; all things full of gods 411 a 8; water as the first principle 983 b 19-984 a 4; his proof that philosophers could be wealthy 1259 a 7-22; referred to 984 a 28, 996 a 9

Thales, the Cretan poet, 1274 a 29

Thapsia, 864 a 6; as treatment for bruises 890 b 7-19

Thargelia, Festival of 1023 b 11

Thargelion, 543 b 7, 575 b 15, 611 b 9

Thasos, 549 b 16, 839 b 5, 1448 a 13, 1461 a 21

'Thaten,' 1033 a 7, 1049 a 20

'That in virtue of which' (καθ'ὅ), meanings of 1022 a 14-36

'That which is,' meanings of 1009 a 32, 1017 b 1

'That which is not,' meanings of 1067 b 26

THEAETETUS of Plato, 76 b 25, 1010 b 12

Theagenes, tyrant at Megara, 1305 a 24, 1357 b 33

Theatre, 832 b 19, 1175 b 12, 1449 a 9; why spread with straw 901 b 30-35; theatrical artists generally of bad character 956 b 11-15. Cf. Actors

Thebanas. *See* Apeliotes, Caecias

Thebe, Plain of, 973 a 10

Thebes, Thebans, 69 a 1, 202 b 13, 231 b 29, 351 b 35, 500 a 4, 843 b 22, 1093 a 16, 1269 b 37, 1274 a 32, 35, 1397 b 9, 33, 1398 b 3, 18, 1423 a 1, 7, 1429 b 13; law at Thebes that no one could hold office until he had retired from business for ten years 1278 a 25; revolution at 1302 b 29, 1306 a 37; oligarchy at 1321 a 29

Theft, penalties for 952 a 17-b 35, 953 a 3-9; has no mean 1107 a 11

Themis, 838 a 25

Themiscyra, 554 b 10

Themistocles, 176 a 1, 569 b 13, 1233 b 12, 1376 a 2

Theodamas, 1406 b 30

Theodectes, 1150 b 9, 1255 a 37, 1397 b 3, 1398 b 5, 1399 a 8, b 1, 27, 1400 a 27, 1401 a 35, 1421 b 2, 1455 a 9, b 30. Cf. *Lynceus*

THEODECTES of Theodectes, 1410 b 3

Theodorus River, gold of 833 b 17

Theodorus, the rhetorician, 183 b 33, 1412 a 25, 34, 1414 b 13, 1457 a 13; the *Art of Rhetoric* of 1400 b 16

Theodorus, the tragic actor, 1336 b 28, 1404 b 22

Theognis, 1129 b 29, 1170 a 12, 1172 a 14, 1179 b 5, 1230 a 11, 1237 b 14, 1234 a 17

Theology, distinguished from mathematics and physics 1025 b 1-1026 a 33, 1064 a 1-b 13

Theopompus, king of Sparta, established Ephoralty 1313 a 25-33

Theory (θεωρία), secondary to observed facts 293 a 27-31, 760 b 28-32; must harmonize with facts 698 a 14; contrasted to experience 981 a 13-b 9

Thera, government at 1290 b 12

Thermodon River, 554 b 10, 567 b 17

THESEID, 1451 a 21

Theseus, 1363 a 18, 1397 b 21, 1399 a 3

Thesis, an immediate basic truth of a syllogism is a thesis 72 a 15; dialectical problems and theses 104 b 1-105 a 9; defined 104 b 20, 34; not every thesis needs to be examined 105 a 2; relation of dialectical problems and theses to demonstration 105 a 8; when terms are familiar the thesis is easy to attack 111 a 11; rules for selecting and maintaining a thesis 160 b 14-22

Thespiadea, 838 b 17

Thessaly, 841 b 9, 842 b 10, 1269 a 37, b 5, 1373 a 26; serpents of 832 a 14-18, 846 b 10; sacred-snake of 845 b 17-33; the freemen's agora in 1331 a 2

Thetis, 1124 b 16

Thettaliscus, 1398 b 3

Thibron, praised the Spartan government 1333 b 18

Thigh-bone, 494 a 4

Thighs, 499 b 4, 504 a 1, 809 b 7; of birds 710 b 21, 712 b 32; as a physiognomic sign 810 a 35, 36, 811 a 1; fatigue in 882 b 25-883 a 2, 29-b 2, 885 a 30

Thinking, thought (νόησις, διάνοια), 430 a 26, 1052 a 30, 1072 a 18-1073 a 12, 1189 a 19, 22, b 33-1190 a 1, 1204 b 17, 1224 a 6, 1225 b 3, 1248 a 21; teleological nature of 407 a 8; faculty of the soul 414 a 30, 413 a 14-416 b 31; akin to perceiving 427 a 20; always involves images 431 a 16; man the only animal that thinks 433 a 12, 641 b 8; why sometimes followed by action, sometimes not 701 a 7-b 33; objects of 968 a 17, 1072 a 26; movement of thought is quickest movement 968 a 25; contact of thought with objects 968 b 1, 969 a 31; thinking and making 1032 b 15-17; nature of the divine thought 1074 b 15-1075 a 11; the most divine of things 1074 b 16; involuntary actions are not accompanied by thought 1188 b 26-38, 1189 a 32, 36

'Third man,' 990 b 17, 1039 a 2, 1059 b 8, 1079 a 14

Thirst, caused by snake bite 846 b 15; caused by fear 947 b 15-22, 35-948 a 8, b 14-19; better satisfied by wine than by water 948 a 22; can tolerate hunger easier than thirst 949 b 26-36

Thirty, the, at Athens, 1305 b 26, 1400 a 18, 33, 1401 a 34

'This somewhat.' *See* Substance

Thistles, 593 a 1, 610 a 5

Thoön, 513 b 26

Thorax, 491 a 28

Thorns, 820 a 20, 827 b 7-17; poisonous thorns 845 a 15

Thorn-tree, 819 b 7

Thos. *See* Civet

Thought. *See* Reason, Thinking

Thought as an element in tragedy, 1450 a 2, 7, 14, 29, b 5-12, 1456 a 33-b 8, 1459 b 12, 17, 1460 b 3

Thrace, 519 a 16, 595 a 25, 606 b 4, 620 a 32, 782 b 33, 805 a 27, 832 b 28, 841 b 15, 973 b 18, 1274 b 24, 1351 a 24, 1412 a 34; honey of 831 b 30-34; firestone in 833 a 25-28; burning stones of 841 a 27-b 2; barley of 841 b 3-8; fatal spring in 842 a 12-14; counting of the Thracians 911 a 2, 3; holds military power in esteem 1324 b 12

Thracias (N.N.W. wind), 363 b 25, 29, 364 a 14, b 4, 22, 29, 365 a 2, 394 b 25, 30, 973 b 18-23; called Sciron in the Megarid 973 b 19; called Circias in Italy and Sicily 973 b 20; called Olympias in Euboea and Lesbos 973 b 22

Thrasippus, choragus to Ecphantides, 1341 a 36

Thrasybulus of Athens, 1400 a 31, b 18, 1401 a 34

Thrasybulus, tyrant of Miletus, 1284 a 27, 32, 1311 a 21

Thrasybulus, tyrant of Syracuse, 1312 b 12, 1315 b 38

Thrasymachus, 183 b 33, 1400 b 19, 1409 a 3, 1413 a 7; overthrew democracy at Cyme 1304 a 2; the 'Appeals to Pity' of 1404 a 14

Thrattai, vari-coloured 785 b 24

Thraupis, 592 b 29

Threshing-floors, 835 b 10, 842 a 7, 973 a 15

Thriasian Plain, 942 a 19

Thritta, 621 b 16

Throat, 493 b 6, 804 b 26

Thrush, 615 a 6, 617 a 17-23, 632 b 18; nest of 559 a 5; hibernation of 600 a 26

Thumb, of man 687 b 12-18

Thunder, 803 a 3; caused by quenching of the fire in clouds 93 b 8, 94 a 5, b 32; its noise splits rocks 290 b 35; Aristotle's theory of 369 a 13-b 4, 370 a 25-32; Empedocles' theory of 369 b 12; Anaxagoras' theory of 369 b 14-24; splits things not by its noise but by its exhalation 371 b 12; cause of 395 a 13; heard after lightning 395 a 16-21; effect on the hatching of eggs 560 a 3

Thunderbolts, 371 a 18-b 13, 395 a 22, 401 a 18, 836 b 2; fall downward 342 a 14, 397 a 21; sacred 937 b 28

Thuria, 1409 a 27

Thurii, revolution at 1303 a 32, 1307 a 28, b 6-18

Thurium, 846 b 33

Thyestes, 1453 a 11, 21

THYESTES of Carcinus, 1454 b 23

Thyme, 554 a 10, 626 b 21, 627 b 18, 821 a 31; in Attica 925 a 8-18

Tick, generation of 552 a 15

Tickling, in armpits and soles of feet 964 b 30-32, 965 a 23; no one can tickle himself 965 a 11-18; on lips 965 a 19-22

Tiger, 607 a 4

Tigris River, stone in 846 a 33

Tilon, 602 b 26; spawning of 568 b 25

Timaeus, identification of matter and space 209 b 11, 36; earth rolled about the axis of the whole heaven 293 b 33; the 'all-receptive' 306 b 19; use of 'heavier' and 'lighter' 308 b 6; primary reals are planes 315 b 31, 325 b 25-34; view of soul 404 b 16-26; on movement of soul 406 b 17-407 a 2; eye composed of fire 437 b 12; respiration as pushing 472 b 6; the Locrian Timaeus 847 b 8

TIMAEUS of Plato, 209 b 11, 34, 280 a 30, 293 b 32, 300 a 1, b 18, 306 b 19, 308 b 6, 315 b 32, 325 b 25, 329 a 13, 332 a 30, 472 b 7, 1057 b 9, 1071 b 32, 1072 a 2, 1092 a 1

Time ($\pi o \tau \acute{e}$, $\chi \rho \acute{o} \nu o s$), 103 b 22, 217 b 29-224 a 16, 231 a 10, 426 b 24-30, 1020 a 29, 1071 b 9; examples of 2 a 1, 11 b 10; a continuous quantity 5 a 6; prior in time 14 a 27, 1028 a 32, 1038 b 27, 1049 b 12; universal not limited by 34 b 18; and causality 95 a 10-96 a 19; as test of accidents 111 b 24 (Cf. 115 b 12); season ($\kappa \alpha \iota \rho \acute{o} s$) or time as a determiner of values 117 a 26-40; its relation to movement 120 b 1, 218 b 1-219 b 8; a necessary condition of movement 200 b 20; infinity of 203 b 17, 232 a 23-233 b 32; its relation to the 'now' 218 a 6-29, 219 b 9-220 a 26, 971 a 16-20, b 3; defined as number of movement in respect of the before and after 219 b 2, 220 a 24; does its existence depend upon soul? 223 a 16-28; the number of movement *qua* movement 223 a 33; thought to be a circle 223 b 29; relation of finite and infinite space and time 233 a 22-b 15, 237 b 23-238 b 22, 239 b 5-240 b

8, 969 a 29; defined as that which is intermediate between moments 237 a 5; always divisible 237 a 10, 26, 241 a 16, 263 a 21, 430 b 8; no minimum time 274 a 9; no time outside the heaven 279 a 12-b 3; defined as the number of some continuous movement 337 a 24; perceptions of 449 b 28, 450 a 11, 451 a 18

Timidity. *See* Cowardice

Timocracy. *See* Commonwealth

Timophanes of Corinth, 1306 a 24

Timophanes of Mytilene, 1304 a 7

Timotheus, the Athenian, 1435 a 14; his scheme for raising money 1350 a 24-b 15

Timotheus, the poet, 993 b 15, 1448 a 17; referred to 1407 a 17, 1413 a 1. Cf. *Scylla*

Tin, 388 a 14, 389 a 8, 443 a 20, 794 b 9, 835 a 10, 836 a 27; Celtic 834 a 6-12; coinage of tin by Dionysius of Syracuse 1347 a 33-37

Tiphe. *See* Spelt

Tisias, 183 b 32

Tithe, 1345 b 33

Titmouse, diet of 592 b 18, 626 a 8; habits of 616 b 3

Tityus, the giant, 698 b 24

Tlepolemus, 840 a 25

Tmolus, Mount, changing stone on 847 a 8-11

Toad, 530 b 34, 673 b 32; spleen of 506 a 19; copulation of 540 a 32; habits of 609 a 24, 626 a 31

Toes, 494 a 13; of man 690 b 2-11; many-toed animals bear many young 774 a 33, b 10; as a physiognomic sign 810 a 20

Together, defined 226 b 22

Tomb, at Lipara 838 b 30-839 a 11; at Deïope 843 b 4

Tongue, 492 b 27-33, 533 a 25, 660 a 14-661 a 30, 801 b 8, 804 b 28; uses of 420 b 17, 423 a 18, 476 a 19; of elephant 502 a 3; of birds 504 b 1-3, 660 a 30; of serpent 505 a 20-27, 660 b 7; of fish 505 a 29, 660 b 14; softest, widest, and freest in man 660 a 18; used by man in speech and as organ of taste 660 a 19-22; colour of 786 a 21-29, 963 b 36, 964 a 4-9; effect of

drunkenness on 875 b 19-33; effect of cold on 888 b 7-15; never fat 892 b 33-35; effect of sourness on 931 a 12-15; indicative of many things 963 b 33-40; never becomes sweet 964 a 1-3. Cf. Taste

Tonsils, 492 b 34

Tool, defined as an inanimate slave 1241 b 24

Topics. *See* Argument

'Torches,' 395 b 12; cause of 341 b 1-342 a 35

Torch-races, 228 a 28, 1437 b 2

Torone, 548 b 15; cows of 523 a 7; sea-urchins of 530 b 10

Torpedo fish, narce, electric ray, 540 b 18; gills of 505 a 4; gall-bladder of 506 b 8; breeding of 543 b 9, 565 b 24, 566 a 23; habits of 620 b 19; tail of 695 b 9; fins of 696 a 27-32; swimming of 696 a 32

Tortoise, 468 b 15, 479 a 5, 529 a 23, 530 b 34, 720 a 5; lung of 475 b 28, 669 a 29, 671 a 18; habits of 503 b 9, 612 a 24, 831 a 26-31; spleen of 506 a 19; stomach and intestines of 508 a 5; testicles of 509 b 8, 716 b 25; womb of 510 b 35; only oviparous animal that has a bladder 519 b 15, 541 a 11; sound of 536 a 7; copulation of 540 a 29; generation of 558 a 4-14; sloughing of 600 b 22; shell of 654 a 9; bladder of 671 a 15-26, 676 a 30, 720 a 6; kidneys of 671 a 26; liver of 673 b 30; ears of 691 a 13-18; eyelids of 691 a 21; legs of 713 a 17; eggs of 732 b 4

Torture, as a form of persuasion 1375 a 24, 1376 b 32-1377 a 8; evidence given under torture 1428 a 22, 1442 b 37, 1443 b 28; how to credit and discredit evidence given under torture 1432 a 12-32

Touch (ἀφή), 532 b 33, 803 b 14, 1150 a 10, 1202 a 32; the basic sense 413 b 4, 414 a 3, 435 a 12-b 26; all animals have sense of touch 414 b 3, 415 a 4 (Cf. 433 b 32), 455 a 7, 27, 489 a 17, 533 a 17, 535 a 5; medium is necessary 419 a 30-b 2, 653 b 28; taste is a sort of touch 421 a 18, 422 a 8, 434 b 18, 439 a 1, 441 a 2, 656 b 37, 660 a 22; nature and objects of 422 b 17-

424 a 15; single or group of senses? 422 b 19; only sense to perceive by immediate contact 435 a 18; loss of sense of touch brings about death 435 b 4; sense of touch consists of earth 438 b 30; man's sense of touch exceeds that of the animals 441 a 2, 494 b 17, 660 a 13; most complex sense-organ 647 a 16; most corporeal sense-organ 647 a 20; flesh is organ and medium of 653 b 24-29, 744 a 1; taste and touch are in immediate connection with the heart 656 a 30; organ of touch lies internally 656 b 36; incontinence of 949 b 6-11, 37-950 a 17; problems connected with 964 b 21-965 a 39; object held between two crossed fingers appears to be two 965 a 36-39; temperance limited to sense of touch 1117 b 23-1118 b 7, 1230 b 21-1231 a 25

Touchstone, 793 b 1

Trade. See Commerce

Traders, lead an ignoble life 1319 a 26, 1328 b 40; admitted to citizenship at Thebes after retiring 1278 a 25, 1321 a 28

Trade winds, 395 a 2

Tragaena, 770 b 36

Tragedy (τραγῳδία), 920 a 12, 1403 b 23, 1404 a 32, 1415 a 19, 1447 a 14, b 26, 1449 a 3, 8, 15, 19; portrays men better than in actual life 1448 a 18, 1454 b 8; compared with epic 1449 b 9-19, 1459 b 8-1460 b 5; defined 1449 b 23-31, 1450 b 24; six parts of: (1) Plot, (2) Character, (3) Thought, (4) Diction, (5) Melody, (6) Spectacle 1449 b 32-1450 b 20; an imitation of action not of persons 1450 a 16, b 2, 1452 a 1; plot is the purpose of 1450 a 23; impossible without action 1450 a 24; arrangement and length of 1450 b 21-1451 a 15 (Cf. 1459 b 18-31); unity of 1451 a 16-35; pity and fear in 1452 a 2, b 1, 32, 35, 38, 1453 a 4-7, b 1, 12, 1456 a 38; quantitative parts of 1452 b 14-27; four kinds of 1455 b 32-1456 a 10; requires the marvellous 1460 a 12; the epic is a higher form of imitation than the tragedy 1461 b 26-1462 b 15

Tragic, 1450 a 30, 1456 a 21, 1461 b 27; the tragic hero 1452 b 30-1453 a 39; the tragic deed 1453 b 1-1454 a 13

Translucency, 442 b 30; has no separate existence 439 a 18-28; translucent medium 794 a 1-15

Transparent, described 418 b 4-13; transparent liquid 779 b 30, 780 a 5

Trapezus, honey of 831 b 24-26

Treadles, 560 a 28

Treasurers, 1321 b 34; of the sacred revenues 1322 b 25

Tree-creeper, grub-picker, 593 a 13, 616 b 28

Trees, enduring constitution of 467 a 10; must not bear too much fruit 750 a 22; parts of 818 a 4-13; propagation of 818 b 9, 820 a 29-821 a 25, 827 a 8; defined 819 b 4; aromatic trees 820 b 26-28; sweet odour of certain trees 906 a 36-b 34. Cf. Plants

Trembling, of drunkards 871 a 27-b 31, 874 b 22-875 a 28; of shadows 913 a 5-16; from fear 947 b 12-14, 948 a 35-b 12

'Trenches,' cause of 342 a 35-b 24

Triangle, 110 b 21-25, 168 b 1-5, 287 a 1, 308 b 15, 309 b 34, 402 b 20, 414 b 31, 851 a 24, 1183 b 2, 1187 a 38-b 3, 1189 b 12; the ideal triangle 968 a 12; any three given straight lines can form a triangle 970 a 8; proof that angles are equal to two right angles 1051 a 23-26

Triangle, the musical instrument, 1341 a 41

Triballi, 115 b 23, 26

Trichia, a disease, 587 b 26

Trichias, breeding of 543 a 4, 569 b 25; migration of 598 b 12

Tridents, 837 b 15

Trierarchs at Rhodes, 1304 b 27

Trigle. See Mullet, red

Trimeter, 1447 b 12

Triopium, 1271 b 37

Tripolis, Gulf of, 973 a 19

Triptolemus, 843 b 5

Trite, 918 a 15, 920 a 17

Trochaic, 1404 a 31, 1408 b 38, 1449 a 22; a metre of movement 1459 b 38

Trochee, 1408 b 36, 1452 b 24

Trochilus. See Sandpiper

Trochus, generation of 757 a 2-13

Troezenians, 1303 a 29, 1335 a 20

Trojan Cycle, 1100 a 7

Trojans, 840 a 16, b 10, 1116 a 25, 1396 b 17

Trojan War, 1018 b 16, 1459 a 32

Troy, Ilium, 222 a 26, 840 a 18, 916 a 19, 39, 1139 b 6, 1363 a 6, 16, 1396 b 13, 1414 a 3, 1456 a 17; wooden horse of 840 a 31

Trumpet-shell. *See* Ceryx

Truth (ἀλήθεια), 430 a 27, 431 b 10; and falsity of propositions 16 a 9-18, 18 a 26, 24 a 30; that which is true must agree with itself 27 a 9; popular acceptance or rejection no criterion of 74 b 23; not all truth is appropriate 74 b 25; may get a true conclusion from false premisses 53 b 4-57 b 17; cannot obtain false conclusion from true premisses 53 b 7; dialectics aid in distinguishing truth and error 101 a 35; eternal truth 742 b 28; and falsity in cognition 980 a 8-b 17; study of the truth is both difficult and easy 993 a 30-b 11; philosophy called knowledge of the truth 993 b 19; the end of theoretical knowledge 993 b 21; Democritus said there is no truth 1009 b 12; not everything which appears is true 1010 b 1-1011 a 2; relative truth 1011 b 3; being as truth 1027 b 17-1028 a 5, 1051 a 34-1052 a 12, 1065 a 21; not in all things 1027 b 25; must honour truth above friends 1096 a 16; in a true view all data harmonize 1098 b 11; controlling factors of action and truth 1139 a 18; states of mind by which we reach truth 1139 b 14-1142 a 31

Truthfulness, sincerity, 1108 a 21, 1124 b 30, 1127 a 13-b 32, 1186 a 27, 1193 a 28-36, 1221 a 6, 1234 a 1-3

Trygon. *See* Sting-ray

Tug-of-war, 888 a 21

Tunny, 537 a 19, 844 a 24-34; gregarious 488 a 6; smooth-skinned 505 a 27; as bait 533 a 33; breeding of 543 a 1, 9, b 3, 13, 571 a 8; parasites in 557 a 28, 602 a 27-34; growth of 571 a 16; diet of 591 a 10, b 18; migration of 597 a 24, 598 a 26, b 20; eyes of 598 b

21; hibernation of 399 b 9; not edible 607 b 29; habits of 610 b 4. Cf. Orcys

Turbinata, whorls of 763 a 22

Turpentine, 837 a 33

Turtle, 589 a 26; kidneys and bladder of 506 b 28; stomach and intestines of 508 a 5; copulation of 540 a 28; eggs of 558 a 11-14; diet of 590 b 4; legs of 713 a 17

Turtle-dove, 633 b 8, 830 b 14; size of 544 b 8, 617 a 31; eggs of 558 b 23, 562 b 4; diet of 593 a 16; migration of 593 a 17, 597 b 4; hibernation of 600 a 19-24; habits of 609 a 18, 25, 610 a 13, 613 a 12-26; young of 774 b 31

Twins, women of Egypt often have twins 584 b 31; generally resemble one another 586 a 8-12; cause of 772 b 14-26; sex in 894 a 7-11

Two. *See* Dyad

Tyana, sacred water of 845 b 34-846 a 6

Tydeides, 1116 a 26

Tydeus of Theodectes, 1455 a 9

Tydidae, 840 a 7

Tyndareus, sons of 1397 b 22

Tyranny (τυραννίς), 1160 a 36-b 11, 1161 b 9, 1241 b 31, 1266 a 2, 1372 b 2; rule of master over slave 1160 b 29; the perversion of royalty 1279 b 5, 1287 b 39, 1289 b 1, 1292 a 18, 1295 a 18, 1310 b 2; rule of a master in political society 1279 b 16; the worst form of government 1289 a 39-b 2; the extreme form of democracy 1292 a 17, 1312 b 5; akin to democracy 1292 a 18-22; forms of 1295 a 1-24; no freeman will endure a tyranny 1295 a 22; democracy may become a tyranny 1296 a 3, 1305 a 7-34, 1308 a 21; revolutions in 1310 a 39-1315 b 10; compound of oligarchy and democracy in their most extreme forms 1310 b 4, 1311 a 9; ways in which it may be preserved 1313 a 39-1315 b 11; enjoyed by women and slaves 1313 b 33-38; short-lived 1315 b 12-39; its end is the protection of the tyrant 1366 a 6

Tyrant, must kill his rivals 1284 a 26-b 2, 1311 a 21, 1313 a 40; guarded by mercenaries 1285 a 26, 1311 a 7; rules over involuntary subjects 1285 a 27; influenced by flattery 1292 a 21, 1314 a 2; most ancient tyrants were originally demagogues 1305 a 8-12, 1310 b 14; aims at pleasure 1311 a 4; uses spies 1313 b 11; wages continual war 1313 b 28; fond of bad men 1314 a 1; the tyrants on the Bosporus 1347 b 4

Tyro of Euripides, 1454 b 25

Tyrrhenia, 1329 b 19, 1349 b 33; commercial treaty with Carthage 1280 a 37

Tyrrhenian Sea, 354 a 22, 839 b 23, 843 a 4

Tyrrhias, copper in 833 b 1-3

Tyrtaeus, wrote poem entitled 'Good Order' 1307 a 1

U

Ugly, the, 1449 a 34

Ulysses, 575 a 1, 1454 a 30, b 27, 1455 a 2, 1457 b 12, 1460 a 36, 1461 b 6

Ulysses as Beggar, 1459 b 6

Ulysses the False Messenger, 1455 a 14

Ulysses Wounded, 1453 b 34

Umbilical cord, 745 b 22, 746 a 11, 751 a 7, 752 a 26, b 7, 753 b 20, 30, 754 a 11, 777 a 23

Umbria, 359 b 1; fertility of 836 a 20-24

Unambiguous, univocal (συνώνυμος), when things are named univocally 1 a 6, 3 b 7; substances and differentia predicated univocally 3 a 33. Cf. Ambiguity, Ambiguous terms

Unambitiousness, 1107 b 29, 1125 b 10-13, 22

Unanimity, 1155 a 24; and friendship 1167 a 22-b 15, 1212 a 14-26, 1241 a 15-35

Understanding. See Intelligence

Understatement. See Mock-modesty

Unfortunate, 1195 a 22, 1213 b 15

Unfriendliness, churlishness, contentiousness, habit of dislike, 1126 b 17, 1127 a 11, 1193 a 23, 1221 a 7, 27, 1233 b 30

Unguents, 1118 a 13; stupefy bees 832 a 4; fatal to vultures 845 a 35; give per-

spiration an evil odour 867 b 8-11; induce perspiration 908 b 24-28; odour of 908 b 34-909 a 7

Unit (μονάς), 108 b 24, 968 a 8, b 6, 991 b 24, 1080 a 13-1085 a 2; prior to number 141 b 8; defined 1016 b 25, 1084 b 26, 1089 b 35; a limit of a body 1028 b 17

Unity (τὸ ἕν), 121 a 16, 169 a 24; numerical 1 b 6; of meaning 20 b 15; conjunct and immediate 93 b 36; of soul 411 a 24-b 30; of body and soul 412 b 7, 413 a 3; has many senses 412 b 8; unity and being 996 a 5-8, 1001 a 4-b 25, 1060 a 36-b 19; sense in which being and unity are same 1003 b 23-1004 a 1; of definition 1037 b 8-1038 a 35, 1044 a 2-6, 1045 a 7-b 24, 1087 b 12; not a substance 1040 b 16-27; things that have no matter are unities 1045 b 23; being and unity are most universal of predicates 1053 b 20; in a state 1261 a 10-b 15, 1263 b 30-1264 a 8; of plot 1451 a 1, 16, 1459 a 19-21. Cf. One

Universal (καθόλου), 17 b 29, 67 a 17, 141 a 15, 1028 b 34, 1042 a 15, 1110 b 32, 1180 b 22, 1236 a 23, 1450 b 12; defined 17 a 38, 1023 b 29, 1038 b 11; without time limitation 34 b 18; one premiss of syllogism must be universal 41 b 7, 47 b 26; universal conclusions most difficult to establish, easiest to overthrow 43 a 1; implicit in particular 71 a 7; explicit in particular 71 a 18; knowledge of universals gained by induction 81 b 1, 108 b 10; has no separate existence 85 a 31; in establishing a thing universally we also show it in particular 119 a 35; impossible to reason without using universals 164 a 10, 1103 a 14; more knowable than particular in order of explanation 189 a 6; sensation apprehends particulars, knowledge universals 417 b 22; most universal things hardest to know 982 a 23; no universal can be a substance 1003 a 7, 1038 b 1-1039 a 23, 1053 b 17, 1060 b 21, 1069 a 27, 1087 a 2; definition by 1018 b 30-36, 1036 a 28; every science is of universals 1059 b 26, 1140 b 31;

knowledge impossible without universals 1060 b 20, 1086 b 6; doctrine of Forms assigns separate existence to universals 1086 a 18-1087 a 25; the universal good 1096 a 11; two kinds of universal terms 1147 a 4; poetry deals with universals, history with singulars 1451 b 7. Cf. Attribute, Demonstration, Knowledge, Particular, Premiss

Universe. *See* Heaven

Univocal. *See* Unambiguous

Unjust. *See* Injustice

Unlimited, Being is unlimited 974 a 9, b 7, 22, 975 b 37, 976 a 4, 22, b 9, 979 b 22; Melissus' use of the term 975 a 30; Anaxagoras' view of 975 b 16-19, 976 a 14; Not-being is unlimited 977 b 3-5, 978 a 25-39; nature of 978 a 17-19

Unmanliness, 1251 a 14

Unscrupulousness, 1251 a 2

Up, 365 a 26; defined as the direction in which fire moves 208 b 19; not for all things what it is for the Cosmos 416 a 2

Upper-arm, 493 b 26

Uranion Mountains, 841 a 10-19

Urethra, 493 b 4, 895 b 9

Uria, 753 a 22. Cf. Wind-eggs

Urine, 380 a 1, b 5, 382 b 13, 389 a 11, 689 a 6, 32, 866 b 26; contains salt 357 b 3; passages for 719 b 29-720 a 36; drugs that promote the flow of 865 a 19-24; concoction of 865 b 6-17; why those who wish to pass urine cannot have sexual intercourse 878 b 33-35; shiver after urinating 887 b 35-38, 888 b 1-5, 963 b 33-37; female passes urine with effort 892 b 36-893 a 2; sweet-smelling plants promote flow of 907 b 4-13, 924 b 18-27; garlic promotes flow of 907 b 7, 908 a 28-b 10, 924 b 22, 949 a 5; odor of 907 b 21-26; fear makes men desire to pass urine 948 b 35-949 a 7; anise and wormwood promote flow of 949 a 2

Use, natural and unnatural 1246 a 26-b 36; often the user is the best judge of an art 1282 a 17-23

Useful (ὠφέλιμον), as a test of desirability 117 a 35, 118 a 35; defined as productive of good 124 a 16, 147 a 34, 153 b 38; exists for sake of the honourable 1333 a 36; Hellenes often regarded usefulness as the test of a government 1333 b 9; not only end of education 1337 b 5, 1338 a 38; free and exalted souls do not seek the useful 1338 b 4

Usury, 1121 b 33; the most unnatural means of acquiring wealth 1258 b 2-7, 25

Uterus, womb, 493 a 24, 497 a 32, 510 b 6-511 a 36, 716 a 32, 738 a 9-739 b 33, 754 b 31, 756 b 9-13, 764 a 34, 765 a 19, 771 b 32; of fish 564 b 19, 565 a 13-22, 718 b 18, 755 b 17-23; varies in different animals 716 b 33-717 a 12, 718 a 35-719 a 30; double 716 b 33; position of 719 a 31-b 28, 749 a 28-34; discharge from 728 a 1; termination of many blood vessels 738 a 11, 745 b 29; part by which female differs from male 766 b 25; of women and mares is large 773 b 28

Utica, salt in 844 a 7-16

Utility, friendships of 1156 a 10, 13-31, 1157 a 2, 13, b 1, 1158 a 21, 29, 1159 b 12, 1162 a 25, b 5-12, 17-20, 22-1163 a 23, 1164 a 8, 1165 b 2, 1167 a 12, 1169 b 23, 1170 b 24, 1171 a 24, 1209 a 4-b 27, 1210 a 6-23, 1235 a 36-b 2, 1236 a 33-37, 1239 b 22-29, 1242 a 6, 31, b 32-1243 a 14; aim of deliberative oratory 1362 a 18

Uvula, 493 a 3

V

Vacuum, 471 a 2

Vanity, vaingloriousness, 1107 b 22, 1123 b 8, 25, 1125 a 17, 28-32, 1192 a 21, 1221 a 10, 32, 1233 a 16; physiognomic signs of 810 b 32, 813 a 12

Vapour, surrounds the earth 340 a 34; moist and cold 340 b 27; hoar-frost when frozen 347 a 16, b 24 (Cf. 784 b 15); defined 387 a 25; in the earth 822 b 28-31; in plants 824 b 6

An Index to Aristotle

Vapour baths, 822 b 19-21, 824 b 25-35, 867 a 29, 869 a 19-23, b 20-31. Cf. Baths

Vargariaton tree, 819 a 12

Varicocele, prevents any animal from procreation 878 b 36-879 a 3; eunuchs never have varicocele 894 b 39-895 a 3

Varicose veins 518 b 26, 521 a 29, 587 a 34, 895 a 3

Vegetables, 270 a 33, 828 b 15; defined 819 b 9; problems concerning shrubs and vegetables 923 a 5-927 a 8; older seeds produce more stalk than fresh seeds 924 b 28-34

Veins, 489 a 22, 511 b 1-515 a 26, 520 b 10-521 b 2, 804 b 27; place of the blood 456 b 1; persons with inconspicuous veins are addicted to sleep 457 a 22; and heart 474 b 7; bodily heat resides in pores of 483 b 19; connect with intestines and belly 483 b 25; as a physiognomic sign 812 a 29; of plants 818 a 6, 819 a 36; swollen veins 885 b 31. Cf. Blood vessels

Vengeance, 1229 b 32, 1250 a 41, 1378 b 26

Venom-spider, phalangium, 550 b 33, 555 b 12, 611 b 21; female larger than male 538 a 27; copulation of 542 a 11-17; habits of 609 a 5; species of 622 b 28

Venus, 1073 b 31

Verb, 19 b 11, 1404 b 27, 1456 b 22, 1457 a 14-18, 25; defined 16 b 6; indefinite verbs 16 b 14

Vermilion, 559 a 26

Vermiparous animals, 489 a 34, 538 a 26, 601 a 5, 1256 b 12

Verse, 1447 a 29, b 25, 1448 a 11, 1449 b 10-12, 31, 35, 1450 b 15, 1451 b 28; historian writes prose, poet writes verse 1451 b 1

Vertebrae, 516 a 11

Vertex, 491 b 3

Vetch, 568 b 22, 595 b 6, 596 a 25; makes milk copious 522 b 27

Vice. See Evil

Village, formed by union of families 1252 b 15-27

Villainy, physiognomic signs of 811 b 24, 814 a 2

Vine, 818 b 37, 820 a 16, b 39; mad-vine of Libya 846 b 1

Vinegar, 552 b 5; cures inflammation 889 b 19; makes inner flesh smart 959 b 7; stops hiccups 961 b 20, 962 a 1-16, 963 b 5

Violets, 909 a 1

Viper, adder, 490 b 25, 676 b 2, 831 a 27, 844 b 32, 845 a 1, b 20; generation of 511 a 16, 558 a 25-33; hibernation of 599 b 2; sloughing of 600 b 25; bite of 607 a 28; oviparous internally, viviparous externally 676 b 2, 718 b 32; copulation of 846 b 18-21; never tame 895 b 26. Cf. Serpent

Virtue, intellectual, 1138 b 18-1145 a 12, 1196 b 4-1198 a 20, 1221 b 29; two kinds of virtue: intellectual and moral 1103 a 4-10, 1220 a 5-12; intellectual element thought to be the man himself 1166 a 17

Virtue, moral (ἠθικὴ ἀρετή), 13 a 26, 1095 b 30, 1098 b 30, 1120 a 11, 1190 b 9-1196 b 3, 1220 a 13-1234 b 13, 1255 a 13, 1283 a 25, 1440 b 18, 1448 a 3; not easily dislodged 8 b 34; contrary of vice 113 b 31; better than pleasure 118 b 33; the genus of justice 121 b 26, 123 b 15, 21, 32, 127 b 20; a kind of state and disposition 121 b 38; the genus of temperance 139 b 39-140 a 2; soul as well as body has its virtue 153 b 10; virtuous activity is most permanent function of man 1100 b 13; two kinds: intellectual and moral 1103 a 4-10, 1220 a 5-12; moral virtue produced by doing virtuous acts 1103 a 14-b 26, 1105 a 18, 1220 a 38-b 6; concerned with pleasures and pains 1104 b 4-1105 a 17, 1220 a 39, 1221 b 7-1222 a 5, b 11, 1227 b 1-11; always concerned with the harder 1105 a 9; distinction between acts that create moral virtue and those that flow from it 1105 a 18-b 18; moral virtue defined as a disposition to choose the mean 1105 b 19-1108 b 10, 1220 b 21-1221 b 3; involves choice 1106 a 4, b 36, 1230 a 27; concerned with passions and actions 1109 b 30; has to do with voluntary acts 1113 b 3-1115 a 6, 1222 b 15-1223 a 20; its end is honour 1115 b 13; sub-species of moral states 1126 a 8-31, 1221 b 10-15; how related to practical wisdom 1144 b 1-1145 a 11, 1198 a 10-b 20; superhuman virtue 1145 a 19-29, 1200 b 17; natural or produced by habit 1151 a 18; friendship based on 1156 b 6-1157 a 24, b 25-37, 1162 a 26, 1209 a 4-b 37, 1236 a 32, b 2-27, 1237 a 10, 1238 a 30; contemplation is the best virtue 1177 a 17, 28; found in the soul 1184 b 23, 1219 b 26; a habit of the soul 1184 b 33; the best state 1185 a 37; moral virtue destroyed by defect and excess 1185 b 14-32; moral virtue determined by pleasure and pain 1185 b 33-37, 1186 a 35, 1204 a 29, 1206 a 20; moral virtues do not come by nature 1186 a 3-8; a mean with respect to feelings 1186 a 20-33, b 33; virtue is in man's power 1187 a 5-b 19; more concerned with ends than means 1190 a 8-b 6; natural impulse to 1197 b 37-1198 a 9; natural virtue 1198 a 3, 1199 b 38; two virtues cannot be in conflict 1199 b 36-1200 a 10; cannot have too much 1200 a 11-35; defined as harmony of reason and passion 1206 a 36-b 29; defined as acting in accordance with right reason 1208 a 5-b 1; difficulty in deciding what is virtuous 1215 b 15-1216 b 25; defined as the best state or condition or faculty of all things that have a use and work 1218 b 38; mean of pleasure and pain 1222 a 6-22; objects of praise 1249 a 26; general effect of 1251 b 26-39; power of 1255 a 13; of slave, woman, and child 1259 b 21-32; men and women have different virtues 1259 b 28-1260 a 31, 1277 b 20; of ruler and ruled 1259 b 33-1260 a 9; is the virtue of a good man and a good citizen the same? 1276 b 16-1277 b 32, 1278 a 40, 1288 a 38, 1293 b 5, 1333 a 12; no one can practice virtue while living the life of a mechanic or labourer 1278 a 20; the happy life is the life of virtue 1295 a 36; a mean 1295 a 37; of state and individual are the same 1323 a 14-1325 b 31; leisure necessary for the development of 1329 a 1; not a matter of chance 1332 a 31; three things make men virtuous: (1) habit, (2) nature, (3) rational principle 1332 a 39-b 11, 1334 b 7; depends on rational principle 1333 a 18; requires training and habituation 1337 a 20; is virtue the aim of education? 1337 a 33-b 23; consists in rejoicing, loving, and hating aright 1340 a 17; all good things may be abused except virtue 1355 b 5; a constituent of happiness 1360 b 24, 1362 a 13, 14; the subject of epideictic oratory 1366 a 23-1368 a 39; forms of 1366 b 1

Viscera, 647 a 36; none in bloodless animals 665 a 29, b 5, 678 a 29; differs in different animals 673 b 13-674 a 3; compared with flesh 674 a 4-8; peculiarities of viscera in ovipara 676 a 22-b 15; formed out of blood 678 a 32

Viscous, 387 a 12-14

Vision, 1218 a 32, 1219 a 17; copper beneficial to 834 b 28; effects of drunkenness upon 872 a 18-b 14, 874 a 5-21, 875 b 9-18; has shape of a cone 872 a 37, 911 b 6, 16, 20; effect of sexual excess upon 876 b 24-32; cannot pass through hard objects 905 a 35-b 22; cannot pass through porous objects 939 a 12; yellow and green beneficial to 959 a 23-37; white and black harmful to 959 a 27; see better if shield eyes from sun 960 a 21-28. Cf. Sight

Vituperation, 1425 b 37-1426 b 21; one of the genera of oratory 1421 b 9, 1428 a 4; methods of 1440 b 5-1441 b 29

Viviparous animals, 489 b 1-502 b 27; have lungs 475 b 20; not all are hair-coated 490 b 26; ears of 492 a 27; only animals that have mammae 504 b 19; womb of 511 a 23, 719 a 13-30; generation of 571 b 2-588 a 12, 718 b 29-31, 752 b 13, 774 b 5; stronger and larger than other animals 655 a 7; have two eyelids 657 a 26; only animals that have horns 662 b 24; more erect than other quadrupeds 669 b 7; testicles in 716 b 26, 717 b 26; catamenia in some 726 a 30; all are sanguineous 732 b 8; choria in 739 b 32; milk in 1256 b 13

Voice, 426 a 27, 660 a 31, 948 b 27, 1403 b 27, 1404 b 22, 1408 b 7; defined as a kind of sound characteristic of what has soul in it 420 b 5; many animals are voiceless 420 b 9; 'sound with meaning' 420 b 33; in animals 535 a 27-536 b 23, 786 b 8-788 b 2; voice of female is sharper-toned than voice of male 538 b 12, 544 b 33; change of voice in man indicates maturity 544 b 22, 581 a 18, 776 b 23-26; after castration 632 a 5, 787 b 20-788 a 17; changes in both sexes when they begin to bear seed 776 b 16; dim 800 a 14; misty 800 a 14; causes of differences in 800 a 17-801 a 20; hard 801 a 17, 802 b 30-803 b 1, 813 b 1; causes of distinctness in 801 b 2-22; clearness in 801 b 23-802 a 7; 'grey' 802 a 1; 'white' 802 a 2; rough 803 b 2-17; thin 803 b 18-804 a 8; thick 804 a 9-21; piping 804 a 22-32; cracked 804 a 33-b 8; aspirated 804 b 9; smooth 804 b 10; stammering 804 b 27-39; as a physiognomic sign 806 a 31, b 27, 807 a 13-24, b 36, 813 a 32-b 5; man utters many voices 895 a 5, 6; problems connected with the voice 898 b 27-906 a 20; hot-tempered men have big voices 899 a 10-14; sounds shriller at a distance 899 a 22-b 17; rougher after a sleepless night 900 a 10-15; effect of meals on 900 a 16-19; of children 900 a 32-b 6, 902 a 5-35, b 16-29; shrillness of 900 b 15-28, 901 a 7-34, 903 a 26-38, b 30-33, 904 b 7-10, 905 a 24-30, 906 a 2-20; of eunuchs, boys, women, and old men 900 b 15-28, 903 a 26-28, 906 a 2-20; deeper in winter 900 b 29-901 a 6, 905 b 38-906 a 2; effect of drinking on 900 b 39-901 a 6, 903 b 7-12, 904 b 1-6, 905 a 24-30; deep voice more audible close at hand, less so at a distance 901 a 7-19; effect of exercise on 901 a 30-34; effect of illness on 901 a 30-34; shouting after meals spoils the voice 901 a 35-b 15; compared to echo 901 b 16-23, 904 b 27-33; effect of fear on 902 b 30-903 a 6, 905 a 5-15; trembling of

902 b 30-35, 906 a 10, 948 a 35-b 12; effect of nervousness on 902 b 30-903 a 6, b 7-12, 905 a 5-15; effect of leeks on 903 b 27-29; effect of garlic on 903 b 27-29; more audible from above than from below 904 a 23-39; compared to flute 918 a 29-34. Cf. Speech

Void (κενόν), 188 a 22, 213 a 11-217 b 28, 265 b 23, 310 b 10, 976 b 5; a necessary condition of movement 200 b 20; defined as place bereft of body 208 b 26, 214 a 1-17; arguments for and against its existence 213 a 11-b 29; refutation of arguments for existence of void 214 a 16-b 11; there is no void existing separately 214 b 11-216 b 20, 320 b 27, 321 a 7; not the condition of locomotion 214 b 16, 216 b 34-217 a 4; no void in bodies 216 b 21-217 b 28; no void outside the heaven 279 a 12-b 3; as explaining expansion 305 b 17; some think objects are light because they contain so much void 309 a 7, 14, 28-310 a 13, 311 b 1; has no natural movement 309 b 18; not the matter of things 312 b 21; defined as a non-perceptible body 320 b 2; denial of its existence 324 b 25-326 b 28; theories of Empedocles and Leucippus 325 a 3-b 12, 976 b 23-33, 985 b 5; Melissus' view of 976 b 12-18; Anaxagoras' view of 976 b 19-22; Democritus' view of 985 b 5, 1009 a 27; how potential 1048 b 9

Volcanoes, 395 b 21, 400 a 33, 840 a 1-5, 841 a 20-26; in Pithecusae 833 a 15; in Etna 833 a 18, 846 a 9-17

Voluntary (ἑκούσιον), 1187 a 5-1188 a 37, 1195 a 28, 1199 a 20, 1368 b 10; and involuntary 1109 b 30-1111 b 3, 1132 b 30, 1135 a 15-1136 a 9, 1196 a 8, 1223 a 21-1224 a 9, 1225 a 33-b 16; is everything in accord with appetite voluntary? 1111 a 25-b 2, 1223 a 29-b 17; virtue has to do with voluntary acts 1113 b 3-1115 a 6, 1222 b 15-1223 a 20; voluntary exchange 1132 b 12; all just action is voluntary 1136 a 13-b 14; defined as that not done under compulsion 1187 b 35; accompanied with thought 1188 b 25-38; distinction between voluntary act and purposive act 1189 b 1; no one voluntarily injures himself 1195 b 5-34, 1196 a 14; not all voluntary acts are deliberate 1368 b 11; voluntary acts seem good or pleasant 1369 b 21-26. Cf. Involuntary

Voluptuousness, has no mean 1107 a 19

Vomiting, effect on voice 804 a 18, 900 b 39-901 a 6, 903 b 7-12, 904 b 1-6, 905 a 24-30; lightens the body 868 b 7, 965 b 29; caused when one is cooled while perspiring 868 a 5-9; watery wine apt to cause 873 b 24-37; one ought to be in a turgid state to vomit 877 a 35-b 4; as a cure of fatigue 881 a 12-39

Vote, methods of voting 1300 a 9-b 4; election by 1424 a 14, b 2; of jury 1433 a 24, 1443 a 18; right to vote 1446 b 22

Vowel, 535 a 32, 895 a 10, 1434 b 36, 1435 a 35, b 17, 1456 b 25, 1458 a 1, 11, 15

Vulgarity, lack of taste, extravagance, lavishness, 1107 b 19, 1122 a 31, 1123 a 19, 1209 b 19, 1221 a 11, 34

Vulpanser, 593 b 22; wind-eggs in 559 b 28

Vulture, 592 b 6, 835 a 6; breeding of 563 a 5-12, 615 a 8-14; habits of 609 b 8, 34, 845 a 35

W

Wagtail, habits of 615 a 20

Waist, as a physiognomic sign 810 b 5-7

Waking, 778 b 32; a non-voluntary movement 703 b 9; an effect of sensation 816 b 29

Walking, 109 b 4, 122 a 22, 128 a 33, 227 b 17, 228 a 17, 249 a 17; fatigue in 880 b 15-28, 881 b 18-27, 37-882 a 2, 29-39, 883 a 21-28, 884 b 9, 10, 885 a 14-b 9; difference between running and walking 882 b 23, 24, 883 b 37-40

Wallcreeper. *See* Blue-bird

Walls of a city, 1330 b 32-1331 a 18; officers in charge of 1321 b 26, 1322 a 36

Walnuts, 820 b 11

Wandering Islands, 839 b 20

Want, 1205 b 22, 1210 a 11; is pain 1205 a 2

Wantonness, 1202 b 28

War, 1096 a 32, 1115 a 34, 1116 b 7, 1117 b 14, 1160 a 17, 1177 b 9-11, 1331 a 2, 1334 a 7, 1366 b 6, 1447 a 2-7; ought captives of war to be made slaves? 1255 a 3-b 3; art of acquiring slaves is a species of hunting or war 1255 b 37-40, 1333 b 38; just wars 1256 b 23-26; war tactics 1297 b 21; tyrant wages continual war 1313 b 28; peace is the end of 1333 a 35, 1334 a 15; a subject of political oratory 1359 b 33-1360 a 5; and peace as subjects of deliberative oratory 1423 a 25, 1425 a 9-b 15; pretexts for waging 1425 a 10-16. Cf. Peace, Persian War

Wardens, of the agora 1299 b 17, 1300 b 12, 1322 a 14, b 33, 1331 b 9; of the city 1321 b 23, 1322 a 13, b 33, 1331 b 10; of the country 1321 b 29, 1322 b 33, 1331 b 15. Cf. Magistrates

Warm, all things having souls are warm 416 b 29, 470 a 21; warm climate promotes cowardice 909 b 9-24, 910 a 37-b 8

Warmth, cause of digestion 466 b 32, 469 b 25. Cf. Heat

Wasp, 523 b 19, 531 b 32, 552 b 27, 623 b 10; gregarious 488 a 10; bloodless 489 a 32; sting of 532 a 15, 628 b 3-30, 629 a 26, 683 a 8; generation of 551 a 29, 554 b 22-555 a 11, 627 b 23-628 b 30, 721 a 5, 761 a 2; habits of 622 b 21, 629 a 4-27, 844 b 32-34; flight of 710 a 11; scolex of 758 b 18, 32; have no monstrosities 770 a 29. Cf. Hornet, Ichneumon

Water, 103 a 15-23, 127 a 14, 519 a 10-19; naturally moves to center of earth 269 a 18; its surface is spherical 287 b 1; Thales thought water supports the earth 294 a 28; thought by some to be the one element 303 b 11; cold and moist 330 b 5, 389 b 16; an intermediate element 330 b 24-331 a 1; contrary to fire 331 a 1, 335 a 5; readily adaptable in shape 334 b 35; and earth are heaviest and coldest elements 340 b 20; water carried up comes down again 355 a 26; sweet water lighter than salt water 355 a 33, 359 a 5, 824 a 31, b 15 (Cf. 824 a 19); acid water 359 b 14; does not thicken 380 a 34; subterranean sources of 395 b 20; all liquids contain 423 a 25; and air form sense organs 425 a 4; eye composed of 437 b 5-438 b 29; more easily confined and condensed than air 438 a 15; tasteless 441 a 3-29; inodorous 443 a 11; will not suffice for food 445 a 21; continuous 446 b 14; cause of generation and decay 465 a 15; has less heat than air 477 b 4; contains no air 482 a 23; hard water causes infertility 767 a 34; cold water causes birth of females 767 a 35; colours of 779 b 32, 791 a 20-25, 792 a 21, 793 b 9, 794 b 26, 796 a 11-17; affects colour of hair 786 a 5; naturally white 791 a 2, 795 a 11; a translucent medium 794 a 1; effect on plants 821 a 37, 824 b 37-40; natural position of 823 b 2, 824 a 8; sacred water of Tyana 845 b 34-846 a 6; change of drinking water is unhealthy 860 b 26-861 a 19; problems connected with salt water 931 a 35-936 a 10; more transparent than oil 932 b 23, 935 b 22; appears less white when in motion 934 a 13-24; problems connected with hot water 936 a 12-937 b 28; in wells becomes warm after midday 936 a 16-20; boiling water does not melt things 936 a 26-31; does not boil so much in winter as in summer 936 a 38-b 9; hot water causes wrinkles 936 b 10-13, 937 a 1-11; does not form scum when boiled 936 b 22-39; unfit for washing purposes when heated by sun 937 a 34-b 6; the universal element 975 b 23, 976 a 18, b 1; Anaximander said the All is water 975 b 23; good water supply is essential for a town 1330 b 4-17. Cf. Moisture, Salt water

Water-clock, 294 b 22, 866 b 12, 868 b 23, 914 b 9-915 a 24

Water-lily, 825 b 35

Water-raven. *See* Cormorant

Water-snake, 487 a 23, 508 b 1

Waves, no ripples in open sea 931 a 35-37, 933 b 5-10, 934 a 25-29; move before wind reaches them 931 a 38-b 8, 932 b 38-933 a 8, 934 b 4-8; an indication of wind 932 b 29-37; effect on the ground 934 b 9-23

Wax, 623 b 25; impressible 386 a 18, 424 a 19, 435 a 9; squeezable 386 b 6; inflammable 387 b 22; meltable 388 b 33; bleached by sun 966 b 21

Weakness, 1146 a 15, 1150 b 19, 1176 a 14; the weaker always ask for equality 1318 b 4

Weals, problems connected with 889 b 10-891 a 5; prevention of 889 b 10-19

Wealth, 180 b 9, 1120 a 8, 1123 a 25, 1124 a 17, 1147 b 30, 1199 b 19, 1200 a 16, 1202 a 30, 1207 b 31, 1208 a 3, 1210 b 4, 1212 a 36, 1230 a 12, 1232 a 1, 1362 b 18, 1365 b 16, 1447 b 5; happiness better than 116 a 6; friendship more desirable than 116 b 38; to be a philosopher better than to make money, but not if the man lacks the necessities of life 118 a 11; excess of friendship better than excess of 118 b 6; more often found in hands of the wicked than of the good 950 b 36-39; its effect on the character of men 1094 b 19, 1387 a 23, 1390 b 32-1391 a 19; thought by some to be happiness 1095 a 22; not an end in itself 1096 a 5-10, 1097 a 27 (Cf. 1199 b 7); a constituent of happiness 1099 b 1, 1360 b 21, 1361 a 12-24; defined 1119 b 26; a useful thing 1120 a 5; the unnatural means of acquiring wealth 1121 b 34, 1256 b 40-1258 b 7; the end of oligarchy 1131 a 28, 1161 a 2, 1366 a 4; a potency 1183 b 28, 34; the natural means of acquiring wealth 1256 a 15-1257 a 41, 1258 a 19-40, b 9-20; valued too highly at Sparta and Carthage 1269 b 24, 1273 a 23-b 7; the many desire wealth more than honour 1318 b 16; qualities of economist in relation to 1344 b 23-1345 b 3. Cf. Acquisition, Poverty, Rich

Weasel, 605 b 30, 1149 a 8; genitals of 500 b 24; habits of 609 b 28, 612 a 28, b 1, 756 b 34; generation of 756 b 16; legs of 808 a 33

Weather, effect on disease 859 b 21-860 b 25; calm weather most often at midnight and midday 938 a 23-31; of Pontus 938 a 37-b 4; cloudy weather hotter than clear 939 b 15-22, 33-940 a 2

Weaver-fish, habitat of 598 a 11

Wedge, 853 a 19-32, b 23, 24

Weight, 250 a 8; infinite weight impossible 273 b 27-274 a 18; not everything has weight 276 a 16; all elements except fire have weight 311 b 5, 312 b 16; force of weight increased by movement 853 a 18-23; meanings of 1052 b 28

Wells, 857 a 34; in Pythopolis 834 a 34-b 2

West winds. See Iapyx, Leuconotus, Lips, Thracias, Wind, Zephyrus

Whale, 476 b 13-29, 589 a 33-b 20, 669 a 9; mammae of 521 b 24; blow-hole of 489 b 3, 537 b 1, 566 b 3, 697 a 16; generation of 566 b 3; lung of 697 a 16, 26-31; viviparous externally and internally 718 b 30

What, 1022 a 27, 1025 b 31, 1026 a 36, 1028 a 17; meanings of 1030 a 18-26; starting-point of syllogisms 1034 a 31, 1078 b 24

Wheat, 819 b 14, 820 b 7, 821 a 32; said to have originated in Enna 836 b 21-27; barley a better food for sick person than 863 a 34-b 10; more nourishing than barley 927 a 17-22; grinding of 927 a 23-26, b 15-20; wheat bread more digestible the more it is kneaded 927 b 23-31; gruel takes up more water than the wheat 929 b 1-7; those who handle wheat are healthy 929 b 26-29, 967 b 19-22; flour becomes less closely packed when cool 929 b 35-930 a 4

Whelk, 679 b 14; operculum of 679 b 22; shell of 683 b 14; generation of 761 b 31; 'eggs' of 763 b 9

Whey, 521 b 27

Whirlpool, in Cilicia 832 b 4-6; objects in whirlpools are carried into the middle 858 b 5-32

Whirlwind, 371 a 1; cause of 371 a 10; described 395 a 7

White, 102 b 9, 103 b 31, 109 a 36, 115 b 1, 123 b 26, 126 a 4, 149 a 39; contrary to black 105 b 36, 119 a 27; defined as a colour which pierces the vision 119 a 31, 153 a 39; cannot be a genus 127 a 23; some animals have white hair (albinos) 786 a 9-14, 798 a 25-b 15, 831 b 14; a simple colour 791 a 3-7, 794 a 4, 795 a 12; harmful to vision 959 a 27

Whitebait, 569 a 20

White-fish, 567 a 20

White gull, 593 b 15

White-leaved rod, 846 a 29-32

White-rump, 593 b 4

Whole (ὅλον), 195 a 21, 218 a 35, 1013 b 23, 1052 a 22; inclusion in a whole 24 b 26, 25 b 32; not the sum of its parts 150 a 15-21; defined as that of which nothing is outside 207 a 12; Melissus defined whole as infinite 207 a 16; Parmenides defined whole as 'equally balanced from the middle' 207 a 17; meanings of 1023 b 26-1024 a 10; relation of whole and its parts 1034 b 20-1037 b 6, 1337 a 29; prior to its parts 1253 a 18-28; interests of whole and parts are same 1255 b 10; whole cannot be happy unless parts are happy 1264 b 17, 1329 a 23; 'if each part is little, then the whole is little' 1307 b 36. Cf. Complete

Why, the four meanings of 'why' same as the four causes 198 a 14-22

Wife, 1134 b 16, 1158 b 14, 1160 b 33, 1161 a 23, 1162 a 16-33; proper possession of all freemen 1343 a 22; position in the household 1343 b 8-1344 a 7, 1345 a 6; rules for treatment of 1344 a 8-22

Will, the will of man is an unsafe guide 1272 b 6

Willow, 726 a 7, 820 a 8

Wind, defined as movement of air 127 a 4, 146 b 29, 387 a 29, 394 b 12; does not blow above highest mountains 340 b 37; prevents formation of dew and hoar-frost 347 a 27; causes of 349 a 17-25, 359 b 26-363 a 20, 394 a 17, b 7; the winds named 363 b 11-364 a 4, 394 b 19-34, 973 a 1-b 25; more from north than south 364 a 5; the cause of earthquakes 365 b 21-369 a 9; both inside and outside the earth 365 b 26; described 394 b 8-18; types of 395 a 5-16; subterranean sources of 395 b 20; effect on breeding of sheep 574 a 1; its effect on bodies of water 777 b 32; in a sense has life, birth, and death 778 a 2; effect on health and disease 859 a 9-24, 862 a 17-34, 945 a 13-17; waves are an indication of 932 b 29-37; cold in morning from rivers but not from sea 933 a 28-b 4, 943 b 4-20; result of air being moved by heat 939 b 1; problems connected with the winds 940 a 16-947 b 9; cause of alternating winds 940 b 16-29; cloud-winds 940 b 30-32, 941 b 37; same winds not everywhere rainy 940 b 33-39; usually occurs during eclipses 942 a 22-28; come from east in winter 942 b 3-12; shooting stars a sign of 942 b 16-19; strongest when ending 942 b 23, 24; cause dryness 943 a 28-31; rises and falls at sunrise 944 a 25-30; does it have a source? 944 b 4-20; alternating winds blow where there are bays 945 a 1-7; why cold 945 b 8-34; periodical winds 946 a 10-16; blow in winter early and from east 946 a 35-b 21; blow in summer in evening and from west 946 a 35-b 21; different winds rainy in different places 946 b 32-947 a 6; of Arcadia 947 a 15-24; lasts a long time when it begins at dawn 947 a 25-27; spiders' webs as sign of 947 a 33-b 2; sometimes thought to be but two winds: north and south 1290 a 14. Cf. East, North, South, and West winds

Wind-egg, cynosura, 539 a 31, 559 b 21-560 a 19, 730 a 5, 32, 737 a 30, 749 b 1, 757 b 1-31; has nutritive but not sensitive soul 741 a 17-31; nature of 750 b 2-751 a 24; colour of 751 b 22

Windlass, 852 b 11-20, 853 b 12

Windpipe, 420 b 23-421 a 6, 471 a 21, 473 a 19, 476 a 31, 481 b 13, 483 a 23, 492 b 12, 493 a 8, 495 a 21-b 18, 505 b 33, 507 a 24, 960 b 36; position and functions of 664 b 3-21, 665 a 11; moisture in 788 a 27; relation to voice

800 b 20-801 a 9, 803 a 10-20, 804 a 19, b 18, 901 b 7

Wine, 111 a 3, 358 b 19, 382 b 13, 384 a 4, 388 b 1, 389 a 11, 460 a 29, 842 a 25-33, 930 b 5-11, 931 a 6-15, 1225 b 4, 1229 a 20, 1404 b 21; not 'fermented water' 127 a 18; sweet wine 387 b 9, 872 b 26-873 a 3, 874 b 11, 875 b 1-4; productive of sleep 457 a 14-b 19, 874 b 14-21; differences in 485 b 26; not good for children 588 a 5, 1336 a 8; souring of 753 a 23; honey-wine 832 a 6-13; as cure of disease 859 a 7; has heating effect 871 a 28, b 32, 874 b 23, 35; mixed wine causes worse after effects than unmixed 871 a 16-23, 872 b 26-31, 873 a 4-11, 874 a 28-34, b 11-13; why children who have a hot temperament are not fond of wine 872 a 3-8; has the effect both of stupefying and of driving to frenzy 873 a 23-36; watery wine apt to cause vomiting 873 b 24-37; has effect of repression 873 b 27; makes the stomach drier 874 a 22-27; unmixed wine has stronger odour 907 b 14-19; made more pleasant with oxymel 922 a 6; sweetened by marjoram 926 b 32-927 a 2; to be taken while eating fruit 930 b 20-32; contains air 938 b 25, 953 b 26, 955 a 35; brave men generally fond of wine 948 a 13-30; naturally hot 948 a 21; satisfies thirst better than water 948 a 22; effects of 953 a 33-954 a 11; excites men 1342 b 26; ought not to be given to slaves 1344 a 32-35

Wings, of insects 682 b 5-19, 710 a 16, 713 a 11; of birds 693 a 27, b 14, 27, 709 b 10, 712 b 24-29, 713 a 10, 806 b 11; why impossible for man 711 a 1-7; of Cupid 711 a 2; made from residual matter 749 b 8

Winter, 348 a 1; due to sun's motion 361 a 13; illness is rarer but more fatal in winter than in summer 862 b 16-24; winds come from east in winter 942 b 3-12, 946 a 35-b 21; winds blow early in winter 946 a 35-b 21; best season for marriage 1335 a 35-b 2

Wisdom, philosophic wisdom (σοφία), 149 b 33, 163 b 9, 995 b 12, 1098 b 24, 1103 a 5, 1139 b 17, 1185 b 6, 1243 b 33, 1323 b 34, 1366 b 1, 3, 1371 b 27, 1440 b 20, 1441 b 6, 1447 b 4; problems connected with prudence, intelligence, and wisdom 953 a 10-957 a 35; why man becomes wiser as he grows older 955 b 22-956 a 11; ancients had no prizes for 956 b 16-33; depends on knowledge 981 a 26; none of senses regarded as 981 b 10; deals with first causes 981 b 28, 982 a 1; characteristics of 982 a 5-983 a 23, 996 b 8-14; a science of first principles 1059 a 18; as union of intuitive reason and science 1141 a 9-b 22; defined 1141 a 19, b 2, 1197 a 11-16; utility of 1143 b 18-1144 a 36; and practical wisdom 1145 a 7-11, 1197 a 32-b 11; pleasantest of virtuous activities 1177 a 25; practicality of 1198 a 32-b 8; the steward of philosophy 1198 b 9-20

Wisdom, practical, prudence (φρόνησις), 89 b 8, 116 b 25, 119 b 33, 121 b 31, 136 b 11, 137 a 12, 141 a 8, 145 a 28-32, 180 a 8, 1025 b 21-26, 1103 a 6, 1139 a 27, 1142 b 32, 1145 b 18, 1146 a 3, 1152 b 16, 1153 a 27, 1172 b 30, 1178 a 16, 1180 a 22, b 28, 1197 b 18-27, 36, 1218 b 13, 34, 1221 a 12, 1246 b 4, 34, 1249 b 27, 1250 a 3, 30-39, 1277 b 25, 1323 a 28, 1366 b 1, 20, 1447 b 4; more desirable in old age 117 a 28; even desirable without power 118 a 18; way to show that prudence is not knowledge 120 a 26-31; problems connected with intelligence, wisdom, and prudence 953 a 10-957 a 35; man has more practical wisdom than any other animal 955 b 4-8; its end is action 993 b 21; some identify happiness with 1098 b 24; the knowledge of human goods 1140 a 24-b 30, 1141 b 8-22, 29; and political wisdom 1141 b 23-1142 a 31; concerned with particulars 1142 a 27; utility of 1143 b 18-1144 a 36; how related to virtue 1144 b 1-1145 a 11, 1198 a 10-b 20; incompatible with incontinence 1152 a 6-15, 1204 a 5-18; deals with matters of action in which

there is a choice and avoidance 1197 a 1, 11, 15; a virtue 1197 a 17-19; and philosophy compared 1197 a 32-b 11; some say prudence is the highest good 1214 a 34, 1215 a 34; not irrational 1247 a 14; a characteristic of the ruler 1277 b 25; inspires confidence in the orator's character 1378 a 8

Wish (βούλησις), 700 b 18, 1111 b 11-30, 1155 b 30, 1178 a 31, 1226 a 7, 16, b 1, 1227 a 2, 28; found in faculty of reason 126 a 13, 432 b 6; defined as conation for an apparent good 146 b 5, 27-147 a 5; a form of appetite 433 a 23, 434 a 12; related to action 701 a 39, 1187 b 16, 1212 a 8, 25; object of wish is the good or apparent good 1113 a 15-b 2; contrary to wish 1136 b 5, 7, 24; a form of impulse 1187 b 37; are acts due to wish voluntary? 1188 a 27-35, 1223 b 26-1224 a 4; we wish for ends 1189 a 5-12; a kind of desire 1223 a 27, 1225 b 25; what is done from wish is more voluntary than that done from passion or anger 1223 b 24-37, 1224 a 1; in children 1334 b 23

Withy, 627 a 8

Witness. See Testimony

Wittiness, 1234 a 4-23, 1389 b 11

Wolf, temper of 488 a 28, b 17, 571 b 28, 811 a 17; genitals of 500 b 24; stomach of 507 b 17; copulation of 540 a 9; reproduction of 580 a 11-31, 742 a 9, 771 a 22; diet of 594 a 25-31; in Egypt 606 a 23; hybrid 607 a 2; habits of 609 b 1, 612 b 2, 620 b 6, 1338 b 30; neck of 686 a 22; digits of 688 a 4-12; crossed with dogs 746 a 34; development of young at birth 774 b 17

Wolf-spider, 622 b 30

Woman, 809 b 1, 812 b 17, 813 a 27, 840 a 10, 1162 a 23, 1171 b 10; Parmenides thinks women hotter than men 648 a 30; Empedocles thinks men hotter than women 648 a 32; uterus of 716 b 34, 718 a 37, 719 b 26, 773 b 28, 776 a 11; fat women are less fertile 726 a 4; why smaller than men 727 a 20; menstrual flow greater in women than in any other animal 727 a 22, 728 b 14, 776 b 26 (Cf. 774 a 27); woman an impotent male 728 a 18; colder than men in nature 738 a 12; women and mares only animals that admit male during gestation 773 b 27; differences between men and women 775 a 5-b 24, 1343 b 8-1344 a 7 (Cf. Female, Male); a sort of natural deficiency 775 a 16; *mola uteri* in 775 b 24-776 a 14; voice of 803 b 20, 813 b 1; gait of 813 a 15; of Liguria 837 b 20-23; Trojan women 840 b 10-18; why more terrible to kill a woman than a man 951 b 11-14; play passive role in copulation 1148 b 32; rule by 1161 a 1; has a different virtue than man 1259 b 28-1260 a 31, 1277 b 20; deliberative faculty in 1260 a 11; women and children to be held in common in Plato's ideal state 1261 a 5-1262 b 36, 1264 b 1-4; importance of disciplining women 1269 b 13-1270 a 14; Spartan women 1269 b 13-1270 a 14, 1361 a 11; Guardians of Women 1299 b 19, 1300 a 4, 1322 b 38; enjoy democracies and tyrannies 1313 b 33-38, 1319 b 28; time of generation in 1335 a 10; care of women during pregnancy 1335 b 12-19; must be trained in virtue 1361 a 11. Cf. Female, Sex

Womb. *See* Uterus

WOMEN OF TROY, 1459 b 7

Wonder, excited by nature and art 847 a 10; the origin of philosophy 982 b 12-27; implies desire to learn 1371 a 30-b 10

Wood, 818 a 7, 819 a 33, 821 b 10, 827 b 26; nature of 384 b 15; as source of dye 794 a 18; method of testing 802 a 30-36; piece of wood more easily broken if ends are held equidistant from knee 852 b 21-28; cutting of 853 b 14-24; weight carried on wood by two persons 857 b 9-21

Woodcock, 614 a 33, 617 b 24

Wood-lice, 557 a 24

Woodpecker, 504 a 18; diet of 593 a 5; habits of 609 a 7, 30, 614 b 1-17, 831 b 5-9; habitat of 610 a 9; beak of 662 b 8. Cf. Green-pie

Wool, dyeing of 794 a 33-b 9

Words, 1458 a 31-b 4; spoken 16 a 3; written 16 a 4; the spoken word and inward discourse 76 b 25; man is the only animal that uses words 905 a 21; expression of things in 980 b 6-9; things are not words 980 b 18; represent things 1404 a 21; compound words 1404 b 28, 1405 b 35-1406 a 7, 1457 a 12, 34, 1459 a 4, 8; beauty and ugliness of 1405 b 7; bad taste to use strange words 1406 a 8-11; three kinds of: (1) simple, (2) composite, (3) metaphorical 1434 b 33; three ways in which words can be put together 1434 b 34-37; arrangement of 1434 b 38-1435 a 2. Cf. Ambiguous terms

Work. *See* Function

World, 206 b 23, 252 b 26; worlds 196 a 26, 203 b 26, 250 b 19; width of inhabited world 393 b 19; its divisions: Europe, Asia, and Libya 393 b 22; has existed from eternity 817 b 39

Wormwood, 820 a 36; promotes flow of urine 949 a 2

Wound, circular wounds heal more slowly 79 a 15; heal more quickly in the young 961 a 5

Wrasse, gills of 505 a 16; habitat of 598 a 10; hibernation of 599 b 8; changes of colour in 607 b 15. Cf. Scarus

Wren, golden crested wren 592 b 23; habits of 609 a 12, 17, b 12, 615 a 17

Wrestlers, train by crawling in sand 709 a 14

Wrestling, 1361 b 16, 24

Wrist, 494 a 2, 702 b 4, 11, 705 a 18; flexion of 712 a 15

Writing, a customary branch of education 1337 b 24

Wrong-doing, 1368 b 1-1375 b 21; defined as injury voluntarily inflicted contrary to law 1368 b 7; motives of 1368 b 28-1372 a 2 (Cf. 1362 a 15-1365 b 21); the circumstances and characters that cause wrong-doing 1372 a 3-1373 a 39

Wryneck, yunx, 504 a 11-18; toes of 695 a 23

X

Xenarchus, 1447 b 11

Xenocrates, 112 a 38, 141 a 7; the happy life and the good life are the same 152 a 7, 27; referred to 1028 b 25, 1069 a 35, 1076 a 20, 1080 b 22, 29, 1083 b 1, 1085 b 7, 1086 a 6, 1088 b 28, 1090 b 30, 1091 b 35

Xenophanes, 833 a 16, 976 a 33, 986 b 22, 27, 1010 a 6, 1377 a 19, 1399 b 6, 1400 b 6, 1460 b 37; earth below us is infinite 294 a 23; views of 977 a 13-b 20; criticism of 977 b 21-979 a 9

Xenophantus, 1150 b 12

Xerxes, 398 a 13, 1393 b 2, 1406 a 8; the assassination of 1311 b 37-39

Xuthus of Croton, 216 b 26

Y

Yard-arm, ship travels faster when yard-arm is raised 850 b 38-851 a 5

Yawning, 945 b 18; infectious 886 a 24-36, 887 a 4-14; one hears less when yawning 902 a 9-15, 904 a 16-22, 961 a 39; affects the ears 961 a 37-b 6

Yellow, beneficial to vision 959 a 23-37

Young, of mutilated parents 724 a 3-6, 737 a 27; care of 753 a 8-16; no animal that copulates has many young 755 b 25; number produced at birth 771 a 18-772 b 12; development at birth varies in different animals 774 b 5-775 a 4; time for young to be born 777 a 22-27

Youth, 436 a 14, 1142 a 12-16, 1155 a 12, 1179 b 31; defined 479 a 30; young man is not a proper hearer of lectures on politics 1095 a 2-11; live by feeling, rather than reason 1118 b 11, 1128 b 17, 1156 a 32, 1172 a 21; youth is pleasant 1154 b 10; friendships of 1156 a 32-b 5, 1157 a 8, 1158 a 4, 20; desire that everything be sweetened with pleasure 1340 b 15; influenced by anger and appetite 1369 a 9; character of 1389 a 2-b 11; rhetorical excuses of a young man 1437 a 39-b 8

Yunx. *See* Wryneck

Z

Zaleucus, legislator of Locri, 1274 a 22, 29

Zancle, seized by the Samians 1303 a 35

Zeno, 65 b 18, 250 a 20, 325 a 2-23(?), 979 a 5, b 26, 1001 b 7, 1372 b 6; refutation of Zeno's proof of the impossibility of movement 160 b 8, 172 a 9, 179 b 19, 233 a 22-b 15, 239 b 5-240 b 8, 263 a 5-264 a 7, 272 a 29; problem of being 182 b 26, 976 a 26; his difficulty with the concept of place 209 a 24, 210 b 23; argument for simple magnitudes 968 a18-21; refutation of Zeno's argument for simple magnitudes 969 b 6-25

Zephyrus (W. wind), 363 b 12, 364 b 3, 23, 394 b 21, 27, 946 a 17-33, 973 b 13; blows at evening 942 b 6, 944 a 10-24, 31-35; dispenses scent 942 b 13-15; drives largest clouds 942 b 20-22; pleasantest of the winds 943 b 21-944 a 3, 946 b 22-31

Zeugitae, a class in Solon's constitution 1274 a 20

Zeus (the god), 166 b 7, 673 a 19, 700 a 1, 838 a 25, 844 b 1, 1091 b 6, 1124 b 16, 1160 b 26, 1165 a 16, 1208 b 32, 1242 a 39, 1244 a 14, 1284 b 32, 1313 b 23, 1339 b 7, 1346 a 33, 1379 a 4, 1387 a 34, 1398 b 32, 1418 a 36, 1461 a 30; titles of 401 a 14-26; etymology of the word 401 a 15; Orphic Hymn describing Zeus 401 a 28-b 7; born in Crete 836 b 29; temple of 840 b 24, 844 b 7; fountain of Zeus Horcias 845 b 34; the 'father of gods and men' 1259 b 13

Zeus (the star), 392 a 24, 399 a 10

Zeuxis, 1450 a 27, 1461 b 12

Ziara (Sahara ?), 820 a 5

Zignis. *See* Chalis

Zodiac, 343 a 24, 345 a 19, 346 a 12, 392 a 12

Zoophytes, compared with molluscs 714 b 16

Zostera, 591 a 16